DILEMMAS OF ACTIVISM

Class, Community and
the Politics of Local Mobilization

DILEMMAS OF ACTIVISM

Class, Community, and
the Politics of
Local Mobilization
Edited by Joseph M. Kling
and Prudence S. Posner

TEMPLE UNIVERSITY PRESS   Philadelphia

HN
65
.D493
1990
152190
May 1991

Temple University Press, Philadelphia 19122
Copyright ©1990 by Temple University. All rights reserved
Published 1990
Printed in the United States of America

The paper used in this publication meets the minimum
requirements of American National Standard for Information
Sciences—Permanence of Paper for Printed Library Materials,
ANSI Z39.48—1984

Library of Congress Cataloging-in-Publication Data
Dilemmas of activism : class, community, and the politics of local
  mobilization / edited by Joseph M. Kling and Prudence S. Posner.
      p.   cm.
    Includes bibliographical references.
    ISBN 0-87722-696-2 (alk. paper)
    1. Community organization—United States.   2. Social action—
  United States.   3. Social classes—United States.   4. Community
  power—United States.   I. Kling, Joseph M.   II. Posner, Prudence
  Sarah.
  HN65.D493   1990   89-27678
  305.5'0973—dc20   CIP

To our parents

*To Harold and Ronah Posner, whose lifelong commitment to social justice
has been a support and inspiration,
and to the memory of Selma Lefkowitz Kling, whose love and laughter was
a constant reminder of what it is all about anyway.*

Contents

Preface

All books, no matter how scholarly or technically oriented, are intensely personal to their authors. But this one is personal because its contributors are men and women who have tried since first reaching adulthood to integrate their concerns for participating as activists in the world with their interest in "figuring it out." It ties together for us the struggles we fought, and continue to fight, to make a better world—said without irony—with the efforts we make as writers and teachers to understand what is going on now, why things happen in communities as they do, and what actions might be taken. It has been our intention in this collection, therefore, to unite the concerns of theory and practice in ways that we believe few books have done in recent years.

The 1960s were a time when such issues as race and exploitation and imperialism and the possibilities of change were right in front of you. There was a sense of common struggle, of a community of concern—no matter how infuriating one group found another group's ideas to be, and despite the fact that some chose destructive paths. What counted was that people could talk of "the movement" and be understood. Gender had not yet emerged as a source of conflict, but it too was there, underneath the organizing and internal struggling. We are lucky because we know what it feels like to live in a time when "revolution was in the air."

Many of us remained fortunate in that we were subsequently able to pursue scholarly and intellectual studies related to our activist concerns. Some of the writers in this volume still have their feet in the worlds of both analysis and action. No matter where we stand, we feel that the intellectual investment required to "figure it out" is never as compatible with the energy and time commitments of activism as we would like. The pulls in one direction seem always to be overwhelming the pulls in the other.

For the editors, working on this collection has offered an opportunity to rethink issues of community organization with which we have been involved directly for fifteen years. It has given us the time, away from the immediacies of political action, to confront questions having to do with the role of power, ideology, class, race, and gender in the working out of change at the level of people's daily lives. We have been fortunate in being able to collaborate with a group of people who shared these concerns. We were only able to address both the practical and theoretical problems of this collection because of the extraordinary cooperation and patience of Bob Fisher, James Jennings, Bruce Palmer, Rona Weiss, Sid Plotkin, Bill Scheuerman, Tony Schuman, Svi Shapiro, Marie Kennedy, and Chris Tilly. We also want to thank Ira Katznelson for his warm encouragement when we sought his permission to excerpt material from his writing for the essay on class and the community–workplace dichotomy. We are particularly grateful to Sid Plotkin, Bill Scheuerman, and Rona Weiss. They helped initiate the plans for this book. Without Rona's indomitable faith in us, and in the uncounted versions of the Prospectus and Introduction that she read and criticized, the collection would not have gotten under way. Thanks also to friends Martin Eisenberg and Barbara Shollar for reading and criticizing many versions of the editors' papers. And Bob Fisher's generosity of intellect and spirit was more important to the final realization of this volume than he would ever grant.

We would also like to acknowledge the very important influence on both of us of a small group of people who have maintained an interracial community center in Brooklyn since 1954. The late executive director, Morris L. Eisenstein, brought a love of philosophy to the everyday work of a storefront community center. It was Morris's dual commitment—to the role of ideas and to the role of conflict (the presence of choice between alternative behaviors and alternative value systems)—that, more than any other single factor, influenced both our thinking and the subsequent direction of our lives. Another person from the United Community Centers who had a special impact on us was its former Board president, Evelyn Millman. Evelyn embodied the values, ideas, and traditions of the radical generation that preceded our own—with both its strengths and weaknesses. Finally, we wish to acknowledge the role of Rose Marie Hernandez, who became executive director of the Center after Morris's death. Her quiet understanding has made it possible for the organization to keep on going—an organization that, according to conventional wisdom, shouldn't have existed at all, let alone continued for over thirty-five years. Of course, without the dedication and willingness of the staff and volunteers of that organization, we ourselves could not have grown to understand what we have about the daily, tedious, time-consuming, and sometimes thrilling work of organizing people to take some control over the conditions under which they live.

At least one set of our respective children is not overly impressed by The Book, which has taken up so much of their parent's time and energy. Prue Posner's teenage daughters, Angela and Sarah, wondered why their mother wasn't writing about something more interesting—like women's problems. Heidi and Rachel Kling, in their early twenties, are perhaps more sympathetic to its content because they are both wrestling with issues of the meaning of activism in a world that seems to provide no organizational support. Each generation has its own concerns but if we listen carefully, our children can teach us how to connect the puzzles of the past to those of the present, and avoid the prison of addressing only the people who have shared one's own life experiences. Our children have tried hard to teach us to listen, even as they sense the fragility of their own approaches to the world.

Prue Posner would not have survived her first years in the teaching profession (coinciding with the beginning of work on this collection) without the support and friendship of teachers in the Social Studies Department of Franklin Delano Roosevelt High School in Brooklyn. In similar fashion, Joe Kling found tremendous support from his colleagues at St. Lawrence University.

We are especially grateful for the conviction of our editor at Temple University Press, Michael Ames, that there really was a book here, and for his determination to see that it got out. We hope that whatever insights it provides from the work of one generation of activists will have resonance in the work of another.

DILEMMAS OF ACTIVISM
Class, Community, and
the Politics of Local Mobilization

Introduction

Prudence S. Posner

The essays in this volume focus on collective action in communities and neighborhoods, not in the workplace. We made this choice for two reasons. First, community organization has become the subject of ideological debate primarily between those identified as new populists (or neopopulists)[1] and those identified as Marxists—the former focusing primarily on issues of community and citizenship, the latter on issues of class. Second, the theoretical issues of race and class and gender and class are being debated and examined,[2] while the theorizing that has followed more than a decade of "neighborhood" community organizing has often been more celebration than analysis (with the notable exception of Delgado's *Organizing the Movement*, 1986).[3]

Disagreements between new populists and Marxists involve genuine alternatives. Nevertheless, *both* alternatives are present in the actual situations of community organizing. We refer to these alternatives as the *dilemmas of activism*. In their challenge to what is referred to as "traditional" Marxism (or "leftism"), the new populists have raised, in a polemical fashion, important issues for the theory and practice of organizing people for democratic social change. Rather than simply attempt to resolve this debate in favor of one side or the other, the essays in this volume explore, on both a theoretical and a practical level, the implications of these dilemmas for activism.

For example, it has been obvious for a long time that American working people have not undertaken collective action in terms of a class-identified politics. Indeed, the major social movements since World War II have been organized around nonclass collectivities: the civil rights and black empowerment movements, the student/anti-war movement, the women's movement, and, in recent decades, the community organization and citizen action movement. At the same time, the contributors to this volume argue that there is a *structural framework* within which the grievances addressed by these postwar social movements must be understood. That structural framework is most clearly delineated in a number of contemporary efforts to reformulate the Marxist concept of class conflict.[4] As the essays collected here indicate, in order to understand contemporary social movements, both the agency of activism—primarily community organization in recent decades—and the structural roots of the grievances/issues must be explored. This constitutes the first dilemma of activism, which for convenience we have labeled *class–community*. How can the immediacy of "community" as a vehicle of mobilization be related to the reality of "class" as the dynamic of conflict through which not only labor but land, air, and water are appropriated for profit?

The second dilemma lies in the tension between the traditional wisdom and values of the people and a systematic critique of conditions by intellectuals. New populists emphasize the importance of the traditional ideas through which people explain and evaluate their condition. This is an important counterweight to the use of such a concept as *false consciousness* (identified with Marxism) to explain the difference between an understanding of the structural cause of a grievance and the ideas, values, and language in which the aggrieved formulate their condition. But reliance solely on ideas that have common currency creates a trap for the activist because the everyday discourse through which people understand their condition is, in large part, a product of the structural relationships that are the source of the grievance. At the same time, reference to the common discourse is a necessary part of the process by which people can be mobilized into collective action. For example, the Jeffersonian vision of independent freeholders directing the affairs of the commonwealth has provided an important ideological weapon with which to transform undemocratic institutions. At the same time, this vision has created the ideological scaffolding according to which the defense of property is equated with the defense of freedom. Too often, American ideology, as well as jurisprudence, lumps together personal property—a house or a car—and the productive assets of corporations.

The problem of power is at the heart of the third dilemma. Certainly governance by bureaucracy is debilitating to democracy. The democratic spirit atrophies in the absence of effective public decision making and the democratic administration of decisions. Periodic voting is no substitute for engaging in debate and determining public policy regarding issues of significance to one's daily life or to a vision of a better future. But the degree of public power necessary to counter the power of corporations—evidenced in plant closings, toxic waste dumps, air pollution, overdevelopment of rural areas, and the like—is far greater than that exercised by a group of citizens associated in a voluntary organization, or even through local governmental agencies. It is important to recall, for example, that during the civil rights movement (with its organized and committed mass involvement) the power of the federal government was needed in order to counter that of local and state segregationist forces. The third dilemma, therefore, is rooted in the fact that the activist mobilizes people democratically and locally to exercise power in a corporate-based, technologically complex society.

Do Activists Need Theory?

People who want to persuade, organize, and mobilize others to undertake collective action—whether in relation to a major social injustice like racial segregation or to particular issues, such as halting the construction of an incinerator near a residential area—ask themselves certain questions about the task they confront. Among these questions are "What will make people willing to spend time and energy on an activity whose outcome is far from certain?" "Are some groups more likely than others to expend that effort?" "What ideas do people have about the proper relationship between themselves and government (or, alternatively, corporations) that will support or inhibit collective action for change?" "In what ways are these grievances the result of corporate, individual or bureaucratic incompetence, ill will, and possibly evil—and to what extent are they a function of structural processes occurring at an economic, geographic, and political level far beyond the particular locale where the grievance is experienced?"

Not one of these questions is simply strategic or tactical. Each is embedded in a theoretical framework. The answers proposed within the context of a particular contested issue (schools, toxic waste disposal, affordable housing) have a powerful impact on the degree to which that struggle opens up possibilities for further democratic efforts.

It is to theory, and the empirical validation of theory, that activists must look for guidelines in working through the dilemmas they confront as they work out tactics and strategies in specific situations. Neither the new populist focus on the theory that embeds popular resistance in communal loyalties and affections nor the Marxist reliance on changing structural conditions to alter popular consciousness provides adequate theoretical frameworks for activism. Negotiating the dilemmas of class–community, traditional and critical ideologies, democratic control and state power requires theory that integrates without subsuming one or the other "horn" of each dilemma. At the level of issue-oriented social action and community organization, this kind of theoretical integration and sustaining of opposites can serve to encourage the continuous opening of possibilities for struggle, instead of serving (as theory unfortunately too often has) as a measure of "right" or "wrong" practice.

Dilemmas of Activism

We have distinguished three "dilemmas" for the sake of conceptual clarity and analysis. We recognize that they are interrelated. The ideologies by which we explain our past and present, and plan our futures, are woven into our sense of who we are, individually, ethnically, racially, in relation to gender and to the status and class structure of our society. In turn, that identity is shaped by class structures and by daily habits of place, or community. The exercise of governmental power is simultaneously a function of the historical formation of the decentralized "community" politics of the American system and of the broad class dynamic of capital accumulation. We exercise some measure of power through our politically defined communities; we are subject to the exercise of state power in relation to our position in the multileveled class structure of American society.

Class and Community

The black urban uprisings of the 1960s established the terms in which the politics of "community" would be discussed for the next twenty years. Black demands for "community control" (primarily over publicly funded service institutions such as schools, police, welfare agencies) were ultimately channeled into what Ira Katznelson referred to as the established "trenches" of urban politics.[5] Nevertheless, the idea that subordinate groups could resist undesirable changes in their lives, as experienced at the place of residence, became the basis for activism during the next two decades.

Meanwhile, the dynamic of global capitalism was leading to downtown redevelopment and the withdrawal of public investment in the services and amenities required for working-class (black or white) life in urban areas.

This has been described by Manuel Castells as the "reappropriation of urban space" and is here discussed by the editors in "Class and Community in an Era of Urban Transformation." In "Transformative Populism," Marie Kennedy and Chris Tilly examine the particular response to this process in Boston as it devastated the black and Latino neighborhood of Roxbury. The global movement of capital, with its disastrous consequences for working class neighborhoods, confronted community organizers with the vast distance between the locus of power that created the grievances and the locus of organizing. The dilemma created by this situation extends beyond the urban neighborhood, as Sidney Plotkin and William E. Scheuerman point out in their study of resistance to plant closings in the Monongahela Valley of Pennsylvania centering in Pittsburgh along the Monongahela River. With steel mills as the industrial focus, the Mon Valley as a region becomes defined as a "community," and the response to the withdrawal of capital and shutdown of the steel plants is understood as a community response.

The dilemma is rendered more difficult by the confusion of meanings that surround both *class* and *community*. We turn to Ira Katznelson's suggestion that *class* must be understood as a layered, rather than a unified, concept. The dynamic of class conflict (as collective capital vs. collective labor) is inherent in the structures of capitalist society. This dynamic does not describe particular events, relationships, or attitudes. Instead, it functions as a constraint on the ways in which any capitalist society produces and distributes its wealth. The class structure as lived experience is a function of the national, racial, immigrant, gender, political structures and other specifics of history as they are shaped by these constraints. The feelings and ideas ("dispositions" in Katznelson) that people have about their situation is yet another layer through which class may (or may not) be a useful referent. Mobilization for collective action (the goal of activism), then, is contingent on all three meanings of class: (1) the dynamic of class conflict at the most abstract level of social structure, (2) the historically developed formations of class through which people actually live their lives, and (3) the dispositions (ideas, values, ideologies) by which people make sense of their condition.

The difficulties with the word *community* primarily stem from the utopian meanings attached to it. Yet it is from these meanings that community activism derives much of its power. I say "utopian" here in the sense that Joseph R. Gusfield (1975) uses it in his critical study *Community*, that is, a poetic term embodying feelings and hopes that cannot be semantically mapped onto the word itself but that surround it in everyday usage. The utopian meaning of community is expressed in the pain of Pat Barker's heroine Liza, "the century's daughter," in her novel of that title (Barker 1986). Past eighty, dying in the ancient rooms soon to be knocked down to make way for apartment blocks, Liza recalls the poverty and misery of her working-class youth, yet feels something missing:

> *Not* the good old days, but still she rocked to and fro, for the broken streets and scattered people, for the cold hearth and the cracked furnace, for the river flowing between empty wharves. (Barker 1986, 269)

What was missing? With all the visible improvements in the standard of living and in the (collective consumption) services available for working people, something was missing. Liza observes to a woman friend who remained a Labour party activist,

> Where are we going? And you know there was a lot of good going on. New hospitals, new schools . . . because that's where it went wrong you know. It was all *money*. You'd've thought we had nowt else to offer. But we *did*. We had a way of life, a way of treating people. You didn't just go to church one day a week and jabber on about loving your neighbour. You got stuck in seven days a week and bloody did it, because you knew if you didn't you wouldn't survive and neither would she. We had all that. We had pride. We were poor, but we were proud. (Barker 1986, 226)

New populists argue that this sense of solidarity, of neighborliness—of "community"—is missing in class-based social reform schemes of social democrats; Liza points to this as something "we had" that was not passed on in the struggle to improve living conditions. According to social historians, this sense of solidarity also fueled the struggles of the past. While we recognize the importance of community in this sense of solidary grouping, noncommodified relationships, we cannot confuse the appropriate and poetic use of "utopian"—by which we articulate our hopes for the future—with the inappropriate use, by which we replace our understanding of the material (and class) constraints of the present with our wishes. The social historian Craig Calhoun warns that "the social foundations for this (earlier) radical democratic vision and action have not often been made part of the life of modern workers. . . . New social foundations for radicalism may yet be made, but they are no longer inherited as they were before and during industrialization."[6] In other words, the genuine human needs met by older (often preindustrial) forms of community have to find new expression and new ways of weaving people together in meaningful bonds of connectedness.

The dilemma of class and community takes on a special form when the aggrieved "community" is defined racially, or when we examine community activism in relation to gender. This is not a reversion to the use of community as a self-identified grouping (e.g., blacks or women) but to (1) issues that, because of the role of women in our society, are identified particularly with the needs and responsibilities of women; or (2) neighborhoods, residential areas, identified as black or, in some cases, "minority" (usually meaning black and Latino).

Obviously, women do not live in geographically distinct communities (except, perhaps, convents or a few college dormitories). But as Rayna Rapp's "Family and Class in Contemporary America" shows, the "community" off-work residence site is the place of *work* of women who are responsible for the organization and maintenance of a household (whether or not they hold jobs outside the home). Issues that address grievances related to the raising and educating of children or health and safety in the residential neighborhood (environment, zoning, health services) tend to be seen as women's responsibility, and with these kinds of neighborhood/community issues, women predominate as activists. This reflects the way in which the economic function of the household (the site of the reproduction of labor) is tied to the ideology of the family and position of women, both economically and ideologically, therein. Rapp's essay, written in the mid 1970s, remains the seminal discussion of the socially constructed nature of the family, although the particular issues that exercised the women's movement at that time have given way to others today.

Ida Susser's study of women community activists in Greenpoint (Brooklyn), "Working-Class Women, Social Protest, and Changing Ideologies," concretely illustrates the relationship between women's roles in the family and the structures of labor and reproduction in our society. Susser also introduces the element of the welfare state and transfer payments, both as context of women's class experience and as object of activism.

Although the off-work, residential/community life of blacks seems to conform in structure (homeownership, tenancy, workplace-residence separation, and so on) to that of whites of a similar economic status, the problems confronting blacks in their neighborhoods are not the same as those of whites. The fact of race, both as a source of the grievance and as an element in the disposition and mobilization of community residents, is of vital importance. In "The Politics of Black Empowerment," James Jennings argues that in terms of the African-American community, as subject—organizing, struggling, suffering, changing—race is *not* simply one more factor (like ethnicity or geography). Community organization in African-American neighborhoods cannot be understood as simply community organization with a black face. The role of racial discrimination and domination, over and above class processes, in creating urban black neighborhoods gives a different meaning to collective action at the community level. For the black neighborhood (as well as the black community in the larger sense), the dilemma of community and class is always filtered through the prism of race. As Jennings suggests, this can be an asset in the struggle to alter the structures that cause the grievance, since there can be no illusion that racial inequalities and injustices are local in origin. Neither can there be any illusion that "politics as usual," in the form of competition among interest groups for position and spoils, will effect significant change in the African-American or "minority" community. Both Jennings, in his theoretical paper, and Kennedy and Tilly, in their study of the Roxbury, Massachusetts, community, describe the way in which an understanding of class processes interpenetrates the racial identity and striving for racial equality of black community activism. In "Transformative Populism and the Development of a Community of Color," Kennedy and Tilly introduce a new perspective on the kind of community organization that retains both a class framework and a consciousness of racial diversity. By distinguishing between "transformative populism" and "redistributive populism," they not only name but make visible the distinctions the editors have been developing from a more formal/theoretical perspective. In "Class and Community," we introduce the concept of "organized publics," borrowing from John Dewey and C. Wright Mills. Like Kennedy and Tilly, we are offering a possible conceptual resolution of the class—community dichotomy as a framework within which empirical analysis and programmatic development might take place.

Traditional and Derived Ideologies

The role of ideas and ideologies in collective action has been somewhat obscured for the current generation by the fact that two of the major social movements of the postwar era, the civil rights movement and the women's movement, could be understood in terms of a demand for inclusion in the structures of rights and benefits that existed for less subordinated groups.

Much of the potency of this demand derives from its reliance on what are generally accepted ideas about the equality of individuals and the elimination of ascriptive barriers to civic and economic participation. Society cannot reject claims made in the name of equality without undermining its own legitimacy, since a demand for equality is part of the ideology that provides the framework for majority rule and representative democracy.

The historical success, however limited, of social movements that seek the realization of existing values is not the only reason why the role of ideas in collective action is obscure. Both Marxism and the new populism have sought shortcuts around the inescapable fact that subordinated groups, suffering clearly identifiable grievances, think about their position and their grievances in terms established by those in power. In cliché form: The dominant ideas of the society are the ideas of those in power. These ideas mark out the terrain on which political struggle takes place.

Marxists accept this formulation, at least in general terms. Nicos Poulantzas, Erik Olin Wright, and others have undertaken the task of identifying and describing contradictory ideological elements among different sectors of the working population.[7] Since people's ideas and values are related to (although not determined by) their concrete material situation, as the condition of working people worsens (as it has since the 1970s with the decline of a manufacturing economy and the rise of a service-oriented city), the tendency remains among Marxists to imagine that significant changes in ideological orientation will emerge.[8] Despite the increased sophistication of analysis that separates contemporary Marxism from economic determinism, there has been no theory of collective action tying together class structure, ideology, and collective mobilization. As a result, these social theorists have been unable to offer more than a generalized optimism in the way of explaining the potential emergence of an oppositional movement.

The new populist, in contrast, identifies oppositional strains within the dominant idea systems (often rooted in older values that no longer serve a legitimating function). These oppositional strains generate a disruptive tension and sustain what Plotkin, in his essay on environmentalism, "Enclave Consciousness and Neighborhood Activism," refers to as the "functional unruliness" of much community activism. But while Plotkin emphasizes the *contradictory* nature of these traditional oppositional strains, the new populists assume that since these strains exist, all that is necessary is to identify them in order to create an oppositional discourse. The new populists do not take into account differences in ideas and values that are a function of real differences in material conditions of life. For them, the "discourse" of democracy and equality is an undifferentiated discourse, arising out of a common history, rather than a conflicted and self-contradictory one in relation to the different experiences of different groups in society.

Svi Shapiro's "Changing the Conversation" suggests an approach that utilizes these conflicts within popular experience, attempting to create a discourse that both speaks to real grievances and contests dominant interpretations of their sources and meanings.

Although the new populist emphasis on traditional American (even Judeo-Christian) values as "the wellspring of American politics" is to some extent a reaction to Marxist economic determinism as a theory of social change, it is equally a victim of its own optimism and desires. While the Marxist looks for the answer in the right group of people, the new populist looks for it in the right discourse. While the new populists have astutely recognized that the idea systems that inform collective action are closely tied to the sense of one's own identity and self-esteem, they have looked to the traditional values and ideologies to form the basis of an oppositional identity that can sustain collective action. Calhoun's warning—that the solidary communities and the values they bred are no longer part of the experience of working people—goes unheeded.

In their essay on ideology and activism, "Leading the People," Robert Fisher and Joseph M. Kling suggest that the formulation proposed by the historian George Rudé offers a useful way out of the either/or situation posed by determinist Marxism and the new populism. Rudé (1980) distinguishes between two kinds of ideologies: (1) *traditional*, or *inherent*, ideologies composed of the commonsense beliefs of most people; and (2) *structured*, or *derived*, ideologies, which are a systematic critique of conditions and present that critique in a coherent fashion. Rudé argues that although the traditional ideology can become the focus of political resistance when the rights and liberties of subaltern classes are attacked, such resistance has transformative potential only when the traditional ideology has become strongly suffused with the derived ideology.

Without the *interplay* of traditional democratic commitments and a coherent oppositional ideology, the moments of resistance remain a way of checking a move by capital here or there, but leaving the game unchanged and its rules unchallenged ideologically. As Tony Schuman indicates in his study of housing activism, "The Agony and the Equity," existing ideological commitments to property rights and the concept of housing (and land) as commodity are important factors in the failure to develop an adequate housing policy in the United States. The establishment of community land trusts or, as described by Schuman, the Mutual Housing Association of New York (MHANY), constitutes efforts to resolve this dilemma through policies that draw on the (frequently conflicting) values of home ownership and community responsibility. Similarly, in environmental conflicts discussed by Plotkin, commitment to property rights supports environmental activism locally while at the same time undercutting the development of broad-based policy to control the environmentally destructive activities of real estate boards, manufacturing corporations, and, too often, government agencies.

Three papers that focus on land use—Kennedy and Tilly, Plotkin, and Schuman—emphasize the role of the organizer as the bearer of oppositional ideas and values. All three also stress the importance of supportive planning institutions: Pratt Institute in the case of ACORN's organizing efforts in the East New York section of Brooklyn and the Center for Community Planning at the University of Massachusetts College for Public and Community Service in the case of neighborhood activism in Roxbury, Boston. The historical contribution from Bruce Palmer, examining "the first and last large-scale political movement to come to grips with these dilemmas (created by the rise of corporate capitalism)" also stresses the role of "derived" ideology. Palmer argues that it was the *absence* of ideological clarity in the face of the national banking, commercial, and Democratic party interests that contributed to the downfall of the agrarian populists of the 1890s.

The role of ideology in shaping activism becomes even more complex when the "good" that is at issue is not simply a service, however necessary. As the only public institution funded and, to some extent, governed locally, schools are frequently the focus of neighborhood activism. Education, or at least schooling, plays a dominant role in the American democratic mythology of upward mobility. Yet education is not only a "good," it is a cultural process, resonating with meanings having to do with personal identity, feelings of control over the future of one's children and the validity of one's own philosophical world view. As the engine of social reproduction, schools simultaneously offer some people an avenue to success in the world of work and impose a value system that denigrates the lives of those who are not "successful" in those terms. Shapiro's essay on education activism shows how the terms of the political debate in which education issues are formulated ("excellence," "equality," "a nation at risk") consistently reinforce the dominant ideas and relationships of our society. The fears and concerns of citizens/parents are articulated by established groups into a political language that appears to offer answers. Shapiro argues that it is possible to "change the conversation," that is, to insert new meanings into the debate over educational excellence and equality, meanings that contribute to the empowerment of students and the validation of their families' hopes and dreams. He examines specifically the issue of curricular reform as it emerged in Philadelphia.

Bruce Palmer and Rona Weiss respectively introduce the question of ideology in relation to agricultural organizing: Palmer reviewing the struggles of agrarian populists of the 1890s, Weiss examining the agricultural movements of the 1980s. Palmer suggests that as early as the end of the nineteenth century, the Jeffersonian idyll of an agrarian republic was wishful thinking in terms of the economic realities in newly industrializing America. Weiss examines the ideological basis of the various programs advanced by agricultural activists, identifying the role of myth in shaping public attitudes toward agricultural issues. Weiss argues that without government intervention, the middle-size (family) farm cannot escape absorption by large agribusiness complexes. This is significant for more than the sentimental reasons that posit the family farm as the bedrock of American values. Weiss argues that unless agriculture is able to break its bonds to the corporate-dominated market, the environmental damage, to the soil and to the agricultural product itself, will be irreversible.

State Power, Community Empowerment, and Democratic Participation

How does the activist mobilize people in relation to the dilemma inherent in democratic public power? Democratic efficacy is experienced at the local level, yet in the world of corporate capitalism, the power necessary to achieve democratic and egalitarian goals exists, if anywhere, only at the level of the bureaucratic national state. The dilemma reflects the conflict between the need for enlarged social power in order to achieve democratic projects and the goal of increased democratic participation in decision making. The Marxist approach has tended to push the problem off to "after the revolution," when presumably state power would be in the hands of well-meaning representatives of the working class. The new populists have tried to get around the problem by ignoring the power of those who benefit from the current inequalities and injustices. Identifying statism, and the concentration of power in the bureaucratic state, as the major obstacle to democratic participation, they offer "community power" as the force that can oppose the decisions of global capital.

Economists Samuel Bowles and Herbert Gintis (1984, 179) look to "workplace and community empowerment as opposed to state expansion" in order to avoid the "dead-end" of the welfare state. While the contributors are not unaware of the hazards of enlarged government power, a central thesis of this collection is that under certain conditions we cannot avoid the question of state power, specifically in the form of the federal government and its agencies. Resolution of the grievances experienced at the level of communities requires the exercise of power that can enforce policies, regulations, and restrictions on very powerful economic entities. Furthermore, programs that would meet the need for more equitably distributed public goods, such as health care or housing, are necessarily implicated in the important power relationships of our society.

The dilemma of democratic process and state power is most sharply articulated from a Marxist perspective, since it insists on the role of class structures and the dynamic of capital accumulation in shaping community, consciousness, and ideology. Without entering into contemporary debates about the autonomy, relative autonomy, or lack of autonomy of the state, we would simply argue that, from an activist perspective, "It's the only game in town."[9] The historical development of government has made it an arena of struggle in which the tilt of state power can be (in general terms) toward capital or toward labor (understood in the broad generic sense, not as the trade union movement alone). The state (through the agencies of government) has appropriated for itself the collective powers of society; for better or worse, it is the only instrument through which those without economic power can exercise some controls over those who have it.

Although this collection does not address questions of factory and industrial organization, the dilemma there is similar. Without government regulation of health and safety conditions (on a federal level), workers have only temporary means of enforcing what they know to be necessary for their own, and their community's, good health. The oversight and vigilance necessary to maintain enforcement within a particular factory may stimulate democratic processes on the shop floor, but the legislation and its administration are bureaucratic functions. Worse, a self-managed shop, confronting the exigencies of the market directly, may be *less* likely to maintain costly health and safety measures than one in which the workers are clearly organized in opposition to the owners.

In the more familiar realm of social services, the American health care system is a two-tier system that separates health care for the indigent from that provided to those who can pay (or have the requisite medical insurance).

If we want a system that does not segregate patients based on income, we will have to place some limits on the freedom of choice of those who currently can obtain "the best medical care money can buy." Such a system may be administered through a wide variety of local, community, union, and other voluntary or decentralized governmental agencies; but only the taxing power of the federal government could finance it. Only national policy can provide the structures through which class and racial equality is, if not guaranteed, at least possible. Only national enforcement agencies can protect a public system from the ill will of segments of the medical, pharmaceutical, medical technology, and other professions and industries that would lose significant advantages as a result of such changes. The experience of the Reagan administration's withdrawal of federal financing and supervision over such areas of health care as nursing homes and public hospitals shows how readily this arena succumbs to the predation of private corporations seeking to profit from human suffering.

In order to provide affordable housing for all Americans, limits would have to be placed on the functioning of the real estate market. Those who currently own houses would find their freedom to profit from the sale of their property limited. This issue has already emerged with reference to sweat-equity housing (discussed in Tony Schuman's article in this collection). The question whether the new "homeowners" should have the right to sell their homes on the open market poses serious problems. Given the definition of homeownership as "property," resolution of the problem of homelessness and inadequate housing will require the exercise of governmental power on a large scale. This does not mean construction of large blocks of apartments; it means expanding what is defined as public (and thereby subject to political decision making) into an arena that is jealously guarded as private by most homeowners *and* community governmental units as representatives of homeowners and taxpayers. (See the reference above to community land trusts and the MHANY.)

For the activist, this dilemma does not arise in the *process* of organization, which is by definition participatory and democratic. Nevertheless, it must be confronted at the level of program, that is, the articulation of goals, promulgated as "demands," whose satisfaction is the purpose of the rallies, lobbying, picketing, putting forth candidates, sit-ins, leafletting, and so forth. An organized community group, exercising the rights of citizens, is demanding that government enact, implement, modify, or cease the undertaking of some kind of public policy. To the extent that such mobilized collectivities focus only on the locally available power (e.g., city ordinances, community boycott), they are hopelessly outclassed. Yet, successful community activism can also reproduce the original dilemma. The exercise of bureaucratic power in the interest of community or public needs (e.g., to stop a polluting industry or congested construction, or to promote better schools, more comprehensive public health care, or affordable housing) dilutes the feeling of efficacy and the daily practice of democratic decision making that the new populists correctly identify as so important to the preservation and enlargement of a democratic polity.

We offer no neat resolutions. To the contributors to this collection, these dilemmas are inevitably a part of modern social life and therefore of the struggle to improve the conditions of that life. It is our hope that by delineating them at the theoretical level and examining them in relation to particular issues, we can grasp the nettle of what we see as unavoidable contradictions. We also hope to show that struggle in the face of these dilemmas is not futile. The process of struggle for change is itself a factor in the creation of a democratic culture and perhaps even in the creation of new social foundations for a radicalism that is no longer inherited.

Notes

1. Books that come under the "new populist" category would include Boyte (1980, 1984), Boyte and Evans (1986), Carnoy and Shearer (1980), Bowles, Gordon, and Weisskopf (1984), Bowles and Gintis (1987), Goodwyn (1978), and Boyte and Reissman (1986).

2. Even a cursory listing includes such work as Marable (1980, 1983) and Outlaw (1983). Or, more recently, Bloom (1987). On the relationship of gender and class, see Eisenstein (1983), Hartsock (1983), or Swerdlo and Lessinger (1983).

3. For a discussion of the community/citizen activism of the 1970s, see Boyte (1980, 1984). Also see "Organizing Neighborhoods" (1979) and "Neighborhood Action" (1980). And see the letters, articles, and special features in *Social Policy* from November/December 1980 through May/June 1981; the Summer 1984 and Winter 1984 issues; and the editorials on populism by Frank Riessman and S. M. Miller in the Summer 1985 issue. In addition, new populist organizations and individuals have published a number of "how-to" manuals for organizers; see, e.g., *Midwest Academy Organizing Manual* (1984), Kahn (1982), and Burghart (1982).

4. One might begin with O'Connor (1975) and Fainstein and Fainstein (1974) and follow through with such contemporary work as Logan and Molotch (1987) or Castells (see, esp., 1983). We find, informing these studies, the Marxist concept of a constraining class structure and dynamic of capital accumulation. For those

concerned with the application of theory, the problem arises when these structural explanations are understood as determinants and direct causes rather than as constraining frameworks within which a wide variety of alternative actions and outcomes are possible.

5. For a full discussion of the channeling of black community protest into the "trenches" of urban politics as usual, see Katznelson (1981, esp. Chap. 8).

6. Calhoun, one of the strongest proponents of the view that collective action during the formation of the working class was a function of *resistance* to becoming part of the proletariat, not *class action* on the part of an existing working class, warns against imposing the past on the future: "Nonetheless, the social foundations for this radical democratic vision and action have not often been made part of the life of modern workers. Whether well-paid or poor, the new workers have different personal experiences and social capabilities. They are a class in a way their predecessors were not, but that is more an indicator of isolation as individuals, than of unity. New social foundations for radicalism may yet be made, but they are no longer inherited as they were before and during industrialization" (Calhoun 1982, 239).

7. Poulantzas (1975, 290) examines the contradictory oppositional ideological elements found among the stratum he identifies as the new petit bourgeoisie, the technical elites. Wright, too, insists that "the effects of class structure are mediated by politics. Class relations may define the terrain upon which interests are formed and collective capacities forged, but the outcome of that process of class formation cannot be 'read off' the class structure itself" (Wright 1985, 286).

8. Thus we find in Smith and Judd the argument that "objective conditions are currently present for the political mobilization of the newly marginalized, who once had reasonable expectations of middle income employment, but whose expectations have been (or are being) shattered. Furthermore, the new structural conditions of urban labor markets also make possible the forging of previously unlikely alliances between newly marginalized workers who are direct victims of growth-induced restructuring, traditional secondary labor market workers, and both old and new immigrant workers, in major central cities" (1984, 189). What Smith and Judd say about the changes in the condition of the once-secure old immigrant working class is true; what their political economy leaves unexamined is the historical processes that connect changes in material conditions with changes in the ideas necessary for the mobilization of collective action. The existence of such lacunae in neo-Marxist thought is precisely why structured and rigorous theories of political activism need formulation and development.

9. The old debate between "instrumentalists" and "structuralists" about whether the state was the immediate captive of business elites or was capable of autonomous action in opposition to the interests of capital has lost its salience. It has become apparent that there is no reason to suppose any fundamental contradiction between the two points of view: "We regard the state and capital as the two major initiators of redevelopment activity and think that in some cases a purely

instrumentalist explanation of state action, whereby the state acts at the direct bidding of capital applies," write Norman and Susan Fainstein. "But we also accept a class-struggle model of the state, in which the state incorporates the gains that have been won by popular movements" (Fainstein and Fainstein 1983).

References

Bloom, Jack M. 1987. *Class, Race, and the Civil Rights Movement*. Bloomington: Indiana University Press.

Booth, Heather, Harry Boyte, and Steve Max. 1986. *Citizen Action*. Philadelphia: Temple University Press.

Bowles, Samuel, and Herbert Gintis. 1987. *Democracy and Capitalism: Property, Community, and the Contradictions of Modern Social Thought*. New York: Basic Books.

Bowles, Samuel, David M. Gordon, and Thomas E. Weisskopf, eds. 1984. *Beyond the Wasteland*. New York: Doubleday Anchor.

Boyte, Harry. 1980. *Backyard Revolution*. Philadelphia: Temple University Press.

———. 1984. *Community Is Possible*. New York: Harper Colophon.

Boyte, Harry, and Frank Riessman, eds. 1986. *The New Populism: The Politics of Empowerment*. Philadelphia: Temple University Press.

Burghart, Steven. 1982. *The Other Side of Organizing*. Cambridge, Mass.: Schenckman.

Calhoun, Craig. 1982. *The Question of Class Struggle: Social Foundations of Popular Radicalism during the Industrial Revolution*. Chicago: University of Chicago Press.

Carnoy, Martin, and Derek Shearer. 1980. *Economic Democracy: The Challenge of the 1980s*. Armonk, N.Y.: Sharpe.

Castells, Manuel. 1983. *The City and the Grassroots*. Berkeley and Los Angeles: University of California Press.

Delgado, Gary. 1986. *Organizing the Movement: The Roots and Growth of ACORN*. Philadelphia: Temple University Press.

Eisenstein, Zillah. 1987. *Capitalist Patriarchy and the Case for Socialist Feminism*. New York: Monthly Review Press.

Evans, Sara, and Harry Boyte. 1986. *Free Spaces: The Sources of Democratic Change in America*. New York: Harper & Row.

Fainstein, Norman I., and Susan S. Fainstein. 1974. *Urban Political Movements*. Englewood Cliffs, N.J.: Prentice-Hall.

———. 1983. "Regime Strategies, Communal Resistance, and Economic Forces." In *Restructuring the City*, edited by S. Fainstein et al. New York: Longman.

Fisher, Robert, and Peter Romanofsky, eds. 1981. *Community Organization for Urban Social Change: A Historical Perspective*. Westport, Conn.: Greenwood.

Geertz, Clifford. 1973. "Ideology as a Cultural System." In *The Interpretation of Cultures*. New York: Basic Books.

Goodwyn, Lawrence. 1978. *The Populist Movement*. New York: Oxford University Press.

————. 1981. "Organizing Democracy." *Democracy* 1.

Gusfield, Joseph R. 1975. *Community: A Critical Response*. New York: Harper & Row.

Hartsock, Nancy. 1983. *Money, Sex, and Power: Toward a Feminist Historical Materialism*. New York: Longman.

Kahn, Si. 1982. *Organizing*. New York: McGraw-Hill.

Katznelson, Ira. 1981. *City Trenches: Urban Politics and the Patterning of Class in the United States*. Chicago: University of Chicago Press.

Logan, John R., and Harvey L. Molotch. 1987. *Urban Fortunes: The Political Economy of Place*. Berkeley: University of California Press.

Marable, Manning. 1980. "Through the Prism of Race and Class: Modern Black Nationalism in the U.S." *Socialist Review*, May/June.

————. 1983. *How Capitalism Underdeveloped Black America*. Boston: South End Press.

Midwest Academy Organizing Manual. 1984. 600 W. Fullerton Avenue, Chicago, Illinois.

"Neighborhood Action." 1980. *Social Policy*, Special Issue, September/October.

O'Connor, James. 1975. *The Fiscal Crisis of the State*. New York: St. Martin's Press.

"Organizing Neighborhoods." 1979. *Social Policy*, Special Issue, September/October.

Outlaw, Lucius T. 1983. "Race and Class in the Theory and Practice of Emancipatory Social Transformation." In *Philosophy Born of Struggle: Anthology of Afro-American Philosophy from 1917*, edited by Leonard Harris. Dubuque, Iowa: Kendall/Hunt.

Poulantzas, Nicos. 1975. *Classes in Contemporary Capitalism*. London: New Left Books.

Rudé, George. 1980. *Ideology and Popular Protest*. New York: Pantheon.

Swerdlo, Amy, and Hanna Lessinger. 1983. *Class, Race, and Sex: The Dynamics of Control*. Boston: Hall.

Smith, Michael Peter, and Dennis Judd. 1984. "American Cities: The Production of Ideology." In *Cities in Transformation*, edited by M. P. Smith. Beverly Hills: Sage Publications, Urban Affairs Annual Reviews, vol. 26.

Wright, Erik Olin. 1985. *Classes*. London: Verso Books.

PART I

Figuring It Out
Theoretical Frameworks for Activism

The knowledgeable man in the genuine public is
able to turn his personal troubles into social
issues, to see their relevance for his community
and his community's relevance for them. He
understands that what he thinks and feels are
personal troubles are very often . . . not subject
to solution by any one individual but only by modi-
fications of the structures of the groups in which
he lives and sometimes the structure of the
entire society.

Mills, *The Power Elite*

CHAPTER 1

Class and Community in an Era of Urban Transformation

Joseph M. Kling
and Prudence S. Posner

Moving the People: Class or Community?

In recent decades, one of the most controversial debates relating to the problem of activism has focused on the groups to be mobilized for change. Does one seek to organize the working class? What of "new" working classes? Or has the fundamental locus of struggle become nonclass groups, such as women and racial and ethnic minorities?

Membership in the working class is usually defined, in these debates, by the fact that surplus value is extracted from a person's particular activity as producer of goods or services. This follows, in broad outline, Marxist-oriented understandings of class. Yet collective grievances exist that cannot be traced directly to an individual's class position. These grievances yield identities that we refer to as *citizen-based* or *constituency-based*. Constituency members are tied to social action either because they are socially singled out and subjected to discrimination as persons or because they reside in a common area (usually a neighborhood) that generates communal identity and locally based political interests. For example, women, in the face of market and workplace discrimination or repressive traditions regarding family roles, have common social interests as women; at the same time, women who live in the same neighborhood may be brought together around specific needs for, say, a local day-care center or health clinic.

While the activist debate might be described generally as one between those who look primarily to class as the basis for political action and those

A slightly different version of this paper appears in *Comparative Urban and Community Research* 3 (1990).

who look to constituency or aggrieved citizenship, it can also be approached in terms of the distinction between class and community. The locus of class-based organizing is clear: the workplace and areas where workers reside, neighborhoods resting somewhere in the vicinity of the plants that dominate the classic industrial city and mill town. Citizens and constituency members, in contrast, are not necessarily identifiable as workers in the strict sense of direct producers who exchange their labor power for a wage. The locus of constituency-based organizing, therefore, is often "the community"—where these citizens live and, frequently, commute to all sorts of work in a variety of settings. Since most constituency interests transcend locality, the need to think in terms of a locus of organizing leads to the terminological class–community distinction in contemporary discussions of social movements.

Overview of the Debate: The New Populism or the New Marxism?

There is a long tradition in the United States that relies on citizenship as the basic category through which to understand collective political action. This tradition challenges the primacy of the Marxist notion of class as the key to the emergence and direction of social movements.[1] It is a tradition associated with the middle-class Progressivism and agrarian populism of the decades preceding World War I, and traces its roots back to Jeffersonian ideas of the American commonwealth (Evans and Boyte 1986, esp. Chaps. 1, 4, 5). Its significance declined between the world wars, because, in response to the Great Depression, class issues came to the fore. Labor unions, led by the CIO, became the primary social movers, and the American Communist party exercised a significant impact on progressive politics.

After World War II, labor's influence diminished, and class concepts of organization lost salience. Community organizer Saul Alinsky put forth a concept of workers as citizens, whose first responsibility was to society as a whole, not to a union and certainly not to a "class."[2] The American labor movement embraced both Cold War ideology and corporate unionism.[3] In these years, C. Wright Mills (1967 [1951]) wrote *White Collar*, which introduced the notion of an exploited, or new, middle class and challenged traditional Marxist notions of class struggle and collective organization.

In the early 1950s, under the batterings of McCarthyism and a general antileft hysteria, there was no large-scale organizing presence of populist or class-based orientation. Then, in May 1954 *Brown v. Board of Education* was decided. A year and a half later, on December 1, 1955, in Birmingham, Alabama, Rosa Parks refused to move to the back of the bus. The civil rights movement was under way.[4]

This essay cannot do justice to the history of post–World War II American social movements. Their history is not, in any event, an unfamiliar story. In summary, there have been four major social movements in America since the silences of the McCarthy era: civil rights and black power, student/ antiwar, women's, and community action.[5] What is notable is that none of these movements has been class-based. All have built on the citizenship notion of populism, rather than the class-identity concept of Marxism.

The resurgence of citizen-based movements led to a resurgence of populist theory in the realm of social and historical analysis. For example, the agrarian movement of the 1880s and 1890s once was analyzed in terms of farmers as a kind of peasant class of small landowners caught in the jaws of an expanding industrial capitalism: now it came to be seen as a people's movement not subject to categorization in terms of class.[6]

Organizers such as Mike Miller of the Organize Training Center in San Francisco and Wade Rathke of ACORN (Associated Community Organizations for Reform Now), the policy theorist Frank Riessman of *Social Policy* magazine, and the historian and social theorist Harry Boyte took emerging neopopulist ideas and applied them to the community and public-interest movements that began to appear in the 1970s. Boyte explicitly reintroduced the notion that what was occurring was citizen- or constituency-based political action. "Elements of a democratic, populist sensibility grew through the 1970's," he wrote:

> a renewed vision of direct democracy coupled with a mistrust of large institutions, both public and private. Such a democratic vision represented a rekindled faith in the citizenry itself. . . . In turn, the building blocks for a *revitalized ethos of citizenship* are to be found in the voluntary structures of all kinds at the base of American society. (Boyte 1980, 7)

There was much force to the populist argument. Certainly traditional Marxist analyses could not sufficiently account for the emergence and character of postwar social movements except through a crude class reductionism and a monotonous insistence that working people simply did not know what their true interests were.

Still, many observers argued against the abandonment of class-based social analysis. Robert Fisher (1984) wrote a history of neighborhood organizing in which he was critical of neopopulist historians and activists because, unlike Marxists, they "tended to ignore political and economic developments at the national level which directly affected the lives of working people" (pp. xvi–xvii).

Erik Olin Wright and Ira Katznelson worked at reconceptualizing the notion of class. Wright, taken with the breaches made in the armor of the Marxist framework by the rise of a middle class that seemed, in its way, to be as exploited by the new bureaucratic capitalism as workers were by early capitalism, attempted an ambitious reformulation of class theory built to incorporate what he called "contradictory class positions" (Wright 1979, Chap. 2; 1985, 26–37).

Katznelson's (1981, 1986) deconstruction of the notion of class into four levels almost precisely parallels Wright's. A major difference is that Katznelson tied his reconceptualization directly to the emergence of non-class-based social movements, particularly those in the urban black community. For this reason, his approach proves somewhat more fruitful in attempting to understand the relationship between class structures and constituency-based organizing.

So brief an overview cannot indicate the complexity of the ways in which class theory has been reworked since the 1970s. The point is to suggest that class-based theories recognizing the basic insights of neopopulist thinking exist. They provide a starting point for attempts to reconcile, at least partially, the activist dilemma precipitated by the class–community split. To this effort at consolidation we now turn.

Castells: The Capitalist City and Constituency Mobilization

If Marxism is so powerful a tool of analysis, neopopulist theory properly inquires, why has it failed to account for the character of many major social movements in the industrialized West? To Manual Castells, the answer is simple: Marxism was never a *unified* theory of change. Its first part dealt comprehensively with the concept of class structure; its second, however, dealt with the notion of class *struggle* and, given the historical juncture at which Marx wrote, was unable to elicit an adequate account of the ways in which working people would become mobilized.

Since the two parts of Marxist theory are, in many ways, logically distinct, it is possible to reassess Marxism's understanding of social movements while retaining its basic analysis of the role of surplus appropriation in shaping social structure. For those unwilling to abandon the centrality of class when shifting perspective from social structure to social movements, the essential theoretical question becomes, in the formulation of Castells (1983, 298), How is the connection to be established between the structure and the practices?[7]

The traditional Marxist answer has always been through the class-based vanguard party. "Leninism became an integral part of Marxism," Castells (1983) writes, "not only because of the triumph of the Soviet revolution, but because only the theory of the party can establish a bridge between structures and practices in the marxist construction" (p. 299). The problem, of course, is that the class-based party movement has never been the sole form of resistance to political domination. This historical fact becomes especially clear after World War II, with the worldwide unfolding of constituency movements built around such issues as black nationalism, ethnic nationalisms, community resistance to industrial encroachments, feminism, and environmentalism.

In the face of these disconfirming realities, a number of responses are possible. Marxism can insist that all social movements, at bottom, are class movements. Or it can dismiss these movements as having no independent historical significance. But these arguments are variants of a mechanical and logically indefensible reductionism. A third response is to attempt to retain the fundamental impact of class on historical development while incorporating the relevance of nonclass-based movements into the theoretical and empirical understanding of social change.

Castells's contribution is to have conceptually and empirically linked constituency movements to class structures through the notion of urban space. Space, he reminds us, is as much a material dimension of production as are land, labor, and capital, for the ways in which goods are produced are inseparable from the ways in which space is appropriated to produce them. The story of how this process of spatial reorganization worked in terms of the development of industrial capitalism is a well-known one: With the invention of the steam engine and the emergence of the factory system, family producers are uprooted from their cottages in and around the rural village. They are forced by social conditions to locate in concentrated regions organized and structured in terms of the interests of the owners and controllers of the newly industrialized means of production. Thus is born the capitalist city, whether a manufacturing center, like Manchester, or a market and financial one, like London.

How people experience the domination and control that flow from the spatial form associated with the modern capitalist city leads to urban-based social movements. In such cities, these movements need not be class derived, since they are more likely to emerge out of what a group sharing a common residential area perceives as a threat to its cultural identity or neighborhood autonomy. One cannot predict what form these nonclass movements will take in response to pressures generated by the class structure; they are contingent rather than determined. What is crucial to understand is that whatever the value or interest or goal at the base of the nonclass movement, it has been precipitated by the workings of a particular mode of production on the shape of people's lives.

Castells thus presents us with a developed theory of the relation between class structure, urban space, and urban-oriented social movements. In the late capitalist city, with its access to modern technologies of transportation and information flow, people's experience of surplus extraction is determined and shaped by the way in which the spaces where they live and consume are separated from the spaces where they work and produce. In this situation, social movements grounded in the experience of neighborhood, family, or racial and cultural identity should be the expected norm. Once Castells's insight is recognized, the significant question for students of social change shifts from whether class or community is the more fundamental source of collective action. Instead, one must try to discover the relation in which nonclass mobilizations stand to the class structure that shuttles through, and environs, them.

Based on a wide range of movements researched and studied, Castells and his staff concluded that urban social movements in the era of late capitalism usually form around three goals: collective consumption, community solidarity, and citizen action. *Collective consumption* refers to the attempt to expand the social wage, to bring to localities such social services as housing, improved education, and health and child-care centers. Movements of *community solidarity* seek to protect racial or cultural identity, or resist perceived threats against the integrity of the family and neighborhood. *Citizen action* movements fight for local autonomy, decentralization, and neighborhood self-management. These three kinds of movement are not class based, as Castells (1983) points out, "for the very simple reason that they do not relate directly to the relationships of production but to the relationships of consumption, communication, power" (p. 320).

John Logan and Harvey Molotch (1987, 38; Molotch 1984) are correct in warning against the "romanticism of the grass-roots" from which Castells's work suffers. Castells seems conveniently to assume that all neighborhood groups—including service-oriented and "preservationist" ones—may be understood as activist and progressive. Still, the three goals Castells selects as shaping recent community action are close to the mark; they are the concerns, specifically urban based or not, that mobilized many neighborhoods in the decades following the War on Poverty. Critically, for our purposes, they are tied precisely to the issues that neopopulism sees as generated out of "the interests of the community." The problem is that neopopulism conceives of these goals, and the issues around which they are built, as the basic elements of social struggle. It does not understand the ways in which they are molded by the urban form of the capitalist class structure. It thus identifies the surface expression of the resistance to capitalist modes of domination as the essential substance of that resistance.

Neopopulism does not have to recognize the connection between constituency movements and the exigencies of capitalist control. But if the Castellian framework is correct, unless it does, and makes such linkages explicit and manifest in its organizing activity, neopopulism will continually undermine itself and the organizational movements that follow from its principles. Castells (1983) somewhat wearily points out near the conclusion of his massive work that "urban social movements are not agents of structural social change, but symptoms of resistance to the social domination even if, in their effort to resist, they do have major effects on cities and societies" (1983: 329).[8]

We are now in position both to examine critically the term community, and locate it within the multilayered framework for analyzing class developed by Ira Katznelson. We hope to show that while community signifies too many different things to be useful either for the analysis of power relationships or as the basis for democratic social change, once placed in a framework of class analysis it can be a helpful instrument for understanding and engaging in social action.

The Limits of the New Populist Concept of Community

When people find themselves unable to control the world, they simply shrink the world to the size of their community. (Castells 1983, 331)

Lacking the ability to deal meaningfully with the large-scale organizational and institutional structures that characterize our society, many of those we talked to turned to the small town not only as an ideal but as a solution to our present political difficulties. (Bellah et al. 1985, 204)

We begin this section by quoting these authors because they are intimately associated with the discussion of community, as a unit of resistance and as a basis for social transformation. Yet they recognize the limitations of that concept as a tool for either understanding or changing a world dominated by multinational corporate power. Like other social thinkers, Castells and Bellah use *community* in both its descriptive and utopian meanings—in the words of Joseph Gusfield (1975), its semantic and poetic meanings. The poetic or utopian meanings of community refer to the value placed on it as a normative concept, echoing the *gemeinschaft–gesellschaft* debate of an earlier era.

As a value-term, community refers to a relationship of persons as "ends", rather than as means or instruments. It stands in opposition to the notion of working people as "hands," or "costs of production." It challenges the idea that land, whether urban dwelling space or rural farm land, is a commodity whose value is measured purely in exchange terms. It encompasses the idea that housing is a human need, to be met as such, not merely a product to be supplied if the price is right. Clearly, the idea of community is a powerful one that draws on deep human desires and commitments that are fundamentally opposed, not only to the needs of capitalist organization of production, consumption, and reproduction but perhaps even to industrial organization in general. Nevertheless, the power of the concept as a value commitment does not, in itself, warrant our use of the term, either in an analysis of contemporary conditions or as a prescription of resistance to them and of transformation.

As we argued earlier, the concept of community as a basis for social activism is the product of the particular kinds of social changes and social movements that have emerged since World War II. Theorists of this latter form of social-change action call it *new populism*. From the new populist perspective, the major agent of social transformation must be the community. For them, "the community" becomes a substitute for the older Marxist notion of the proletariat as the agent of revolution *and* for the social democratic program of seeking state intervention in the market on behalf of human needs. For example, Bowles and Gintis (1987) explain the feasibility of their image of "postliberal democracy":

By stressing workplace and community empowerment as opposed to state expansion, the vision of postliberal democracy avoids one of the great dead

ends encountered in the expansion of personal rights and simultaneously
addresses a key weakness of social democracy. By stressing that the extension
of democracy is not synonymous with the extension of state power, postliberal
democracy affirms the sentiment that neither the centralized state nor the
capitalist corporation will be the vehicle of human liberation. (p. 179)

Without turning a blind eye to the manifest evils of state bureaucracy, we
believe that the ease with which an idea such as "community empowerment"
seems to avoid the "weakness of social democracy" is more a function of its
ambiguity than of its superior utility as a concept.

There is an irreducible reality to *community* as it applies to geographical
units that constitute the American local political landscape. These units
have taxing power, authority over schooling, and the power to zone for land
use, thereby obtaining certain regulatory powers. But most analysts (and
activists) concerned with social change are not interested in community
primarily as it exists at the level of the 650 separate taxing bodies on
suburban Long Island. Nor are they referring to the 73 Primary Metropolitan
Statistical Areas in the United States (each of which is economically integrated into one of the 21 Consolidated Metropolitan Statistical Areas (U.S.
Bureau of the Census 1986). The complexity of levels of governance and
common interest is prohibitive. Instead, to the extent that its meaning is
made explicit, community is viewed as a collectivity in need of empowerment
or as a relationship of persons in which we are neighbors ("ends") rather
than buyers and sellers ("means"). As such, community refers to a process,
not to a thing or place.

Turning again to Gusfield's discussion of community, we would say that
what is meant is something that emerges as the product of people consciously
acting in common, defining themselves as an "us," different from, and
frequently opposed to, "them." Given the importance to homeowners of the
power to exclude "them" through zoning (a political/community function),
obviously the different meanings sometimes coalesce. Nevertheless, the
political patchwork of communities capable of legally exercising that power
hardly exhausts the meaning of the term. As Gusfield (1975) puts it: "The
nature of the social bond and the selection of bondsmen is not a fixed and
given fact; a part of the *essence* of the group. Instead it is a facet of historical
situations; a part of the *existence* of acting persons" (p. 39). We leave aside
the use of the term to mean "interest group," as in a Jewish community, a
gay community, or a community of scholars. In this usage it is fairly obvious
that community membership is voluntary (more or less) and that the existence

of a community capable of acting in common to achieve goals requires the
conscious recognition of "bondsmen" and the deliberate forging of such a
bond. Nevertheless, even if we look only at uses that are tied to a geographical location, we are using a term that has moral meanings attached to it. A
community school, community hospital, or community center, however
bureaucratic and impersonal it may be, is on some level expected to "belong"
to the people in the locality it is supposed to serve.

The community most frequently cited as the model of resistance during
the past two decades is the urban neighborhood (Boyte 1980; Castells 1983;
Plotkin 1987). The emergence of urban communities that self-consciously
resisted efforts to remove poor and working-class residents from central
cities in the name of urban renewal is a function of the macroeconomic
trends of the 1950s through the 1970s. The rapid growth of community
organization through the 1970s was largely a response to what Castells
(1983) calls "the reappropriation of urban space." Cutbacks in housing
subsidies for the poor, the "redlining" of working-class areas to eliminate
private mortgages and home improvement loans, and the diversion of public
funds into "downtown development" and middle- and upper-income housing
would all serve as mechanisms for making the central cities "safe" for
investment and profitable construction. This process took place in the
context of a shrinking public pot, as the corporate tax share of the national
budget decreased from 23 percent in 1960 to less than 8 percent in 1984.[9]

The urban communities galvanized into collective action as a result of
the pressures of urban renewal and redevelopment (including the pressure
from central-city black families to find housing in nearby, exclusively white
neighborhoods) were not political subdivisions with taxing and zoning power.
Sometimes they had neighborhood designations (Chelsea, Dorchester,
Southside, Washington Heights); sometimes the embattled community was
a subsection of a larger neighborhood. Their self-identity as a community
combined a sense of historical continuity with the immediacy of the threat
from "them"—the City Hall planners advocating downtown development at
the expense of low-cost housing and services, and the financial interests
eager to invest in desirable central-city locations once the land became
available.

As veterans of innumerable public meetings at which the microphone
was seized from city officials with the demand that "the community" be
heard, we are reluctant to abandon such a politically powerful concept. At
the same time, that experience brings home forcibly the degree to which
"community" is in the eyes of the beholder. It includes those who agree to
undertake collective action in order to achieve some public goal—the

modification or elimination of existing policy, the inauguration of new policy—the introduction or augmentation of public services, or the elimination of a public nuisance. Other than as a convenient political slogan, the idea that power *ought* to inhere to communities is, to say the least, problematic. The upper-class "community" of Irvine, California, fighting to prevent further development in the vicinity of the multiacre lots of their community, is not the same as the working-class communities of Chelsea (Manhattan) or Cobble Hill (Brooklyn), fighting to hold on to affordable housing units in the face of gentrification. The lower-middle-class white Brooklyn "community" of Canarsie, tightly organized to control the movement of black families into the area, is not the same as the neighboring "community" of East New York, trying to prevent the location of halfway houses and juvenile homes in a low- and middle-income black residential area. And obviously, none of these is the same as the "community" of Pittsburgh, which has included business, unemployed, service employees, and practically all residents in the effort to figure out how to reindustrialize the Monongahela Valley.

The fact that "communities" cut across lines of social stratification within a residence area, for example when a community organizes to keep an industrial employer in the area, to control a polluting industry, or to keep out a dangerous or polluting plant or dump, does not tell us much about the relationship between community and class. Obviously many communities, especially homeowning suburbs, equate the values of community with the maintenance of their expensively purchased life style. But sometimes, as in the well-documented and closely watched case of Santa Monica, renters and homeowners join forces in order to exercise control over growth and development.

Sidney Plotkin (1987) has shown the complex intertwining of class interests in any given land-use conflict. Despite the complexity, however, we think it is possible and helpful to situate community, as a concept, within a framework premised on the central notion of class conflict in capitalist society.

"Community" within the Framework of a Layered Class Model

Our focus is less on grand schemas of class or other relationships than it is on the ways in which class and community are both articulating terms and ways of understanding issues that may or may not mobilize people into collective action. We stress *issues* because mobilization for collective action takes place in response to a particular event or in order to achieve a particular goal, not to alter the general structure of the game. At the same time, the major grievances that in fact mobilize people cannot be eliminated within the rules of that game, the game of capitalism. As we showed earlier, the categories of class alone, however finely drawn, do not sufficiently articulate the kinds of grievances people experience. At the same time, although community is frequently the self-defined locus of the grievance and the vehicle for collective action, as a term it lacks sufficient clarity and explanatory power to serve the purposes some new populist analysts would have it serve.

The urban social movements to which discussions of community organization and community empowerment refer represent the community or residence side of the community–workplace dichotomy in American political life and social consciousness. This side of our lives is not insulated from class, however; it is merely not experienced in class terms. It is experienced in the language and action of ethnicity and community, race, social status, and political affiliation. It is not merely experienced as such (to the extent that experience can be relegated to the "mere"), for these are the "trenches" (in Katznelson's 1981 terminology) of urban civic life through which struggles for change are channeled and contained.

Rather than try to read the breakdown of class fragments or strata within a community, or worse, simply to dismiss class as irrelevant to struggles related to issues of consumption and distribution, we want to use Katznelson's layered concept of class in order to clarify the function of community (with its penumbra of meanings) in a society whose essential characteristic remains that of class conflict over the appropriation of surplus value (Katznelson 1981, 1986).

Briefly, Katznelson argues that the notion of class suffers from conceptual overload: Too many different meanings are packed into a single term. He seeks to break the concept apart, to crack it open along lines of fault not visible until history provides the opportunity to test out the original Marxist formulations. Class is not a unified construct, Katznelson suggests, but is composed of "four connected layers." He identifies those layers as (1) structure, (2) ways of life, (3) dispositions, and (4) collective action (Katznelson 1986, 14). We summarize these four levels of meaning as he proposes them.

The first level, *structure*, is shared by all systems based on private capital investment. It refers to the fundamental organization of the economy, whereby collective capital exploits collective labor by appropriating the surplus value produced by the latter. Not only do most Americans not understand capitalism in this form, but it is not experienced in this form by the real people who participate in it. Although it shapes that experience, it lies, by definition, outside the realm of immediate perception and awareness.

What we experience, as workers and as consumers of what is produced, occurs at Katznelson's second level of class, the *way of life* precipitated by the operation of capital and its continuous drive for profit as it has developed historically in our particular society. It is the job one holds, the hours and pay level, the degree of authority over others or submission to others' demands. It includes the kind of neighborhood in which one rents or owns a home, the availability of public and private facilities for recreation and education, and the degree of exclusionary control one exercises in that capacity in order to determine with whom one shares a way of life. As a "way of life" it includes the ways in which our children are prepared to take their place in the organization of society—as job holders, executives, citizens, parents, and so on. It includes the ways in which the society is stratified, using race, ethnicity, educational level, gender, geography, and the like to allocate goods and services.

It has often been noted, with regret by the political left and with satisfaction by the right, that the class position held by persons in the terms described above does not offer much predictability as to what they feel, think, and believe about their situation. Neither does there appear to be any determinate relationship between class position and how people will act in order to preserve or alter that situation. What Katznelson proposes is that we accept that *disposition*, or "consciousness"—feelings, and ideas—is a third level of analysis, one related to class formations but dependent on many other factors. Katznelson argues that in the United States, the off-work "consciousness" of working people developed in relation to community, which is understood primarily as the place of residence that is simultaneously the locus of political representation. Since residence, or geographical community, is historically tied to income strata and, especially *within* urban areas, to ethnicity and race, these identities are often coextensive with locally oriented political party activity and exercise of citizenship. At the level of "consciousness," then, in their off-work lives, Americans operate with nonclass "mental maps."[10] If Katznelson's (1986) thesis is correct, the bad news is that this is a *given* of the American scene and is not likely to change, no matter what strategies for social change are developed.

The good news lies in the recognition that the fourth level of meaning, *collective action,* is no more rigidly determined by beliefs and ideas than these are wholly determined by one's position in a class structure. The fallacy of generations of Marxists was to suppose that disposition, or consciousness, could be deduced from a correct reading of class as way of life. The trick, therefore, was to find the Real Working Class, teach it the correct political understanding and values, and mobilize it into action. The fallacy of the new populists is to suppose that collective action is determined by ideology or disposition, rather than limited or influenced by it. The trick for the new populists, then, becomes identifying the real values and dispositions of the People, and hitching collective action to those.

There are real structures and processes that are a function of capitalism, whether people have constructed the understandings to include them or not. These are the large-scale institutional structures and organizations that people find they cannot control, and according to Castells (1983), "shrink down" to the size of their community.

Obviously people are more likely to mobilize for collective action in terms of familiar identities and beliefs. Any activist knows that in the United States probably the easiest issue to mobilize people around is protection of their property rights. Second easiest is the demand that "the community" participate in decisions that affect the life situation (e.g., property value, child raising and educating, shopping, traffic patterns, environmentally determined health conditions, in-migration of lower-status neighbors due to government housing policy). Even racial solidarity, so powerful as an inspiration to collective action on behalf of black citizenship rights, may pale in the face of these kinds of issues. Yet we also know that in the absence of a commitment to some larger concept of social justice, mobilization for collective action based on these most readily accessible "dispositions" does not necessarily move people in the direction of greater equality or democracy. In fact, it is precisely these readily accessible mobilizing sentiments that lead collective action into the "trenches," the preexisting channels of competitive pluralism and communal defensiveness that assimilate protest into the structures of politics as usual.[11]

Our concern here is not with predicting or planning social movements or upheavals, however. We are trying to see if it is possible for collective action, in the off-work context of American politics, to be related to class issues and conflicts when we know that the consciousness or dispositions of the people whose "toes are pinched" by social conditions is nonclass in nature. In particular, we are looking at issues that are understood in terms of community: the rights of communities as political units and actors, and the privileges of those who dwell within them. We are trying to confront the dilemma posed by the fact that dispositions are oriented toward "community" in relation to many off-work issues, yet collective action that fails to include "class content" (for want of a better term) and that is not directed at the class structures of appropriation consistently fails to address the roots of the problems people face.

The factors that have the possibility of reconnecting collective action to class structures and processes (in the absence of class consciousness) are those of leadership and organization. Since the link between the dispositions, consciousness, and identity of a collectivity and the kind of collective action it undertakes is not rigidly determined (although the two levels are obviously related), there are choices possible at the moment of transformation from a feeling or sentiment of collective grievance into collective action for redress of that grievance. We suggest that this reconnection occurs in the formulation of *program*, that is, the combination of explanation and proposed solution that gives direction to collective action.

Programs informed by class content tie local issues to larger questions of the restructuring of policy at state and federal levels. In the sphere of environmental organizing, for example, the alternative "not in my backyard" has been posed against the demand for stronger and more democratically formulated state and federal controls on industrial production and waste. While these are not necessarily contradictory, the choice of whether to articulate the program primarily in terms of "community" (not in my backyard) or "class" (public controls on private industry) is a matter of emphasis that will determine the overall direction of the collective action or struggle. The existence of these choices has to do with the reconnection of what are understood as community issues to the class processes of a capitalist society.

A similar example can be found in the conflict over control of the San Antonio aquifer discussed by Plotkin (1987). Collective action to protect the city's water supply can remain at the level of competing communal rights; alternatively, the issue of water, like the issue of land use, concerning resources that cannot be reduced to exchange value and property rights, can be moved to the federal level, where there is sufficient power to set limits on private development. Of course, the organization of people to address such an issue takes place at the level of the self-defined community, even though the social power to resolve it resides elsewhere.

Finally, some examples can be taken from the women's movement, at points where it is engaged in the public arena. The need for day care, for example, may be experienced as a women's issue, a community issue, a race issue, or even a work-related issue (as unions are beginning to include provision of day care as an employer-paid benefit). The "class content" of a program demanding day-care facilities, however, is related to the idea that child care and preschool education are social responsibilities. A class perspective rejects the notion that "you can get what you can pay for," so the children from lower economic strata and status groups are entitled only to what their parents can make possible. Again, this should not be understood to mean that other, nonclass issues related to the care and education of children are unimportant (e.g., nonsexist, multiracial pattern of staffing, curricular development), only that these issues do not reconnect what may be experienced as a nonclass issue (e.g., sexual or racial equality) to the class structures.

The strategy of collective action in a particular situation is contingent on many factors, including the dispositions of those who have been moved to undertake the action. Without "class content" of the kind described earlier, the struggle will once again be channeled through the existing trenches, from which little change can be made. The question, then, is whether people whose history and experience and inherited values have rendered close to invisible the impact of class structure on their lives can be moved to organize themselves, not as a class, but at least in terms of class-oriented policy issues. These issues, in their programmatic formulation, specifically seek state reordering of the systemic priorities of both the process of private capital accumulation and the distribution of social surplus within a market economy.

Social Movements as Organized Publics

We have tried to argue that class and community are not oppositional concepts but different modes through which society organizes people's connection to the worlds of production and politics. We need synthesis, therefore, not argument over which is prior, or which is the more valid construct through which collective action should take place. In our search through the literature, the most helpful idea we came across was the old notion of the democratic public, as reformulated by John Dewey in the 1920s and then by C. Wright Mills, writing in the midst of the repressive, anxious, fragmenting America of the 1950s. Both Dewey and Mills sought social change, both were aware of the inadequacies of Marxist analysis to the complexities of twentieth-century capitalism, and both suggested that theorists and practitioners think of social movements as organized *publics*. It is an idea we would like briefly to explore and develop in this concluding section, for it seeks to transcend, at least conceptually, the splintered identities and interests that day-to-day life in the modern polity precipitates for working people.

Dewey (1927, 166) tried to determine the conditions necessary for the emergence of what he called "a democratically organized public." He took his departure "from the objective fact that human acts have consequences upon others, that some of these consequences are perceived, and that their perception leads to subsequent effort to control action so as to secure some consequences and avoid others" (p. 12).

A public is open to formation, then, when a group of actors recognizes that it is being affected—in ways it considers undesirable—by a second group of actors or a set of institutions that operates from a social realm in some manner distinct from those being affected. This is the "us–them" sense in which the experience of community itself becomes rooted.

Dewey further argued that there is a distinction between conditions that objectively create a public and an aggregate's correctly perceiving itself as such. Publics, that is, may not fully comprehend the sources of their grievances. Here, Dewey integrated into his theory of the democratic state the idea that members of a given population may have essential interests and concerns that are systemically generated, but of which they are plainly and simply unaware. Collective action, and corrective social policy, will not emerge, therefore, unless affected aggregates become conscious of themselves as a public (Dewey 1927, 131). The organized public takes shape as people come together to take action to change the structures.

In the 1950s, C. Wright Mills returned to the notion of publics. In those dark years of McCarthyism and the pronouncement of the end of ideology, those years of the happy suburban family and juvenile delinquency, social critics were fully confronting the phenomenon of mass society. Mills had the prescience to recognize that the search for community was a reaction to the sense of disconnection from larger societal institutions. "This loss of any structural view or position," he argued, "is the decisive meaning of the lament over the loss of community." Mills was insistent: "The political structure of a democratic state requires the public; and, the democratic man, in his rhetoric, must assert that this public is the very seat of sovereignty" (Mills 1959, 322, 323).

The recognition of social alienation—the sense of powerlessness and inefficacy—as a malaise more profound and general than that associated with "alienated labor" forced Mills to probe deeply into what the internal structures of a public were all about. This was a task for which history had provided John Dewey and other progressives of his era neither the empirical social conditions (the full emergence of the bureaucratic state) nor the conceptual language to undertake.

In the world examined by Mills, public discourse over alternatives of social life had been displaced by conformist-oriented and corporate-controlled mass media as the major sources of public opinion. Labor unions and political parties had become unresponsive bureaucratic machines. The voluntary associations of local politics—the traditional publics of classic democratic thought—had been taken over by experts and the philosophy of professional administration. The "man in the mass," Mills (1959, 307–308) wrote, "is without any sense of political belonging."

The reconstituted public was the only possible form of social organization that could meaningfully reconnect people to their world and provide them with some degree of control over its political directions. A public, for Mills, had three decisive characteristics: It was "a context in which reasonable opinions may be formulated; . . . an agency by which reasonable activities may be undertaken; . . . a powerful enough unit, in comparison with other organizations of power, to make a difference" (Mills 1956, 308). A public, in other words, provided people with an arena in which to deal with ideas, to act collectively on those ideas, and to develop a sense of effectiveness in the struggle to transform those ideas into reality.

Overall, the key to the fabric of the public, what differentiates it from any other form of political or voluntary association, is that its members understand and experience social grievances as "public issues" rather than "private troubles."

> The knowledgeable man in a genuine public . . . understands that what he thinks and feels to be personal troubles are very often also problems shared by others, and more importantly, not capable of solution by any one individual but only by modifications of the structure of the groups in which he lives and sometimes the structure of the entire society. (Mills 1959, 187)

Organized publics emerge, and structures are challenged, only when people come to believe that what they first considered to be personal grievances are, in fact, socially grounded; that others, outside their immediately identified peers, suffer the same undue treatment; and that some form of broad-based collective action may result in policies to regulate or redirect the sources of anxiety and frustration.

Organized publics, in the discourse we are proposing here, function as social movements, but as movements that link constituent- and community-based action groups to policies and programs that can have class content and orientation. The organized public describes social movements that seek to reshape political rules in broader democratic directions and that have core structures rooted in any kind of social base, whether class, constituency, or community. The labor movement of the 1930s, and the civil rights movements of the 1950s and 1960s, may be understood as organized publics in this sense. Indeed, any mass-based group that has a program aimed at extending the protections of the state to groups threatened by private and bureaucratic decision making exhibits, to one degree or another, the elements of a public.

What we are looking for are ways to move from within the daily lived currents of a particular constituency, from dispositions rooted in the immediacy of inherited political experience, to policies and programs that tap into the structures of class and state that set these movements in the context of market capitalism. This task, we suggest, falls precisely to the political organizer, and returns to the notion that people must often be educated to the larger, structural sources of social grievance. Otherwise, public issues remain, if not private troubles, then localized ones.

People must *be* organized. Jo Freeman (1983, 26) writes that "social movements do not simply occur." But the organizer cannot simply reflect the existing level of consciousness of a given constituency. The new populists are correct in asserting that nonclass movements are essential in building social change. They are also correct when they trace the origin of social movements back to community networks and inherited cultural traditions. At the same time, it is myopic to lose sight of Dewey's and Mill's arguments that the knowledge available to people, and the ways in which their experience has been historically structured, obscure the larger nature of the social forces at work on them. Reliance on inherited values and free spaces alone prevents constituencies organized as publics from arriving at informed understandings of what policies and programs will most directly attack the sources of their grievance. This is simply to recognize that societies do, in fact, mystify and that the ability of people to control their world demands demystification. It is a key role of the organizer, no matter the nature of the public to which he or she is attached, to aid in that process, "continually to translate," in Mill's words, "personal troubles into public issues, and public issues into the terms of their human meaning for a variety of individuals" (Mills 1959, 187).

There are no guarantees. Especially in America, the holds of localism, family identity, and racial and ethnic political consciousness may be so strong as to preclude constituent and community-based publics from generally projecting programs aimed at state regulation of the social surplus. Even then, the hold of global capitalism over our resources and political structures may be too great for class-oriented programs to make a significant difference in the quality of people's lives. But the only alternative is acquiescence to a set of political and economic arrangements that continually deny people economic dignity, pit them against each other, and dehumanize social life.

Notes

1. For a classic statement of this argument, see Hartz (1955).

2. Alinsky had begun to break with the Communists, and their vision of community organization as an extension of the class-party, sometime in the late 1930s. The Back of the Yards (BYO), which Alinsky referred to as "the first real People's Organization," held its founding meeting in July 1939, which means that Alinsky was developing the ideas on which it was based much earlier. In *Reveille for Radicals*, published at the beginning of the Cold War period, Alinsky made about as formal a statement of his theoretical principles regarding class-based organizing as he ever did. "It is not just trying to deal with the factory manager," he wrote, "but with every element and aspect, whether it be political, economical or social, that makes up the life of the worker. This will mean a complete change in the philosophy of the labor movement, so that instead of viewing itself as a separate section of the American people engaged in a separate craft in a particular industry, it will think of itself as an organization of *American citizens*" (Alinsky [1946] 1969, 36; for BYO founding, see 47).

3. This story has been told many times. See, for example, Green (1980, 208) and Bluestone and Harrison (1980, Chap. 5).

4. Parks's decision not to get up was spontaneous. But the fact that she was a long-time member of the NAACP, and no stranger to activism, is key to the event. The presence of organized movements may not always be obvious when social action takes place, but their role in *preparing* people for such action has historically proven itself again and again. This is one of the overlooked lessons of Thompson's *The Making of the English Working Class* (1963). For Parks's action, see Sitkoff (1981, Chap. 2), Raines (1983, 37–51), Parks ([1956] 1974).

5. For some histories of the New Left, see Ferber and Lynd (1971), Sale

(1973), Unger (1975). For two general histories of the 1960s, which include penetrating discussions of both the civil rights and student movements, but from differing political perspectives, see Hodgson (1978) and Matusow (1984).

For the women's movement see Evans (1980); Ferree and Hess (1985), and Freeman (1975). For histories of the community organizing movement, see Adamson and Burgos (1984), Delgado (1986), and Fisher (1984).

In America, environmentalism has never had the sort of generalized activist base associated with these four; its concerns have most often been expressed through locally based community action programs, or consumer protectionist interest groups such as PIRG. But see Logan and Molotch (1987). In Europe, of course, the Greens remain an autonomous and large-scale political presence.

6. For one of the best class-oriented studies of Populism, see Rogin (1967). More classic works include Destler ([1946] 1966), and Quint (1953).

7. "Marxism," Castells writes, "has been, at the same time, the theory of capital and the development of history through the development of productive forces, while also being the theory of class struggle between social actors fighting for the appropriation of the product and deciding the organization of society" (Castells 1983, 298).

8. What "major effects" means in this context is unclear. Castells, one suspects, is trying to have it both ways: Urban social movements are not *structurally* significant, but they are "significant."

9. Gary Delgado summarizes: "It was the resistance to this phenomenon, the reappropriation of urban space, that became the context for the formation of community organizations in the 1970s. . . . Community organizations were set up to fight evictions, resist urban removal, control schools and police, and address neighborhood safety, zoning and the threat of superhighways dividing the neighborhood." (Delgado 1986, 4–9).

10. The phrase "mental maps" is that of Geertz (1973, Chap. 8).

11. See Katznelson (1981) for a cogent discussion of exactly this process in New York City (Washington Heights) during the "community control" and other communal uprisings of the late 1960s. See also Mollenkopf (1983, esp. Chap. 5, "Consequences of the Neighborhood Revolt Against Renewal"). The "consequences" were cooptation of the community organizations and their leaderships. Leaders came, Mollenkopf wrote, "to view neighborhood needs in programmatic rather than political terms. . . . In the most extreme cases, these tendencies have produced what might be called 'programmatic tribalism,' with fragmented clans, each with its own patrons and clients, maneuvering against the next." At the same time, Mollenkopf recognizes that once the Nixon administration undermined the community action program, these leaders did not have much choice. Many of them, by seeking to "become more influential in city-wide decision-making," were simply trying to do what they could to preserve "the values and visions with which they emerged on the political scene in the mid-1960's" (Mollenkopf 1983, 197).

References

Adamson, Madeleine, and Seth Burgos. 1984. *This Mighty Dream*. Boston: Routledge and Kegan Paul.

Alinsky, Saul. 1969. *Reveille for Radicals*. New York: Random House. Originally published 1946.

Bellah, Robert, et al. 1985. *Habits of the Heart*. New York: Harper & Row.

Bluestone, Barry, and Bennett Harrison. 1982. *The Deindustrialization of America*. New York: Basic Books.

Bowles, Samuel, and Herbert Gintis. 1987. *Democracy and Capitalism*. New York: Basic Books.

Boyte, Harry. 1980. *The Backyard Revolution*. Philadelphia: Temple University Press.

Castells, Manuel. 1983. *The City and the Grassroots*. Berkeley: University of California Press.

Delgado, Gary. 1986. *Organizing the Movement: The Roots and Growth of Acorn*. Philadelphia: Temple University Press.

Destler, Chester McArthur. 1966. *American Radicalism*. Chicago: Quadrangle Press. Originally published 1946.

Dewey, John. 1927. *The Public and Its Problems*. Denver: Swallow Press.

Evans, Sara M. 1980. *Personal Politics*. New York: Vintage Books.

Evans, Sara M., and Harry Boyte. 1986. *Free Spaces*. New York: Harper & Row.

Ferber, Michael, and Staughton Lynd. 1971. *The Resistance*. Boston: Beacon Press.

Ferree, Myra Marx, and Beth B. Hess, 1985. *Controversy and Coalition: The New Feminist Movement*. Boston: Twayne.

Fisher, Robert. 1984. *Let the People Decide: Neighborhood Organizing in America*. Boston: Twayne.

Freeman, Jo. 1975. *The Politics of Women's Liberation*. New York: Longman.

———. 1983. "On the Origins of Social Movements." In *Social Movements of the Sixties and Seventies*, edited by Jo Freeman, 8–30. New York: Longman.

Geertz, Clifford. 1973. *The Interpretation of Cultures*. New York: Basic Books.

Green, James R. 1980. *The World of the Worker*. New York: Hill and Wang.

Gusfield, Joseph R. 1975. *Community: A Critical Response*. New York: Harper & Row.

Hartz, Louis. 1955. *The Liberal Tradition in America*. New York: Harcourt Brace Jovanovich.

Hodgson, Godfrey. 1978. *American in Our Time*. New York: Vintage Books.

Katznelson, Ira. 1981. *City Trenches, Urban Politics and the Patterning of Class in the United States*. Chicago: University of Chicago Press.

———. 1986. Working-Class Formation: Constructing Cases and Comparisons. In *Working-Class Formation*, edited by Ira Katznelson and Aristide Zolberg, 3–41. Princeton: Princeton University Press.

Logan, John, and Harvey Molotch. 1987. *Urban Fortunes*. Berkeley: University of California Press.

Matusow, Alan J. 1984. *The Unraveling of America*. New York: Harper & Row.

Mills, C. Wright. 1956. *The Power Elite*. New York: Oxford University Press.

———. 1959. *The Sociological Imagination*. New York: Oxford University Press.

———. 1967. *White Collar*. New York: Oxford University Press. Originally published 1951.

Mollenkopf, John. 1983. *The Contested City*. Princeton: Princeton University Press.

Molotch, Harvey. 1984. "Romantic Marxism: Love Is (Still) Not Enough." *Contemporary Sociology* 13, no. 2: 141–143.

Parks, Rosa. 1974. "Montgomery Bus Boycott" (interview with Myles Horton at Highlander Folk School). In *Black Protest*, edited by Joanne Grant, 276–280. New York: Fawcett Premier. Mimeographed 1956.

Polotkin, Sidney. 1987. *Keep Out: The Struggle for Land Use Control*. Berkeley: University of California Press.

Quint, Howard H. 1953. *The Forging of American Socialism*. Indianapolis: Bobbs-Merrill.

Raines, Howell. 1983. *My Soul Is Rested*. New York: Penguin.

Rogin, Michael. 1967. *The Intellectuals and McCarthy: The Radical Spectre*. Cambridge, Mass.: MIT Press.

Sale, Kirkpatrick. 1973. *SDS*. New York: Vintage Books.

Sitkoff, Harvard. 1981. The Struggle for Black Equality, 1954–1980. New York: Hill and Wang.

Thompson, Edward P. 1963. *The Making of the English Working Class*. New York: Random House.

Unger, Irwin. 1975. *The Movement: A History of the American New Left, 1959–1972*. New York: Dodd, Mead.

U.S. Bureau of the Census. 1986. *State and Metropolitan Data Book*. Washington D.C.: GPO.

Wright, Erik Olin. 1979. *Class, Crisis and the State*. London: Verso Books.

———. 1985. *Classes*. London: Verso Books.

CHAPTER 2

The American Working Class and the Community–Workplace Dichotomy

Selections from the Writings of Ira Katznelson

Edited by Prudence S. Posner

"The Trenches": Class Conflict on the American Terrain

The main elements of explanations for the boundaries and rules of American urban politics, and for what has been special about class relations in the United States, may be found in the ways in which workers understood the objective separation of work and home in early industrial cities and acted on that understanding. The major societies of the West have shared a very similar history of the spatial patterning of workplaces and communities from the development of feudal towns to modern industrial cities. . . . I contend that differences between these societies in the ways their working classes have interpreted the growing division between work and community date from the period of rapid industrial urbanization—roughly from the beginning of the nineteenth century to the 1870s. At that time modern

" 'The Trenches': Class Conflict on the American Terrain" and "Separate Consciousness, Community Politics, and the Politics of Social Change" are reprinted from Ira Katznelson, *City Trenches: Urban Politics and the Patterning of Class in the United States* (Chicago: University of Chicago Press, 1981), 17–21, 193–194; copyright © 1981 by Ira Katznelson and reprinted by permission of Pantheon Books, a division of Random House. "The Theoretical Problem: Four Levels of Class" and "Digging the 'Trenches' of Contemporary Urban Politics: The Formation of the American Working Class" are reprinted from Ira Katznelson with Aristide Zolberg, eds., *Working Class Formation: 19th Century Patterns in Western Europe and the United States* (Princeton: Princeton University Press, 1986), 13–27, 35–38; reprinted by permission. "Class Conflict, the Social Democratic Minimum, and the Social Democratic Surplus" is reprinted from Ira Katznelson, "Considerations on Social Democracy in the United States," *Comparative Politics* 11 (October 1978): 85–93; reprinted by permission.

working classes (characterized by their situation as people who work in exchange for a wage and who neither own nor control investments, capital, or the labor of others), modern cities (characterized by the separation of work and community, in space and by role, for all social classes), and modern politics (characterized by the duties and rights of citizenship, including the possibility of the vote) all made their simultaneous appearance. How workers mapped this new and problematical situation, and why, are questions of comparative history.

The objective separation of work and home in the pre–Civil War city presented American workers with three logical and empirical choices. They might have come to see themselves (as workers did in England, for example) as workers not only at work but also at home; or (as in the "plural societies" of Belgium and Holland) as ethnics at work and ethnics at home. Although these two configurations were in fact lively possibilities at the time, they gave way to a third, and distinctively American, pattern. The two main European definitions of work and home used the same coordinates for both realms. In the United States, by contrast, they were quite separate: Most members of the working class thought of themselves as workers at work but as ethnics (and residents of this or that residential community) at home. To borrow Amy Bridges's phrase, the American working class was formed as labor; outside of work, nonclass identifications and institutions predominated.[1]

Some of the distinctive features of American political and social history have been noticed so often that their very familiarity has been a barrier to systematic understanding. They include (in relative, comparative terms) the failure of attempts to create socialist and labor parties on the various continental and European models, and an ordinary political language that treats class as only one of a larger number of competing bases of affiliation. . . . I argue . . . that these commonly observed realities are aspects of a sharply divided consciousness about class in American society that finds many Americans acting on the basis of the shared solidarities of class at work, but on that of ethnic and territorial affinities in their residential communities. The links between work and community-based conflicts have been unusually tenuous. Each kind of conflict has had its own separate vocabulary and set of institutions: work, class, and trade unions; community, ethnicity, local parties, churches, and voluntary associations. Class, in short, has been lived and fought as a series of partial relationships, and it has therefore been experienced and talked about as only one of a number of competing bases of social life. *What is distinctive about the American experience is that the linguistic, cultural, and institutional meaning given to the differentiation of work and community, a characteristic of all industrial capitalist societies, has taken a sharply divided form, and that it has done so for a very long time.*

This system of values and customary practices, elaborated over time, has provided the main political formula of ideas, organizations, and activities that has protected the core arrangements of capitalism in the United States from challenge. Writing in a prison cell in Fascist Italy, Antonio Gramsci, this century's most original Marxist thinker, argued that in the advanced industrial societies such clusters of ideas and behaviors "are like the trench systems of modern warfare" (Gramsci 1971, 235). In wars of position—like World War I—the system of trenches defines the terrain of battle and thus imparts a logic to the war itself. Because each system of trenches is distinctive, it defines both the place and the content of conflict.

Gramsci's metaphor for what he called "the superstructures of civil society" is apt. All the capitalist democracies of Western Europe and North America are defined politically by their country-specific systems of political and social "trenches," which delineate what is special about class and politics in each society and which help shape the country's rules of conflict. In the United States the most important set of rules has been urban. This American urban-class system of "city trenches" has defined what is exceptional about class (and race) in the United States, and it has made very difficult the emergence of socialist, social democratic, or labor parties on the European model of the late nineteenth and early twentieth centuries.

Elsewhere in the West, mass-membership party and union organizations have succeeded, at least much of the time and in varying degrees, in connecting the segmented dimensions of class, even if usually in distributive, reformist ways. As both a cause and a reflection of this comparative success, ordinary politics in virtually all the European democracies is defined by institutionalized class-based party competition, in which social democratic, socialist, and communist parties use, with different degrees of intensity, a *global* rhetoric and analysis of class, and mobilizing strategies that join economics and politics, and link together the struggles of workers where they labor and where they live. Such parties or movements require that supporters see themselves as workers not only at work but also at home. The separate consciousness of early American industrialization thus impeded a global class politics in later industrialization.

Community Politics and the Politics of Social Change

In the early and middle 1960s, urban liberals and radicals were terribly optimistic about neighborhood and community politics. Armed with little more than Saul Alinsky's view of a world divided between "haves" and "have-nots," they embraced a politics of local action convinced, as Alinsky was, that the community could overcome the malaise of the Eisenhower years and the sterility of the labor movement (Alinsky 1942, 1962; Levi 1974). In the neighborhoods of urban America, genuinely radical movements for social change could be forged. With the collapse of the community-control efforts of the late 1960s and their envelopment by the public policy responses of local authorities, most of the activists of the 1960s became considerably more skeptical as the expected promise of community action was not redeemed.

Today, however, a radical politics of the neighborhood is again in vogue. Underpinned this time by a much more sophisticated understanding of the connections between urban crisis and capitalist development than the one Alinsky provided, the prescriptive thrust is nevertheless the same: Utilize community organization and community movements as vehicles of radical change. A remarkable consensus of activists is once again turning to the place of residence rather than to the place of work as the main locus of insurgent activity. In part this orientation is opportunistic. Many local self-help, consumer, environmental, and neighborhood organizations (many of which have discovered each other) have once again appeared on the scene.[2] In a period of declining union membership, growing attacks on the welfare state, and the growing capacity of conservative political philosophy to define political choices, this mass activity provides the main possibilities for a creative politics of the left, or at least, so it seems. In part, too, this orientation is principled. It is grounded in the expansion of Marxist social theory beyond the narrowly economic and beyond simple versions of determinism that accord a uniquely privileged role to workplace relations.

The strategic and theoretical return to a politics of community makes an understanding of the politics of the urban crisis of the 1960s and early 1970s even more pressing. If this book [City Trenches] makes no other argument, it surely insists that community-based strategies for social change in the United States cannot succeed unless they pay attention to the country's special pattern of class formation in the United States; to the split in the practical consciousness of American workers between the language and practice of a politics of work and those of a politics of community. If we do not self-consciously understand and address this key feature of our urban-class inheritance, we shall continue to play a losing game whose very rules will remain obscure. . . .

The failure of political organizers to come to terms with the special American understandings of work and community reflects not merely dogged obtuseness, or even the fact that they, like the rest of us, are deeply embedded in implicit cultural rules that produce conduct. This failure is also a theoretical one, and it is to this shortcoming that I wish to speak.

The Terminology of Class

The concept "class" provides the obvious starting point. As a term, "class" has been used too often in a congested way, encompassing meanings and questions that badly need to be distinguished from each other. I suggest that class in capitalist societies be thought of as a concept with four connected layers of theory and history: those of structure, ways of life, dispositions, and collective action. . . .

As a concept, class has soaked up so much meaning that it has become bulky to use. Because it is often employed without a clearly specified definition, debates about class often become conversations in which people talk past each other because they are talking about different dimensions of class. Without clear analytical distinctions between levels or layers of class, it is hard to improve on the "class in itself–for itself" model.[3] With the specification of different levels it becomes possible to construct the various cases of class formation in their own terms and to explore the competing capacities of various macrohypotheses about linkages between the levels. Above all, the distinctions that follow are meant to be aids to concrete description and explanation.

Structure

The *first* level is the structure of capitalist economic development, whose main elements include an economy based on privately owned autonomous firms that seek to make profit-maximizing decisions. These enterprises employ labor for a wage and sell what they produce in the market. This process of economic development contains some elements shared by all capitalist societies and others that are distinctive to each. As Karl Polanyi pointed out, this "great transformation" (from precapitalist forms to capitalism) entailed the commodification of money, land, and labor. Capitalism is unthinkable without proletarianization; and, as Marx observed as the centerpiece of his political economy, capitalism is impossible without a quite specific mechanism of exploitation.

Because these key properties are shared by all capitalisms, it is appropriate at this first level of class analysis to propose such distinctions as collective capital and collective labor, and productive and unproductive labor. And it is at this level that the heuristic model building Marx did in his mature works of political economy must test its mettle against other competing accounts.

Structural analyses of capitalism at this level use class analytically as a construct that is "experience-distant" (i.e., as a concept employed by specialists to further scientific, philosophical, or practical aims). Used in this way as a tool to analyze the "motion" of capitalist development, class has no direct or unmediated phenomenological referents.

But economic development, of course, occurs not just in theory or in capitalism in general, but in real places at real times. Each specific national history of capitalist development is shaped by the shared impulses and boundaries of all capitalisms; but each national economy is shaped not only by these tendencies. Family patterns, demography, cultural traditions, inherited practices, state organization and policies, geopolitics, and other factors help determine the specific empirical contours of macroscopic economic development at this first level of class.

Even as we pay attention to these variations, however (as, for example, Aristide Zolberg does in the concluding essay of *Working Class Formation*), at this level of economic structure class remains an experience-distant analytical concept, needed to describe and explain what happened because class is a constitutive element of any capitalist structure. Distinctive national histories of capitalist economic development perforce are structural histories of class formation in the sense of Charles Tilly's "thin" definition in his treatment of the demographic origins of the European proletariat: "people who work for wages, using means of production over whose disposition they have little or no control" (Tilly 1984). Proletarianization at this level provides a necessary, indeed the necessary condition for class formation in the more thickly textured senses of ways of life, dispositions, or patterns of collective action. But even when we take variations in macrolevel economic development into account it is not a sufficient condition for explaining the other layers of class formation. It is impossible to infer ways of life, dispositions, or collective action directly from analyses of class at the first level.

Ways of Life

Nevertheless, broad patterns of economic development are of central importance in shaping patterns of life and social relations in specific capitalist societies. This *second* level, determined in part by the structure of capitalist development, refers to the social organization of society lived by actual people in real social formations. For this reason, theories that deal with this level of class must be "experience-near."

Because this second level includes such economic phenomena as workplace social relations and labor markets, it is tempting to collapse the first two levels of class into the single category of the "economy." Such a conflation, however, eliminates in one stroke a series of important questions about the connections between key aspects of capitalist accumulation and national economic histories on one side and the organization of labor markets and workplaces on the other. As any student of capitalist industrialization knows, the growth and expansion of capitalism has proved capable of fostering many different kinds of workplaces and work. . . .

Although the second level of class includes work settings and labor markets (here classes can be stacked up and counted according to criteria that distinguish between various active members of the labor force),[4] it is not coextensive with these social relationships. The level of ways of life refers to how actual capitalist societies develop at work *and* away from it.

One of the hallmarks of industrial capitalist societies is that they tend to foster ways of life that differentiate between the location and social organization of these two realms. Over time, this distinction is expressed in the social geography of industrial cities. Work leaves the home. Cross-class households break up. Whole regions of cities come to be defined as areas of residence or of production. Further, residential communities segregate by the class position of their residents (in both the Marxist sense of location in a system of production and in the Weberian sense of capacity to consume goods and services in the marketplace). With these separations between work and home and between the social classes in space, class relations are lived and experienced not only at work but also off-work in residence communities.

The first two levels of class are closely related, of course, in that it is something of a conceit to separate too starkly the structure of capitalist accumulation and the self-sustaining development of the economy at the first level from how such broad patterns of economic development exist for working people where they labor and where they live at the second level. Moreover, if we understand that neither level of social relations is purely economic, then it makes sense to see the second level as an attribute of the first. But however closely connected, they are separate nonetheless and, many debates, such as the one between Erik Olin Wright and Nicos Poulantzas about mappings of class, suffer from failure to make this distinction.[5]

At the first two levels of class it is appropriate to construct classifications of class relations, and the literature of social science is full of them. At both levels class is defined, from an orthodox Marxist position, as G. A. Cohen writes, solely "with reference to the position of its members in the economic structure, their effective rights and duties within it. A person's class is established by nothing but his objective place in the network of ownership relations, however difficult it may be to identify such places neatly." Even if the criteria used in such definitions are expanded to other bases of class relations and to patterns of class embedded in residence communities, Cohen is right to stress that at these levels of analysis a person's "consciousness, culture, and politics do not enter the *definition* of his class position. . . . nor even his behavior is an essential part of it" (Cohen 1978, 73). Yet by themselves no such schemata, however compelling, can tell us how class exists distinct from other bases of solidarity and action in specific societies at specific times. This level of analysis may tell us how workers exist and live in certain circumstances, but not how they will think or act in those experienced circumstances.

Dispositions

At a *third* level, social classes are not heuristic or analytical constructs nor do they consist of members of this or that cell of a typology. At this level, classes are formed groups, sharing dispositions. Such cognitive constructs map the terrain of lived experience and define the boundaries between the probable and improbable. Note that I am deliberately avoiding the term "class consciousness" in order to make clear my rejection of any notion of degrees of consciousness, with the highest corresponding to the "real" interests of the working class. Further, the scheme of four levels of class does not imply a series of necessary stages or a natural progression (after all, ways of life are not independent of thought or action). It is, rather, a classification that aims to promote the development of theory free from developmental assumptions.

I take it that the third level of class is what Thompson means when he writes:

> Class is a social and cultural formation (often finding institutional expression) which cannot be defined abstractly, or in isolation, but only in terms of relationship with other classes; and, ultimately, the definition can only be made in the medium of *time*—that is, action and reaction, change and conflict. When we speak of *a* class we are thinking of a very loosely-defined body of people who share the same congeries of interests, social experiences, traditions, and value-system, who have a *disposition* to *behave* as a class, to define themselves in their actions and in their consciousness in relation to other groups of people in class ways. (Thompson 1965, 357).

This suggestive formulation condenses a number of significant issues. To say that people share dispositions can mean that they have come to share understandings of the social system or that they have come to share values of justice and goodness. These two kinds of disposition are at least partially independent. Further, whether they are class dispositions is a contingent matter. Members of a class may share dispositions of either kind, but they need not necessarily be class based analytically or normatively. Further, either knowledge- or norm-based dispositions may view the current situation as the outcome of circumstances that cannot be altered or as posing the possibility of something better.

Much of the variation between the French, American, and German cases consists of variations in the ways working people, confronting changes in the conditions of life at the second level of class, mapped and interpreted these changes at the level of dispositions. Most new social history joins the story of class formation here, studying situations from the point of view of a specific working class in a specific place at a specific time. It is at this level that a Geertzian cultural analysis of the ways people construct meaning to make their way through the experienced world is most compelling,[6] especially because shared dispositions are interactive. They are formed by the manner in which people interact with each other. Thus dispositions are transindividual, not merely opinions or views of individual actors. They constitute cultural configurations within which people act. In Bernard Cohn's terms, "there can be no practical realities without the symbolic coding of them as *practical*. . . . People cannot act as maximizers—either out of self interest or out of deep psychological conditionings . . . without the preexistence of meaning in cultural terms." (Cohn 1980).[7]

The third level of class, that of dispositions, is not coextensive with class structures and class-based ways of life; nor, however, do dispositions simply mirror reality. Rather, they are plausible and meaningful responses to the circumstances workers find themselves in.

A number of important recent discussions in philosophy concern the issue of "correspondence." Analytical philosophers, much like some orthodox Marxists, have taken very seriously the idea that for something to be "right" it must correspond to something "real." Some efforts have recently been made, especially by Hilary Putnam and Nelson Goodman, to transcend this assumption of correspondence. Putnam (1984, 270) proposes that the key issue is "how can language or thought connect up to what is outside the mind"; and Goodman (1984, 284) insists that "philosophy must take into account all the ways and means of worldmaking." But though such worlds are made, they are not constructed from scratch. Meaning is the result of the interaction between the world and human efforts to signify it. If the construction of meaning is not entirely an open or contingent matter, what are the causes of the construction of different kinds of meaning systems about class? I will return to this question shortly.

Collective Action

Thompson follows his discussion of class dispositions by adding, "but class itself is not a thing, it is a happening" (Thompson 1966, 357). Here he moves much too quickly from this third level of class to a *fourth*, collective action. Groups of people sharing motivational constructs ("dispositions to behave") may or may not act collectively to transform disposition to behavior. Even where workers have close contact at work and in their residential communities; even if this interaction promotes strong collective identities; and even if these workers share common systems of meaning that incline them to act in class ways, they may not necessarily act together to produce collective action. For this reason it is useful to distinguish between class at the third level and at the fourth, which refers to classes that are organized and that act through movements and organizations to affect society and the position of the class within it. This kind of behavior is self-conscious and refers to activity that is more than just the common but, unself-conscious shared behavior of members of a class. After all, members of categorical classes must immanently share certain behaviors, but they do not necessarily act consciously and collectively in pursuit of common goals.

The "class in itself–for itself" formulation makes thinking about the links between the social organization of class, class dispositions, and collective action superfluous. But in fact class conflict of any particular kind is not necessarily entailed in the class organization of patterns of social life, nor even in the development of groups of people inclined to act in class ways. The one broad exception to this general rule of contingency is the development of trade unions to fight for better wages and working conditions at the place of work. Although here too there are wide variations between the experiences of different working classes, there are no examples of national histories of class formation utterly lacking in the effort to create trade unions.

There are always impediments to collective action,[8] to those occasions when "sets of people commit pooled resources, including their own efforts, to common ends." A key feature of the historical study of class must consist "of discovering which sets of people, which resources, which common ends, and which forms of commitment were involved in different places and times. Did the configurations change systematically with the advances of capitalism and large organizations?" (Tilly 1981, "Introduction").[9] Both the content and the form of collective action are highly variable, and this variation demands explanation. Class, Thompson suggestively points out, is a "junction term" which lies at the intersection of structure and process, social being and social consciousness. Structural change gives rise to changed experience: that is, both to a set of subjective perceptions of objectively ordered realities and to a more active process of learning, possibly leading to action to modify the objective realities. I have already noted that Thompson, in my view, makes the movement from class structure to class action too certain a passage, but this teleological element can be extruded from his formulation.

The distinctions drawn here between the four levels of class may be read as an elaboration of Thompson's insight that class is a junction term. They allow us to specify more precisely the points of connection *between* the structure of class relations at the macroeconomic level; the lived experience of class in the workplace and in the residence community; groups of people disposed to act in class ways; and class-based collective action. These points of contact specify the possibility of alternative kinds of relationships between the levels, a problem best approached by asking what we mean by class formation after moving beyond "class in itself–for itself" formulations.

It is possible, of course, to continue to define class formation in terms of specific outcomes, rather than to leave open the content of class formation. We might say that class formation has occurred only when class exists at all four levels of structure, patterns of life, dispositions, and action simultaneously. This would have a number of advantages. It would turn our attention to the links between class levels, and it would treat class formation as only one of a number of possible outcomes. It would dispose of the Hobson's choice between structuralist formulations that claim, at least implicitly, that experience is ideology, and culturalist stances fashionable in much current linguistic and semiotic theory in which class society is said only to exist when it is signified.

But despite these advantages, such a definition would be unsatisfactory. An outcome approach hinging on the appearance of class at each of the four levels without specifying the components of class and the range of both class and nonclass possibilities at each of the levels too starkly posits a dichotomous outcome (and in this way resembles the tradition of "revolutionary consciousness"): class either exists or does not as a basis of social solidarity and action. This distinction does not appear to be terribly helpful in explicating the puzzles posed by . . . (the three cases of advanced industrialized nations examined in *Working Class Formation*, France, Germany, and the United States).

Class formation may be thought of more fully and more variably as concerned with the conditional (but not random) process of connection between the four levels of class. The specification of four levels of class allows us to keep the advantages of defining class formation in terms of outcomes while providing a more elaborated and variable object of comparative historical analysis. The content of each of the four levels of necessity will vary from society to society; no level need be understood or analyzed exclusively in class terms; and the connections between the levels are problematical and conditional.

The Formation of the American Working Class: Digging the Trenches of Contemporary Urban Politics

Working classes of the early to mid nineteenth century in the industrializing nations of Europe and in the United States had to make sense of and deal with a cluster of fundamental changes in the organization of production, conditions of work, community organization, and politics. These basic

alterations in the structure and conditions of life were so massive and
multifaceted in character that they invariably provoked basic changes in
language, consciousness, and institutions—in short, in the symbolic and
organizational aspects of culture. If we are prepared to see culture as "webs
of significance" spun by people in society and if, in consequence, culture
demands interpretation, these webs were spun by working people suspended
between very hard and jagged economic, social, and political rocks.[10]

The broad outlines of these changes were shared across political boundaries. Skilled artisan production based on traditions and obligations centuries old was disrupted irretrievably. New kinds of social relationships of
production, new forms of exploitation, and new dimensions to the process
of proletarianization ushered in vigorous defenses of the old order as well
as new thoughts and deeds concerning the conditions of workers within the
new order.

Working people, for the first time, altered their vocabularies and world
views to speak and think of themselves as workers, rather than just as
members of this or that trade. They generalized the sense of solidarity of
trade beyond specific and segmented crafts. The timing of this transformation
is rather similar in the three countries considered in this book [*Working
Class Formation*]: in the early 1830s in France and in the United States,
and in the late 1840s in Germany. But the extent and content of this new
collective awareness varied considerably. This diversity, at class levels
three and four, is the principal object of our analysis of working-class
formation. . . .

In constructing our objects of analysis at the third and fourth levels of
class, we ask: What rhetoric did workers use in presenting their demands
to employers and the state? What forms of organization were used to make
their claims? What was the character of the relationship between the two
sets of claims in rhetorical and organizational terms? Did such rhetorics and
organizational forms embody a unity of dispositions and action about the
social relations of work and the residence community or did they embody
divisions, expressed in dichotomous politics of work and off-work? To what
extent did workers, in placing their demands before their employers and
the state, interpret their concerns in terms of the division between capital
and labor? How attractive were various radical, socialist, and, in the middle
and later years of the period, Marxist perspectives? To what extent did
workers regard themselves as part of national groups or movements? How
did workers, in making demands, reveal the outer limits of the working
class? And if there were dominant national patterns, what were the secondary

ones? In no case was there only a single outcome of class formation that encompassed artisans, marginal workers like those in construction, and people who worked in the new, large-scale industrialized plants. . . .

No single clear direction to working-class sentiments or organizational activity emerged in the United States before the Civil War. Mass political action included the short-lived Workingmen's parties of the late 1820s and early 1830s, which sought to articulate a class-based republican response to the degradation of artisan life; a nativist response in the mid 1830s and early 1840s, which interpreted these changes in cultural, ethnic, and religious terms; various labor movement attempts to secure a shorter work-day, free public schooling, and democratic political reforms; militant strikes; and cross-class collaborative party politics.

This variety of political forms crystallized after the Civil War into a distinctive, recognizable, and clearly institutionalized system of class dispositions and organizations. Martin Shefter summarizes these developments. . . .

> Differences between the interests, values, and behavioral dispositions of workers and employers sparked conflicts during the post–Civil War years that at times approached full-scale class warfare. The labor union and the political machine institutionalized an accommodation between these warring forces. By no means did the emergence of these organizations put an end to such conflicts. Nonetheless, the institutionalization of the trade union and the political machine established the characteristic manner in which class conflicts in the United States could be channelled and thereby contained. (Shefter 1986, 199)

These two predominant organizations crystallized a division between the politics of work and off-work. Although they often pressed policy demands on the state in addition to the demands they made to employers, American unions were, on the whole, disconnected from partisan electoral activity. Their domain came to be restricted largely to the workplace and to political demands that directly affected work or their right to organize.[11] In reciprocal fashion, public officials tolerated strikes only when they were limited to workplace concerns, and the trade unions increasingly diminished the scope of their activity to bread-and-butter unionism.

The political machine, in turn, was a transclass institution, which mobi-lized supporters where they lived on the basis of territorial and ethnic identities. Political mobilization based on the neighborhood (here class and ethnicity intertwined) and on demands for city services provided the basis for an accommodation between the working classes and the political and economic order. Led by professional politicians, these organizations downplayed class and class conflict in the interest of a politics of patronage and distribution. Even where union leaders sought to organize third parties to fight for social change, they virtually always did so in alliance with middle-class reformers, under the banner of middle-class slogans and ideas. Such trade unionists frequently became detached from the rank and file.

All in all, the central hallmark of nineteenth-century class formation in the United States was the development, in the words of Shefter's essay, of "a division between the organizations through which workers pursued their interests at the workplace, on the one hand, and in the realm of politics, on the other" (Shefter 1986). By 1860, the dominant forms of working-class collective action had been established clearly: votes for Republicans or Democrats, and trade union mobilization.

Even the role of American socialists was divided in this way, in spite of the holistic interpretation of capitalist development that the various strains of socialist ideology promoted. Many socialists (including Samuel Gompers!) were absorbed into the trade union movement and became leading promoters of a vigorous bread-and-butter craft unionism. Others sought to build social-ist parties. When the conditions of work permitted close relationships between work and home, as in the garment industry at the turn of the century, and where there was a large concentration of new immigrants who brought a socialist political culture with them, as in the case of Lower East Side Jews in New York City, efforts to create electoral alternatives to the Democrats and Republicans succeeded. But in the more typical cases, where these conditions did not obtain, socialist electoral efforts failed. . . .

The social geography of large American cities changed in fundamental ways. By the Civil War, the majority of workers no longer labored in their homes or in immediate proximity to them. Rather, they lived in increasingly well defined, class-specific communities that contained a plethora of institutions—gangs, fire companies, self-help insurance societies, saloons, and clubs—that divided the organizational and social lives of workers from nonworkers. Even more, they provided bases for subtle variations within the working class, as different workers with different market positions came to live in different areas of the city. These were defined by income, skill level, and, increasingly, by ethnicity (see Katznelson 1981; also relevant is Scobey 1984).

These divisions by themselves were necessary but not sufficient to produce a divided pattern of class formation. In fact, there was a remarkable similarity between the social geography of mid-nineteenth-century English and American cities.[12] As the English case makes clear, such spatial demarcations are not incompatible with the emergence of class as a category of disposition and action spanning the divide between work and off-work. But if, by themselves, spatial demarcations do not produce dichotomous working-class politics, they clearly make such a pattern possible. Nevertheless, an explanation for the American outcome remains to be identified.

Like their English and French counterparts, American artisans did produce anticapitalist political visions, and they did build labor organizations that resembled social movements. What distinguished American craft workers, however, was their incapacity to transfer their leadership, their language, or their orientation to the new proletariat. To be sure, there were instances when radical artisans did instruct and lead the new working class. But the discontinuities, concretized in many settings by different partisan loyalties, are much more impressive in a comparative context. It is this failure of transmission that opened the way to the separate and reformist politics of craft labor and political party machines.

How is the hiatus between traditional artisan perspectives and those of the modern proletariat to be explained? Amy Bridges (1986) offers two principal hypotheses. The first is demographic. As a result of massive immigration from Germany and especially from Ireland and as a consequence of a clear cultural division of labor at the workplace, "in the most literal ways the American working classes did not have artisan origins."[13] Most workers of the 1850s had been born outside the United States. The persistent importance of artisan traditions stressed in studies on France (see Sewell 1986; Perrot 1986; Cottereau 1986) thus could not easily find a counterpart in the United States.

This point, obvious once made, turns Hartz's argument about the absence of a feudal tradition in America on its side, if not on its head. The importance of the liberal tradition in America could not have had its imputed effect by an easy intergenerational transfer of values. Indeed the societies from which most American proletarians came did have a feudal tradition. Rather, if the liberal tradition had an effect, it was that of facilitating the very early introduction of suffrage for adult white males.

Bridges proposes an especially interesting formulation of the importance of the franchise.

I am not saying here, as Reinhard Bendix did, that workers in the United States were less angry about industrialization than voters elsewhere because they had the vote as "compensation." Nor am I saying, with Alan Dawley and Paul Faler, that the vote offered a "ritual" of democracy that made politics a safety valve for working-class discontent. I am arguing that when workers had political goals (e.g., laws limiting the workday or the abolition of contract labor), were entitled to vote, and were an urban minority, they were inevitably drawn into electoral politics and party politics—and those practices just as inevitably shaped their consciousness and their culture. (Bridges 1986, 192).

This point is a telling one, but it is incomplete. The issue is not only whether workers were necessarily absorbed under these conditions into electoral politics as a means to pursue their working-class goals in a mass franchise democracy. The fact that the demand for the vote did not have to be a central feature of working-class politics meant, first, that the state was not defined as "them" and thus was not a target of constitutionally oriented collective action; second, that the regime had a high degree of legitimacy based on shared citizenship; and, third, that working-class politics could more easily fragment between proletarian–employer conflict at the workplace and a politics organized by cross-class political parties away from work.

Additional features of state structure and public policy also affected the formation of the American working class. The American state is decentralized and fragmented. Because the central state was relatively underdeveloped,[14] it did not present a concrete target for attention or attack. Rather, government was experienced as both nearby and accessible; it was made even more so by the close interpenetration of local political parties and bureaucracies. Workers were thus mobilized through the country's political institutions, not against them.

This incorporation was reinforced by the early access workers had to mass public education. In the United States workers did not have to fight on a class basis either for inclusion in the system or for control as citizens over its direction.[15]

Even state repression was "soft." Although American trade unions faced the same common law as their English counterparts, proscriptions against combinations were usually rendered moot by sympathetic working-class juries and by judges who feared the wrath of working-class citizens. Local police forces and penal institutions were controlled at the city level by ward politicians, that is, by people who were familiar, reachable, and malleable.

Workers in the United States, Shefter concludes, "did not find themselves subjugated by an official, and officious, class. This in conjunction with the relatively narrow domain of government in the United States during the late nineteenth century meant that on the whole, whatever oppression American workers experienced was not oppression by the State" (Shefter 1986).

Class Conflict, the Social Democratic Minimum, and the Social Democratic Surplus

[Editor's Note: In this final section, Katznelson discusses the implications for activism of his layered concept of class in the context of the American "trenches." By identifying the "cluster of anti-market policies"—policies, that is, that address the needs of people as workers and consumers, rather than the needs of capital—with the notion of developing a "social democratic surplus," the author begins the process of connecting the four layers of class discussed above *through the medium of political action*.]

Class, in all its levels, intersects history, structure, daily life, biography, and dispositions. The relative capacities of classes to shape the social order generally, and to effect state policy more particularly, are thus in large but not exclusive measure, the product of class relations in this total sense. Not exclusively, because political class capacity is also shaped by the state itself, by its organization, accumulated history, and practices, and by the degree of autonomy it possesses.

The formulation of competing class capacities provides the potential to connect the structural and volitional in political analysis. At any given moment, the political capacity of a class to secure its interests depends primarily, *but not only*, on its position with respect to production. Class capacities are also the result of the accumulated heritage of previous political decisions,[16] the relative capacities of competing ideologies, value systems and cultural practices; available mechanisms of physical repression; the distributional features of labor and consumption markets; and the patterns of political institutionalization by which different classes are connected to the policy (Skocpol, 1973; Silver, 1971). The dimensions of political conflict, seen this way, are neither disconnected from the conflicts immanent in the social structure nor are they givens or outcomes, but parts of an ongoing dialectical process of cohesion and challenge.

This perspective implies a way of thinking about the state that is distinctive from traditional pluralist analysis as well as from instrumentalist or structuralist Marxism. The state itself is seen neither as a neutral switchboard for competing claims nor as a perfect mechanism for reproducing capitalist society. Rather, the state itself is seen as a distinctive "product" and "determinant" of both class reproduction requirements and class conflict. The problem facing advanced capitalist social formations is how can the capitalist state be structured so as to perform functions dictated by economic contradictions given the actual or potential existence of a politically organized working class (Esping-Anderson et al., 1976, 191, 192). The state, in these terms, is understood as the product of the distinctive calculus of tension in a given society between objective developmental tendencies and the dynamics of volitional class organization and demands.

From this perspective, the sources of the expansion of the state's macroeconomic, planning, and social welfare functions inform the character of those policies—which in turn are an element in determining relative class capacity. The state's social democratic, potentially antimarket, cluster of policies[17] develops in two interrelated ways. First, the ordinary operation of the capitalist political economy requires a variety of state activities for the re-creation of capitalist productive and social relations. We do not possess a precise understanding of what these requirements are; we lack such a theory. What we do have, in the work of James O'Connor, Ian Gough, and others, is a plausible statement about how the reproduction of relations in and of production is assisted by a particular configuration of state policies. Even if its precise content is not known in every instance, it seems beyond doubt that a reproduction minimum of social democratic state policies is required to ensure the accumulation process and to give it broad social acceptance.

The level of the social democratic minimum varies from time to time and from state to state. It represents an amalgam of what has come to be both economically and culturally necessary. The minimum is in part genuinely a minimum by intention; it connotes a widely shared set of meanings and understandings about the appropriate dimensions and character of state interventions in the market. Although largely the result of past class and group struggles, the minimum at any given moment is no longer the subject of struggle. While the National Health Service in Britain, for example, could hardly be said to be necessary to reproduce capitalism, it is today part of that country's social democratic minimum both in the sense that if it were revoked mass disruption threatening productive relations would be likely, and because it is now an assumed integral part of the social scene, accepted as such by all classes in the society.[18]

In political terms policy developments within the framework of the reproduction minimum are principally the result of attempts to solve "problems" that appear technically and socially neutral. The inflation rate is high, investment in a given region too low, rivers are polluted, and so on. To such problems administrators and contestants for the vote are compelled to respond in a manner that resembled political learning (Heclo 1974). They also must not overturn previous social democratic gains in fundamental ways because once enacted policies become part of the reproduction minimum. The agenda of social democracy thus may be enacted into law, made government practice, and be protected from attack by anti-social democratic political forces even where no social democratic party or movement exists. *Under certain conditions, however, such parties and movements may succeed in moving social democratic reforms forward at a pace more rapid than that dictated by the emergence of manifest "problems" of past concessions of the capitalist order.* When such attempts succeed, it makes sense to speak of a *social democratic surplus*. The level of social democracy in a given moment is the sum of the reproduction minimum about which there is broad communal consensus, and the results of current contentious, factional group and class conflicts. The dimensions of the minimum inherited from the past, and struggles about whether and to what extent a surplus will be fashioned in the present, are functions of the strength of a nation's social democratic movement. . . .

The Social Democratic Minimum as a Determinant and a Product of Class Dispositions and Collective Action

Interpreting Antonio Gramsci's concept of hegemony, Raymond Williams has stressed the depth to which values, institutions, ordinary language, and routine patterns of daily behavior create cohesion—not by externalized compulsion, but by internalized compulsive practices "which are lived at such a depth, which saturate society to such an extent," that capitalist hegemony "constitutes the limit of common sense for most people under its sway" (Williams 1973, 8, 9). European social democracy has nowhere created socialism, but it has shifted the locus of the dual patterning of class, discussed above, sufficiently to make socialism conceivable, because in limited ways it is part of the experienced social reality of most people. The capitalist–socialist antinomy in societies such as Sweden or even West Germany is thus qualitatively different from that in the United States, because the existence of social democratic movements and their successes in fashioning surplus social democracies has altered the terms of the conflict of class capacities. . . .

[In the United States] more than in any other Western society, *the expansion of the state has been determined in pace and scope by the interests, needs and capacities of the dominant class*. We may infer that the role of the state may be understood as being very close to the structural minimum necessary for system reproduction. *A surplus social democracy does not exist because those who would be served by it lack the capacity—that is, both the disposition and the ability—to bring it into being*.[19]

Frances Piven and Richard Cloward have stressed that important expansions of the social democratic role of the state have occurred during periods of political crisis in response to mass disruption, defiance, and protest by ad hoc social movements in the 1930s and 1960s. Major initiatives in social policy are the product of such special times and activities; but the internal logic of such movements leads to their demise and to a very limited residue of reform (Piven and Cloward 1971, 1977). They stress that irregular action, not organization, is the key to understanding the development of the welfare state, and that the organizational phase of irregular movements substantially produces the close of periods of reform. Within the American context their work is persuasive, but only in that context. That is, *in the absence of a regular vehicle for social democratic reform*, the achievement of social democratic surplus is rare, and when it occurs it is an outcome of elite fears and concessions to ad hoc, disruptive movements. Their limited impact is likewise assured by the absence of more regular and enduring mass organization. Thus, a general conclusion about the relative efficacy of disruption versus organization is not warranted. They are right, however, to stress that in the United States only relatively expressive and inchoate defiance has been a recurring, if fleeting, vehicle for creating a social democratic surplus.

Notes

1. For an expanded discussion of these themes, see Bridges (n.d.), but cf. Evansohn (1975).

2. A good guide to this new mood and to the seductiveness of community organization strategies is "Organizing Neighborhoods" (1979). Especially useful

and revealing are the articles by Harry Boyte, John Mollenkopf, Janice Perlman, Gar Alperowitz and Jeff Faux, and the concluding "Profile of Some Neighborhood and Community Organizations."

3. The "class in itself–for itself" model in Marxist theory refers to the relationship between the actual class structure of a society and the emergence of "actors with the potential to achieve class consciousness, understood in terms of understanding and acting on fundamental class interests" (Katznelson 1981, 202).

4. For an extended theoretically informed empirical analysis along such lines, see Wright (1979).

5. Theoretical discussions of the base–superstructure metaphor within Marxism also suffer from a collapse of these two levels into "the economy." A brilliant attempt at "bringing workers back in" at the point of production through an analysis of the labor process, which succeeds in overcoming the theoretical problems I have alluded to—albeit a treatment rather different in emphasis than that of this essay and book—is Burawoy (1985).

6. In Geertz's work there is some ambiguity about whether he wishes to claim that culture is the encompassing concept or whether culture is a distinctive mapping of society. See Geertz (1973) and Rabinow and Sullivan (1979).

7. William Roseberry puts the point this way: "People do not simply act in terms of objective limits or positions but also in terms of apparently subjective evaluations of limits, positions, and possibilities. As they do so, the 'subjective' becomes 'objective'; culture becomes material. Action is, in short, meaningful, as Weber long ago insisted" (Roseberry 1984).

8. The best-known treatment of these impediments is Olson (1965). See also Hardin (1982). For a stunning treatment of related issues of strategy and rationality, see Elster (1979).

9. Also see the discussion of collective action in Tilly (1978).

10. See the sections on culture in Williams (1979, 1981) for discussions that locate cultural forms in material context much more explicitly than Geertz, who defines culture in semiotic terms: "Believing that . . . man is an animal suspended in webs of significance that he himself has spun, I take culture to be those webs, and the analysis of it to be therefore not an experimental science in search of law, but an interpretive one in search of meaning" (Geertz 1973, 5).

11. This is an argument I develop in Katznelson (1981, esp. chap. 3). See also Bridges (1984).

12. One of the few instances of a systematic linkage between spatial development and class formation is Dennis's (1984) synthetic work.

13. For a detailed and thoughtful treatment of the development of craft labor markets and a distinctively American accommodation between wage labor and employers, see Jackson (1984).

14. An influential discussion is Skowronek (1982).

15. These questions are discussed at length in Katznelson and Weir (1985).

16. The English gentry of 1832, for example, was ill-placed to resist reform

precisely because its victory in the seventeenth century had produced a weak central state.

17. The term *social democracy* refers here to a "substantive historical *process* of modifying and reshaping market patterns, which for many—but by no means all—of its adherents promises an end to capitalism in the distant and dimly seen future. Social democracy in Western Europe has thus been a strategy of reform intended to make capitalism more tolerable and less ruthless." This is in contrast to the term "socialism" which "refers to an *outcome*, which negates the basic features of capitalist productive and social relations associated with the private control of capital and the extraction of a surplus from labor by capital. Accordingly, the social command of capital and the democratization of production relations have been at the core of the various analytical and political approaches to socialism" (Katznelson 1978, 77).

18. [Despite the victories of the Right in the United States and Britain since 1980] "Thatcherite Conservatives in England do not dismantle the British Health Service to return to fee for service medicine, though they might try to reduce increases in health spending. Conservative Republicans in the White House and Congress are equally unlikely to dismantle social security, or Medicare and Medicaid, which they once fought so hard to prevent, even though they will work to stop their expansion. The costs to the social order of doing so simply would be too high" (Katznelson 1981b, 320).

19. Daniel Patrick Moynihan (1969) argues that state officials themselves, together with social service professionals, may have this capacity. I think it more accurate, however, to place their activities in the problem-solving mode.

References

Alinsky, Saul. 1942. *Reveille for Radicals*. Chicago: University of Chicago Press.

————. 1962. *Citizen Participation and Community Organization in Planning and Urban Renewal*. Chicago: Industrial Areas Foundation. Bridges, Amy. 1984. *A City in the Republic: Antebellum New York and the Origins of Machine Politics*. New York: Cambridge University Press.

————. 1986. "Becoming American: The Working Classes in the United States Before the Civil War." In *Working Class Formation*, edited by Ira Katznelson with Aristide Zolberg, 157–196. Princeton: Princeton University Press.

————. n.d. "Ethnicity and Class Structure: Notes on United States Ethnic Studies." Manuscript.

Burawoy, Michael. 1985. *The Politics of Production: Factory Regimes under Capitalism and Socialism*. London: Verso Books.

Cohen, G. A. 1978. *Karl Marx's Theory of History: A Defense*. Princeton: Princeton University Press.

Cohn, Bernard S. 1980. "History and Anthropology: The State of Play." *Comparative Studies in Society and History* 22 (April).

Cottereau, Alain, 1986. "The Distinctiveness of Working-Class Cultures in France, 1848–1900." In *Working Class Formation*, edited by Ira Katznelson with Aristide Zolberg. Princeton: Princeton University Press.

Dennis, Richard. 1984. *English Industrial Cities of the Nineteenth Century: A Social Geography*. London: Cambridge University Press.

Elster, Jon. 1979. *Ulysses and the Sirens: Studies in Rationality and Irrationality*. New York: Cambridge University Press.

Esping-Andersen, Gosta, Roger Friedland, and Erik Olin Wright. 1976. "Modes of Class Struggle and the Capitalist State." *Kapitalistate* 4–5 (Summer).

Evansohn, John. 1975. "Promises, Promises: A Critical Review of *False Promises*." *Radical History Review* 2 (Summer).

Geertz, Clifford. 1973. *The Interpretation of Culture*. New York: Basic Books.

Goodman, Nelson. 1984. "Notes on the Well-Made World." *Partisan Review* 51, no. 2.

Gramsci, Antonio. 1971. *Selections from the Prison Notebooks*. New York: International Publishers.

Hardin, Russell. 1982. *Collective Action*. Baltimore: Johns Hopkins University Press.

Heclo, Hugh. 1974. *Modern Social Politics in Britain and Sweden*. New Haven: Yale University Press.

Jackson, Robert. 1984. *The Formation of Craft Labor Markets*. New York: Academic Press.

Katznelson, Ira. 1978. "Considerations on Social Democracy in the United States," *Comparative Politics* (October).

————. 1981a. *City Trenches: Urban Politics and the Patterning of Class in the United States*. Chicago: University of Chicago Press.

————. 1981b. "A Radical Departure: Social Welfare and the Election." In *The Hidden Election*, edited by Thomas Ferguson and Joel Rogers. New York: Pantheon.

Katznelson, Ira, and Margaret Weir. 1985. *Schooling for All: Class, Race, and the Decline of the Democratic Ideal*. New York: Basic Books.

Levi, Margaret. 1974. "Poor People Against the State." *Review of Radical Political Economics* 6 (Spring).

Moynihan, Daniel Patrick. 1969. *Maximum Feasible Misunderstanding*. New York: Free Press.

Olson, Mancur. 1965. *The Logic of Collective Action*. Cambridge, Mass.: Harvard University Press.

"Organizing Neighborhoods." 1979. *Social Policy*, Special Issue, September/October.

Perrot, Michelle. 1986. "On the Formation of the French Working Class." In *Working Class Formation*, edited by Ira Katznelson with Aristide Zolberg. Princeton: Princeton University Press.

Piven, Frances Fox, and Richard A. Cloward. 1971. *Regulating the Poor: The Functions of Public Welfare*. New York: Vintage Books.

———. 1977. *Poor People's Movements: Why They Succeed, How They Fail*. New York: Vintage Books.

Putnam, Hilary. 1984. "After Ayer, After Empiricism." *Partisan Review* 51, no. 2.

Rabinow, Paul, and William M. Sullivan, eds. 1979. *Interpretive Social Science: A Reader*. Berkeley: University of California Press.

Roseberry, William. 1984. "Why Marxists Should Take Culture Seriously." Paper presented at the annual meeting of the American Anthropological Society, November.

Scobey, David. 1984. "Boycotting the Politics Factory: Labor Radicalism and the New York City Mayoral Election of 1886." *Radical History Review*, nos. 28–30 (September).

Sewell, William H., Jr. 1986. "Artisans, Factory Workers, and the Formation of the French Working Class, 1789–1848." In *Working Class Formation*, edited by Ira Katznelson with Aristide Zolberg. Princeton: Princeton University Press.

Shefter, Martin. 1986. "Trade Unions and Political Machines: The Organization and Disorganization of the American Working Class in the Late Nineteenth Century." In *Working Class Formation*, edited by Ira Katznelson with Aristide Zolberg. Princeton: Princeton University Press.

Silver, Alan. 1971 . "Social and Ideological Bases of British Elite Reactions to Domestic Crisis in 1829–32." *Politics and Society* 1 (February).

Skocpol, Theda. 1973. "A Critical Review of Barrington Moore's Social Origins of Dictatorship and Democracy." *Politics and Society* 4 (Fall).

Skowronek, Stephen. 1982. *Building a New American State: The Expansion of National Administrative Capacities, 1877–1920*. New York: Cambridge University Press.

Thompson, E. P. 1966. "The Peculiarities of the English." In *Socialist Register 1965*, edited by Ralph Miliband and John Saville. London: Merlin Press.

Tilly, Charles. 1981. "Introduction." In *Class Conflict and Collective Action*, edited by Louise A. Tilly and Charles Tilly. Beverly Hills, Calif.: Sage.

———. 1984. "Demographic Origins of the European Proletariat." In *Proletarianization and Family Life*, edited by David Levine. New York: Academic Press.

Williams, Raymond. 1973. "Base and Superstructure in Marxist Cultural Theory." *New Left Review*, no. 82 (November–December).

———. 1979. *Politics and Letters: Interviews with New Left Review*. London: New Left Books.

———. 1981. *Culture*. London: Fontana.

Wright, Erik Olin. 1979. *Class Structure and Income Determination*. New York: Academic Press.

CHAPTER 3

Leading the People

Two Approaches to the Role of Ideology in Community Organizing

**Robert Fisher
and Joseph M. Kling**

> Why weep or slumber America,
> Land of brave and true?
> With castles and clothing and food for all
> All belongs to you.
> Ev'ry man a king, ev'ry man a king
> For you can be a millionaire . . .
>
>   Huey Long, "Every Man a King"

An organizer offers a familiar complaint. One million people show up in New York City in June 1984 for an antinuclear rally. It is the largest march in U.S. history, writes the activist, but "three months later, on-going organizational activity is at a snail's pace," (Burghardt 1984, 31). Over the past decade, no broad-based movements for change have emerged out of the organizing occurring on local, regional, and national levels. Yet, clearly, grass-roots organizing has continued, and even grown, since the progressive social policies of the Great Society were turned back by the American electorate with the promotion of Richard Nixon to the presidency in 1968. But the wide array of community activism, and large-scale organizing around such issues as Nicaragua, nuclear disarmament, the ERA and women's choice, and South Africa, to cite some of the more visible examples, have not brought the kind of national movement that could save the limited social

An earlier version of this paper was presented to the Society for the Study of Social Problems, New York, August 27, 1986, and later published in *Radical America* 21, no. 1 (1987).

welfare agenda that has existed in this country since the New Deal, let alone move beyond it. Much argument and debate has emerged about what is wrong, and about how to correct it.[1]

Our own proposal is that a critical element is being ignored and must be addressed in the debate over activist theory and practice: a movement's *attitude toward the concept of ideology*. Progressive organizing, we argue, is best understood and assessed by the extent to which it seeks to both elicit and strengthen those maps and evaluations of social reality—ideologies— that challenge existing arrangements of political and economic domination. New concepts must be close to, and consistent with, a population's experience. And they should be geared to reorienting members' fundamental assumptions regarding the source and character of their condition in society.[2]

Following Gramsci's schema, we recognize (1) that differing ideologies will often be in competition for the allegiance of the same populations, (2) that certain of these belief systems attain hegemonic status, and that (3) in consequence, people find themselves adhering to conceptual systems that are inconsistent with each other (Gramsci 1971, 323–343).

Reliance on inherited ideology alone is insufficient to mobilize oppressed groups toward fundamental change. In this paper, we consider alternate theoretical approaches to the question of the relation between ideology and political organizing. Sara Evans and Harry Boyte's (1986) notion of "free social space" ties into a tradition that is suspicious of articulated ideology. The premise is that the traditions of local autonomy that shape the consciousness of working people are the sources of democratic change and need only to be freed, enhanced, and supported, not transformed. George Rudé's (1980) distinction between "inherent" and derived ideology, in contrast, is closely allied to Gramsci.

George Rudé: The Role of "Derived" Ideologies

To develop his theory of effective intervention, George Rudé (1980) turns from the immediacy of contemporary activism to a survey and analysis of protests going back to the Middle Ages. He finds that movements of social *transformation*, as opposed to ones based on *defense of inherited right*, most frequently emerge out of the intensification of material oppression (enclosures, hoarding and high prices, rack renting, etc.) combined with the introduction of what he calls a *derived* ideology into the system of community moral and political beliefs.

Rudé makes a distinction between two general kinds of ideology, one relatively structured and the other composed of more simple attitudes, *mentalités*, or outlooks. This latter Rudé refers to as *popular* or traditional or "inherent" ideology; it is "based on direct experience, oral tradition or folk-memory and not learned by listening to sermons or speeches or reading books" and may, in fact, be identified with "the culture of the people at large" (Rudé 1980, 28, 29).

The derived ideology comes to the ordinary classes—whether peasants or freeholders or artisans or workers—from outside their inherited sense of right and immediate traditions. Rudé describes this second element as "the stock of ideas and beliefs that are 'derived' or borrowed from others, often taking the form of a more structured system of ideas, political or religious, such as the Rights of Man, Popular Sovereignty, *Laissez-faire* and the Sacred Rights of Property, Nationalism, Socialism or the various versions of justification by Faith" (Rudé 1980, 28).

From this rather simple distinction, Rudé develops two central propositions. First, there is no hard-and-fast division between popular and derived ideologies; one cannot, therefore, "simply describe the second as being 'superior' or at a higher level than the first." There is considerable overlap between them, but, in many cases, "the derived or more 'structured' ideas are often a more sophisticated distillation of popular experience and the people's 'inherent' beliefs" (Rudé 1980, 28–29).

The second proposition Rudé offers is that although popular ideology can become the focus of political *resistance* when the rights and liberties of subaltern classes are attacked, such resistance has transformative potential only when an inherent ideology has become strongly suffused with a derived one. There is a mixture of disparate beliefs in such cases. Rudé cites, for example, portraits drawn by Eric Hobsbawn in *Primitive Rebels:* the Italian brigand leader of the 1860s who proclaimed "long live the fair kingdom of Naples with its most religious sovereign, long live the vicar of Christ, Pius IX, and long live our ardent Republican brothers." Or the plea of the rebellious peasants to the army general sent by Alexander II to wipe them out: "Don't fire on us, you are shooting on Alexander Nikoleyevich, you are shedding the blood of the Tsar" (Rudé 1980, 31–32).

Thus, when faced with political encroachments on the terrain of what has become to be accepted as just—the right to a grazing commons or a customary price for bread—exploited groups, given certain historical contexts, will organize and rise up in defense of what they identify as their inherited rights and liberties. But such actions—the food riots of early

industrial France and England, for example, or the Luddite machine-break-
ing in early-nineteenth-century England—need have nothing to do with
goals of fundamental change (Rudé 1980, 28–29).

Unless a derived ideology is at work somewhere in the mix of beliefs that
forms the consciousness of vulnerable classes, popular organization will not
move beyond existing social and political parameters. In modern terms,
one gets the populism of a Huey Long that promises to make everyone a
millionaire. Or there emerges the pseudo populism of the new right, with
its poorly disguised promise to the white lower-middle and working classes
to protect them against the encroachments of minorities and changes in the
family structure.

Rudé provides a theoretical discourse that assumes that the consciousness of working people is neither progressive nor reactionary. Instead, it is
defensive, and thus subject to movement in any of a number of political
directions. People desire to protect what they have, and to keep or secure
those things to which they fervently believe they have a right. For Rudé,
then, the introduction of a formally developed ideology that can transcend
existing belief systems is a necessary condition for the transition from simply
resistive to progressive mobilization.

Sara Evans and Harry Boyte: Free Spaces as the Sources of Democratic Activism

Sara Evans and Harry Boyte (1986) argue that the true sources of democratic
change reside in the particular histories and inherited values of locally
based groups, as shaped and expressed through such organic institutions as
the family, ethnic ties, religious communities, civic and workers' organizations, and mutual aid societies. At crucial moments, these coalesce to create
what Evans and Boyte call "free social spaces." Here, within church meeting
halls or on town squares or at any community gathering place where people
come to discuss and mutter and talk things over, ancient beliefs in inherited
rights can be transmuted into collective action and demands for political
autonomy. In free social spaces, the ideas that lead to organization, resistance, and, finally, fundamental change, are able to percolate precisely
because there are no controlling elites present, and because the constantly
felt pressure of authoritative social institutions toward approved behavior is
blocked out.

The most recent work of Evans and Boyte (1986) demonstrates the importance of community and tradition in social movements. In example after example, including the black struggle for equality, the woman's and labor movements, and agrarian populism, they illustrate how free spaces were the seedbed—the source of strength and action—and how community values, traditions, and institutions were sometimes reactionary but more often the basis of progressive change.

Evans and Boyte conceive of free spaces as ideologically grounded. For Rudé, such social spaces give organizational form to the "inherent ideology" of producing classes. The determining difference with Rudé is that Evans and Boyte do not see the belief systems of working people as essentially defensive and in need, therefore, of larger, more articulated social visions to ensure their progressive character. On the contrary, the ideas, beliefs, and traditions to which the common people are inherently drawn, according to these authors, come out of a vision of popular democracy rooted in their experience. The argument is that transformative social change depends far more on inherent ideology than on the introduction into existing world views of new and derived ideological perceptions from its grass-roots sustenance. For Evans and Boyte, in fact, a major explanation for the left's failure is precisely its attempt to inject what they define as external, inappropriate, and often foreign ideologies into the everyday lives of working people.

Evans and Boyte believe that democracy has throughout history denoted the idea of *popular power*, "locating control over the institutions of society and government in the majority of the population, the common people" (1986, 3). Further, the traditional notion of democracy implies not only the *rights* of participation but also the *responsibilities* and *values* of citizenship. These include a concern for the common good; a willingness to honor the same rights for others that one possesses for oneself; tolerance of diverse religious, political, and social beliefs; an acceptance of the primacy of the community's decisions over one's private inclinations, and recognition of an obligation to serve the public (Evans and Boyte 1986, 3, 5).

The inherent notion of popular and participatory democracy takes on different meanings in different hands and under varying historical conditions. Evans and Boyte recognize this problem. Free spaces, they concede, can nurture reactionary efforts as well as progressive ones. "Examples of defensive and limited protests abound," they write, citing the nativist movements of the nineteenth century, the National Union for Social Justice of the 1930s, the Ku Klux Klan and the White Citizens Councils of the 1950s, fights against "dangerous books" in the present (Evans and Boyte

1986, 15). But they fail to offer a persuasive explanation as to why free spaces are sometimes progressive and at other times reactionary.

We are told that "in democratic populist movements, as people are moved first in defense of their rights, traditions, and institutions, they change."

> They discover in themselves and their traditions new resources and potentials. They repair their capacity to work together for collective problem solving. They find out new political facts about the world, build networks, and seek contacts with other groups of the powerless. . . . In sum, communities deepen the meaning of what they are doing, from understanding it merely as a protest against threats, to coming to see the need for a struggle for a new vision of the common good. (Evans and Boyte 1986, 158)

If indigenous groups do not develop a democratic ideology, it is because they are subject to manipulative control by elites in power or because they have no history of an open public life. For example, the Knights of Labor, and the populist cooperatives they supported, were defeated in the South "in large part because of successful elite manipulation of racist traditions" (Evans and Boyte 1986, 189). But this does not explain why some popular movements become subject to elite manipulation, while others do not.

Evans and Boyte tend to overlook, in their conception of the sources of grass-roots movements, the articulated ideology that organizers and activists actually brought to, or used to create, the free spaces at issue, a derived ideology present in the movements they discuss. The contradiction between received wisdom and immediate experience *prepares ground* for the emergence of an alternative vision. But whether it can do more than that is highly problematic. The combination of inherent and derived ideology—the mixture of community traditions, values, and vision, on the one hand, with the politics and vision of the progressive organizer on the other—is not only an essential bulwark against reactionary trends but serves as a critical element in mobilizing people to get involved, and stay involved, in movements for democratic change.

Two major organizing philosophies since the 1930s have influenced the left in this country: the ideas and strategies for local activism developed by the American Communist party during the Great Depression, and those formed under the direction of Saul Alinsky and his associates since 1938. The first, of course, represents an approach that sees overtly ideological leadership as essential to effective organization. Alinsky, who in much of his work was reacting, at least indirectly, to the ideologically directive practice of the Communists, held that leaders and organizers should keep their ideas to themselves and should work solely on the basis of what their constituents saw as their existing values and believed their interests to be.

Grass-Roots Organizing and the American Communist Party

The major controversy that seems to swirl around any study of the American Communist party is whether, in the years of its political ascendance, it was simply an agent of Soviet and Comintern interests or whether it had original and innovative contributions to make to American radicalism and social movement formation. We suggest that it was *both* subservient to the Comintern *and* a significant and original force in the shaping of an American left movement.

The Communist party's major legacy to American radicalism can be found in its organizing technique and its insistence that specific tasks be related to international contexts and the broad-based theoretical concerns. That its uncritical acceptance of the Comintern line undermined its efficacy on the shop floor and at community levels does not mean that valuable insights were not discovered in these local arenas and that the party has nothing to teach the contemporary left. In fact, the idea that something of value has been overlooked is precisely what has led many young academics back to the experience of the party in the 1930s.[3]

The Communist party was crippled in essential ways by its grounding in Comintern doctrine, but in direct functioning in organizing campaigns and strikes, rank-and-file party members could be innovative, resourceful, spontaneous, and courageous.[4] The Comintern never issued specific instructions on putting together militant shop-floor and grievance committees, establishing Unemployed Councils, mobilizing antieviction drives, precipitating mass demonstrations, developing community associations, organizing and leading strikes, or prromulgating slogans, programs, and nationwide campaigns that would push social agendas leftward and challenge existing levels of political consciousness. These are the sorts of things that Communist militants did more consistently, with greater visibility, and to more powerful effect than any other left organization of the depression era.

The key to understanding Communist party political organization is recognizing that it operated on different *levels of practice*. By connecting these different levels, the party hoped both to elevate local and particularized activity into a component part of international social struggle and to charge it with ideological resonance.

The most comprehensive level of the Communists' overall political practice loosely corresponds to the overarching, theoretical framework of the movement—ideological principles such as general commitment to socialization of the means of production, the nature of class conflict, and promotion of the concept of working-class democracy. These ideas get expressed in the classic writings, in movement literature or the party press, or at forums and plenums and ritual celebrations such as May Day. Here is the level out of which the "derived ideology" identified by Rudé operates. Organizing at more specific and immediate levels takes on effectiveness as an instrument for transitional social change only to the extent to which it relates back to broader principles and analysis.

The next level is composed of the specific campaigns, programs, and organizational forms intended to lend the articulated ideology its historic substance and force. Thus, in the 1930s, the Communists organized nationwide demonstrations against unemployment and hunger. There were constant campaigns for social insurance, housing for the poor, better home relief, free milk for children of the unemployed. There was steady agitation, among both whites and blacks, to get workers to become part of groups protesting against discrimination in hiring, Jim Crow, lynching, the Scottsboro boys' trial, the imprisonment of Angelo Herndon. These campaigns were structured through union locals in the Communist-based Trade Union Unity League, neighborhood Unemployed Councils, and Communist-led community groups, and they were promoted on national, state, and local levels.

The third level of practice encompasses the day-to-day involvement with people that makes up and defines the quality of struggle in its most immediately felt mode. Here are local efforts to stop an eviction, get a family help from the downtown relief bureau, organize a demonstration at City Hall. The "Jimmy Higgins" work, the Communists used to call it—the simple, grinding, aggravating tasks of making phone calls, knocking on doors, handing out leaflets. Or one worked and waited week after week on an assembly line, making acquaintances and looking for some dramatic issue to break. Organizers helped create issues too, by mobilizing people around small grievances that then gave entry to larger social and political problems.

The party's organizational movements, such as the Trade Union Unity

League and the Unemployed Councils, linked the three levels of practice. These mass organizations expressed the general ideological line, carried out what the party called the political tasks of the moment, and sought to attract new members by organizing in the community and on the shop floor. They were the arenas in which the derived ideology of class struggle was mixed with inherent traditions and value orientations that justified action on the part of working people to protect what they perceived as their basic rights.

The concept of using the immediate as entree to the systemic was essential to Communist organizing theory. It was not only the courage and commitment of party organizers that were central to effective organizing, but the party's insistence that particular grievances be related through the broader political movement to theory and general principle. This shared analysis, this derived world view, helped provide the glue and rationale for the democratic elements in Communist organizing work.

If students of community and political organization are not to lose what is most valuable in the experience of the American Communist Party, they must focus on the actual process through which party militants worked with people. As activists went into local communities and shops to organize around immediate problems, they fought to connect daily struggles to broad political campaigns and ideological issues. As long as what they were doing did *not intrude on Comintern policy*, front-line workers had a free hand, a limited but localized autonomy.

One of the most thorough discussions of how the process worked can be found in the autobiography of Steve Nelson (Nelson, Barrett, and Ruck 1981). Nelson, born Stjepan Mesaros in 1903, came to the United States from Croatia after World War I, joined the party while he was working in the auto industry in Detroit in the mid 1920s, and in 1929 went to Chicago where he became one of the earliest organizers of the unemployed.

According to Nelson, the experience of the Unemployed Councils taught the Communists that they were going to have to talk less about the coming revolution and more about ways of helping people survive in the here and now. "We learned to shift away from a narrow, dogmatic approach to what might be called a grievance approach to the organizing" (Nelson et al. 1981, 76).

The practice of mobilizing people around locally based political demands—grievances—was supplemented by the practice of helping them out on the most immediate level of their problems. People would come into the Unemployed Council office looking for help to stay an eviction. Or a

Polish worker, who spoke no English, might come and say that his wife was sick and needed a doctor. One of the organizers would go down with the man to the welfare office and act as interpreter. "We spent much of our time simply learning the welfare rules in order to be effective" (Nelson et al. 1981, 76, 77, 78). The revolution waited while Communists learned welfare regulations, acted as advocates of the poor, and explained to neighborhood people what their rights were. Communists tried to make their work an integral part of neighborhood existence. "For fundraising we tried to stage events that fit into the cultural life of the community," Nelson wrote. Bingo, raffles, picnics, and block parties were common. The Unemployed Council sponsored dances for young people. The hall at the church was sometimes available, "and we could usually dig up an accordion player somewhere" (Nelson et al. 1981, 76–78). In these ways, the Communists tried to establish the presence of their street units, block committees, and Unemployed Councils, not just as the advance guard of socialism but as palpable agencies of community life.

The fatal flaw in Communist practice, of course, was that local campaigns and techniques could be manipulative rather than sincere, and were subject at a moment's notice to reversal by higher party organs and, ultimately, by Comintern determination of overall policy. But there were strengths to the party's organizing theory as well. The Communists consciously incorporated into their practice the recognition that what moves people to action—their sense of what they perceive as legitimately an injustice or grievance—is itself a function of an implicit ideology. To broaden the base of what popular constituencies will take action to change, therefore, requires a broadening of their ideological perspective. At the same time, rank-and-file Communist activists knew how to draw on local traditions and values as they struggled to organize people. They recognized that to enable constituencies to move beyond inherent ideologies, organizers had to enter into the flow of daily life and the immediate community experience those ideologies shaped, limited, and legitimized.

Activities of block committees, Unemployed Councils, and shop groups in the 1930s, the nature of the organizing experiences they produced, compose a set of variations on a common theme. The Communists, in order to discover the kinds of grievances that would draw local constituencies to action, had to be aware of, and sensitive to, the existing values and political beliefs through which these constituencies understood their lives. All Communist practice concerned itself, then, with the immediate grievance as the wedge for opening the door to larger political consciousness.

There were destructive and crippling aspects to Communist practice. Their theories of political and economic repression were crude, and the movement's achievements were irrevocably distorted by its attachment to Stalinism. The party insisted on introducing issues extraneous and alien to the immediate concerns of the American working class. Top leadership, should it suddenly devise a new policy or receive instructions from the next higher level, would readily sabotage campaigns and alliances already in place. And ideological pressures toward behavior consistent with socialist values were used to intrude into people's lives, and exercise social and political control over areas of personal choice.[5] Still, a fruitful and provocative theory of community action is buried along with much that was antidemocratic and controlling.

Saul Alinsky and "Nonideological" Organizing

Few organizers have had an impact on social-change efforts equal to that of Saul Alinsky. Although the tangible results of his personal organizing from the late 1930s to the early 1970s are mixed, Alinsky is the father of modern community organizing. His organizing method is the basis of what Boyte (1980) labeled the "backyard revolution" of the past fifteen years. Alinsky is equally important because his method foreshadowed and embodies two major changes in movement organizing in the United States since the late 1940s: (1) a shift from the workplace to the community as the locus of organizing, and (2) a move from consciously ideological organizing to an approach assumed to be "nonideological." It is the second part of this practice, the so-called nonideological element, that attracts our attention here.

Since the early 1960s, from the early days of the New Left to current neopopulist efforts, the dominant thinking has held that successful organizing must be nonideological. Bruce Payne, a Student Nonviolent Coordinating Committee (SNCC) staffer, put it this way:

> SNCC people generally refer to themselves and their organizations as "nonideological." By this they mean that they do not have a total view of political and social life that enables them to offer a blueprint for the kind of society they would like to see in the future. . . . The absence of full-scale program has as its concomitant an emphasis on immediate action. (Cited in Fisher 1984, 99)

Saul Alinsky encouraged the trend toward nonideological organizing. In an oft-cited statement, Alinsky declared that "the only reason people have ever banded together, and the only reason they will, is the fact that organization gives them the power to satisfy their desires or realize their needs. There never has been any other reason" (Silberman 1964, 324). Nevertheless, while Alinsky may have been "true to the American pragmatic tradition, which exalts action over theory," it does not follow that either he or his organizing method were nonideological (Aronowitz 1964, 104). All organizing is ideological. And by insisting on a nonideological reading of his work, Alinsky set the terms by which his own most basic philosophical commitments could be undermined.

Critics of the Alinsky method assert, correctly, that if individual material advantage is all that counts, then Alinsky's organizing could lead to reactionary as well as progressive ends, which is what happened in Back of the Yards.[6] But we need to remember that Alinsky was very disheartened by the results of his Back of the Yards organizing. Alinsky was not involved in the organizing process simply to let people decide to organize effectively to keep blacks out of the neighborhoods that hired him, and, depending on the situation, he used his politics and ideology in varying degrees to guide the organizing process.[7]

One of Alinsky's great contributions to community organizing was his emphasis on the importance of grounding the organizing process in community values and traditions, what Rudé calls the popular, traditional, or inherent ideology. Alinsky did not fear, though well he might have, reactionary elements in such traditions. With community traditions as a base, he counseled, the mixture of conservative neighborhood agencies and a progressive People's Organization "will result in a progressive product." Only community organization grounded in the people's traditions, Alinsky thought, was "truly representative of the people and truly in keeping with the spirit of democracy."

> A People's Organization actually is built upon all of the diverse loyalties—
> to the church, to the labor union, to the social groups, to the nationality
> groups, to the myriad other groups and institutions which comprise the
> constellation of the American way of life. These loyalties combine to effect
> an abiding faith in, and a profound loyalty to, the democratic way of life.
> (Alinsky 1946, 88)

In the late 1930s, Alinsky's emphasis on popular ideology combined with a derived ideology that changed over time to create some extraordinary organizing successes. This was most evident in the first years of organizing in Back of the Yards in the late 1930s. Then, still influenced by the radical politics of the Congress of Industrial Organizations (CIO) and the Communist party in Chicago (especially the Popular Front days of the party after 1935), Alinsky emphasized the need to build "broad general People's Organizations whose very character would involve an *over all philosophy* and attack" (Alinsky 1946, 37; italics added). From 1938 through the late 1940s, Alinsky's form of organizing was to borrow heavily from the community-based, multi-issue, confrontational organizing he learned from the CIO and the Unemployment Councils of the Communist party. While he consciously rejected the party line, it was in this first period, when he referred to himself in classic Popular Front terms as a "professional antifascist," that he understood the need for program and vision in the organizing process, the need for derived as well as traditional ideology.[8]

But the Back of the Yards Neighborhood Council (BYNC) also stands as Alinsky's great failure. During the initial period when Alinsky was directly involved with the council, he made excellent use of a blend of militant tactics and both popular and derived ideology. But it did not last long. Alinsky's direct contact as leading organizer in Back of the Yards was relatively brief, though he did keep in touch with BYNC for many years. The legacy of the Alinsky method, as was to be the case in almost every succeeding project, was an emphasis on tactics and organization building rather than political education. With his departure from the organizing in Back of the Yards, a let-the-people-decide creed came to dominate. The derived ideology of antifascism disappeared. For it had resided almost exclusively in Alinsky the individual, never as an organizational program or collective vision. And in Back of the Yards the popular ideology grounded in community traditions ultimately resulted in a well-organized white working-class group becoming not only a recognized part of the political machine in Chicago but a segregationist neighborhood organization.

In the history of community organizing, instances in which community and workplace struggles united effectively have been rare. Such a radical action in Back of the Yards did not come about solely from militant tactics, community traditions, or letting the people decide. Alinsky emphasized community values and traditions to form the organizing base and then coupled it with a radical Popular Front style of politics.

What characterized Alinsky's practice before 1946 was the infusion of a derived ideology coupled with a sense of people's traditions and experiences. After 1946, the emphasis on community action as part of a larger ideological

progressivism disappeared, and Alinsky vehemently promoted his "nonideological" position. This rejection of consciously introduced ideology as an
aspect of organizing practice must be understood as falling within a larger
tradition of American activism, especially the impact of the Cold War and
anticommunism on activism.

Since the Bolshevik revolution in 1917 and the periodic anticommunist
"red scares" in the United States that followed it, being ideological has
come to be associated with supporting un-American, statist, Communist
and Socialist parties. Historically, the nonideological stances of Alinsky
(and the early New Left and current neopopulists) have served as clear public
rejections of traditional left (essentially communist) organizing efforts. The
impact of anticommunism and anti-Stalinism on community organizing is
an episode in the history of the American left that needs a separate telling.
Suffice it to say that by the late 1940s, an increasingly militant Alinsky
method deemphasized all ideology and substituted a focus on organizing
technique and skills, on the "highly trained, politically sophisticated, creative organizer" (Sanders 1970, 68–69).

In the postwar years, Alinsky did everything he could to distance himself
and his organizing method from the radicals (i.e., communists). For example, the Community Political Organization (CPO), which Alinsky and Fred
Ross organized in East Los Angeles, changed its name in 1947 to Community
Service Organization (CSO) so that it would not be confused with the
Communist party (CP) (Fisher 1984, 61). One tactic Alinsky employed to
distance his organizing method was to deny the existence of any derived
ideology; his was to be a democratic organizing project, not one with a
dogmatic, authoritarian ideology like that of the Communist Party.[9]

With the advent of the Cold War, Alinsky organizing, always heavily
oriented toward tactics and organizational skill development, consciously
sought to exclude any derived ideology from the organizing process. (Yet,
we reiterate, there is no such thing as nonideological organizing.) What
remained was a hard-nosed, interest-group style of organizing *and* a popular
ideology that professed that people's values and traditions were somehow
intrinsically democratic and progressive.

Ultimately the Alinsky method, devoid of the radical ideology of its early
years, expressed a tacit faith in pluralistic politics, a model of democracy
in which organizations compete for resources and pressure the system in
behalf of their own interests. This is true of Alinsky organizing efforts from
the Woodlawn Organization in Chicago to COPS in San Antonio, Texas.

What has become most important in Alinsky-based organizing is to give community people a sufficient sense of their own dignity and power so that they can argue on their behalf, and then to get these newly empowered people to the interest-group bargaining table (Fisher 1984, 58). In a society more than willing to ignore and exclude people from the decision-making process, this is no small achievement. But because there is no room in such an approach for questioning the economic foundations of the existing order, Alinsky-based organizing is unable to confront the possibility that capitalism is not set up to serve the poor and the working class, that it is inherently undemocratic.

Alinsky-type organizing has won many victories and empowered many people. And neopopulist organizers have improved on the basic method, especially in recognizing the limits of organizing solely at the community level and understanding the potential in electoral politics. But without an emphasis on bringing the radical ideology of the organizer to the organizing process, without a commitment to raising the political consciousness of the organized by both challenging and refining community values and traditional ideology, the legacy of Alinsky to his current neopopulist supporters, most of whom continue to follow in his "nonideological" footsteps—has been limited.

Conclusion

Organizers are left with the problem of how to move people to progressive ideas in an era rife with reactionary politics. We argue that whatever strategies emerge, somehow the conscious use of ideology must be part of them. Organizing, past and present, has suffered from a mistaken belief in the existence of something called nonideological organizing.

This theme is gaining greater recognition among those who have been involved in the organizing struggles of the 1960s and 1970s. Gary Delgado, seeking to assess the strengths and weaknesses of one of the most significant organizing agencies of recent years, Association of Community Organizations for Reform Now (ACORN), recounts the group's efforts to develop a People's Platform in 1980. The goal was not primarily to influence the Democratic National Convention but to use the task of platform development as a way of forging some ideological unity within the movement.

According to Delgado (1982), ACORN was only partially successful.

> The process did develop the knowledge and skills of both the members and
> staff of the organization. It was not an insignificant step to get low-income
> people to speculate on how banking *should* be regulated or how a national
> health plan conceived in their interests might work. ACORN members were
> given the opportunity to start where they were at experientially and expand
> the scope of vision through a collective process. . . . However, in terms of
> advancing ideological unity within the organization, the platform was at best
> a starting place. At worst, it represented a hodgepodge of progressive notions
> without an underlying ideology. [Delgado 1982, 63.]

All the conflicts buried in American populism, and its unrecognized mixture
of inherent and derived political ideas, erupted. ACORN members in Mem-
phis sought local control over both school spending and school closings,
while avoiding the issue of busing. Texas constituents supported a proposal
that worker representatives and low-income community residents be on the
boards of all corporations with assets of over $10 million; however, they
opposed both Mexican immigration and the ERA.

ACORN's final platform reflected two things: "local experience in specific
areas, and ambivalence between anti-corporate populism and the social
democratic state." The process exposed some of the sharp political differences that exist within American popular movements. Since these differences will not disappear of their own accord, bringing them to the fore at
least had the virtue "of forcing ACORN members and allies to address
policies instead of personalities." Delgado remains convinced that if progressive political organizing is to move beyond its present stagnation, coalitions must develop programs that stem from examining particular issues
within the context of larger political directions (Delgado 1982; 79–80).

Activists must begin to integrate the lessons of both conscious and
implicit approaches into the role of ideology in organizing. We find the work
of Sara Evans and Harry Boyte regarding the necessary role of free spaces
to be valuable, but we disagree with the idea that such spaces are, of
themselves, prime factors in movement building. As Back of the Yards and,
more recently, the white ethnic community of Howard Beach, New York,
demonstrate, reactionary political forms can readily emerge from unmediated reliance on the free spaces of communal association. In the development
of progressive movements, free spaces must be understood as loci where
popular and derived ideology can meet, interact, and be reformulated.

The American Communist party's skillful understanding of the value of community traditions and institutions was undermined by its unyielding subordination to the national leadership and, ultimately, to the Comintern. Alinsky, in contrast, used both inherent and derived forms skillfully and effectively (if not as systematically as the party) in his very early work in Back of the Yards. But for a variety of reasons, he abandoned his antifascist ideology and replaced it with an emphasis on organizing method, popular values, and community traditions. This seriously limited Alinsky projects in the 1960s. Such limitations, we think, continue to haunt neopopulists today.

Notes

1. For example, Frances Fox Piven and Richard Cloward (1979) look to mass movements, social disruption, and empowerment through voter registration. Sara Evans and Harry Boyte (1982, 55–65) emphasize the importance of what they call free social spaces. Mike Miller (1982, 185–196), of the Organize Training Center in San Francisco, seeks the creation of local self-help groups and their involvement in electoral politics. Some see a nationwide program demanding full employment as essential to the growth of a new movement; others insist that the working-class poor will mobilize only in response to demands for an expanding social wage and a strengthened system of social supports (Block et al. 1986, 694–697).

2. By *ideology* we do not envision a static program of political theory that is somehow committed to its own extrascientific truth. We follow Clifford Geertz, who describes ideologies as "maps of problematic social reality and matrices for the creation of a collective conscience. Whether, in any particular case, the map is accurate or the conscience creditable is a separate question" (Geertz 1964, 64). We combine Geertz's notion of ideology as an overarching conceptual and normative system with Gramsci's insight that in the consciousness of what the latter called subaltern groups, conflicting beliefs exist about how societies are and should be organized.

For a less complex definition, but one within the same tradition, see Easton (1967). Ideologies, Easton writes, "are articulated sets of ideals, ends, and purposes which help the members of [a] system interpret the past, explain the present, and offer a vision of the future" (p. 45).

3. Theodore Draper acidly implies that the interest of these scholars in the American communist movement flows from their disappointments with the New Left, disappointments that have led them to seek, in Draper's terms, a "vicarious radicalism." He writes that this "new burst of interest in the history of American

Communism . . . apparently derives from the need of former New Leftists to find a new political home or at least a source of hope. . . . If ever a radicalism could be lived vicariously, it is this one" (Draper 1985b, 49). For responses to Draper, see Buhle et al., 1985).

4. See Howe and Coser (1962, Chap. 11). Also see Draper (1972). Whatever else, Draper points out, during the Harlan County strike the Communists were the only organization prepared to take a principled stand on the unity of black and white workers. The courage white miners demonstrated in sitting and eating with black miners at meals is beyond question. This was not the behavior of automatons.

5. For documentation, see such authors as Dennis (1977), Charney (1968), Gornick (1977), and Wright (1952).

6. Back of the Yards is a Chicago working-class neighborhood just west of the stockyards. In the late 1930s, Alinsky was sent by the Chicago Area Project to work in the community. In 1939 he set up a multi-issue neighborhood organization known as the Back of the Yards Neighborhood Council. Alinsky envisioned the BYNC as a first step in building a chain of "people's organizations" nationwide.

7. As Myles Horton, founder of the Highlander Research and Education Center, put it: "Alinsky was very sad about what happened in the Back of the Yards in terms of their racial prejudice, because the goal of racial equality was very important to him. I just don't want people to think that the material is all Alinsky meant about self-interest" (quoted in Wellstone 1978, 203).

8. There is no room in this paper to go into specifics regarding the nature of Alinsky's derived ideology. Essentially, the broad-based ideology under which Alinsky operated had its roots in the populism that emerged, over the course of the 1930s, out of the earlier agrarian populist movement. Alan Brinkley identifies populism as containing the following precepts: It seeks to (1) affirm the ideal of community, (2) restore power back to the local level and the individual, (3) decentralize power in order to provide access to all, (4) oppose the tyranny of excess power, and (5) identify enemy targets that seek to destroy community or ignore the needs of community residents. Brinkley discusses urban populism in the 1930s as it emerged out of the efforts of Huey Long and Father Coughlin (see Brinkley 1982, 142–160).

The difficulty with populism is that even when it is consciously used as a mobilizing ideology, it is severely limited because if offers little critique of the political and economic system within or outside the neighborhood. There is little analysis, other than the self-evident assertion that neighborhoods are "powerless" and in need of "self-determination," of what causes and perpetuates problems in the locality. It thus provides no solutions to the grievances of communities beyond "getting power."

9. It should be noted that Alinsky's anticommunism was not simply a product of his practical response to Cold War pressures. Even in Chicago in the 1930s he was deeply opposed to what he viewed as a fundamentally undemocratic and manipulative organizing method. American populism has always positioned itself

as a native radical movement to the left of liberal capitalism but opposed to noncapitalist, Marxist alternatives, and Alinsky's populism was no exception.

References

Alinsky, Saul. 1946. *Reveille for Radicals*. Chicago: University of Chicago Press.
Aronowitz, Stanley. 1964. "Poverty, Politics, and Community Organization." *Studies on the Left*, No. 4 (Summer).
Block, Fred, Richard A. Cloward, Barbara Ehrenreich and Frances Fox Piven 1986. "Expand the Social Programs: The Trouble with Full Employment." *Nation* 242, no. 19.
Boyte, Harry C. 1980. *The Backyard Revolution*. Philadelphia: Temple University Press.
Brinkley, Alan. 1982. *Voices of Protest*. New York: Oxford University Press.
Buhle, Paul, James R. Prickett, James R. Barrett and Rob Ruck, Norman Markowitz, Al Richmond, Mark Naison, Roy Rosenzweig, Gary Gerstle, Murray Bookchin, and Theodore Draper. 1985. "Revisiting American Communism: An Exchange." *New York Review of Books*. August 9.
Burghardt, Steve. 1984. "The Strategic Crisis of Grass Roots Organizing." *Against the Current* 3 (Fall): 31.
Charney, George. 1968. *A Long Journey*. Chicago: Quadrangle Books.
Delgado, Gary. 1982. "Taking it to the Streets: Community Organizing and National Politics." *Socialist Review* 12, nos. 3–4: 59.
Dennis, Peggy. 1977. *The Autobiography of an American Communist*. Westport, Conn.: Lawrence Hill.
Draper, Theodore. 1972. "Communists and Miners." *Dissent* 16 (Spring).
————. 1985a. "American Communism Revisited." *New York Review of Books*, May 9.
————. 1985b. "The Popular Front Revisited." *New York Review of Books*, May 30.
Easton, David. 1967. *A Systems Analysis of Political Life*. New York: Wiley.
Evans, Sara M., and Harry C. Boyte. 1982. "Schools for Action: Radical Uses for Social Space." *Democracy* 2 (Fall).
————. 1986. *Free Spaces: The Sources of Democratic Change in America*. New York: Harper & Row.
Fisher, Robert. 1984. *Let the People Decide: Neighborhood Organizing in America*. Boston: Twayne.
Geertz, Clifford. 1964. "Ideology as a Cultural System." In *Ideology and Discontent*, edited by David Apter. Glencoe, Ill.: Free Press.
Gornick, Vivian. 1977. *The Romance of American Communism*. New York: Basic Books.

Gramsci, Antonio. 1971. *Selections from the Prison Notebooks*, edited by Q. W. Hoare and G. Nowell Smith. New York: International Publishers.

Howe, Irving and Lewis, Coser. 1962. *The American Communist Party*. New York: Praeger.

Miller, Mike. 1982. "Community Organization Vision and the Electoral Tactic." *Socialist Review* 12, nos. 3–4.

Nelson, Steve, James R. Barrett, and Bob Ruck. 1981. *Steve Nelson. American Radical*. Pittsburgh: University of Pittsburgh Press.

Piven, Frances Fox, and Richard A. Cloward. 1979. *Poor People's Movements*. New York: Vintage.

Rudé, George. 1980. *Ideology and Popular Protest*. New York: Pantheon.

Sanders, Marion K. 1970. "The Professional Radical: Conversations with Saul Alinsky." *Harper's* 240 (January).

Silberman, Charles. 1964. *Crisis in Black and White*. New York: Random House.

Wellstone, Paul. 1978. *How the Rural Poor Got Power*. Amherst: University of Massachusetts Press.

Wright, Richard. 1952. *The God That Failed*, edited by Richard Crossman. New York: Bantam.

CHAPTER 4

Family and Class in Contemporary America
Notes toward an Understanding of Ideology

Rayna Rapp

[Editor's Note: The years between the first appearance of "Family and Class in Contemporary America" (1978) and its inclusion in this collection have witnessed a shift in the political context in which this essay is grounded. The context has moved from the living rooms of women's movement meetings to the floors of state legislatures and Congress. At the same time that reproductive rights, especially abortion, are under attack from an increasingly antifeminist judiciary and state legislatures, demand is broadening and escalating for state support for reproductive activities—childbearing and childrearing—that traditionally have been women's lot. Under the "family policy" label, gender-neutral parenting leaves and extensive childcare programs have become the object of widely supported legislative activity.

Obviously, we cannot attribute to Rapp's essay the shift in feminist policy concerns from equal rights to what are popularly identified as "family" issues. Nevertheless, Rapp's insistence on understanding the family as a *construct*, serving ideological purposes in relation to the needs of class-differentiated households, provided the seminal concepts needed to understand the conflicts in the feminist movement referred to in her opening paragraphs. Although the conflict between liberation *from* the family and liberation *for* the family are no longer major division among feminists, these questions, which were so painful for the women's movement in the mid 1970s, now require formulation in terms comprehensible in the political

Originally published in a special issue of *The University of Michigan Papers in Woman's Studies*, this article subsequently appeared in *Science and Society* 42 (1978): 278–300 and is reprinted with permission of the author and *Science and Society*.

arena. Through her integration of gender, class, and community, Rapp provides what is still the most coherent theoretical framework for making sense out of the competing claims presented as "family" versus "liberation."]

This essay is grounded in two contexts, one political and one academic. The political context is that of the women's movement, in which a debate seems always to be raging concerning the future of the family. Many of us have been to an archetypical meeting in which someone stands up and asserts that the nuclear family ought to be abolished because it is degrading and constraining to women. Usually, someone else (often representing a Third World position) follows on her heels, pointing out that the attack on the family represents a white middle-class position and that other women need their families for support and survival. Evidently both speakers are, in some sense, right. And just as evidently they aren't talking about the same families. We need to explore those different notions of family if we are to heal an important split in our movement. To do so, we must take seriously the things women say about their experiences in their families, especially as they vary by class.

The second context out of which this essay grows is the academic study of the contemporary American family. Over the last few years, in reading eclectically in sociology, demography, urban planning, and policy literature, I've been trying to sort out what is known (or not known) about women's experiences in their families. Here, too, a debate is raging over the future of the family. On the one hand, there is a tremendous alarmism that presages the end of the family—recent books have included titles such as *The Fractured Family*; journals on family coordination and counseling, and courses at every level from high school through graduate studies speak of the family in crisis. On the other hand, *Here to Stay* (to name but one title) and a spate of studies reanalyzing the divorce rates reassure us that the American family is simply changing, but not disappearing. This debate seems to mystify the subject it claims to clarify.[1] This is not surprising, since the family is a topic that is ideologically charged. In order to get some understanding of the importance of ideology in analyses of the family, there are two fields to which we ought to turn for perspective. One is the recent work that has been done on the history of the family.[2] A great many innovative studies reveal similar issues in historical perspective; for as long as modern records have been kept concerning families, it seems that people have been speculating on the future of the institution. The last decade of social history should caution us to moderate our alarmism. At the least, we have learned that all societies contain a multiplicity of family forms whose structural arrangements respond to complex conditions.

The second field that adds perspective to the issue is anthropology, which studies the family and kinship systems both at home and abroad. Anthropology reminds us that we are *all* participant observers when we study the American family. It has been pointed out that our understandings often get in the way and more often express the ideology and norms of our culture than an analysis. This word of warning leads me to examine not only what differing groups of people *say* about their families but what they actually *do* in their families. It also leads me to examine the ways in which I think the concept of family itself is ideological in social science.

The archetypical political debaters arguing over the meaning of the family aren't talking about the same families. Neither are the social scientists. We need to make a distinction between families and households, and to examine their relation to one another. The entities in which people actually live are not families, but households (as any census taker, demographer, or fieldworking anthropologist will tell you). Households are the empirically measurable units within which people pool resources and perform certain tasks. Goody analyzes them as units of production, reproduction, and consumption (Goody 1972). They are residential units within which personnel and resources get distributed and connected. Households may vary in their membership composition and in their relation to resource allocation, especially in a system such as our own. That is, they vary systematically in their ability to hook into, accumulate, and transmit wealth, wages, or welfare. This seems a simple unit to define.

Families, on the other hand, are a bit more slippery. In English we tend to gloss "family" to mean household. But analytically, the concept means something else. For all classes of Americans, the word has at least two levels of meaning (Goody 1972; Schneider and Smith 1973). One is normative: Husbands, wives, and children are a set of relatives who should live together (i. e., the nuclear family). The other meaning includes a more extended network of kin relations that people may activate selectively. That is, the American family includes the narrower and broader webs of kin ties that are "the nuclear family" and all relations by blood and marriage. The concept of family is presumed in America to carry a heavy load of affect. We say "blood is thicker than water," "till death do us part," "you can choose your friends, but not your relatives," and so on. What I argue in this essay is that the concept of family also carries a heavy load of ideology.

The reason for this is that the family is the normative, correct way in which people get recruited into households. It is through families that people enter into productive, reproductive, and consumption relations. The two genders enter them differently. Families organize households, and it is within families that people experience the absence or presence, the sharing or withholding, of basic poolable resources. "Family" (as a normative concept in our culture) reflects those material relations; it also distorts them. As such, the concept of family is a socially necessary illusion that simultaneously expresses and masks recruitment to relations of production, reproduction, and consumption—relations that condition different kinds of household resource bases in different class sectors. Our notions of family absorb the conflicts, contradictions, and tensions actually generated by those material, class-structured relations that households hold to resources in advanced capitalism. "Family," as we understand (and misunderstand) the term, is conditioned by the exigencies of household formation, and serves as a shock absorber to keep households functioning. People are recruited and kept in households by families in all classes, yet the families they have (or don't have) are not the same.

Having asserted that households and families vary by class, we now need to consider that third concept, class. If ever a concept carried a heavy weight of ideology, it is the concept of class in American social science. We have a huge and muddled literature that attempts to reconcile objective and subjective criteria, to sort people into lowers, uppers, and middles, to argue about the relation of consciousness to material reality.[3] I will say only the following: "Social class" is a shorthand for a process, not a thing. That process is the one by which different social relations to the means of production are inherited and reproduced under capitalism. As the concept is developed by Marx, the process of capital accumulation generates and constantly deepens relations between two categories of people: those who are both available and forced to work for wages because they own no means of production, and those who control those means of production. The concept of class expresses a historical process of expanding capital. In the process, categories of people get swept up at different times and places and deposited into different relations to the means of production and to one another. People then get labeled blue collar or white collar; they may experience their social existence as mediated by ethnicity or the overwhelming legacy of slavery and racism. Yet all these categories must be viewed in the light of the historic process of capitalist accumulation in the United States. To a large extent, what are actually being accumulated are changing categories of proletarians. Class formation and composition is always in flux; what gets accumulated in it are relationships. Under advanced capitalism, there are shifting frontiers that separate poverty, stable wage-earning, affluent salaries, and inherited wealth. The frontiers may be crossed by individuals, and in either direction. That is, both upward and downward mobility are real processes. The point is, "class" isn't a static place that individuals inhabit. It is a process determined by the relationships set up in capital accumulation.

Returning to the initial distinction between family and household, I want to explore how these two vary among differing class sectors in contemporary America and to draw a composite picture of the households formed around material relations by class, and the families that organize those households. I argue that those families mean different things by class, and by genders as well, because classes and genders stand in differing material relations to one another. I further argue that their meanings are highly ideological.

I'd like to begin with a review and interpretation of the studies done on the working-class family. Studies span the postwar decades from the late 1940s to the present. They are regionally diverse, and report on both cities and suburbs. The data provided by researchers such as Berger, Gans, Komarovsky, Howell, Rubin, and others reveal a composite portrait.[4] The most salient characteristic of household organization in the working class is dependency on hourly wages. Stable working-class households participate in relations of production, reproduction, and consumption by sending out their labor power in exchange for wages. "Sending out" is important: There is a radical split between household and workplace, yet the resources upon which the household depends come from participation in production outside of itself. How much labor power a working-class household needs to send out is determined by many things: the cost of reproducing (or maintaining) the household, the work careers and earning trajectories of individual members, and the domestic cycle (that is, the relations between the genders and the generations, which specify when and if wives and adolescent children are available to work outside the home). Braverman estimates that the average working-class household now sends out 1.7 full-time equivalent workers (Braverman 1974). That figure tells us that a high percentage of married women and teenaged children are contributing their wages to the household. In many ways, the work patterns for nineteenth-century European capitalism described by Tilly and Scott still leave their mark on the contemporary American working-class household; it is not only male heads of households upon whom survival depends (Tilly and Scott 1975).

What the working class sends out in exchange for basic resources is labor power. Labor power is the only commodity without which there can be no capitalism. It is also the only commodity for which the working class controls its own means of production (Gernstein 1973). Control over the production of labor power undoubtedly affected women's experiences historically, as it does today (Gordon 1976). In the early stages of industrialization, it appears that working-class households literally produced a lot of babies (future labor power) as their strategy for dealing with a market economy (Tilly 1977). Now workers produce fewer children, but the work of servicing them (social reproduction) is still a major process that goes on in the household. Households are the basic units in which labor power is reproduced and maintained. This takes place in a location radically removed from the workplace. Such relations therefore appear as autonomous from capital, but of course they are not; without wages, households are hard to form and keep functioning; without the production of a disciplined labor force, factories cannot produce and profit.

The work that gets done in households (primarily by women) is not simply about babies. Housework itself has recently been rediscovered as work, and its contribution to arenas beyond the household is clear.[5] At the least, housework cuts the reproduction costs of wage workers. Imagine if all those meals had to be bought at restaurants, those clothes cleaned at laundry rates, those beds made by hotel employees! Housework is also what women do in exchange for access to resources that are bought by their husband's wages. As such, it is a coin of exchange between men and women. As housework is wageless, it keeps its workers dependent on others for access to commodities bought with wages. It makes them extremely vulnerable to the work conditions of their men. When women work (as increasingly they do), their primary definition as houseworker contributes to the problems they encounter in entering the paid labor force. They are available for part-time (or full-time) work in the lowest-paid sectors of the labor market, in jobs that leave them less economically secure than men. Participation in the "sexregated" labor market then reinforces dependency upon the earnings of other household members and the continued importance of women's domestic labor.[6]

Of course, these rather abstract notions of "household participation" in the labor market or in housework are experienced concretely by family members. Working-class families are normatively nuclear. They are formed via marriage, which links men and women "for love" and not "for money" (Schneider and Smith 1973). This relation is of course both real and a socially necessary illusion. As such, it is central to the ideology of the family. The cultural distinction between love and money corresponds to the distinction between private family life in the home and work life outside the home. The two are experienced as opposite; in fact they are interpenetrating. The seeming autonomy to exchange love at home expresses something ideological about the relation between home and work: One must work for the sake of the family, and having a family is the "payoff" for leading a good life. Founding a family is what people do for personal gratification, for love, and for autonomy. The working-class family literature is full of life histories in which young women saw "love" as a way to get out of their own, often difficult families. Rubin's interviews, for example, are full of teenaged girls who said, "When I grow up, I'll marry for love, and it will be better than my parents' marriage." You may marry for love, but what you mainly get is babies. Forty to 60 percent of teenaged pregnancies are conceived premaritally, and approximately 50 percent of working-class women marry in their teen years (Rubin 1976). It's a common experience to go from being someone's child to having someone's child in under a year. This is not exactly a situation that leads to autonomy.

For men, the situation is complementary. As one of the young working-class men in Rubin's study puts it:

> I had to work from the time I was thirteen and turn over most of my pay to my mother to help pay the bills. By the time I was nineteen, I had been working for all those years and I didn't have anything—not a thing. I used to think a lot about how when I got married, I would finally get to keep my money for myself. I guess that sounds a little crazy when I think about it now because I have to support the wife and kids. I don't know *what* I was thinking about, but I never thought about that then. (Rubin 1976, Chap. 4)

What you get from the romance of love and marriage is in fact not simply a family but a household, and that's quite another matter. Romance is implicated in gender identity and ideology. We are all aware of the cultural distinction made between the sexual identity of a good and a bad girl; a good girl is one who accumulates her sexual resource for later investment. Autonomy means escaping your childhood family to become an adult with your own nuclear family. For young men, the identity process includes the cultural role of wild boy—one who "sows some wild oats," hangs out on street corners, perhaps gets in trouble with the police, and drinks (Rubin 1976, 56ff.). Ideally, the good girl domesticates the wild boy; she gives him love, and he settles downs and goes out to work. Autonomy means becoming an adult with your own nuclear family as an escape. But of course, autonomy is illusive. The family is classically seen as an escape from production, but in fact it is what sends people into relations of production, for they need to work to support their families. The meaning of production is simultaneously denied and experienced through family relations; working-class wives say of a good husband that he works steadily, provides for the kids, and never harms anyone in the family. The complementary statement is uttered by working-class husbands, who define a good wife as one who keeps the kids under control when he comes home from a hard day's work, and who runs the household well (Rubin 1976; Shostak 1969; Sennett and Cobb 1972; Terkel 1972). To exchange love is also to underwrite both the necessity and the ability to keep on working. *This* is the heritage that working-class families pass on, in lieu of property, to their children.

The family expresses ideology in another sense as well—the distinction between norms and realities. The norms concerning families are that people should be loving and sharing within them and that they should be protective. The reality is too often otherwise, as the recent rising consciousness of domestic violence indicates. Even without domestic violence, there are more commonplace stresses to which families are often subjected. Rubin found in her study that 40 percent of the adults she interviewed had an alcoholic parent (Rubin 1976). Fifty percent had experienced parental desertion or divorce in their childhood. National statistics confirm these figures (U. S. Bureau of the Census 1974, 221f.). About half the adults in her study had seriously destabilizing experiences within their families. The tension generated by relations to resource base can often tear households apart. Under these conditions, to label the working-class personality "authoritarian" seems a cruel hoax. When the household is working, it expresses work discipline.

Ideology is expressed in gender role in families in another sense as well. Throughout the urban kinship literature, across classes and ethnic groups, the work of reproducing families is in part undertaken by larger kinship groups (the family in the broader sense of relatives). Family networks in this larger sense are women centered and tend to be serviced by women. There exists a large literature on women-centered kinship networks in which it is usually assumed that women minister to kinship because they minister to families in general. Sylvia Yanagisako suggests that there is also a symbolic level to the kinship work that women do; ideologically, women are assigned to "inside, home, private" domains, while men are seen to represent the outside world (Yanigasako 1977, 207–226). Nuclear families are under cultural constraints to appear as autonomous and private. Yet they are never as private in reality as such values might indicate. The ideal autonomy of an independent nuclear family is constantly being contradicted by the realities of social need, in which resources must be pooled, borrowed, shared. It is women who bridge the gap between what a household's resources really are and what a family's position is supposed to be. Women exchange babysitting, share meals, lend small amounts of money. When a married child is out of work, his (or her) nuclear family turns to the mother, and often moves in for a while. The working-class family literature is filled with examples of such pooling.[7] To the extent that women "represent" the family, they facilitate the pooling needed at various points in the domestic cycle. Men maintain, at least symbolically, the autonomy of their families. Pooling is a norm in family behavior, but it's a hard norm to live with, to either meet or ignore. To comply with the demands of the extended family completely is to lose control over material and emotional resources; to refuse is very dangerous, as people know they will need one another. The tightrope act that ensues is well characterized in the classic mother-in-law story, which usually concerns a young wife and her husband's mother. The two women must figure out a way to share the small services, the material benefits, and the emotional satisfactions one man brings to them both in their separate roles of mother and wife. The autonomy of the younger woman is often compromised by the elder's needs; the authority of the mother is sometimes undermined by the demands of the wife. Women must constantly test, strain, and repair the fibers of the kinship networks.

Such women-centered networks are implicated in a process that has not yet been discussed. We have spoken of production and reproduction as they affect the working-class household and family. We ought briefly to mention consumption as well. As a household function, consumption includes turning an amount of wages into commodities so that labor power may be reproduced. This is often women's work. And work it really is. Weinbaum and Bridges tell us that the centralization and rationalization of services and industry under advanced capitalism may be most efficient from the point of view of capital, but it leaves a lot of unrewarding, technical work to be done by women in supermarkets, in paying bills, in dealing with huge bureaucracies (Weinbaum and Bridges 1976, 88–103). Women experience the pay packet in terms of the use values it will buy. Yet their consumption work is done in the world of exchange value. They mediate the tension between use and exchange, as exemplified in the classic tales concerning domestic quarrels over money in which the man blames the woman for not

making his paycheck stretch far enough. In stable working-class neighborhoods, the consumption work is in part done by women united by family
ties who exchange services, recipes, sales information, and general life-
style skills. Kinship networks are part of "community control" for women.
As Seifer notes, working-class women become involved in political issues
that threaten the stability of their neighborhoods (Seifer 1973, 1976). Perhaps one reason is that their neighborhoods are the locus of extended
families within which both work needs and emotional needs are so often
met.

When everyone submits to the conditions described here "for the sake
of the family," we see the pattern that Howell labels settled living (Howell
1973). Its opposite, in his words, is hard living, a family life style that
includes a lot of domestic instability, alcohol, and rootlessness. I want to
stress that I am here departing from a "culture of poverty" approach. The
value of a label like hard living is that it stresses a continuum made up of
many attributes. It is composed of many processes with which the working
class has a lot of experience. Given the national statistics on alcoholism,
desertion, divorce, premarital pregnancy, and the like, everyone's family
has included such experiences, either in its own domestic cycle or in the
wider family network.[8] Everyone had a wild brother, or was a bad girl, or
had an uncle who drank too much or cousins who got divorced. In each of
such cases, everyone experienced the pooling of resources (or the lack of
pooling) as families attempted to cope with difficult, destabilizing situations.
In a sense, the hard livers keep the settled livers more settled: The consequences of leaving the normative path are well-known and are not appealing.
This, too, is part of the working-class heritage. In studies by Seifer, Howell,
and Rubin, young women express their hopes of leaving a difficult family
situation by finding the right man to marry. They therefore marry young,
with little formal education, possibly about to become parents, and the cycle
begins again.

Of course, hard living is most consistently associated with poverty in the
urban family literature. For essentially political reasons, black poverty has
more frequently been the subject of social science analysis than has white
poverty, but the pattern is found across races. Black Americans have
survived under extremely difficult conditions; many of their household and
family patterns have evolved to deal with their specific history, while others
are shared with Americans of similar class and regional backgrounds. The
problems of household formation under poverty conditions are not unique
to any group of people; some of the specific, resilient solutions to those

problems may be. Because we know far more about black families in poverty than we do about whites, I'll draw a composite picture of households and families using studies that are primarily black.[9] Even when talking about very poor people, analysts such as Liebow, Hannerz, Valentine, and Stack note that there are multiple household types, based on domestic cycles and the relative ability to draw on resources. Hannerz, for example, divides his black sample into four categories (Hannerz 1969). Mainstreamers live in stable households composed of husband, wife, and children. The adults are employed, and either own their own homes or aspire to do so. Their households don't look very different from the rest of the working class. Swingers (Hannerz's second type) are younger, single persons who may be on their way into mainstream life, or they may be tending toward street-families (type three), whose households are headed by women. This type is most important for our study. The fourth category is composed of street men who are peer oriented, and predominantly hard-core unemployed or underemployed. They are similar to the men of *Tally's Corner* (Liebow 1967). While Hannerz and Liebow both give us a wealth of information about what men are doing, they don't analyze their domestic arrangements in detail. Carol Stack, who did her fieldwork from the perspective of female-centered households, most clearly analyzes household formation of the very poor (Stack 1974). She presents us with domestic networks: extremely flexible and fluctuating groups of people committed to resource pooling, to sharing, to mutual aid, who move in and out from under one another's roofs.

Given the state of the job market, welfare legislation, and segregated slum housing, households are unstable. There are people essentially living below socially necessary reproduction costs. They therefore reproduce themselves by spreading out the aid and the risks involved in daily life. For the disproportionally high numbers who are prevented from obtaining steady employment, being part of what Marx called the floating surplus population is a perilous endeavor. What this means in human terms is not only that the poor pay more (Caplowitz 1967) but that the poor share more as well. Stack's monograph contains richly textured descriptions of the way that food, furniture, clothing, appliances, kids, and money make the rounds between individuals and households. She subtitles one chapter, "What Goes Round Comes Round" and describes the velocity with which pooling takes place. People try to give what they can and take what they need. Meeting consumption requirements is hard work under these conditions, and domestic networks get the task done. The pleasure and pressures of such survival networks are predominantly organized around the notion of family.

Meyer Fortes tells us that "domestic groups are the workshops of social reproduction" (Fortes 1972). Whatever else they do, the families that organize domestic networks are responsible for children. As Ladner and Stack remind us, poverty, low levels of formal education, and early age for first pregnancy are highly correlated; a lot of young girls have children while they are not fully adults (Ladner 1971; Stack 1974). Under these circumstances, at least among black families, there is a tremendous sharing of the children themselves. On the whole, these are not kids who grow up in "isolated nuclear families." Stack, for example, found that 20 percent of the ADC (Aid to Dependent Children) children in her study were being raised in a household other than that which contained the biological mother. In the vast majority of cases, the household was related through the biological mother's family. Organizing kinship networks so that children are cared for is a primary function of families. Men, too, often contribute to childrearing. Like women, they share out bits and pieces of whatever they have. While some men make no contribution, others may be simultaneously contributing to sisters, to a mother and aunt, as well as to wives or lovers. They may sleep in one household, but bring groceries, money, and affection to several others (Stack 1974, Chap. 7). Both Stack and Ladner analyze the importance of a father's recognition of his children, by which act he links the baby to his own kinship network. It is family in the broader sense of the term that organizes social reproduction.

Family may be a conscious construction of its participants. Liebow, Stack, Ladner and others describe fictive kinship, by which friends are turned into family. Since family is supposed to be more reliable than friendship, "going for brothers," "for sisters," "for cousins," increases the commitment of a relationship, and makes people ideally more responsible for one another. Fictive kinship is a serious relationship. Stack (who is white) describes her own experience with Ruby, a black woman with whom she "went for sisters." When Ruby's child was seriously ill, Stack became deeply involved in the crisis. When the baby was admitted to the hospital, she and Ruby rushed over for visiting hours. They were stopped by a nurse, who insisted that only the immediate family could enter. Ruby responded, "Caroline here is my sister, and nothing's stopping her from visiting this baby." And they entered, unchallenged. Ruby was correct; under the circumstances, white Caroline was her sister (Stack 1974, 21).

Liebow notes that fictive kinship increases the intensity of relationships to the point where they occasionally explode: The demands of brothers and sisters for constant emotional and material aid may lead to situations that shatter the bonds. Fictive kinship is a prime example of family-as-ideology. In this process, reality is inverted. "Everybody" gets a continuous family, even though the strains and mobility associated with poverty may conspire to keep biological families apart. The idiom of kinship brings people together despite centrifugal circumstances.

It is important not to romanticize this pattern. It has enormous benefits, but its participants also pay high costs. One of the most obvious costs is leveling: Resources must be available for all and none may get ahead. Variations in the chance for survival are smoothed out in domestic networks via sharing. Stack tells the story of a central couple, Calvin and Magnolia, who unexpectedly inherit a sum of money. While the money might have enabled them to ensure their own security, it is gone within a few months. It disappears into the network to pay off bills, buy clothing for children, allow people to eat better (Stack 1974, 105–107). Similar stories are told by Hannerz, Liebow, and Howell. No one gets ahead because individual upward mobility can be bought only at the price of cutting off the very people who have contributed to one's survival. Upward mobility becomes a terribly scarring experience under these circumstances. To get out, a person must stop sharing, which is unfamilial, unfriendly, and quite dangerous. It also requires exceptional circumstances. Gans speaks of the pain that working-class children face if they attempt to use school as a means to achieve mobility, for they run into the danger of being cut off from their peer group (Gans 1962). The chance for mobility may occur only once or twice in a lifetime—for example, at specific moments in a school career or in marriage. People rarely get the occasion, and when they do, to grasp it may simply be too costly. The pressures to stay in a supportive and constraining network, and to level out differences, may be immense. They contribute to the instability of marriage and the normative nuclear family, for the old networks compete with the new unit for precious resources.

The family as an ideological construction is extremely important to poor people. Many studies show that the poor don't aspire to less "stable families," if that term is understood as nuclear families. They are simply much more realistic about their life chances. Ties to family, including fictive family, are the lifelines that simultaneously hold together and sustain individuals. My guess is that among the poor, families do not exhibit the radical split between "private, at home" and "public, at work" found in families of the stable working class. Neither work relations nor household relations are as continuous or as distinct. What *is* continuous is the sharing of reproduction costs throughout a network whose resources are known to all. There can be no privatization when survival may depend on rapid circulation of limited resources. In this process, women don't "represent" kinship to the outside world. They become the nodal points in family nets that span whatever control very poor people have over domestic and resource-getting arrangements. Families are what make the huge gap between norm and reality survivable.

It is particularly ironic that the ideology of family, so important to poor people, is used by ruling-class ideologues to blame the poor for their own condition. In a society in which *all* American subscribe to some version of the normative nuclear family, it is cruelty to attack "the black family" as pathological. Mainstream culture, seeing the family as "what you work for" (and what works for you), uses "family language" to stigmatize those who are structurally prevented from accumulating stable resources. The very poor have used their families to cement and patch tenuous relations to survival; out of their belief in "family" they have invented networks capable of making next-to-nothing go a long way.[10] In response, they are told that their notion of family is inadequate. It isn't their notion of family that is deficient, but the relationship between household and productive resources.

If we now return to the political debate that opened this essay, I believe we can see that there are two different concepts of family at work. To achieve a normative family is something many categories of Americans are prevented from doing because of the ways that their households plug into tenuous resource bases. And when normative families are achieved, it is at substantial and differential costs to both men and women.

Having considered the meaning of family and household among class sectors with regular or unstable relations to wages, we should now consider those sectors for whom resource bases are more affluent. Analyzing the family and household life of the middle class is a tricky business. The term "middle class" is ambiguous; a majority of Americans identify themselves as part of it whenever they answer questionnaires, and the category obviously carries positive connotations. Historically, we take the notion from the Marxian definition of the petty bourgeoisie: that category of people who own small amounts of productive resources and have control over their working conditions in ways that proletarians do not. The term signifies a stage in proletarianization in which small-scale entrepreneurs, tradesfolk, artisans, and professionals essentially stand outside the wage-labor/capital relation. That stage is virtually over: There are ever fewer small-scale proprietors or artisans working on their own account in post–World War II America. We now use the term to refer to a different sector—employees in corporate management, government and organizational bureaucrats of various kinds, and professionals, many of whom work directly or indirectly for big business, the state, and semipublic institutions. On the whole, this "new middle class" is dependent on wages; as such, it bears the mark of proletarianization. Yet the group lives at a level that is quite different from the wage levels of workers (Braverman 1974). Such a category is obviously hard to define; like all class sectors, it must be historically situated, for the middle class of early-twentieth-century America differs markedly from that of our own times. To understand what middle class means for the different groups, we need to know not only their present status but also the ethnic and regional variations in class structure within which their families entered America.

In a sense, the middle class is a highly ideological construction that pervades American culture; it is, among other things, the perspective from which mainstream social scientists approach the experiences of all the other sectors they attempt to analyze. To analyze the middle class's household formations and family patterns, we have to examine not only the data available on all the people who claim to be middle class but also explore the biases inherent in much of social science. This is a task beyond the scope of the present essay. Instead, I merely suggest a few tentative ideas as notes toward future research.

Households among the middle class are obviously based on a stable resource base that allows for some amount of luxury and discretionary spending. When exceptional economic resources are called for, nonfamilial institutions usually are available in the form of better medical coverage, expense accounts, pension plans, credit at banks, and so on. Such households may maintain their economic stability at the cost of geographical instability; male career choices may move households around like pieces on a chessboard. When far from family support networks, such households may get transitional aid from professional moving specialists, or institutions like the Welcome Wagon (Packard 1977). Middle-class households probably are able to rely on commodity forms rather than kinship processes to ease both economic and geographic transitions.

The families that organize such households are commonly thought to be characterized by egalitarian marriages (Schneider and Smith 1973). Rubin comments that "egalitarian marriage" may be a biased gloss for a communication pattern in which the husband's career is in part reflected in the presentation of his wife (Rubin 1976). To entertain intelligently, and instill the proper educational and social values in the children, women may need to know more about the male world. They represent the private credentials of family to the public world of their men at work. If this is the case, then "instrumental communication" might be a more appropriate term.

I am not prepared at this point of offer an analysis of middle-class kinship patterns, but I have a few hunches to present:

1. At this level, kinship probably shifts from the lateral toward the lineal. That is, resources (material and economic) are invested lineally, between parents, children, and grandchildren, and not dispersed into larger networks, as happens with working-class and poor families. Such a pattern would of course vary with geographical mobility, and possibly with ethnicity. There is usually a greater investment across generations, and a careful accumulation within them. This kind of pattern can be seen, for example, in the sums invested in children's educations, setting up professional practices, wedding gifts (in which major devolvement of property may occur), and so forth.

2. Perhaps friendship, rather than kinship, is the nexus within which the middle class invests its psychic and "familial" energies. Friendship allows for a great deal of affective support and exchange but usually does not include major resource pooling. It is a relation consistent with resource accumulation rather than dispersal. If the poor convert friendship into kinship to equalize pooling, it seems to me that the middle class does the converse: It reduces kinship exchanges, and replaces them with friendship, which protects them from pooling and leveling.[11]

There is one last sector of the American class system whose household and family patterns would be interesting to examine—the upper class, sometimes identified as the ruling class or the very rich. Once again, I limit myself to a few tentative observations. As one sociologist (either naive or sardonic) commented, "We know so little about the very wealthy because they don't answer our questionnaires." Indeed! They fund them rather than answer them. The few studies we do have (by authors such as Domhoff, Amory, Baltzell, Veblen) are highly suggestive. The upper class, they tell us, seems to hang together as a cultural phenomenon. They defend their own interests corporately, and have tremendous ideological importance.

We know very little about the household structure of the very rich. They are described as having multiple households that are recomposed seasonally (Hoffman 1971; Baltzell 1958) and filled with service workers rather than exclusively with kin and friends. While there is a general tendency toward "conspicuous consumption," we have no basic information on the relation of their resource bases to domestic arrangements.

When we turn to the family structure of the very rich, some interesting bits and pieces emerge (which may possibly be out of date). Families are described as extremely lineal and concerned with who they are rather than what they do. People have access to one another through their control of neighborhoods, schools, universities, clubs, churches, and ritual events. They are ancestor oriented and conscious of the boundaries that separate the "best" families from all others. Families are obviously the units within which wealth is accumulated and transmitted. Yet the line between wealth and class is not so simple; some of the "best" families lose fortunes but remain in the upper class. Mobility is also possible. According to Baltzell, under certain circumstances it is possible for nonmembers to enter the class via educational and work-related contacts. What emerges from the literature is a sketch of a group that is perhaps the only face-to-face subculture that America contains.

Women serve as gatekeepers of many of the institutions of the very rich (Domhoff 1971). They launch children, serve as board members at private school-run clubs, and facilitate marriage pools through events like debuts and charity balls. Men also preside over exclusive clubs and schools, but different ones. The upper class appears to live in a world that is very sex segregated. Domhoff mentions several other functions that very rich women fulfill. These include (1) setting social and cultural standards and (2) softening the rough edges of capitalism by doing charity and cultural work. While he trivializes the cultural standards that women set to things like dress and high art, I think he has alerted us to something more important. In the upper class, women "represent" the family to the outside world. But here, it is an outside world that is in many senses created by their own class (in the form of high cultural institutions, education, social welfare, and charity). Their public presence is an inversion of reality; they appear as wives and mothers, but it is not really their family roles but their class roles that dictate those appearances. To the extent that "everyone else" either has a wife/mother or is a wife/mother, upper-class women are available to be perceived as something both true and false. What they can do because of their families (and, ultimately, for their families) is utterly, radically different from what other women who "represent" their families can do. Yet what everyone sees is their womanness as family members rather than class members. They influence our cultural notions of what feminine and familial behavior should be. They simultaneously become symbols of domesticity and public service to which others may aspire. The very tiny percentage of very wealthy women who live in a sex-segregated world and have no need to work are thus perceived as benevolent and admirable by a much larger group of women whose relation to sex-role segregation and work is not nearly so benign.

"Everybody" can yearn for a family in which sex-role segregation is valued; nobody else can have a family in which it is valued as highly as theirs. In upper-class families, at least as they present themselves to "the public," we see a systematic confusion of cultural values with the values of family fortunes. We have here an excellent illustration of how the ideas of the ruling class become part of the ruling ideas of society.

At each level of American society, households vary systematically as to resource base and their ability to tap wealth, wages, and welfare. Households are organized by families (which means relatives both distant and close, imaginary and real). Families both reflect and distort the material relations within which households are embedded. The working-class and middle-class households may *appear* isolated from the arenas in which production takes place. But, in fact, their families are formed to generate and deepen relations to those work processes that underwrite their illusion of autonomy. Women's experience with "the family" varies systematically by class because class expresses the material and social relations upon which their household bases rest. We need to explore their transformatory potential as well as the constraints that differential family patterns provide.

Women have structurally been put in the position of representing the contradictions between autonomy and dependence, between love and money, in the relations of families to capitalism. The ideological role that women have played needs to be demystified as we struggle toward a future in which consumption and reproduction will not be determined by capitalist production, in which households will not have access to such uneven resource bases, and in which women will neither symbolically nor in their real relations be forced to bridge the gap between affective norms and contradictory realities under the name of love. To liberate the notion of voluntary relations that the normative family is supposed to represent, we have to stop paying workers off in a coin called love.

Notes

1. The demographic concerns are clearly outlined in Bane (1976); historical issues of rapid change are briefly reviewed in O'Neill (1977); the political issues and public policy concerns are presented with polemical flair in Novak (1976).

2. Overviews of the history of the family literature may be found in Pleck (1976), Lasch (1975–1976), and Tilly and Scott (1978). They all stress the complex relations between political–economic and ideological change that both condition and are conditioned by family patterns.

3. There is a vast literature on this subject. Its mainstream interpretations in relation to family research are reviewed in Otto (1975). Marxist perspectives are presented in Anderson (1974a, 1974b), Szymanski (1972), and Braverman (1974).

4. This composite is drawn from the works of Berger (1968), Gans (1962, 1967), Howe (1970), Howell (1973), Komarovsky (1962), Rubin (1976), Ryan (1973), Seifer (1973, 1976), Shostak (1969), Sennett and Cobb (1972), Sexton and Sexton (1971), and Terkel (1972).

5. The economic value of housework has been the subject of vigorous debate in Marxist literature in recent years. The debate was begun with the publication of Dalla Costa (1972) and continued by Secombe (1974), Gardiner (1975), Vogel (1973), Gerstein (1973), among others. See Hartmann (1974) and Vanek (1974) for American case historical materials, and Glazer-Malbin (1976) for a review of the field.

6. For historical, sociological, and political–economic analyses of women's economic position in the labor market, see Reagan and Blaxall (1976). See also U.S. Bureau of the Census (1974) for statistical data on demography and workforce participation rates of women.

7. This literature is reviewed in Yanagisako (1977). Further instances are in Reagan and Blaxall (1976) and U.S. Bureau of the Census (1974). The pattern is given much attention in Wilmott and Young (1957) and Bott (1971).

8. Throughout her work, Rubin is especially sensitive to this issue and provides an excellent discussion of individual life cycles in relation to domestic cycles. She explains why the labeling issue is such a critical one (Rubin 1976, 223).

9. Howell (1973) provides important and sensitive insights into the domestic lives of poor and working-class white families, collected in the style of Oscar Lewis. Composite black family studies include Hannerz (1969), Ladner (1971), Liebow (1967), Rainwater (1970), Scanzoni (1970), Stack (1971), and Valentine (1968, n.d.)

10. It is easier to make this point given Haley's consciousness-raising work *Roots* (Haley 1976) and the work of Herbert Gutman (1976). They point out, in popular and scholarly language respectively, the historical depth and importance of this pattern.

11. I know of no substantial work describing the uses of friendship versus kinship in the middle class. Ingelore Fritsch is currently conducting research on the networks of families in a suburban middle-class, East Coast community; her results should add to this discussion.

References

Anderson, Charles H. 1974a. *The Political Economy of Social Class*. Englewood Cliffs, N. J.: Prentice-Hall.
——. 1974b. *Toward a New Sociology*. Rev. ed. Homewood, Ill.: Dorsey Press.

Baltzell, E. Digby. 1958. *Philadelphia Gentlemen: The Making of a National Upper Class.* Glencoe, Ill.: Free Press.

Bane, Mary Jo. 1976. *Here to Stay: American Families in the Twentieth Century.* New York: Basic Books.

Berger, Bennett. 1968. *Working Class Suburb: A Study of Auto Workers in Suburbia.* Berkeley: University of California Press.

Braverman, Harry. 1974. *Labor and Monopoly Capital: The Degradation of Work in the Twentieth Century.* New York: Monthly Review Press.

Caplowitz, David. 1967. *The Poor Pay More.* New York: Free Press.

Dalla Costa, Mariarosa. 1972. "Women and the Subversion of the Community." *Radical America* 6: 67–102.

Domhoff, G. William. 1971. *The Higher Circles.* New York: Vintage Books.

Fortes, Meyer. 1972. "Introduction." In *The Development Cycle in Domestic Groups*, edited by Jack Goody. Cambridge: Cambridge University Press.

Gans, Herbert J. 1962. *The Urban Villagers.* New York: Free Press.

Gardiner, Jean. 1975. "Women's Domestic Labour." *New Left Review* 89: 47–71.

Gerstein, Ira. 1973. "Domestic Work and Capitalism." *Radical America* 7: 101–130.

Glazer-Malbin, Nona. 1976. "Review Essay: Housework." *Signs* 1: 905–922.

Goody, Jack. 1972. "The Evolution of the Family." In *Household and Family in Past Time*, edited by Peter Laslett and Richard Wall. Cambridge: Cambridge University Press.

Gordon, Linda. 1976. *Women's Body, Women's Right: A Social History of Birth Control in America.* New York: Grossman.

Gutman, Herbert. 1976. *The Black Family: Slavery and Freedom, 1750–1925.* New York: Pantheon.

Haley, Alex. 1976. *Roots.* New York: Doubleday.

Hannerz, Ulf. 1969. *Soulside: Inquiries into Ghetto Culture and Community.* New York: Columbia University Press.

Hartmann, Heidi I. 1974. "Capitalism and Women's Work in the Home, 1900–1930." Ph.D. dissertation, Yale University.

Hoffman, William. 1971. *David: Report on a Rockefeller* Secaucus, N. J.: L. Stuart.

Howe, Louise Kapp, ed. 1970. *The White Majority: Between Poverty and Affluence.* New York: Vintage.

Howell, Joseph. 1973. *Hard Living on Clay Street.* Garden City, N. Y.: Anchor Press.

Komarovsky, Mirra. 1962. *Blue Collar Marriage.* New York: Random House.

Ladner, Joyce. 1971. *Tomorrow's Tomorrow: The Black Woman.* New York: Doubleday.

Lasch, Christopher. 1975–1976. "The Family and History." *New York Review of Books* 22: 18–20.

Liebow, Elliot. 1967. *Tally's Corner.* Boston: Little Brown.

Novak, Michael. 1976. "The Family Out of Favor." *Harper's Magazine*, April.

O'Neill, Lois Decker. 1977. "The Changing Family." *Wilson Quarterly*, Winter.

Otto, Luther B. 1975. "Class and Status in Family Research." *Journal of Marriage and the Family* 37: 315–332.

Packard, Vance. 1977. "Mobility: Restless America." *Mainliner Magazine.*

Pleck, Elizabeth H. 1976. "Two Worlds in One: Work and Family." *Journal of Social History,* December.

Rainwater, Lee. 1970. *Behind Ghetto Walls: Black Families in a Federal Slum.* Chicago: Aldine.

Reagan, Barbara B., and Martha Blaxall, eds. 1976. "Women and the Workplace." *Signs,* Special Issue.

Rubin, Lillian. 1976. *Worlds of Pain.* New York: Basic Books.

Ryan, Joseph A. 1973. *White Ethnics: Life in Working Class America.* Englewood Cliffs, N. J.: Prentice-Hall.

Scanzoni, John. 1970. *The Black Family in Modern Society.* Rockleigh, N. J.: Allyn and Bacon.

Schneider, David M., and Raymond T. Smith. 1973. *Class Differences and Sex Roles in American Kinship and Family Structure.* Englewood Cliffs, N. J.: Prentice-Hall.

Secombe, Wally. 1974. "The Housewife and Her Labour under Capitalism." *New Left Review* 83: 3–24.

Seifer, Nancy. 1973. "Absent from the Majority: Working Class Women in America." Middle America Series, National Project on Ethnic America, American Jewish Committee.

———. 1976. *Nobody Speaks for Me: Self-Portraits of American Working-Class Women.* New York: Simon and Schuster.

Sennett, Richard, and Jonathan Cobb. 1972. *The Hidden Injuries of Class.* New York: Knopf.

Sexton, Patricia Cayo, and Brendan Sexton. 1971. *Blue Collars and Hard Hats.* New York: Random House.

Shostak, Arthur B. 1969. *Blue Collar Life.* New York: Random House.

Stack, Carol B. 1974. *All Our Kin: Strategies for Survival in a Black Community.* New York: Harper & Row.

Szymanski, Alfred. 1972. "Trends in the American Class Structure." *Socialist Revolution,* no. 10 (July–August).

Terkel, Studs. 1972. *Working.* New York: Pantheon Books.

Tilly, Louise. 1977. "Reproduction, Production, and the Family among Textile Workers in Roubaix, France." Paper presented at the Conference on Social History.

Tilly, Louise, and Joan Scott. 1975. "Women's Work in Nineteenth Century Europe." *Comparative Studies in Society and History* 17: 36–64.

———. 1978. *Women, Work, and Family.* New York: Holt, Rinehart, Winston.

U.S. Bureau of the Census. 1974. *Statistical Abstract of the United States.* Washington, D.C.: GPO.

Valentine, Charles. 1968. *Culture and Poverty: Critique and Counter Proposals.* Chicago: University of Chicago Press.

————. n. d. "Black Studies and Anthropology: Scholarly and Political Interests in Afro-American Culture." *McCale Module in Anthropology*, no. 15.

Vanek, Joann. 1974. "Time Spent in Housework." *Scientific American*, November.

Vogel, Lise. 1973. "The Earthly Family." *Radical America* 7.

Weinbaum, Batya, and Amy Bridges. 1976. "The Other Side of the Paycheck: Monopoly Capital and the Structure of Consumption." *Monthly Review* 28: 88–103.

Wilmott, Peter, and Michael Young. 1957. *Family and Kinship in East London.* London: Routledge and Kegan Paul.

Yanagisako, Sylvia Junko. 1977. "Women-Centered Kin Networks in Urban, Bilateral Kinship." *American Ethnologist* 4: 207–226.

CHAPTER 5

The Politics of Black Empowerment in Urban America
Reflections on Race, Class, and Community

James Jennings

Since the end of World War II, black urban activism has been molded by three concepts: race, class, and community, or neighborhood. Although these concepts are inseparable for understanding black political experiences in America, race has certainly been the most prominent element in black activism. This is still true to a large degree. As tensions associated with class and community have emerged in urban America, however, black activism has begun to reflect not only the racial dynamics of society but, increasingly, class and community tensions as well.

The Early Civil Rights Movement

Issues of class and community were muffled in the beginning stages of the civil rights movement because equal access to American institutions of power and influence was the major goal for blacks. Attempts to raise community and even class concerns were discouraged by a liberal-oriented coalition of blacks and whites that dominated the early civil rights movement. At least two instances illustrate how leaders of this coalition sought to underplay class and community: (1) the censoring of parts of John Lewis's speech at the 1963 March on Washington;[1] and (2) the media's deliberate disregard of Malcolm X's critique of the march, which he presented in a classic speech in November 1963, "Message to the Grassroots" (Malcolm X, 1973).

Both Lewis and Malcolm pointed to basic social and class differences within the black community; they rejected the goals of the integrationist leadership as, at best, irrelevant for the black masses. On the basis of a racially identified politics and one that looked to the interests of poor and working-class blacks, Malcolm X and others called for a more radical political activism. They were hostile to organizations advocating integration with established white power structures.

With the emergence of "Black Power," some activists raised issues that reflected neither class nor race exclusively, but the reality of community-based, or neighborhood, interests. By the late 1960s, Stokely Carmichael and Charles Hamilton called for community-based black participation in American economic and political processes as "blacks," not necessarily as workers or as new entrants to the system (Hamilton and Carmichael, 1967). Black communities would be organized and mobilized on the basis of racial identification and community consolidation; blacks would control institutions serving their communities in order to ensure accountability. This was neither a class nor purely a racial strategy, but one of "plural nationalism," which responded foremost to blacks as occupants of identifiable communities or spaces in urban America.[2]

From Civil Rights to Empowerment: The Emergence of Class and Community Issues

A survey of community/neighborhood and class issues in urban America shows that much black political activism today encompasses goals different from those of the civil rights movement in the 1950s and 1960s. As one writer has pointed out:

> While the demands of the civil rights movement were of benefit to all in the sense that they were a step toward the recognition of blacks as worthy of human dignity, it was primarily middle-class blacks, who were financially independent of whites, who led the assault and who were able to make use of its victories. (Bloom 1987, 219)

The goals and demands of the civil rights leadership were primarily intended to overcome the exclusion of blacks as a racially identifiable group in American society. The leaders' vision did not encompass either class struggle or control of land and cultural institutions at the level of community.

Black political participation and behavior essentially represented a response to racism, and therefore class and community dynamics were obscured. This does not mean that these dynamics were absent but that the pervasive impact of racism and racial hierarchy in the United States kept race per se at the forefront of the movement's concerns. In the decades following the apex of the civil rights movement, the shifting dynamic of race, class, and community has led to a black political activism that is more expressive of class- and community-based interests.

The latest stage of black political activism is referred to in this essay as *empowerment*. This term denotes a change in black America's political agenda that is beginning to emphasize *power* rather than mere "access to the powerful." Black empowerment suggests an important distinction between access to the powerful and actual power. There is a difference "between having power and being associated with those who have it, between partici- pating in the decisional process and actually influencing the outcome of that process, and between the symbolic trappings of political power and political power itself" (Jones 1978, 1). Grass-roots activists, frustrated at the incapac- ity of "liberal oriented" politics to alleviate economic and social problems in the black community, are now focusing on power instead of pursuing a politics based on mere proximity to public and private decision makers.

This suggests that black political activism is changing from an orientation primarily determined by race to one that gives class and community greater weight than in previous periods. No longer can a political program based solely on a racial agenda sustain a movement for social change in the black community. The notions of class and community (or culture) have emerged as organizing themes that are increasing in importance in defining, explain- ing, and molding black political activism in urban America. Nonetheless, race is still the major organizing theme—and it will remain so as long as African Americans as a group occupy the bottom rungs of America's social structure. The addition of the elements of class and community to the race consciousness of black political activism illustrates the movement of the black political agenda toward "radical" challenges to the American political and economic systems—as well as to the racially skewed structure and hierarchy of wealth.

Thus the new activism cannot be understood within a framework formu- lated exclusively in terms of race, class, or community. The social reality of black America prohibits using an either/or perspective (either class *or* race *or* community). The increased salience of community or class issues does not diminish the significance of race, or vice versa.

The particular relationship between these concepts has generated much debate. While the new populists have tended to emphasize community and neighborhood, those utilizing a Marxist perspective have argued that class is more important as an explanation of social change in American society. Writers supporting both orientations have many times overlooked or under-emphasized the significance of race; this has produced major conceptual and theoretical problems for both populist and Marxist theory and activism.

Some of the literature from these two schools of thought represents path-breaking analyses but often the analyses are incomplete. Many times, works representing the major ideas of Marxists and populists are built on assumptions and frameworks that exclude the significance of race, racism, and America's racial hierarchy; that is, they exclude a social situation where, for whatever reasons, most blacks do not enjoy the kinds of socioeconomic benefits available to white citizens. This conceptual weakness makes some of this work useless, either for understanding the full spectrum of black political activism and how it is changing or as a guide for building effective coalitions between the black community and potential white allies. Given the social position of the black community within the "metropolitan establishment," the demography of this community, and the historical vanguard role of blacks in movements for social change, this weakness is serious.

Alinsky, the New Populism, and the Organizing of Black Neighborhoods

The life and work of Saul Alinsky, whose practice is discussed in Chapter 3 of this volume, is an outstanding example of an activism that misses the significance of black empowerment. Although Alinsky's theoretical and practical work was very important, his model at times has been implemented in ways that have maintained a racial hierarchy, despite the objective of change based on community agendas. In some settings, his model has been criticized by black activists engaged in "community" struggles because it has allowed, or has excused, a certain degree of racial chauvinism on the part of white activists. In an interview for this essay, for example, Eugene ("Gus") Newport, the former black mayor of Berkeley, California and a long-time activist in Rochester, New York, argued that during the 1960s, Alinsky, working in Rochester, actually hindered the development of a black-led struggle against the city's corporate leadership.

According to Newport, the Alinsky model had the effect, in Rochester, of confining black activists to issues considered by whites as acceptable for blacks. It discouraged black activists from broadening their struggles to public policy issues that encompassed the entire city and its political economy. In 1965, after a series of riots in the city, the Council of Churches funded Alinsky with $75,000 and then followed with a grant of $100,000, basically to pacify the black community. Newport described Alinsky as condescending to blacks who urged a community struggle with a focus broader than localized black issues.[3]

In the early 1980s several black political activists in Brooklyn, New York—among them State Assembly Representatives Al Vann and Roger Green and U. S. Congressman Major Owens—found themselves at odds with white activists who were utilizing the "Alinsky approach" to organize poor people in that borough. According to an article in *In These Times* on May 25, 1982, proponents of the Alinsky model did not readily support the broad-based electoral efforts of these black activists, choosing instead to attempt to mobilize blacks outside the electoral arena and around single issues.

In Boston, several white leftists and populists refused to support Mel King's mayoral bid in 1983 because they felt that it was not realistic to expect a black to get the votes of white citizens. While these activists generally acknowledged that King was the most progressive candidate, and the most consistent in relation to neighborhood empowerment issues, they insisted he could not win because of his color. This argument alienated many black and white progressives, who saw it as but another excuse for racism in Boston. The conclusion that King could not win among white voters, these progressives believed, should have led to a strategy of openly confronting the problem of race rather than accommodating to it (Green 1984, 13).

There are two basic characteristics of American society that white populist and leftist thinkers and activists often refuse to acknowledge. And their refusal is one cause of the friction between activists utilizing the Alinsky approach and those seeking black empowerment. The first, often unacknowledged, characteristic is that blacks have been historically forced to see their political and social realities, to use Manning Marable's term, through the prism of race (Marable 1983). Blacks, exploited as workers, have also been exploited as blacks. The second characteristic is that both history and the current demography of American society combine to create a situation in which white leftists and populists usually cannot be effective in black or

Latino communities; yet because of the social position of blacks and Latinos, this is precisely where the struggle for social change in America begins.

That some white leftists and populists have resisted accepting these conditions may have to do with beliefs they hold about theories of social change and questions of leadership around community-based struggles. For the continuing presence and weight of America's racial hierarchy implies that the black struggle for equality, and its leadership, do hold a *vanguard* position in the movement for change. This situation undermines the priestly and missionary function of white activists who, sometimes unknowingly, seek to define for the black community the parameters and style of social change in American society.

Harry Boyte's *The Backyard Revolution* (1980), despite its strengths in alerting the reader to community as an important factor in explaining the urban political economy exhibits the limitations of new populist analyses that do not specifically address the significance of race. This work is path-breaking in showing how neighborhood organizations in the late 1960s and early 1970s challenged the interests of the wealthy and powerful that were seeking to dislodge and disrupt the stability of communities. But here, too, the black and Latino urban experience is basically tokenized within this "revolution." One of the most dynamic and important movements for neighborhood stability and citizen control within a broadly defined democratic and constitutional setting, for instance, was the "community control" movement in New York City at that time. This episode was precisely about black and Puerto Rican citizens challenging the power and arrogance of giant bureaucracies and insensitive politicians, yet this major episode in the political history of New York City is not even mentioned in Boyte's volume. Luis Fuentes, one of the leaders of the movement and New York City's first Puerto Rican district superintendent, expressed frustration at the conspicuous absence of white populist and leftist groups in the struggle, despite the rhetoric of social change.[4]

In another "populist" work, *Washington, D.C.: Inner City Revitalization and Minority Suburbanization* by Dennis E. Gale, the author spends most of his time describing racial politics in the nation's capital. Somehow he concludes that neither race nor class politics reflects the major political and social issues in the city (Gale 1987, 83). He argues, instead, that in urban planning politics, the battle lines are between white elites debating the city's "environmental fabric." One leaves Gale's work with the impression that the major political confrontation in Washington, D.C., is between white homeowners and community activists seeking to preserve historical landscapes on the one hand, and greedy real estate speculators, on the other. Gale's is another example of a progressive analysis deemphasizing the significance of race, racism, and society's racial hierarchy—and in Washington, D.C., of all places!

Empowerment: A New Policy Question

Black empowerment activism refers to public policy positions or approaches that are different from those that traditionally have called for greater access or equality for minorities within American institutions. The political orientation, substance, and style associated with "black empowerment" differ from patterns associated with both the politics of white ethnic groups in the American city and black electoral activism, which have been based on participation within political and economic mainstream processes. Many of these differences are based on how power and influence are sought, the particular public policies emphasized, the role of the "politically divorced," and the political posture of certain black groups toward the structure and distribution of wealth in American society.[5]

Black empowerment activism seeks to strengthen the black community institutionally, rather than focus on public policies the effects of which may primarily benefit black individuals or improve individual black mobility within the American economic system. It tends to be "redistributive" rather than "developmental" or "allocational" politics, to utilize Paul Peterson's classification (Peterson 1981, 41). But this classification is conceptually limited. The classification of public policy into these three categories does not appreciate that black urban political activism may move beyond a transfer of resources from better-off sectors to poorer ones in society. Black empowerment focuses on *the control of land in black urban communities*. This immediately distinguishes it from traditional white ethnic political activism and from a black political agenda that focuses on integrating blacks into white residential areas. Its emphasis is the economic and cultural strengthening of black communities, not simply more resources taken from middle-class taxpayers.

The political issues generated by activists under black empowerment cannot be neatly confined within Peterson's categories. Issues such as the Mandela movement's call for an independent Roxbury in Boston or the call for an autonomous black school district in Milwaukee not only seek "redistribution" but a fundamental change in the social position of black vis-à-vis white power structures.

Although, in the initial stages of ethnic mobilization, white ethnic politics was based on territoriality and neighborhood turf, eventually, as a result of economic and cultural integration in the American social structure, it moved away from the question of land control. Donald Warren (1975) has pointed out that "white ethnic groups are different not only in the likelihood that many become indistinguishable members of the anonymous majority 'community,' but also that in structural terms territory no longer need be a basis of organization and power" (p. 10). For the emerging black political activism described here, however, the control of land and community is critical; according to several activists interviewed for this essay, it surpasses affirmative action, job discrimination, or school integration as a priority on any black empowerment agenda.

Conrad Worrill, chairman of the National Black United Front, suggested in the *Chicago Defender* on January 13, 1988, that

> the expanding African-American population in the United States' inner cities has been a major concern of white decision makers since the passage of the 1949 Urban Renewal legislation. Since that time, strategies have been attempted to hold down the pattern of African-Americans becoming the majority, or close to the majority, population in cities like Chicago, Philadelphia, Pittsburgh, St. Louis, Washington D.C., New York, Detroit, Cleveland, Kansas City, etc. . . . The question for the African-American community in Chicago and other inner cities of the United States where this trend exists is, why should we again be maneuvered from the land we occupy? Our history in America has been one of forced and manipulated migration. It's obvious that we need a massive organizing strategy to reverse this trend of Black removal.

Chicago offers another example of how racial, class, and community conflict intertwines with an expanding black population and with attempts to control this group's physical expansion. In 1988, a group of white homeowners in that city introduced a "home equity" proposal for the purpose of maintaining "racial integration" in some of the city's neighborhoods. Several black aldermen criticized this program in the *Chicago Defender* on May 10, 1988, calling it nothing more than a way to keep blacks from moving into certain white areas of Chicago.

In Newark, New Jersey, the long-time community activist Amiri Baraka described the struggle over control of land taking place in that city in *Unity* on June 20, 1988:

> By now it is no secret that low income housing is being leveled and eliminated. For the last eight years, the local politicians and the housing authority let $300 million intended for the upgrading of existing public housing sit unused. Why? So finally they could carry out the heinous scam they intended in the late '60s—wipe out the central ward, drive the residents out, and gentrify the area, put up high cost efficiency apartments and coops and condos and attract the yuppies and buppies. Rutgers, NJIT, Seton Hall, St. Benedict's could all serve to remove old housing and residents and turn the central ward into a largely white middle-class area, transforming the politics of the area as well.

Chuck Turner, a long-time community activist in Boston, phrased this issue even more dramatically:

> We are in the midst of a fierce fight over land in Boston. While there are a number of aspects to this struggle, the one that concerns us most is the one between the relatively low income population in most of Boston's neighborhoods and higher income people who desire to move in . . . there is also the issue of institutional expansion, the competition between industrial and commercial uses of land. (Turner 1988)

Dennis Gale also sees the control of land and space as key to urban conflict; he points to the "existence of a fundamental process of competition for space in the nation's capital" (Gale 1987, 43). Policies and economic proposals associated with black empowerment will thus focus on land control and racial and physical consolidation of a community, rather than on integration or dispersal.

Changing the Rules

Another characteristic of black empowerment activism represents a new political development since the 1960s. Black nationalist-oriented and perhaps separatist sectors, which were integral parts of the protest activities of the 1960s, were not fully integrated or institutionalized into the electoral arena; electoral participation on the part of these sectors occurred only sporadically and temporarily. This separatism led Martin Luther King, Jr., to urge the coming together of these two kinds of black leaders, suffering from a "unique and unnatural dichotomy" (King 1967, 149).

This dichotomy has begun to blur in the current black political activism and protest; interestingly, many of the new actors in the electoral arena include black activists who did not trust electoral mobilization. Several successful campaigns have been conducted at the local level (in addition to the Jesse Jackson campaigns) as a result of the marriage between this group and the sector traditionally oriented toward electorally based mobilization. This means that the dichotomy between community and electoral politics that some observers pointed to in earlier periods is no longer appropriate as an analytical tool for understanding black politics in the American city.

Yet another characteristic of black empowerment activism, reflecting a changing relationship between race, class, and community, is the role of the "politically divorced" in the black community. Sectors so described in the literature, or as "alienated" or the "underclass," are being organized by activists in order to encourage their participation in electoral arenas of major urban centers. This is illustrated by the participation of gang members in the successful mayoral election of the late Harold Washington in Chicago, and by the endorsement and participation of the Nation of Islam, under the leadership of Louis Farrakhan, in the 1984 presidential campaign of Jesse Jackson, as well as this organization's growing attraction to the electoral arena. Recently, for example, the Nation of Islam also endorsed a gubernatorial candidate in Missouri's Democratic party primary. These endorsements are noteworthy not because of the controversial figure of Minister Farrakhan but because they represent a new development on the part of a sector in the black community that until now has rejected the utilization of electoral activism as an effective tool for black social advancement.

These developments raise broad questions and problems of governance and the effectiveness of government responses to the needs of blacks in urban settings. Until now, government institutions could respond to a racial agenda that demanded some measure of access to influential and powerful sectors of the social structure. But this becomes more difficult as the racial agenda changes and incorporates more clearly class and community interests of blacks.

The interplay of race, class, and community is reflected in the kinds of issues that are today salient in black urban communities, as well as the kinds of leadership and political mobilization that is emerging in black America. For example, "black nationalism" is more frequently utilized as an organizing foundation for these issues, as are black cultural appeals.

Salim Muwakhil, a long-time observer of black politics, has noted a growing trend for blacks to organize around political and economic issues shrouded in the terminology of self-determination and empowerment. On November 11, 1987, he wrote in *In These Times*:

> Boston and Milwaukee are just two of several cities that have experienced major encounters with this developing black strategy. Others—including East Palo Alto, California, Brooklyn, New York, and Columbia, Maryland— have had similar, though less publicized, encounters. The details vary in every situation, but the theme of self-determination is constant. And the rationale grows increasingly compelling as the economic picture bleakens.

Another example of black empowerment politics may be the Philadelphia Money for Neighborhoods Coalition described in the *Final Call* on July 10, 1988. It has challenged the Wilson Goode administration to spend a larger proportion of the Urban Development Action Grants on neighborhood revital-ization. This community organization also has demanded that the corporate leadership of the city share some of its resources with neighborhood groups. As community activist Michael Blackie has argued in the *Philadelphia Tribune*, "The developers have gotten tens of millions of our tax dollars to build commercial properties downtown, but our neighborhoods are going ignored." The coalition is utilizing electoral processes to seek a "city ordinance that would link downtown commercial development to neighbor-hood revitalization." This suggests another characteristic of black empower-ment activism that involves the relationship between black politics and the corporate sector. As the issue of the politics of land becomes more promi-nent, black community activists will also begin to challenge the leadership of the private sector in terms of the city's agenda.

In Milwaukee, one community activist involved in pressuring black elected officials stated that "downtown interests don't give a damn about the Black community here." Andrew Walker, chair of the NAACP's Discrimina-tion Committee in that city, suggested in an interview that blacks begin to confront the corporate sector, since so much housing and land use is affected by their decisions. He argued that downtown businesses—and Marquette University in particular—should be forced to give back the housing that it eliminated for both black and white working-class citizens of Milwaukee.[6] The gentrification set in motion by Marquette University's decision to take over YMCA facilities to house its students led to the formation of the Task Force on Emergency Shelter and Relocation. As reported in the *Milwaukee*

Courier on June 8, 1988, the task force then called for a boycott of all Milwaukee YMCA health clubs.

Community-based groups and coalitions that attempt to use local government as a means through which to extract benefits from the private sector, or stop the private sector from taking land away from black poor and working-class residents, exist in other large American cities with sizable black populations. These kinds of issues tend to be more responsive to community concerns, and, in many instances, transcend race and class.

The Organization for Black Struggle, which recently held its eighth annual celebration in St. Louis, is one more example of a renewed, and perhaps more radical, local black political activism. This organization was described in February 1988 by Jamala Rogers, a *Unity* journalist, "as a grassroots mass organization whose primary focus is on community empowerment." The political agenda of this group illustrates, in part, the movement away from public policy positions that could be described loosely as "liberal"—positions focusing on access to predominantly white institutions—toward those demanding control of those institutions on the basis of land in a community.

In December 1987, in an instance of reemerging protest and a changing political agenda in the black community, several activists in New York City planned a major political and economic campaign against the city's business community for its general insensitivity to the living conditions of blacks. The Committee for Economic Sanctions Against Racism in New York targeted the giant Macy's department store; picketing and boycotting continued there until store executives agreed to contribute funds for nonprofit, cooperative housing for low-income families. On March 5, 1988, one of the organizers of the campaign proclaimed in the *Chicago Metro News* that "we must let the captains of industry of New York know that there will be no more business as usual." In Chicago, the Citizens United for Better Parks protested to gain more resources in low-income areas of the city. The group protested not only the inequitable level of funds targeted for black and low-income areas but also the lack of citizen input into decisions affecting the management of local parks and recreational facilities. An account of the protest appeared in the *Chicago Defender* on April 3, 1988. Both of the Chicago efforts are being carried out in conjunction with black elected officials.

Civil rights activist Benjamin F. Chavis, Jr., has also pointed to an emergence of activism based on the idea of empowerment. In the December 30, 1987, issue of the *Guardian*, he cited the campaign of blacks in Keysville, Georgia, who organized to hold an election: "the first in 55 years and the first in which African Americans—80% of the population—voted. . . . Administration of Keysville had been turned over to the county during the Depression. African Americans want it back." This is an indication of the significance of race *and* community as organizing themes for blacks.

The election of the late Harold Washington as mayor of Chicago, and the policies of his administration, also illustrate a politics different from the politics usually associated with the liberal public policy agenda for urban America. Abdul Alkalimat points out that "Washington summed up his reform package as having three points of attack: the structure of government, development of the city, and the general mood and direction of government" (Alkalimat 1988, 48). Mayor Washington began to introduce public and governmental policies that would not disadvantage neighborhood groups and, in particular, the black community, as had been the case with previous administrations in that city. Gregory Squires and his associates point out that Washington's approach was especially evident in the area of urban development:

> Viewed in the context of past city administrations' attitudes toward urban redevelopment, the Washington administration's 1984 Chicago development plan represents a substantial shift in course. Principal among its objectives are job creation as the central criterion for assessing the worth of particular projects, and the balancing of downtown and neighborhood groups as agents for development activities. (Squires et al. 1987, 177)

The political activism that propelled Harold Washington to power began to generate an agenda that was different from previous city agendas in terms of blacks and poor people.

Recently, a broad range of black activists held a one-day meeting in Boston to discuss what a black public policy agenda would entail. The discussion had two central concerns: (1) how to make such an agenda more responsive to conditions in the black community; and (2) what kind of agenda would force local government to put greater pressure on the private sector to deal with issues affecting the quality of life in the black community.

Lloyd King, an organizer of the conference and president of the Black Political Task Force (a ten-year-old grass-roots organization in Boston), stated in an interview that such an agenda would be a first step in allowing black leaders to challenge the role of the city's private sector, particularly its political behavior and practices in the black community. King specifically pointed out that until now, the politics of some elected black leaders had not been responding to the needs of poor and working-class blacks, or to the question of who controls the land on which black people live. It was his hope that the development of a black political agenda would begin to formulate issues and activism responsive to blacks, not only as blacks, but also as poor and working-class people whose presence on certain parcels of land is threatened by urban restructuring.[7]

Race, Class, and Community: Implications for Activism

This brief overview of black grass-roots activism around the country offers a picture of the kinds of issues and approaches that are emerging today. These issues are certainly not confined to, or totally defined by, race. At the same time, it is naive and misleading to approach these issues— pregnant with implications for the politics of entire cities—without reference to race. In each of the instances cited, grass-roots activists and organizations have attempted to build alternative public policy agendas that they consider more effective than the agendas put forth by black interest groups aligned with traditional urban liberal coalitions. But equally important, these efforts have also been based on expanding the racial agenda of the civil rights movement and incorporating responses to class and community needs.

The emergence of class and community dimensions in black urban activism does not mean, as several liberal and neoconservative researchers and observers contend, that racism or America's racial hierarchy has been eliminated or even weakened.[8] The racial hierarchy in America remains very much an integral part of the nation's political economy. Historically, black protest after the Civil War focused on access to the prevailing economic and political system rather than any fundamental change in that system.[9] The goals and subsequent legislation adopted as a result of the civil rights and Black Power movements focused on access and enforcement of equal protection of the laws. While black political activism organized on the basis of challenging prevailing economic and social structures—rather than on the basis of access or integration or participation in any such arrangements—has only episodically commanded the allegiance of significant numbers of blacks, it nevertheless has always been an important component of black protest in this country.[10] But demographic and social developments in America have led to a situation in which systemic, not access or participatory, demands, are coming increasingly to characterize urban black political activism.

Not even the many electoral victories of blacks have been able to arrest the growing deterioration of life conditions for poor and working-class sectors in the black community. This is because most of the black electoral victories have concentrated on winning elections and replacing white politicians with black politicians. That is, they have followed a strictly racial agenda. These electoral campaigns have too often been detached from the development of any base of power—rooted in class and community aspects of black life— that could be used to challenge powerful interests that are unresponsive to the needs of blacks.

A good example of this is Atlantic City, New Jersey. The Black mayor has little control over economic activities that determine the quality of life for people in the black neighborhoods that surround the multibillion-dollar casinos. Despite his power over the electoral apparatus of the city, the mayor has minor influence on economic decisions made by its next-door neighbor, the gambling industry. The industry relies heavily on cheap black labor, but black leaders and elected officials have neither the electoral base nor the conceptual framework to challenge the casinos and control them in ways that might be beneficial to poor and working-class communities.

This failure is not limited to Atlantic City. Harold Cruse, for example, emphasizes the fact that black political victories consistently fail to translate into social and economic gains for any but a black elite.

> In the game of electoral politics, black leadership has had no issues of political leverage, only numerical voting strength. However, this voting strength has never been predicated on a political power base grounded in tangible economic, administrative, cultural, or social policy issues with the viability of forcefully influencing *public policy*. Hence, merely winning public office became the one and only tangible good for black political leaders . . . with rare exceptions, they brought nothing with them into political office that bore the least resemblance to a black economic, political, and cultural program that meant much to anybody, friend or foe, black or white, beyond the politically mundane business as usual stance of the liberal consensus. (Cruse 1987, 200)

For the most part, black leadership has not sought to change the game but to make the game more accessible and fair. This can be done, as Cruse says, without bringing into the electoral arena a collective black public agenda. The development of a black power base, and the existence of a collective black political agenda, would allow Black elected officials to offer and pursue public policies responsive to the group needs of black communities.

In summary, I have argued that, although the emergence and development of the civil rights movement could not be separated from class and community dynamics, or from the political economy of the land on which blacks lived, the early leadership basically sought participation in America's social processes without challenging the fundamental structural arrangements of those processes. During the civil rights movement, significant victories for equality were won that, as Samuel Huntington (1969) implies, democratized and modernized American society.[11] But such victories did not respond fully to the class and community tensions faced by blacks in white America. The racial agenda of black America muffled class- and community-based interests. This is understandable, given the caste conditions of blacks living in American society.

As the civil rights movement evolved into the Black Power movement, issues of class and community emerged alongside that of race. Much black activism began to concern itself with the cultural survival of the black community. Indeed, a cultural reawakening occurred, out of which grew several attempts to build alternative community institutions controlled by African Americans. These included efforts to build independent schools and engage in various economic initiatives, as well as more fundamental attempts to change the structural arrangements of decision making. The movement for community control in New York City (and other places), for example, sought political power for local neighborhoods over education, not just access to the downtown structures where decisions were made.

In many ways, life conditions for blacks seem more depressed today than they were a few years ago, despite the presence of black mayors and other high-level elected officials. This does not indict electoral participation per se as a tool of social change, although the disillusionment fostered by the continuing deterioration of life conditions for blacks in America has led some to this conclusion.

Black empowerment activists are not questioning voting as a tool; instead, they are rethinking the conceptualization and goals of electoral mobilization. Since electoral mobilization aimed at *access* to given social and economic structures has not been effective in improving the socioeconomic status of the majority of blacks, activists are suggesting that the goal should shift toward *challenging* structural and institutional arrangements that reflect and protect a system of wealth and power. Black urban activism is conceptually expanding the black agenda, and is becoming more inclusive of class and community needs. What I have proposed in this paper is that only an agenda that seeks change in the accumulation and distribution of wealth and the power of the status quo can respond to the class, community, and race interests of black America.

Conclusion

As the black agenda changes from an emphasis on access to power, electoral mobilization, instead of diminishing in significance, becomes more important as a tool for social change. Thus, we see an increase in black political participation in the electoral arena. But it is crucial to realize that the increasing political participation of African Americans is taking place under a framework different from that suggested by today's liberal agenda or the one under which black electoral gains were made more than twenty years ago.

The guarantee of access provided in the civil rights legislative packages of the 1950s and 1960s was important in moving America toward a more modern and open political society. These advances did not confront basic economic contradictions in America, however; consequent black electoral victories have transformed the character of these contradictions. Victories based on a "politics of rights"—and the resulting breakthroughs, such as the election of black mayors and congressional representatives—were not enough to respond to the depressed economic conditions of blacks. Entry into the electoral arena spoke to aspects of the problems of racism and discrimination, but the larger public policy agendas that followed did not address class- or community-based needs of blacks.

Despite previous limitations, however, there are indications that black grass-roots activists in major cities are now attempting to use the electoral arena not only for traditional "access" to benefits but also as a direct way of challenging structural arrangements. Targets include the private sector, which continues to support public policy frameworks that have been ineffective in changing substantively racial and economic hierarchies in urban America. As but "junior partners" in the grand liberal coalition of urban America, black political actors had not yet mounted fundamental challenges to existing agendas. Black politics basically gravitated toward "piece of the pie" pluralism, its rewards determined by negotiations with the federal government, the liberal wing of big business, and City Hall leaders and their machines.[12]

While much of the electoral activism is still based on race and access, increasingly there are examples of class struggle, as well as struggles based on community dynamics. Local examples reflect developments at the national level. For example, the 1984 and 1988 presidential campaigns of Jesse Jackson indicated increasing political activism among the black electorate along lines that looked beyond traditional pluralist politics.

The involvement of black churches in both Jackson campaigns, as well as that of the Nation of Islam in 1984, demonstrated increased black participation in the electoral arena. But what is particularly significant is that, in both presidential races, much of Jackson's support in the black community was based on his campaign's greater attention to issues related to empowerment. There are indications that if Jackson's campaigns had not stressed populist themes, but had emphasized the traditional black liberal agenda, they would not have received the extraordinary degree of black support they did. In Cleveland, for instance, Jackson won the 1988 Democratic presidential primary campaign; a survey of black voters, reported in *Call and Post* on April 21, 1988, found "that Jackson's support has moved from simply supporting him because he is the 'Black' candidate to more closely examining the issues." This sentiment echoes developments in other major cities as well.

According to Ronald Walters, there may be another illustration of a changing political activism at the national level for blacks.

> There has been a persistent attempt by some Black leaders to appeal to their colleagues not to give away the bargaining leverage of the collective Black community by making individual commitments to the major party candidates in advance of the candidate's public commitment to specific Black issues. In the past this appeal has fallen on deaf ears, largely because of the attractiveness of private incentive and the vulnerability of elected officials to the power of a potential president. (Walters 1988, 106)

Walters argues, however, that a more "independent leverage" approach is gaining wide acceptance among black leaders and activists.

This was echoed in the statement of an activist in Ohio, quoted in the August 7, 1988 *Boston Globe*, who exclaimed that for the general election, "It is like choosing to be eaten by either an alligator or a crocodile. I'm thinking about getting out of the water altogether." Another activist stated, "I've voted in every presidential election since I've had the right to vote; and I'm debating this time whether to use it or not."

These sentiments indicate some support for black political activism not based in Democratic party politics and loyalty. While the proposal for "independent leverage" has a long history, today more and more black activists are discussing this kind of strategy in relation to the Democratic party. It will be interesting to see if, as black America's racial agenda expands to include class and community interests, the Democratic party will be able to incorporate the new agenda. Preliminary indications are negative. While Democratic party politics may have been able to accommodate some of the interests of blacks in terms of a racial agenda, the issues raised by the concept of empowerment seem likely to be too "radical" for the Democrats. The implications of this will shape urban political activism in the coming decades.

Notes

1. The original speech written by John Lewis was redrafted after several coordinators of the march objected to Lewis's criticisms of the federal government's role in diluting the class-oriented demands and momentum of civil rights activists (see Grant 1968, 375).

2. The term "plural nationalism" is defined and explained by Hamilton (1973).

3. Interview with Eugene G. Newport, William Monroe Trotter Institute, University of Massachusetts/Boston, March 14, 1987.

4. Interview with Luis Fuentes, Harvard University, April 9, 1981.

5. The term "politically divorced" is borrowed from Lane (1965).

6. Interview with Andrew Walker, Milwaukee, Wisconsin, April 1988.

7. Interview with Lloyd King, Northeastern University, November 29, 1987.

8. The more popular works associated with this and related arguments include Wilson (1980, 1985); Freeman (1976) could also be included in the genre of "liberal" presentations. For the conservative school of thought, see Banfield (1974) and Sowell (1984).

9. For a brief overview of how black protest has moved from "access" to "power," see Jennings (1984).

10. See Brisbane (1969) for a historical treatment of the "radical" theme in black political activism.

11. Huntington proposed that a partial requirement for a modernized society is one in which political participation is expanding and disenfranchised groups have opportunities to join in the governance of the society. Using this paradigm, American society was modernized during the civil rights period as a result of the expansion

of political participation and the weakening of its racial caste system (see Huntington 1969).

12. For a discussion of how blacks reflected a "junior partner" status in the liberal coalition dominating urban America and the "metropolitan establishment," see Jennings (1984).

References

Alkalimat, Abdul. 1988. "Chicago: Black Power Politics and the Crisis of the Black Middle Class." *Black Scholar* 19 (March/April): 45–54.

Banfield, Edward C. 1974. *The Unheavenly City Revisited*. Boston: Little, Brown.

Bloom, Jack. 1987. *Class, Race, and the Civil Rights Movement*. Bloomington: Indiana University Press.

Boyte, Harry C. 1980. *The Backyard Revolution*. Philadelphia: Temple University Press.

Brisbane, Robert. 1969. *The Black Vanguard: Origins of the Negro Social Revolution, 1900–1960*. New York: Judson Press.

Cruse, Harold. 1987. *Plural but Equal*. New York: Morrow.

Freeman, Richard B. 1976. *The Black Elite*. New York: McGraw-Hill.

Gale, Dennis E. 1987. *Washington D.C.: Inner City Revitalization and Minority Suburbanization*. Philadelphia: Temple University Press.

Grant, Joanne. 1968. *Black Protest*. New York: Fawcett Premier.

Green, James. 1984. "The Making of Mel King's Rainbow Coalition: Political Changes in Boston, 1963–1983." *Radical America* 18 (February).

Hamilton, Charles V. 1973. *The Black Political Experience in America*. New York: Putnam.

Hamilton, Charles V., and Stokely Carmichael. 1967. *Black Power*. New York: Random House.

Huntington, Samuel P. 1969. *Political Order in Changing Societies*. New Haven: Yale University Press.

Jennings, James. 1984. "The Struggle for Equality: From Access to Power." *Suffolk Law Review* (Winter).

Jones, Mack H. 1978. "Black Political Empowerment in Atlanta." *Annals of the American Academy of Political and Social Science* 439: 90–117.

King, Martin Luther, Jr. 1967. *Chaos or Community: Where Do We Go From Here?* Boston: Beacon Press.

Lane, Robert. 1965. *Political Life*. New York: Free Press.

Malcolm X. 1973. "Message to the Grassroots." In *Malcolm X Speaks*, edited by George Breitman. New York: Pathfinder Press.

Marable, Manning. 1983. *How Capitalism Underdeveloped Black America*. Boston: South End Press.

Peterson, Paul. 1981. *City Limits*. Chicago: University of Chicago Press.

Sowell, Thomas. 1984. *Civil Rights: Rhetoric to Reality*. New York: Morrow.

Squires, Gregory D., Larry Bennet, Kathleen McCourt, and Philip Nyden. 1987. *Chicago: Race, Class, and the Response to Urban Decline*. Philadelphia: Temple University Press.

Turner, Chuck. 1988. *Annual Report for the Center for Community Action, Boston*. May.

Walters, Ronald. 1987. *Black Presidential Politics*. Albany: State University of New York Press.

Warren, Donald I. 1975. *Black Neighborhoods: An Assessment of Community Power*. Ann Arbor: University of Michigan Press.

Wilson, William Julius. 1980. *The Declining Significance of Race in America*. Chicago: University of Chicago Press.

———. 1985. *The Truly Disadvantaged*. Chicago: University of Chicago Press.

PART II

Where the Action Is

Issues and Community Activism

> Hope could neither be said to exist . . . nor not to exist. It was like roads crossing the earth. For the earth, of course, had no roads to begin with; but when many men pass one way, a road is made.
>
> Lu Xun, 1921

CHAPTER 6

New Wine in Old Bottles

Southern Populism and the Dilemmas of Class, Ideology, and State Power

Bruce Palmer

The dilemmas of activism have their roots in the historical development of a national, corporate, industrial capitalism in nineteenth-century America. This economic configuration was firmly in place by the 1890s when the Populist party emerged as a response not only to economic problems brought by corporate capitalism but also to associated political, social, and cultural ones.

Because they faced the same opponent—corporate capitalism—though at an earlier stage in its development, Populists encountered problems similar to those faced by oppositional groups today. Corporate capitalism had accelerated the social, political, and cultural fragmenting of communities along lines of race, class, and gender, to name only some of the major divisions. Populists faced the difficulty of addressing national problems while maintaining a democratic polity. Regulating corporations demanded political units operating uniformly over as wide an area as they did. But this requirement tended to divorce the apparently most efficacious democratic unit, the local community, from the most efficacious source of political power, the national state. To make things worse, corporations quickly discovered how to use the national state to promote their own ends, although an organized, coordinated effort to coopt state power waited until the end of the nineteenth and the beginning of the twentieth century (see, especially, Kolko 1963; Weinstein 1968).

Finally, the Populists encountered the dilemma raised by ideology, which Prudence Posner refers to in the Introduction to this volume, that the "everyday discourse through which people *understand* their condition is, in large part, a product of the very structure of relationships which are the source of the grievance." This difficulty was, of course, not new, either to America or to the nineteenth century. But the increasing permeation of all life by capitalism and its vehicle, the possessive market society—a society in which labor (as well as all other things) becomes a commodity (MacPherson 1962, 53–59)—produced an especially difficult, if generally unrecognized, problem for reformers in the latter half of the nineteenth century. Central elements of the republican ideal in the nineteenth century made challenging the emerging corporate order difficult and confusing. The terms of the marketplace, on which that order was based, rest on the idea that freedom, even personal identity, resides in the individual and absolute possession and control of property, a notion intimately associated with the basic premises of the American Revolution.

What makes the Populist party of the 1890s, especially in the South, interesting is that it was the first, and the last, large-scale political movement to try to come to grips with these dilemmas. Its success in building a mass movement between the mid 1880s and 1896 has made it a model for new populist theorists and activists.[1]

That the Populists never succeeded in building a victorious economic or political alternative to corporate America also suggests that the model may have some problems. I want to look specifically at the southern Populists and, in particular, at the issue they identified as critical to their plan to reform American society—the subtreasury plan—and see how they handled the dilemmas of class and community, democracy and state power, and ideology.

Post–Civil War America

In what kind of world did the southern Populists find themselves during the late 1880s and early 1890s? It was a world shaped largely by the needs of an industrializing society, one in which the private sphere controlled and directed most of the investment capital. The sources for this capital were limited. Overseas investment, of which the United States enjoyed a good deal, eventually had to be repaid (and was, during World War I). It also needed to be balanced by exports to prevent too great an imbalance of trade and a subsequent slowing of growth.

The second source of capital was internal savings—put crudely, the difference between what Americans produced and what they consumed. This kind of saving depended on the mechanization of production, which greatly augmented the amount an individual worker or farmer could produce, and on cheap labor. By the early twentieth century, employers had gained, especially from skilled workers, the right to divorce production increases from wages.[2] The advantages of mechanization flowed largely to employers. Mechanization also reduced wages and promoted the control of labor by decreasing the percentage, and sometimes the absolute numbers, of skilled workers in the labor force. Finally, cheap labor was a function of supply, and those who directed the new corporate order found two sources: Europe, especially southern and eastern Europe, and rural America, the largest source.

American agriculture played an important direct role in industrialization and the evolution of corporate America. It, too, was increasingly mechanized, at least outside the South. With fewer farmers needed to produce the food the growing industrial and commercial cities demanded, it served as a source of cheap labor. The increasing capital requirements limited access to farming, and the declining prices of many agricultural products made access more difficult, even while cheaper and more abundant agricultural produce made possible lower wages for industrial workers.

Agriculture, particularly southern agriculture, which furnished fewer of the new industrial workers, served another purpose in American industrialization. Its products helped prevent the growth of a balance of trade so unfavorable that it would discourage the further influx of foreign capital. Cheap cotton especially helped balance the flow of European capital into the United States.

Industrialization did not come smoothly. It created its own opposition in post–Civil War America. Working-class organizations from the National Labor Union of the late 1860s through the Knights of Labor in the 1880s and the new American Federation of Labor in the 1890s, not to speak of the many more local, regional, and even national labor organizations, all posed problems for those directing the industrialization of America under its corporate capitalist aegis. So did more spontaneous reactions, from the great railroad strike of 1876 through the eight-hour demonstrations and the Haymarket riot of the mid 1880s to the Homestead strike of 1892 and the Pullman strike of 1894. These were all matched by widespread, if sporadic, violence and worker resistance to low wages, long working hours, dangerous workplaces, and poor housing and living conditions.[3]

Capitalism generated its own opposition in the countryside as well.

Farmers facing increased costs and declining prices organized themselves again and again into local, state, and then national organizations such as the Patrons of Husbandry (the Grange), the Farmers' Alliance, and, finally, the People's party, often seeking the aid and support of labor.

The political economy of the United States in post–Civil War America evolved within this context. Capitalists and industrialists quickly found ways of making allies of the local, state, and even federal governments. Their money and their candidates frequently dominated elections and appointments. Such arrangements were largely ad hoc, usually based on some sort of corruption or collusion. Nevertheless, from the end of the Civil War, the national government, and most state and local governments, followed a course useful to the interests of capital. Higher and higher tariffs brought windfalls to many manufacturers. Raw materials were given away or sold cheaply to those who could afford to pay for the gifts. Local, state, and federal governments gave railroads millions of acres of public land to be used to finance railroad construction. The federal government made overseas immigration easy. Local, state, and national governments usually followed a policy of hostility to labor organizations and, by the end of the century, often actively intervened, with legal support and sometimes troops, on the side of employers.

Finally, the nation's financial structure, erected during the Civil War, particularly by the National Banking Act of 1862, turned the management of the currency and most of the country's financial system over to large, private bankers. After 1865, the national government, and the national bankers, pursued a policy of long-term contraction of the currency, a long-term deflation, which ended only in 1898 with the discovery of gold in Alaska.[4]

This long-term deflation, in which prices for farm commodities such as wheat and cotton fell faster than the cost of living, turned the farmers, constant credit users in an age of cash crops, toward financial questions. From there they moved to questions of political economy. The dilemmas of class and community, state power and democracy, and ideology and change followed, especially since—and often a thorn in the side of capital—the United States enjoyed universal manhood suffrage, or at least enough of it to promise to the exploited a way out of their exploitation.[5]

Populists articulated their response to this America most succinctly in the famous 1892 Omaha platform. Of its three major planks, the third demanded that land "should not be monopolized for speculative purposes, and alien ownership of land should be prohibited." All land held by corporations "in excess of their actual needs" should be returned to the government and held for "actual settlers only." The second plank demanded that the railroad, telegraph, and telephone systems be owned and operated by the federal government. The first plank demanded that the national banks be eliminated and the monetary system be based solely on a legal tender, fiat currency issued by the federal government to the level of $50 per capita. The Omaha platform's radical core, however, was the subtreasury plan. First made public at the St. Louis convention of the National Farmers' Alliance and Industrial Union in 1889, the plan, if adopted, would have enabled the federal government to extend cheap credit, in the form of currency, to producers of cotton and tobacco in the South.[6]

Deeper in Debt: Southern Populists in the 1890s

Southern farmers faced certain conditions in the post–Civil War era that differed from farmers elsewhere. Efforts to remold the South on the industrial capitalist model of the rest of the country disappeared with the destruction of the Radical Republican (party) governments in the South at the end of Reconstruction and their replacement, in state after state during the 1870s, with Democratic (party) governments dominated by a small landholding and speculative elite (a *comprador* class). The South in 1900 remained a predominantly agricultural semicolony of American capitalism. Within the national system, the South provided cheap raw materials for industrialization elsewhere and, especially, cheap cotton for overseas export to balance the flow of investment capital into the United States.[7]

In this context southern Populism emerged. Concern with cheap credit grew from southern farmers' experience with the lien system, which had its origin in the chaotic agricultural conditions of the post–Civil War era. During Reconstruction, southern landowners, short of cash and credit, began to solve the problem of resecuring black labor for the South's cotton crop by developing a system in which they not only rented land but also took over the mercantile function of advancing credit for seed, fertilizer, and equipment, at considerable interest, to propertyless freed people in return for a large share of the cotton crop those freed people raised. Rent was usually one-half to three-quarters of the crop. Out of the remainder, the freed people would pay, at exorbitant rates, for the credit needed to get from planting to harvest. The declining price of cotton in the years following the war meant that the great majority of black farmers never escaped indebtedness.[8]

By the late 1870s, the collapse of cotton prices, connected to the long-term deflationary policy of the federal government, began to reduce many previously independent white farm owners to a similar state. In the 1870s and 1880s this method of financing the cotton crop, a mortgage system based on a crop lien on cotton, was given legal force in a series of lien laws passed in nearly all the southern states (Hahn 1983, Chaps. 4, 5). According to the census, by 1900 nearly half the farmers, black and white, in the eleven former Confederate states were tenants. The rate of increase was greatest between 1890 and 1900, the Populist decade.[9]

To large numbers of southern farmers this meant immiseration. Once permanently in debt to a landlord or merchant, or both, the standard of living for a farmer, including indebted owners, dropped precipitously. Nothing prevented the creditor from enforcing an absolutely minimum standard of living, barely enough for survival, by controlling what supplies the farmer could purchase. The indebted farmers and their families became, for all intents and purposes, agricultural laborers.[10]

Economic Action: The Farmers' Alliance and Cooperation

To become a Populist in the South of the 1890s often took a great deal of personal courage. At least fifteen blacks and several whites were killed in the Georgia campaigns of 1892. Short of violent death, southern populists faced intimidation, social ostracism, and economic pressure. To warrant this kind of response, southern populism had to be more than just another expression of political self-interest. It was. Out of their experience and heritage, southern Populists had fashioned a wide-ranging critique of southern and American society in the 1890s. Their experience as southern farmers who were falling deeper and deeper into debt directed their attention to fundamental problems in the social and economic order.

Drawing on their Jeffersonian and Jacksonian tradition of equal rights and producerism, they launched an often accurate attack on an expanding industrial capitalism that created immense wealth but failed to distribute it justly or equitably. They criticized a system that left farmers and working people who produced the wealth poor, ill fed, ill housed, and overworked, while a few enjoyed extraordinary luxury. They drew on their evangelical Protestant heritage and experience with producers and marketing cooperatives to suggest that industrialism could be harnessed to the needs of the majority of Americans in a new way. Each person would take a cooperative and personal responsibility for the well-being of every other, and the federal government would begin to assume responsibility for the general welfare of all the country's citizens. Using the same ideas, southern Populists also challenged the central tenet of southern politics—white supremacy—tentatively offering an alternative vision of a rudimentary politics of class built on a biracial coalition of poor white and poor black farmers and tenants.

The economic program emerged first. It appeared in the southern Farmers' Alliance, especially in the mid 1880s in Texas. Texas Alliance members organized around opposition to the lien system and rural debt immiseration. In a massive grass-roots organizing campaign, they developed a program stressing economic cooperation among farmers, designed to bypass the high interest rates on the goods and services furnished by local merchants and landlords, by now usually the same people. Interest rates on supplies could go from 25 to 100 percent above retail prices, and on the lien itself from 20 to 200 percent of the principal.

Opposition from local elites—bankers, merchants, and landowners who controlled credit in southern towns and counties—destroyed the organized farmers' local efforts. In response, the southern Alliance organized statewide business and purchasing agent networks and massive state cooperative exchanges. Regional and national wholesalers, manufacturers, and bankers who had a stake in maintaining the existing supply and marketing system for cotton destroyed the statewide cooperative efforts by refusing to extend credit (Goodwyn 1976, 27–28, 129–131, 169–171; Schwartz 1976, Chaps. 2, 14).

The failure of economic action led the Alliance into politics. Unable to destroy the lien system with cooperation, the Alliance turned in 1889 to the federal government, demanding that it provide southern farmers, through a subtreasury system, with the credit they needed to reestablish control over their land and lives. In turn, the subtreasury plan required a rethinking of America's economic and political condition, a rethinking summarized in 1892 by the Omaha platform. This rethinking brought the southern Populists face to face with our three dilemmas.

Greenback Monetary Theory

The southern Populist alternative to corporate capitalist America was rooted in an analysis of money that itself rested on, and was subsequently sharpened by, a vision of what America should be but was not. The characteristic of the new capitalist order that impressed southern Populists most was the growing maldistribution of wealth. An America formerly devoted to the virtues of liberty and equality (at least the equality of white males, a qualification the southern Populists in most cases simply assumed, as did almost all white male Americans in the nineteenth century) had disappeared. Instead, by the 1880s it was increasingly clear that the few Americans who more and more controlled the wealth of the country were those exhibiting the least virtue. They produced nothing useful, and they bribed and manipulated and stole their way to even larger fortunes. Worse, the people they stole from, and impoverished, were the very ones who made America great and produced the country's wealth through their own labor. These were the people who had constituted the virtuous and independent citizenry that had made America the home of the free and devoted to equality, including economic equality. One person might do better than another in this world, and so possess more worldly goods. But no one ought to have more than they could earn by their own labor. Extreme wealth had to be theft, for no one could "earn," with their own labor, a million dollars. Those who worked, the farmers and laborers, the producers, the "bone and sinew" of the republic, were cheated and robbed by the few in order to build their great fortunes. As the maldistribution of wealth increased, the producing many were slipping into a poverty-stricken mass; the wealthy, immoral, and lazy few increased both their wealth and their power. This imperiled the productive apparatus on which their wealth rested, as well as the political and social order, for the impoverished and increasingly exploited and powerless producing masses would not long continue to labor for nothing but their increasing degradation.[11]

How had the few, the increasingly narrow and increasingly wealthy aristocracy, come into their ill-gotten gains, particularly in an at least formally democratic society? They had seized control of the government through bribery, fraud, and the leverage their increasing wealth brought to politicians, who had to win increasingly expensive elections. Legislation was the key. Bad laws had been passed; good laws had to replace them. In particular, the financial structure of the country, based on national legislation, had been constructed to favor the wealthy few. At the center of this structure lay the currency. Hence the concern of the greenbackers, and the southern Populists, with the currency and the role of the national government.[12]

That the southern Populists were greenbackers meant several things. First, it meant they believed that prices were a direct function of the supply of currency available and the demand for its use. That is, they believed that the purchasing power of the dollar depended on the number of dollars in circulation and that the demand for their use was measured by the number of transactions needing dollars. Agricultural prices had fallen, not because of overproduction, but because of a declining money supply (see Appendix).

Second, greenbackers believed that the currency was created solely by fiat of government law and had nothing to do with the material out of which the currency was made. Their opposition, Democrats and Republicans alike, maintained that currency had to be made of a valuable metal that had "intrinsic" value, value that resided in it because of the inherent value of the metal. Otherwise, they maintained, the currency would be debased or would literally disappear. The southern Populists knew better, most of them. "Gold is not money; silver is not money; nickel is not money," stated the Salisbury, North Carolina, Populist editor of the *Carolina Watchman* in late 1891. "All of them are made money by law."[13] The action of the federal government alone created the currency.[14]

Finally, most southern Populists, particularly the greenbackers, wanted not only an increase in the quantity of money in circulation but a financial system with short-term elasticity to prevent the money supply from lowering prices at harvest and raising them when supplies and credit for the new year had to be purchased.[15] Making such short-term elasticity credit less necessary would help loosen the control of local merchants, bankers, land-lords—and their northern and European suppliers and investors—over farm credit.

In short, only greenbacks would provide the producing classes—farmers and working people, primarily—with the kind of currency they needed to enjoy the fruits of their labor. And because it placed the currency in the hands of the federal government, which the farmers and their allies could potentially control, a greenback currency system appeared to be an excellent tool with which to end the concentration and control of wealth in the hands of a privileged few.

So greenbackism was an integral and necessary part of the change southern Populists considered necessary for the promise of America to survive. The country's currency had to be divorced from its metallic base, and from the control of private bankers (one and the same thing in the 1890s, though not later, after corporate capitalism, thoroughly in control of the political system, saw the uses of a more flexible, purely legal tender currency), and abundant in supply. The financial system that governed money's distribution should respond to demands for currency, make money cheap enough to allow producers easy access to what they needed for the production of tangible wealth, and protect money from the control of a few individuals or groups, leaving it free to circulate widely and easily among the people.

The southern populists justified their analysis of such a financial system with a set of normative values that they inherited and that were supported by their experience as farmers. The greenback heritage helped carry to and reinforced in southern Populism important elements of the Jeffersonian and Jacksonian tradition. One was the notion that the most important division of society was between those who produced tangible goods and those who did not. This notion also carried with it much more widely shared values of a labor theory of value and a republican America based on widespread freedom and relative economic equality.[16] The southern Populists' evangelical Protestant heritage reinforced many of these ideas. Production meant the creation of tangible goods by physical labor. "The creative power of labor," maintained a North Carolina Populist in the Raleigh *Progressive Farmer* on October 13, 1891, "was conferred upon man and fixed by the fiat of Jehovah which went forth from Eden, 'In the sweat of thy face thou shall eat bread.' " The rest of the southern Populists agreed. God's laws confirmed the justice of a labor theory of value and its American producerite manifestation. It also, by implication, condemned the inequity of a world in which the privileged and powerful few ate their bread without sweat, without producing something (Palmer 1980, Chaps. 7, 8).

The Solution: The Simple Market Society and the Subtreasury Plan

The combination of a labor theory of value and the Populists' belief that, in all justice, the producers should receive the value of their labor did not result in a rejection of the competitive market system that underlay American industrial capitalism. The southern Populists' ideal economic order corresponded to what C. B. MacPherson called a simple market society: a capitalist society in which "the production and distribution of goods is regulated by the market but in which labor itself is not a market commodity." Unlike in modern possessive market societies, land and other resources on which to earn a living are available to all, and "the satisfaction of retaining control of one's own labor is greater than the difference between expected wages and expected returns as an independent producer" (MacPherson 1962, 51–53).

In many areas of seventeenth-, eighteenth-, and even early-nineteenth-century America this kind of world seemed to exist. Jefferson's and John Taylor's America of independent and largely self-sufficient yeomen farmers, based on an assumed inexhaustible supply of land, posited a simple market society. The southern Populists inherited this ideal,[17] and it helps explain their uncomplicated advocacy of a labor theory of value. In a simple market society all producers enjoy the full value of their labor because, since a market in labor does not exist, no one can accumulate more than they produce with their own hands. Most southern Populists had been born and raised on the agricultural fringes of a growing industrial capitalism; to them, it still seemed that, with reform, all could become independent producers and maintain a just and equitable distribution of wealth while preserving private property, profit, and a market organization of society. Indeed, this was the world a greenback currency system seemed to make possible, a world where money served to expedite exchanges of produced goods among independent producers, a currency system that favored those producers rather than the few wealthy capitalists.

Paradoxically, however, while the simple market ideal promoted a harsh and often accurate critique of American industrial capitalism, it provided no basis for questioning the competitive market system that underlay the very inequities and injustices the southern Populists attacked. Discussion of how southern Populists thought they could realize this simple market society in America, the way to implement a greenback currency system, reveals the impact of this paradox.

The subtreasury plan was the southern Populists' vehicle for moving America from where it was to where it should be—for realizing a simple market society. The plan worked fairly simply. Though it took some refining, by 1892 the plan's details were well set. It provided for government storage warehouses located in every county that produced a minimum amount of such nonperishable agricultural commodities as cotton, rice, tobacco, and wheat. The federal government would build and operate these warehouses on land donated by counties or states. Any farmer growing such commodities could store them at a warehouse, receiving for the stored crops a loan of 80 percent of their market value in negotiable certificates of deposit payable in legal tender notes (greenbacks). These certificates had to be redeemed within a year, but they could be sold to any purchaser. Storage and operating costs would be covered by a 1 percent charge on the loans.[18]

The plan was an ingenious method for implementing a greenback currency system. It would expand the money supply. By providing access to cheap credit (1 percent), the subtreasury plan would destroy the lien system and return control over their land and labor to the farmers. It would answer the need for short-term currency flexibility, eliminating the price swings that so hurt southern farmers.

More generally, the subtreasury plan would begin to create a simple market society by eliminating the existing financial system and the growing extremes of wealth, giving each producer the capital necessary to produce and denying control over the currency to the wealthy few. In a radical and explicit indictment of American industrial capitalism, it promised to give producers the full value of their labor and release them from dependence on any group or class, all without requiring any alteration of the economic system with which the southern reformers were most comfortable: a competitive, private ownership, market society (Palmer 1980, 104–110).

But the subtreasury plan, while central to southern Populist radicalism, also caused problems. It raised the dilemma of state power and democracy by requiring the federal government to increase greatly its participation in the economic life of the country. Almost all southern Populists, and almost all of their potential supporters, agreed with the South's historical states' rights stand. They also shared Jefferson's fear of the antidemocratic possibilities in a distant and powerful federal government, especially since they had seen how easily the monied few could manipulate it. They never resolved the conflict successfully, though many tried.[19]

Nor were the southern Populists any more successful at transcending their limited experience, raising the connected dilemmas of class, community, and ideology. With some reason, they could still dream of a society where independent producers predominated and labor was not bought or sold on anything more than a temporary basis.[20] Though the southern Populists never rejected industrial America, their limited experience and their Jeffersonian and Jacksonian intellectual heritage helped them overlook the fact that the industrial system was based on exactly the same thing: a market in labor.

As a result, the largely rural southern Populists never developed an alternative to the Omaha platform or the subtreasury plan that would connect the reality of urban working people's lives with political action (Goodwyn 1976, 307–311). The subtreasury plan, the key to the Omaha platform's reform structure, offered little or no immediate benefit to these people. In fact, by appearing to involve a rise in the price of farm commodities, the subtreasury plan seemed to threaten urban working people's already precarious standard of living. To most of them, moreover, the possibilities of someday owning a factory, even with the help of the government, were remote enough to be laughable. Independent entrepreneurship within a competitive, private-property, and profit-governed market society was not a dream with any reality. So not only did the subtreasury plan seem remote to the urban worker, but even the simple market ideal on which it was based, by the 1890s anyway, seemed out of the question, unsupported by urban working-class experience with industrial America.

The limitations of their analysis of American capitalism, however, did not affect the southern Populists' critique of late-nineteenth-century industrial society. They recognized that the growing maldistribution of wealth that had accompanied the tremendous productive expansion of the post–Civil War years called into question American society's claim to basic decency. According to the Raleigh, North Carolina, *Progressive Farmer* in January 1892, the "survival of the fittest" had turned America into "one vast battlefield" for daily survival. Though competition should govern the relations of production and exchange between individuals, it would not serve as an adequate guide for human development. Few southern Populists could choose a system described by the Beaver Dam, North Carolina, *Our Home* in June 1893 as one "where every man is for himself" because "the devil will get most of them."

From their evangelical Protestant heritage and their Alliance cooperative experience, the southern Populists generated a different social rule, one articulated in the Richmond, Virginia, *Seen* on February 13, 1892: "In the ideal of cooperative effort is contained the secret to all true life and progress—the grand emancipating principle of brotherhood." Realization of the Populist program, with its subtreasury centerpiece, would bring a simple market society, with its potential for realizing the brotherhood of men and an end to enforced poverty in a world governed by the survival of the fittest. "With just and equitable laws and a government principle of brotherly love," maintained W. Scott Morgan in his *National Reformer* (Haidy, Arkansas) in November 1895, "neither rich nor poor, anarchist or criminal, could long exist."

The subtreasury plan might work for owner-farmers, even for tenants and croppers. It promised little for rural farm labor and nothing concrete for urban working people. The same tension was evident when the southern Populists justified the subtreasury plan and its simple market society in discourse drawn from their cooperative experience, from evangelical Protestantism and from Jefferson and Jackson. These sources often carried the assumptions of the very system the southern Populists opposed, even while they served an important critical purpose. The brotherhood of men and the cooperative society might have great appeal for agricultural labor and urban working people, but nothing in their intellectual or religious background, and little in their experience, suggested to southern Populists the need to offer rural and urban labor—those whose world was dominated by the need to sell their labor in the marketplace—a vehicle such as the subtreasury plan for the realization of this kind of America.

The Solution: Antimonopoly and the Two-Tier Market Economy

Antimonopoly notions promised a possible escape from the disjuncture between critique and analysis. Almost all southern Populists were antimonopolists, though only the greenbackers articulated a clear rationale for its importance. For these Populists, antimonopoly permeated the whole Omaha platform: the subtreasury plan and a legal tender, fiat currency system, government ownership of the railroad and communication systems, and the prohibition of extensive alien and corporate landownership.[21]

While the southern Populists' antimonopoly position was based on the simple market society's promise of an America of independent producers, it did not harken back to a Jeffersonian yeoman empire. The southern Populists rejected the cries of their opponents for agricultural self-sufficiency through "hog and hominy," maintaining that a healthy society and economy required a general specialization of labor in agriculture. Nor did southern Populists reject what parts of industrial America they found useful and beneficial. They only wanted such "natural monopolies" as the railroad and communication systems owned and operated by a democratic government, in the interest of all.[22]

The result was a kind of two-tier economy, an idea general to most southern Populist thought but one that only a few antimonopoly greenbackers articulated well. Such an economy would combine a competitive market society of small independent producers with democratic ownership and operation of those elements of industrial society that one person alone could or should not control. Judge Thomas Nugent, perhaps the most prominent Texas Populist, an antimonopoly greenbacker and two-time Populist candidate for governor, probably put the notion most clearly in a speech given at Greenville, Texas, in late August 1894 (Nugent 1896, 179–205). He opened his speech by discussing the massive Pullman strike that had taken place in June and July. He supported the Pullman strikers, and their right to strike, without qualification. He noted that the solutions offered by the politicians all favored capital, not labor, and indicted the federal government for what he convincingly argued was unconstitutional interference with the strike.

As a solution, Nugent turned to antimonopoly and the two-tier economy. What underlay labor's discontent and resentment, what drove farmers, artisans, wage workers, clerks, lawyers, and doctors together to oppose monopoly, was their desire to taste once again "the sweet fruits of independence, to find an open door to [their] lost opportunities." The "ascendency of capital," Nugent maintained, derived from legislation that gave it "unjust advantages and enabled it to monopolize both natural resources and public functions and utilities. . . . Give to a few individuals organized into corporations the right to dispense for a price services of a necessary and public character—services essential to the existence and well being of organized society—and you arm them with the power to levy tribute upon the whole community and acquire wealth almost without limit. You, in other words, provide for those consummate products of economic conditions—the millionaire and the tramp." Monopoly, not the marketplace, caused America's ills.

The nation's problem was not industrial development, but the destruction of equitable and decent economic and social relations brought by the particular organization of that development. It was, as Nugent said, "not the excessive production of wealth but its unequal distribution which constitutes the menacing evil of the times." Under normal conditions, industrial progress and the increasing complexity of society would eliminate poverty. It had not done so because "fair opportunities for the exertion of their faculties" had been denied the great mass of people. Monopoly dominated the means of distribution and production—transportation, land, and money—and robbed the producers of the rewards of their labor. The solution had already been learned in the Alliance cooperative experience. Let the people, on a cooperative basis and through the government, own, control, and operate these monopolies, and a society of independent small producers would once again become a reality. Doing this would allow "free play to competition within the proper sphere of individual effort and investment," without the need to resort to "extreme socialistic schemes."

Almost all southern Populists agreed with Nugent; if government owner-ship and operation destroyed private monopoly, the ills of American society could be cured while retaining private property, ownership, and the market system for individual producers. The abolition of land monopoly and implementation of the subtreasury plan would provide them with the tools necessary to produce their own livelihood and enjoy a decent life. Nationalization of the railroads, telegraph, and telephones, and of the currency (a greenback system), would protect individual small producers from private greed and facilitate efficient and effective distribution of the wealth they produced.

The form of antimonopoly, however, like the subtreasury plan that best articulated it, promised little to urban working people, with whom the southern Populists generally sympathized. Their demand that idle land be opened to settlers who would use it and that cheap credit be provided those who needed it demonstrated that the southern reformers could understand the importance of access to the means of production. What they did not understand was that industrial expansion had put these means forever beyond the reach of individual working people, thus denying them access to individual economic independence.

Nevertheless, the southern Populists had a powerful and often accurate critique of urban industrial capitalist America. For one thing, because of their emphasis on distribution rather than production, some southern Popu-lists could propose a crude demand stimulus as a solution to America's economic problems of the 1880s. This proposal did no violence to the market system and although it ran directly counter to the orthodoxy of the day, proved to be more accurate.[23]

The southern Populists' emphasis on antimonopoly, the maldistribution of wealth, and underconsumption (rather than overproduction) as the major causes of poverty in America also reinforced their demand that American society reflect the brotherhood of men, not competition among them. As one Texas Populist wrote in the Dallas *Southern Mercury* in June 1896, "the Christian theory of the survival of all" rather than "the Darwinian theory of the survival of the strongest" ought to be the rule. The emphasis even led some Populists to assert that where the two came into conflict, the interests of humanity should take precedence over those of capital.

Finally, the emphasis on antimonopoly, maldistribution of wealth, and underconsumption, like the greenback position to which they were tied, also led radical southern Populists toward a rudimentary class analysis of American politics and the necessity for a biracial coalition of poor black and white farmers. It was the poor and exploited, blacks and whites, urban and rural, not the favored few or their middle-class retainers, who would benefit from the new world antimonopoly described and demanded.

Class, Race, and Ideology: The Politics of Southern Populism

Like Alliance efforts to escape the lien system—buying agreements, bulking, cooperative stores, and the state exchanges—support of the subtreasury plan implicitly required a crude class consciousness among small farmers and tenants that pitted them against those with the greatest stake in the existing agricultural system: landlords, local merchants, local and regional wholesalers, local and regional bankers. By the 1880s, the commercial and financial components of an expanding industrial capitalism had begun to sharpen class tensions in the southern countryside. Landowners and furnishing merchants, often by the 1880s the same persons, increasingly controlled what essentially was an agricultural labor force removed through the lien system's debt structure from all real control over their land and labor. In the 1880s and 1890s, the Alliance movement and the Populist party in the South were responses by farmers who, because of foresight or because of fairly recent indebtedness, still retained hopes of reversing their situation. They formed the backbone of agrarian protest.

To be successful, however, required that these farmers create a biracial coalition with southern black farmers and tenants along rough class lines, as opposed to uniting across class lines any, or all, of several "communities": the white community, the local county and town versus the "city," the "South" versus the "North and East." Without such a rough class alliance with black farmers and tenants, the white farmers would be (and were) undercut and would eventually be driven from the land or reduced to tenancy.

Perhaps because of their focus on economic action, the Farmers' Alliance in the South did not clearly see the need for a biracial alliance of the black and white poor. Entry into politics and a concern for votes, however, revealed both the need for and the advantages of black support. In the 1892 elections, southern Populists in most parts of the South appealed to black voters. They promised that any relief the white farmer and tenant received from the Populist program, especially the subtreasury plan, the black farmer and tenant would also enjoy. White and black farmers and tenants were "in the same boat" said the Atlanta, Georgia, *People's Party Paper* on March 17, 1892, a sentiment echoed widely among southern Populists. Although they always denied vehemently that they advocated anything resembling social equality, some white southern Populists also promised, especially in the 1892 campaigns, protection of black political and legal rights (Palmer 1980, Chaps. 5, 11, 12).

An important reason for this emphasis in the 1892 elections was the concentration by southern Populists on the more radical elements of the Omaha platform, including the subtreasury plan. This focus was a result of the subtreasury educational campaigns of 1890 and 1891. Because the southern Democrats would not accept the plan,[24] the campaign forced the large body of farmers committed to the subtreasury plan out of the Democratic party (Goodwyn 1976, Chaps. 8, 9; McMath 1975, chap. 8). The emphasis on the subtreasury plan diminished among most southern Populists, however, with the approach of 1892's late summer and fall elections. Of southern Populism's four strongest states—North Carolina, Alabama, Georgia, and Texas—by early 1893, only in Texas was the sub-treasury plan much in evidence.

At the same time, the southern Populists' efforts to attract black voters also dwindled. In North Carolina and Alabama, the Populists had never been too happy with the notion of a biracial coalition. The Georgia Populists tried much harder in 1892 to appeal to black voters, some of them repeating their efforts in the 1894 elections. In most places, however, Populists began falling away from the idea of a biracial coalition with blacks soon after they dropped the subtreasury plan.

The relationship was not coincidental. In North Carolina, the Populists in 1892 did very poorly among black voters, perhaps because of their weak commitment to a biracial political coalition. In Georgia and Alabama, black votes were used to count the Populists out. The Democrats' success in gaining black votes for themselves and keeping black Populist votes from being counted brought a reconsideration of tactics in 1893 and 1894 by southern Populist leaders in these states. Electoral success with a biracial coalition seemed doomed, and so they turned their attention to creating what appeared to be a more promising cross-class alliance, with town and city middle classes, dropping or playing down elements of their platform—especially the sub-treasury plan—that threatened those classes (Palmer 1980 Chaps. 11, 12; Shaw 1984, Chap. 7) "Community" organization took precedence over "class" organization, although class issues remained important.

The cross-class alliance did not work; the emerging southern middle class did not support the Populists. Their interests did not mesh with the interests of those indebted to and dependent on them, no matter how much the southern Populists toned down their program.

Why did most southern Populists in North Carolina, Alabama, and Georgia so quickly begin to ignore the radical elements of their program, elements that required a perception of differing class interests? The difficulty of a biracial political coalition exposed the weak understanding of the greenback analysis among Populists in these states. For Populists in North Carolina and Alabama after 1892, and for many in Georgia by 1894, the major, and in many cases the sole, national issue became free silver. The need for a flexible currency, which free silver could not provide; the fallacy of a redemption currency, which free silver was; the need for low interest government loans on land or crops to destroy the lien system, which free silver would not provide—these things were rarely discussed in Georgia, North Carolina, or Alabama in 1895 and 1896. If they were mentioned, it was to credit free silver, mistakenly, with the power to bring an elastic money supply and thus end the depression and create the producers' simple market society. Gone was the sophisticated greenback analysis of the subtreasury plan and its place in the American economy and social order, and with it went 1892's crude class politics of the subtreasury and the need for a political coalition of poor black and poor white farmers.

With it also went the demand that the federal government involve itself in the social and economic life of the country to protect and promote the interests of the mass of common people, farmers and urban working people. Free silver required no such active intervention; it did not promise to change things much at all, but it had political sex appeal, especially to those who poorly understood the implications of the greenback position.

Only in Texas, where Alliance lessons had been taught longest and to the greatest number of people, did things go differently. The subtreasury plan was defended from 1891 through 1896, and each of the state platforms from 1892 through 1896 explicitly mentioned it. By 1895, when many Texans were saying that the financial issue might be the most important, most of them did not mean free silver but legal tender, fiat greenbacks. Free silver as a solution was consistently rejected on the grounds that it would not provide a sufficient or elastic currency, that it was still part of an intrinsic value monetary system, that it offered no solution to the lien system and would do nothing to provide cheap agricultural credit, and that it would do little to raise prices or solve any of the most serious problems of American society. The *Southern Mercury* led the Texas Populists in a two-year struggle against dropping the subtreasury plan, reducing the Omaha platform to a single issue, or fusing with any other party on the free silver issue.

The continued emphasis among Texas Populists on the subtreasury and a greenback analysis resulted in their rejecting William Jennings Bryan and the sectional politics of free silver in favor of the crude class politics of a biracial coalition of poor whites and blacks. Unlike Populists in the rest of the South, Texans continued through 1896 to increase their share of black votes. Interestingly, the maintenance of a radical program and the continued effort to create a biracial political coalition led to increasing political success. Only in Texas did the Populist party continue to grow following the 1894 elections. Only in Texas did the Populists continue to promise, with some consistency, an end to the impoverishment that the encroachment of American industrial capitalism into the countryside meant for most southern farmers, black and white. Antimonopoly greenbackism, and the crude class consciousness and biracial politics it required, promoted electoral success. Ideology and a class consciousness in this case did not divide people but forged links between them (Palmer 1980, chaps. 11, 12).

But the efforts of the Texas antimonopoly greenbackers left them, by 1896, with no place to turn. In the South, as in the West, most Populists accepted Bryan and free silver fusion with the Democrats. With no national party, the more radical southern Populists were unable to realize their antimonopoly greenback program, for it required national implementation.[25] Bryan, with a Populist rhetoric of conflict between producers and nonproducers, the people and monopoly, led a free silver crusade by the "broader class of businessmen"—wage earners, farmers, employers, merchants, and bankers—of the West and South against the monopolistic East. Taking advantage of a poor understanding of a greenback monetary system, and thus the subtreasury plan, and of the necessity of both for any attack on monopoly within a market system, the southern Democrats sought, successfully, to unite the entire southern white "community," farmer and furnishing merchant and banker, country and town, reinforced by the exclusion of blacks, in a sectional struggle against the East. They defused the rudimentary class politics with appeals to the sectional "community" of all white southerners.

The politics of free silver avoided the issues of class in favor of more traditional "communities," and for that reason avoided any challenge to southern white racism, including the Populists'. So the rudimentary class politics required by the Omaha platform's antimonopoly implications failed, although it was a closer thing than many people now realize. America's elites, and the South's, knew how close it was (Goodwyn 1976, 521–534; Jones 1964, 337–340). The southern Populists' commitment to the marketplace and white supremacy was simply too strong to be overcome in such a short time and with such little room. Divided, the southern farmers and tenants, black and white, fell into the abject poverty that has marked most of the twentieth-century rural South.

Conclusion

What does the experience of the southern Populists have to contribute to a resolution of the dilemmas of ideology, state power and democracy, and class and community? Let's start with the last. A rudimentary class analysis was not only part of the most radical form of southern Populism but an important part of the most successful of the southern state parties, the Texas Populist organization. Southern Populists who did not understand its importance deserted a program that promised them relief, the subtreasury plan, in favor of a cosmetic reform, free silver, which quickly disappeared as an effective political issue. They also abandoned an incipient effort to challenge white supremacy in the South, an abandonment that removed the last major impediment to the emergence of the vicious racism that marked the South after 1900 and had catastrophic results for white southerners, their black neighbors, and Americans in general. If one goal of the new populism is to attack racism, then one lesson of southern Populism is that some class sensibility, if not entirely sufficient, is absolutely necessary. A class sensibility can foster racial tolerance and cooperation by stressing what is *common* in the light of what contemporary politics and culture insist is different.

What about the dilemma of state power and democratic control? The Southern Populist notion that government should serve all the people did not mean the corporate–government partnership we have seen emerge, nor the bureaucratic nightmare that government, in the name of the general welfare, has become.[26] We got government power and an empty paternalism, not democracy. As the Omaha platform makes clear, the southern Populists were committed to democracy, not bureaucracy: "We believe that the power of the government—in other words, of the people—should be expanded (as in the case of the postal service) as rapidly and as far as the good sense of an intelligent people and the teachings of experience shall justify, to the end that oppression, injustice, and poverty shall eventually cease in the land."

This passage also makes clear that the Populists understood the causes of America's misery and the exploitation of every working person and farmer to be national in scope and to require national solutions. Though our experience of the past several generations should make us a great deal more wary of the power of government, especially the central government, than were the southern Populists, it should not mean that we lose our perspective, defining the problem as one of a democratic localism versus a bureaucratic centralism. As the southern Populists realized, many problems of individual farmers could not be solved by the practice of democratic localism. Local cooperatives failed; so did state exchanges. It was these failures that led to the subtreasury plan, a national solution (Goodwyn 1976, 149–153).

In part to resolve the problem of state power and democracy, the southern Populists developed the two-tiered economy. A thoroughly reformed federal government would control land distribution, the railroad, telegraph, and telephone systems, and the currency. The federal government itself would be democratically controlled by the producing many, not by the wealthy few. Antimonopoly greenback reforms would eliminate their sources of wealth and power.

What about the third issue, ideology? The standard notion of ideology seems vague to me, and thus confusing in its application. Is ideology a rigorous analysis of how the world works and how it should work (Marxism comes to mind)? Is it a commitment to ideals such as equality and democracy or "community" (republican America or the revolution in our backyards)? Is it a program for change in the world (the Omaha platform, for one)? Is it a process of change (perhaps the dialectic)? Is it a combination of any or all of these? At one time or another, all these things have been called ideology, though they tend at points to be mutually contradictory.

As a tentative effort to resolve the problem, I would like to offer another definition and work it a bit in relation to the subject of this paper. Let ideology be the description of the world as it is and the world as it should be. It may also include a description of the process of change from the first to the second. Let discourse carry normative values to this description, establishing why the world is bad and should be made better, thus providing the language (or images) that establish the imperative for action. Finally, let the program connect the discourse and the ideology, in the process illuminating the appropriateness of both and making clear to every person affected why the change demanded is not only desirable but necessary.[27] For southern Populism, antimonopoly greenbackism is the ideology. Equality, justice, decency, and human responsibility—and their opposites—serve as subjects of the discourse. The Omaha platform, especially its subtreasury linchpin, is the program.

To ignore ideology and a wide-ranging program in favor of discourse, as Bryan and the Democrats, and to a considerable extent the free silver Populists, did in 1895 and 1896, and as the theorists of the new populism suggest is necessary today, allows for an appeal to large numbers of people and the possibility of quick change in a specific situation. This option is particularly attractive in a formal democracy because the terms of discourse, the normative values, are by definition acceptable to large numbers of people. The republican tradition, Jacksonian producerism to an extent, and evangelical Protestantism provided the discourse surrounding southern Populism. As norms, they had little specific content, making them capable of covering a wide range of different attitudes and acts. Only ideology, as objective a description of the world as possible (though never uninformed by passion or self-interest), gave specificity to the terms of southern Populist discourse. It was, of course, this specificity that introduced the political difficulty. No one could argue with freedom or equal rights to all and special privileges to none, at least not in the abstract. But many could, and did, argue that no freedom, no equality, could be won by eliminating the national banks or instituting the subtreasury to destroy the maldistribution of wealth. America's freedom, the southern Populists' opponents could and did argue, rested on its productive capacity, which in turn depended on the ability of "businessmen" to turn a profit and reinvest their gains in expanding production. They could, and did, argue that equality meant equality of opportunity, not equal shares, and that the demand for elimination of the huge concentrations of individual and corporate wealth and power would destroy America's economic growth (on which rested individual freedom) and, anyway, was sour grapes on the part of the lazy or incompetent.

Given the marketplace definition of individual freedom as a function of alienable property, to which even the antimonopoly greenback southern Populists remained attached, such arguments made sense. The difference between a privately owned farm and a privately owned railroad was difficult to explain if private ownership of property remained unquestionable. Even the antimonopoly greenback southern Populists never successfully resolved the difficulty that Prudence Posner in the introduction to this volume calls the core problem of ideology. At any rate, specificity, the tie between discourse and ideology, appears to divide, not associate, people, and division seems clearly counterproductive if one desires large-scale democratic change. Hence the apparent desirability of focusing on issues with less specificity.

Although the promise of immediate effectiveness supplies the appeal of concentrating on issues of discourse rather than the specifics of ideology and program, it has its weaknesses. A concentration on discourse cedes control of the playing field to one's opponents in the name of a potentially successful contest over a small part of that field, a success that, even if gained, can be contained and neutralized in the long run by those who control the game and can specify the discourse on their terms. Even if, in 1896, the Democrats and their southern Populist supporters had won the campaign for free silver by associating it with widely accepted terms of discourse—the rights of producers, equality, the virtue of labor, the menace of wealth and special interests—the issue could have been easily contained by the opposition. Free silver meant little fundamental change in the lives of those for whom the Populist spoke.[28] Uninformed by an antimonopoly greenback analysis, the content of the normative terms in the discourse could be, and were, defined largely by the southern Populists' opponents.

A focus on discourse at the expense of wide-ranging program and ideology might appear to alleviate the problems of the lack of democratic participation that concentration on ideology, class, and a national focus seems to bring. But while discourse can bring more people together, it also tends to leave the inequitable relations between them untouched. A rhetoric of freedom might unite black and some white Americans, but without ideology, and some specific program linked to it as well as to discourse, any particular successes will prove—have proven—illusory, at least for most blacks. The power to define what "freedom" means, when ceded by default to dominant groups in our society, results in little actually being done for most blacks. Such change can be absorbed by the dominant groups.

Antimonopoly had its own problems. Unless rigorously defined, it tended to include, on the "good" side, not only farmers and urban labor but also small-town merchants and bankers. These groups applied it, for instance, to railroads, as did the southern Populists, but not to themselves. As antimonopoly greenback southern Populists usually understood, small-town merchants and bankers were part of the problem. Antimonopoly, for them, meant the subtreasury, government ownership of the railroad and communication systems, and the restriction of corporate landownership. In short, it meant the Omaha platform. But because of a focus on size rather than on productive relations as a cause of exploitation, antimonopoly failed to address clearly the fundamental conflict between human and property rights, a conflict produced by the marketplace in an industrial society dedicated to private ownership and profit.

The antimonopoly greenback analysis was a start, however. At least it led to a recognition on the part of the more radical antimonopoly greenback southern Populists of the existence of a conflict between property and humanity. It began to suggest that a market society might not be the way to create a new America in which the values of the old one, defined by Jefferson and Jackson, republicanism, and evangelical Protestantism, could be preserved.

What, then, does the southern Populist experience finally have to offer as a resolution to the tension between ideology and discourse, between analysis and normative values, even to the dilemmas of class and community, state power and democracy? It suggests that the issue itself might be a solution, especially if that issue serves to define, and so create, a community of class in terms of individual experience.[29] The issue—the subtreasury plan in the case of the southern Populists—attracts and then educates, making ideology a way of holding people together rather than dividing them. In this sense, the subtreasury plan was ideal, at least for farmers. It tied the necessity for political action to the immediate reality of the lives of southern farmers, individuals who, on other grounds, were divided by political party, by race, by relation to the land, by region, even and especially by individual personality, likes and dislikes, and experience. Larry Goodwyn has demonstrated how the subtreasury plan was used by Alliance radicals to create the Populist party (Goodwyn 1976, Chap. 8). As a result, he also indicates how the subtreasury plan led back to the antimonopoly greenback analysis. Farmers who could understand the need for cheap credit could understand the need for the subtreasury. They could, and did, learn why the subtreasury required a new way of thinking about money and monopoly, about southern and American society in general, including its racism. The program, then, can give content to the terms of the discourse and make ideology unifying rather than divisive. Class identity must grow, dialectically; it cannot spring, whole hog, from the barnyard of experience.

Appendix: The Quantity Theory of Money

Contraction of the money supply brought falling prices and hard times for indebted rural producers, especially when, as in the late nineteenth century, commodity prices fell more steeply than the cost of living. If steep enough, such a contraction could bring panic and depression. The solution to such evils proceeded from the quantity theory of money. To prevent contraction, the supply of currency had to match the demand for its use. To achieve commodity price stability, the most sophisticated of the southern Populists argued, the volume of currency had to expand as fast as the population and the commerce of the country grew. Only a few of the southern Populists' opposition understood the relationship between prices and the amount of money in circulation, and they were absolute opponents of inflation, which would increase prices and promised to benefit debtors, which almost all farmers were, by reducing the amount of goods and services needed to repay debts. This would tend to slow the concentration of wealth, and power, in the hands of the dominant and wealthy few and their allies.

What follows is a *very* simplified demonstration of the quantity theory of money, though it is about as sophisticated as most Southern Populists got.

Let $P = MV/T$, where P = prices, M = the amount of currency in circulation, V = the velocity of currency circulation, and T = the number of transactions involving currency in a specific time.

So, if $M = 5$, $V = 5$, and $T = 5$, then $P = 5$.

Deflation equals the reduction of M while V and T remain constant (or decrease, or decrease more slowly than M). For instance, if $M = 1$, $V = 5$, and $T = 5$, then $P = 1$, and prices have fallen.

Inflation equals the increase of M while V and T remain the same (or increase, or increase more slowly than M). For instance, if $M = 10$, $V = 5$, and $T = 5$, then $P = 10$, and prices have risen.

This relationship can also be described for a farmer in terms of, say, cotton. Farmer A borrows $100, interest free, from Merchant B in 1880, when cotton sells for $.10 a pound. The loan is due in 1890. If there is no inflation or deflation during the ten years, no rise or fall of prices, Farmer A must grow 1000 pounds of cotton to pay off Merchant B.

If *inflation* occurs, and the price of cotton rises to $.20 a pound, Farmer A must grow only 500 pounds of cotton to repay Merchant B. Inflation has made the money received by Merchant A in 1890, in terms of what it will buy, worth half of what it was in 1880, when she loaned the money. To pay off the loan, Farmer A need only work half as hard in 1890 as she would have had to in 1880.

If *deflation* occurs, and the price of cotton falls to $.05 a pound, Farmer A must raise 2000 pounds of cotton to pay off the debt, and Merchant B gets a dollar that will buy twice as much as it would have in 1880.

Deflation, then, tends to transfer income from debtor to creditor. In the South, it worked to transfer income from indebted farmers to the wealthier segments of southern society, where it was available for consumption or private investment. Most of the latter left the South.

Notes

1. The theorists of, and commentators on, the new populism often refer to populism's later successes, which is more problematic. Populism's role in the Progressive movement of the early twentieth century and its bastard reappearance in the 1930s were reflected largely in terms of some of its issues, such as increased federal activity in the economic life of the country, federal regulation of corporations, and legislation aiding agriculture. All these activities, however, were divorced from the ultimate goal of the Populists of the 1890s, which was an effective democratic political and economic order rather than the perpetuation of corporate capitalism through an alliance with a bureaucratic state. For the bastard populism of the 1930s, see Brinkley (1982, esp. 165–168). For the argument that the Progressives by and large carried out the Populist program, see Hicks (1931, Chap. 15).

2. For an excellent discussion of this process, concerning the steel industry and the steelworkers' union, one of the strongest in the United States in the late nineteenth century, see Brody (1960, Chap. 2).

3. A number of books discuss the response of workingmen and workingwomen to industrialization in this country. Among those that elaborate on my point, though in different ways, are Brecher (1972), Montgomery (1979, 1987), and Gutman (1976).

4. On the development of the currency issue, see Nugent (1968) and Unger (1964).

5. For one of the more extended versions of the argument that universal

(in theory) manhood suffrage actually inhibited the development of working-class consciousness, see Dawley (1976, esp. "Conclusion").

6. The Omaha platform can be most easily found in Pollack (1967) or Tindall (1966). For a good, short overview of these developments, though without my particular interpretation, see Degler (1977), esp. Chaps. 1, 2, 3).

7. The Democratic party in the South answered to the needs of a small class of Southerners, the Redeemers and their supporters, whose major interest lay in their continued control of Southern state politics, a control necessary to their economic fortunes. These fortunes were based on handling the movement of capital into the South and the export of raw materials, including agricultural commodities such as cotton, to manufacturing centers in the North and Europe, especially England. Though the South in the late nineteenth century did experience some industrial growth, the gap between this region and the rest of the country did not close.

For the most influential statement of this idea of the colonial South, see Woodward (1951, Chaps. 5, 11).

8. There are numerous discussions of the lien system, including Woodward (1951, Chap. 7). The most detailed is Schwartz (1976, Chaps. 1 to 5).

9. Tenancy rates in the eleven former Confederate states: 1880, 37.9% of all farmers; 1890, 40.4%; 1990, 48.5%; 1910, 49.9%. Michael Schwartz puts the actual figures even higher, arguing that inescapable debt had by 1890 reduced many farmers, who technically owned their own land, to conditions equivalent to tenancy (Schwartz 1976, 76–79).

10. The only recourse these people had was to move, but even moving usually made little difference. Except for a few places in the South—the Birmingham area, for instance—there was no alternative to farming. Nor was migration out of the South possible for most. Northern employers had all they wanted of cheap immigrant labor, labor that often had more industrial and wage-earning experience and was more pliable than southern whites or blacks because of language and cultural differences among the various immigrant groups and between the immigrants and the native population. For blacks, see Mandel (1978, Chaps. 2, 6).

I should add that I do not wish to suggest that oppression alone gave rise to southern Populism. Larry Goodwyn has pointed out the obvious, which almost all American historians of oppositional movements have long failed to point out, that if oppression led automatically and directly to oppositional *movements*, the history of the world would be at the least one of constant revolution (Goodwyn 1978, x).

11. For an extended discussion of this, see Palmer, Chaps. 1, 2, 3).

12. Hence the importance of the greenback analysis. And hence the opposition of the dominant capitalist groups in America. Their control of the currency was an important aspect of their ability to concentrate capital in their own hands, though perhaps not always the most important one. For them, as well as for the Populists,

control of the currency, hence questions of the currency, were central to the issues of economic growth, political power, and America's future.

It is interesting that the greenbackers, two generations later, were vindicated. Their insights, not those of their opposition, triumphed, but—and this is a lesson in the importance of context—well after the dominance of corporate capital was assured, rendering their radical potential harmless. Any one of Paul Samuelson's college economics textbooks will testify to this. Even more strikingly, so will Samuelson's opposition. See Friedman and Schwartz (1963, Chaps. 1, 2, 3).

13. The federal government's fiat declaration that a coin, or a piece of paper, stamped or printed in a specific manner, made money. So, the southern Populists argued, a silver dollar was not worth a dollar because it had silver in it of sufficient fineness and weight to be sold, when melted down for $1. The price of silver depended on the supply, and demand, for it, which fluctuated. Indeed, the silver in a silver dollar always had a value less than or equal to $1. If it were worth more, the holders of silver dollars would melt them down and sell them at a profit, and all silver dollars would disappear. Silver currency, or gold currency, or any metallic currency, if circulated, never contained metal worth more in the market than the face value of the coin. Federal law, not the metal in the coin, made a gold or silver dollar worth $1.

14. The southern Populists' more sophisticated opponents, of course, understood this quite well, though they were happy to foster the idea of an intrinsic-value currency. What these people actually wanted, and generally had, was a currency only loosely tied to bullion, gold, or gold and silver. This allowed the currency to be controlled more easily by the national bankers, who had authority to issue banknotes, and by their allies in the federal Treasury. Beyond this, to permit the government to intervent in behalf of the farmers meant, by implication, that it had the authority to intervene against the farmers' opponents.

15. This idea grew directly out of their experience as farmers and Alliancemen with the crop lien system. Even if they could sell their own crops, farmers were forced to market them when the demand for money to handle the crop pushed prices down. They had to purchase supplies for the coming year, however, when the demand for money was low and prices consequently high. Charles W. Macune, the central figure in the Southern Farmers' Alliance (NFA&IU) between 1886 and the early 1890s and the man who devised the state cooperative exchange idea and the subtreasury plan, estimated in the Tarboro, North Carolina, *Farmers' Advocate* on April 15, 1891, that the price differential between harvest and provisioning could be as much as 40 percent.

16. For the producer ideal in pre–Civil War reform, see Foner (1970, 15) and Pessen (1967, Chaps. 10, 11).

17. Elements of this idea appear later among Jacksonian labor leaders, Radical Republicans, free labor people, and post–Civil War greenbackers (Foner 1970, Chap. 1; Montgomery 1967, Chaps. 10, 11; Pessen 1967, Chaps. 7, 11).

18. The best presentations of details of the subtreasury plan are Tracy ("Appendix" to Davis (1895) and ("Appendix B" in Goodwyn 1976).

19. The importance of the Jeffersonian tradition was so great that it prevented all but a very few southern Populists from seeing the obvious, that legislation such as the subtreasury plan required fell within the scope of federal power because it promoted the general welfare.

20. Many of them had had recent experience with, or could remember, such a world as Hahn (1983, Chap. 7 and "Epilogue") has pointed out.

21. As one Texan put it, a general increase in the money supply without the abolition of the transportation and land monopolies would result in the added currency quickly being absorbed by high corporate salaries, high freight rates, and excessive rents. Land reform without financial reform would mean that most people would be unable to reach the land, and many of those who could do so would be too poor to use it. Those successfully reaching and using the land would not profit because of a contracted currency and high transportation charges. And what good would government ownership of the railroads do those who had no land to till and those who, because of poverty caused by the contraction of the currency, could not purchase what might be shipped? As the Dallas *Southern Mercury* proposed on March 19, 1896, for successful reform, monopoly in all three areas—land, transportation, and finance—had to be destroyed.

22. Antimonopoly did lead the radical editors of two Texas newspapers—the Austin *Argus* and the Austin *People's Advocate*—to socialism in 1894, although both continued to advocate the Omaha platform. Their socialism was of a moderate nature, the result of raising the principle of government ownership to a general level, though they never specified how widely the principle of "government" ownership of the means of production" should spread. In general, an antimonopoly greenback stance did not mean socialism to the southern Populists, even the most radical among them. Instead, their ideal society remained one of independent producers, where individuals owned and controlled the means necessary to their livelihood and thus did not need to sell their labor.

23. In its most common form, the southern Populists' argument ran something like this: An increased circulation of currency, especially if put into the economy through the subtreasury system, would enable farmers to save considerably on credit costs and increase their profits. They would subsequently buy more manufactured goods. As demand for manufactured goods rose, unemployment would turn into a shortage of labor, driving wages up and making working people better customers for farm products, starting the cycle all over again.

24. The subtreasury not only would have meant the loss to the Democrats of any support of the elite and their allies but also would have adversely affected the economic and political power of the existing power leadership in the South.

25. The party in Texas, explicitly antimonopoly in 1894, collapsed more slowly than elsewhere in the South, though just as thoroughly. So, ultimately, antimonopoly proved insufficient. The most radical analysis of southern Populism did better

politically than the less radical, the less "ideological." But it failed all the same. The Texans' effort was not enough.

26. Clearly, analysts of the new populism share some of their attitudes with the southern Populists, if not always for the same reasons. Unlike the southern Populists of the 1890s, the new populists have had at least two generations of experience with "big government" and its bureaucratic, antidemocratic ethos. Given the southern Populists' commitment to democracy and the individual control of productive property, their horror at what has happened might equal that of the new populists. The corporate–government partnership they criticized has grown worse, not gotten better, even though that relationship was almost always sold as democratic reform in the interest of the general welfare.

27. This notion about the role of the program, or issue, was suggested to me by Goodwyn's analysis of the role of the subtreasury in the emergence of the Populist party in the South (Goodwyn 1976, Chaps. 8, 9).

28. Friedman and Schwartz maintain that from the 1870s to 1897, free silver would have meant a more stable, rather than an inflationary, money supply, since it would not have increased the currency supply much. Free silver certainly would not have led to inflation (Friedman and Schwartz, 1963, 134n).

29. Goodwyn implicitly suggests something like this in his discussion of the stages necessary for the development of any democratic movement (see Goodwyn, 1978 xviii, for the stages, and the rest of the book for an elaboration of the model).

References

Brecher, Jeremy. 1972. *Strike*. Boston: South End Press.

Brinkley, Alan. 1982. *Voices of Protest: Huey Long, Father Coughlin, and the Great Depression*. New York: Random House.

Brody, David. 1960. *Steelworkers in America: The Nonunion Era*. Cambridge, Mass.: Harvard University Press.

Dawley, Alan. 1976. *Class and Community: The Industrial Revolution in Lynn*. Cambridge, Mass.: Harvard University Press.

Degler, Carl. 1977. *The Age of Economic Revolution, 1876–1900*. Glenview, Ill.: Scott, Foresman.

Dunning, Nelson A., ed. 1891. *The Farmers' Alliance History and Agricultural Digest*. Washington, D.C.: Alliance Publishing.

Foner, Eric. 1970. *Free Soil, Free Labor, Free Men: The Ideology of the Republican Party Before the Civil War*. New York: Oxford University Press.

Friedman, Milton, and Anna Jacobson Schwartz. 1963. *A Monetary History of the United States, 1867–1960*. Princeton: Princeton University Press.

Goodwyn, Lawrence. 1976. *Democratic Promise: The Populist Moment in America*. New York: Oxford University Press.

————. 1978. *The Populist Moment: A Short History of the Agrarian Revolution in America*. New York: Oxford University Press.

Gutman, Herbert. 1976. *Work, Culture, and Society in Industrialized America: Essays in Working-Class and Social History*. New York: Knopf.

Hahn, Steven. 1983. *The Roots of Southern Populism: Yeoman Farmers and the Transformation of the Georgia UpCountry, 1850–1890*. New York: Oxford University Press.

Hicks, John D. 1931. *The Populist Revolt: A History of the Farmers' Alliance and People's Party*. Minneapolis: University of Minnesota Press.

Jones, Stanley L. 1964. *The Presidential Election of 1896*. Madison University of Wisconsin Press.

Kolko, Gabriel. 1963. *The Triumph of Conservatism*. New York: Free Press.

McMath, Robert C., Jr. 1975. *Populist Vanguard: A History of the Southern Farmers' Alliance*. Chapel Hill: University of North Carolina Press.

MacPherson, C. B. 1962. *The Political Theory of Possessive Individualism: Hobbes to Locke*. London: Oxford University Press.

Mandel, Jay R. 1978. *The Roots of Black Poverty: The Southern Plantation Economy After the Civil War*. Durham, N.C.: Duke University Press.

Montgomery, David. 1967. *Beyond Equality: Labor and the Radical Republicans, 1862–1872*. New York: Random House.

————. 1987. *The Fall of the House of Labor: The Workplace, the State, and American Labor Activism, 1865–1925*. Cambridge, England: Cambridge University Press.

————. 1979. *Workers' Control in America: Studies in the History of Work, Technology, and Labor Struggles*. Cambridge, England: Cambridge University Press.

Nugent, Catherine, ed. 1896. *Life Work of Thomas L. Nugent*. Stephenville, Tex.: privately published.

Nugent, Walter T. K. 1968. *Money and American Society, 1865–1880*. New York: Free Press.

Palmer, Bruce. 1980. *"Man Over Money": The Populist Critique of American Capitalism*. Chapel Hill: University of North Carolina Press.

Pessen, Edward. 1967. *Most Uncommon Jacksonians: The Radical Leaders of the Early Labor Movement*. Albany: State University of New York Press.

Pollack, Norman, ed. 1967. *The Populist Mind*. Indianpolis: Bobbs-Merrill.

Schwartz, Michael. 1976. *Radical Protest and Social Structure: The Southern Farmers' Alliance and Cotton Tenancy, 1800–1890*. New York: Academic Press.

Shaw, Barton C. 1984. *The Wool Hat Boys: Georgia's Populist Party*. Baton Rouge: Louisiana State University Press.

Tindall, George B., ed. 1966. *A Populist Reader*, New York: Harper & Row.

Tracy, Harry. 1895. "Appendix." In James H. Davis, *A Political Revelation*. Dallas: Advance Publishing.

Unger, Irwin. 1964. *The Greenback Era: A Social and Political History of American Finance*. Princeton: Princeton University Press.

Weinstein, James. 1968. *The Corporate Ideal in the Liberal State*. Boston: Beacon Press.

Woodward, C. Vann. 1951. *The Origins of the New South, 1877–1913*. Baton Rouge: Louisiana University Press.

Yohe, William P. 1976. "Appendix B." In Lawrence Goodwyn, *Democratic Promise: The Populist Moment in America*. New York: Oxford University Press.

CHAPTER 7

The Perils of Petty Production: The Agricultural Crisis

Rona S. Weiss

FARM CRISIS ENDANGERING RURAL TOWNS
Robbins, *New York Times*, October 14, 1985

NO END IN SIGHT FOR HARVEST OF DEBT
New York Times, January 14, 1987

FARM POPULATION LOWEST SINCE 1850'S
New York Times, July 20, 1988

"Beware the Farm Crisis!" blares the headline, and a similar message is heard on the evening news. In 1985, nationally noted rock and country singers organized a Farm Aid concert to raise funds that might ease the crisis. From 1985 to 1987, three major motion pictures addressed the problems of rural life associated with a farm crisis. Yet supermarket shelves are brimming over with fruits, vegetables, breads, and meats. Moreover, the prices of these products have temporarily stabilized. So what exactly is the agricultural crisis all about?

On the surface, the agricultural crisis is about the disappearance of the family farm. It is about human suffering, rural poverty, and the decline of rural communities. On the one hand, the farm crisis is about the loss of family farms through bankruptcy and foreclosure, a phenomenon having political implications both because of the impact of these foreclosures on rural communities and because of the ideological role the family farmer plays in democratic mythology. On the other hand, and less noted in mainstream press, the farm crisis is about a profound change in the way food is produced in the United States. This change has resulted in the adulteration of the food supply through the use of hormones, toxic pesticides, and chemical fertilizers, and in the destruction of the natural environment, primarily through soil erosion. This paper examines the structural changes occurring in agricultural production that have caused the situation known as the farm crisis.

Structural changes in agriculture began in the nineteenth century. At that time, the Midwest was settled on the basis of market-oriented commercial agriculture. Crucial links to the capitalist market economy meant that in addition to the vagaries of nature, the agricultural producer was subject to market forces beyond his or her control. The family farmer felt, and responded to, the damaging impact of these forces a century ago. The Populist movement, described in Chapter 6, decried the direction in which agriculture was moving. In 1890, when the Populist party organized thousands of farmers and elected state representatives and senators, approximately 43 percent of the labor force was employed in agriculture (U.S. Department of Commerce 1975, 51, 127). In 1930, that figure was 25 percent. Today, between 2 and 5 percent of the labor force is primarily engaged in agriculture. All indications are that this trend toward decreasing labor force participation in agriculture will continue. Sources suggest that in the past ten years, thousands of farms have gone under each month.[1] In fact, immediately following the election of George Bush in November 1988, 40,000 foreclosure notices were sent to American farmers whose debts to the federally supported Farm Credit System were overdue.

Since the mid 1970s, progressive organizers have been working in rural communities, assisting farmers who faced the loss of their land and homes. These are symptoms of the transition that are being addressed through community organization and collective action. But community organization cannot turn back the clock; 25 to 30 percent of the labor force will never again be engaged in agricultural production. It is unlikely that the family farm can be resurrected as the primary food-producing unit of our society. What some organizers are beginning to recognize is that collective action may be able to affect how food is produced and how land is used or abused. In addition, therefore, to addressing the problem of shattered lives and hopes in the agricultural regions of the United States, rural organizers are raising basic questions about agricultural production.

The Background of the Agricultural Crisis

How did the crisis start? Perhaps this is the wrong question. Commercial agriculture in the United States has always been characterized by instability. Certainly we must look at particular policies and events of the 1970s to understand the current crisis, but the general unpredictability of a market economy meant that once agricultural production became entwined in the market nexus, it, too, would be characterized by imbalance and changeability. In the seventeenth century, the relatively self-sufficient farms of New England were being drawn into the market network. In this region, the process of competition and differentiation caused a qualitative change in agricultural production long before the Civil War (see, e.g., Gates 1960; Handlin and Handlin 1969). By the 1840s and 1850s, thousands of young farmers had left family farms that could no longer support them and traveled west or to the coastal towns. The effects on agriculture of market involvement (in the South and West) were apparent to everyone by the 1880s and 1890s). At that time, the Grange and Populist movements echoed the demands of small landowners and tenant farmers pushed to the brink by, among other things, high costs (especially for credit) and unpredictable prices (see Chapter 6 in this volume and Hicks 1961). Other periods could be pointed to both in past centuries and in the twentieth century, when the general instability of commercial agriculture caused major economic dislocations for family farms.

Market-oriented agricultural production faces two problems: the unpredictable acts of nature and the vagaries of the market. Floods, drought, locusts, frosts, and duststorms are ever-present threats, as is new competition or the unpredictable demand for wheat or corn. Even when farms are "blessed" with agreeable weather conditions and their products are abundant, they are under a possible threat because a bumper crop often means that prices decline, and farm income may be jeopardized. Thus the commercial production of agricultural goods has an inherent potential for instability, which sets the context for the conjunctural conditions that contribute to any particular "downturn."

Trends in Contemporary Agricultural Production

Most of the farms that face bankruptcy today are not small. They are mid- and large-sized operations, with 200 to 1000 acres in production (Kline 1981). They are primarily midwestern grain and livestock producers. That they are in jeopardy is not because they are inefficient; indeed, these farms are among the most efficient in the world. Simply put, they are in trouble because their total revenues rarely exceed, let alone equal, their total costs of production.

Small farms are less vulnerable because their production costs are low and because they are often tended by part-time farmers with nonfarm income. Some very large farms are also shielded from market pressures because they are but one holding of a large corporation with other income sources and/or because their size creates some market advantages.

The general market uncertainty discussed above, coupled with specific events of the postwar era, especially during the 1970s and 1980s, contributed to the increase in costs as well as the downward pressure on revenues for the mid-sized farm. Production costs rose astronomically after World War II as competition led to increased mechanization, especially in the South and Midwest. Also in this period, the number of large agricultural processing and merchant companies grew and established tremendous market power—in many cases, oligopsonistic power (Morgan 1980, 135–170). Most mid-sized farms are now forced to sell their crops to one of a few agricultural processing and wholesaling firms. These firms can dictate prices and some conditions of production, and therefore the costs of production. Through the practice of "contract farming," a farmer agrees to sell a certain amount of grain or a certain number of eggs, for example, by a specified date and at a previously agreed upon price. These commodities must be produced under the specific conditions stipulated in the contract. In this way, the agribusiness "rents" a farm, while the farmer bears most of the risks. By 1980, approximately 30 percent of all farm output was produced under a contractual arrangement, and for particular commodities, the percentage was much higher (Wilson 1986, 50). For example, 94 percent of total sales in dairy, 83 percent of processed vegetables, 34 percent of fruit and nuts, and 21 percent of fed cattle were sold under market contracts between 1980 and 1984; 60 percent of the market value of poultry and eggs was exchanged under production contracts by the late 1970s.[2]

As part of some contractual arrangements, the farmer agrees to use a certain kind of seed, fertilizer, machinery, pesticide, or, in the case of livestock, certain types of chicken coops or barns. These stipulations require the farmer to make certain purchases, in some cases from the same agribusiness that extends the contract or from one of its subsidies. As a consequence, the farmer is often forced to use harmful chemicals, pesticides, fertilizers, or hormones for livestock, additives that eventually reach the human species. Even if the contract were not the compelling force, the commercial farm of today is a highly specialized one. Unlike the diversified farms of yesteryear, today's farmers' entire income is based on the cultivation of one or two crops. Farmers cannot afford to lose part of one crop, so they are "forced" by general market pressures to narrow their risks by using chemical pesticides and the like. As insect pests over the years develop immunities to more "gentle" poisons, more deadly chemicals must be used.

These trends in agriculture undermine the ability of the U.S. population to obtain healthy farm products, and the ability of the middle-sized farm to survive is undermined by cost increases and uncertain prices.

Federal Policy Initiatives and Their Consequences for Food Production

In the 1970s, farmers were encouraged by banks and agencies of the federal government to leverage their operations further and expand. At that time, the U.S. economy faced a tremendous crisis, nationally and internationally. One symptom of the crisis was the deficit in the U.S. trade balance. In the 1970s, as in the 1880s and 1890s, agricultural exports were viewed as a panacea by policymakers (Wessel 1983, 37–81; Burback and Flynn 1980, 41–61). Secretary of Agriculture Earl Butz called on farmers to plant from "fence row to fence row," as production quotas on items were lifted by the government (Lappe 1983, 16). Farmers were courted by private U.S. banks (as well as the Farm Credit System) brimming over with petrodollar deposits and encouraged to borrow money for more land and crop expansion. Land values rose, providing many farmers with more collateral to make their loans. And borrow they did! Some farmers borrowed to expand productive capacity, while others borrowed for the primary purpose of land speculation.

This "official" encouragement to borrow exacerbated the ever-present debt problem many farmers faced. Initially, most farmers borrow money because of the seasonal nature of their work. Harvests come in only a few times a year. So farmers borrow to buy machinery, land, feed, fertilizer, and so on. In the 1970s, some farmers further leveraged their holdings to "gamble" in the market and to benefit from the federal government's need to diminish the unfavorable trade balance. Agricultural production grew, producing millions of dollars worth of food exports. Under the guise of feeding the hungry people of the Third World, such international grain merchants as Cargill and Continental conquered new markets. The costs of U.S. exports were kept low to compete internationally, and the federal government subsidized farm incomes through various kinds of price supports. But the boom of the 1970s could not be sustained. By the late 1970s and early 1980s, the Third World debt crisis put a damper on the demand for U.S. grains. Prices for various commodities fell, and farms were left saddled with huge debts and uncertain revenues. There was no guarantee that foreign markets would provide a steady demand. This set of events, in the context of the nature of present-day commercial agriculture, set the stage for the current crisis.

Although government policies certainly played a role, it would be simplistic to suggest that government policies "caused" the farm crisis. The policies that directly affect agriculture are many and complex, and they sometimes have contradictory effects. Policies change from year to year and from administration to administration. But these policies must not be viewed as exogenous variables; the government is an integral part of the political–economic terrain that supports the agricultural system. What follows is a theoretical elaboration of this terrain with an eye toward its social transformation.

Class Relations in Agriculture: Who's Who?

One of the most provocative theoretical questions for the progressive economic historian, as well as the farm activist, is the conceptualization of a farmer's identity in class terms. What *is* a farmer? Is he or she a worker? a capitalist? a petty producer? none of the above? On what basis can organizers appeal to farmers to join together? Should it be as members of a class? as rural people? Is this type of identity even necessary for a successful political struggle that might improve the chances of the imperiled farmers' survival?

I believe the discussion of farmers' identity in class (and other) terms is a prerequisite to a discussion of policy or strategy. The desired direction of policy change cannot be ascertained unless we have some understanding of the nature of the problematic relationships that have contributed to the current agricultural crisis. Moreover, where people stand with respect to these relationships (i.e., class, community) affects the terms on which they might be mobilized. Class, as I understand it, is one of the critical relationships or processes that might help to explain the present situation in agriculture.

When I use the word *class* in this paper, I am not referring to a sociological category based on income level or status; nor am I using an institutionalist classification based only on type of property ownership or nonownership. I use the word class here to refer to a process, specifically the production, appropriation and distribution of the fruits of necessary and surplus labor.[3] In these terms, *farmers do not constitute a class*. Agricultural producers or farmers engage in a variety of class relations or processes. These include capitalism, independent or petty production, and, in some cases, feudalism.

My use of the class concept to describe agricultural production contradicts the image of the farmer depicted in song and story, as well as contemporary political rhetoric. This "farmer" wears overalls; he has sun and wind-burned skin and calloused hands. He (not she) owns pigs, goats, cows, chickens, and so forth. He grows everything—cabbage, carrots, corn, wheat, green beans, and potatoes. *This* is a farmer. This is the American freeholder, backbone of the republic, personification of fundamental American values! On closer inspection, however, we see that this image overlays several conflicting realities.

Former President Jimmy Carter liked to call himself a farmer. Former Secretary of Agriculture John Block fancied himself a "hog farmer." Yet these "farmers" did not engage in direct production on a daily basis. The appellation obviously is used to obscure clear differences in the circumstances among all farms, particularly in relation to debates over federal farm policy. After all, if all farmers "are in the same boat," then what is good for one farmer is good for all. Farm policies favored by one farmer must benefit all farmers. The use of the title "farmer" by such people as John Block is much like the use of the title "producer" by nineteenth-century captains of industry to describe their activities in manufacture. If they are the producers, then who are the workers? The Jimmy Carters and John Blocks are engaged in forms of capitalist farming and/or various agribusiness operations. As we later see, the needs and interests of the capitalist class process and the agribusiness processing and merchanting firms are not necessarily consistent with those of petty (direct) production. Furthermore, the needs of all those farmers engaged in the capitalist class process do not necessarily coincide.

Agribusinesses engage in various activities such as food processing, storage or marketing, which I call *subsumed class activities*. By this I mean a process or activity that is not direct production of food, clothing, or shelter but is a necessary task or service related to that production, in the context of given social relations. Persons engaged in subsumed class processes receive a portion of the surplus that has already been appropriated through the fundamental class processes (those processes that involve direct production, i.e., capitalism or feudalism).

Most of the farm units that are having difficulties today are engaged in some combination of independent or petty production and capitalism at the same time. Indeed, the contradictory needs of these two separate class processes go a long way toward explaining some of these farmers' problems.

Most of the farmers facing foreclosure are engaged in petty production. That is, they have first claim on the surplus they have produced. They are engaged in direct labor, themselves, on their own land (or, in some cases, on rented or leased land), with their own tools, animals, buildings, machines, and so on. They produce one or two cash crops to sell (unlike their forefathers, who began with self-sufficient farming and moved on to a more diversified form of market production than that of today). Their revenues may cover their costs of production and their family needs for food, clothing, and shelter. Any revenues over this amount are surplus, and the petty producer has first claim on these revenues. One purpose of this kind of farming operation is to produce enough to survive and perhaps to expand. Petty production in U.S. agriculture, from the colonial era to the early twentieth century, also supported a particular "way of life," a regional culture. It was a simple life on the land, and the petty producing and largely self-sufficient families had some control over their own destiny. This reflected their ownership and/or control of the resources of production and their ability to claim the surplus they produced.

The family farmer who engages in petty production may simultaneously participate in the capitalist class process. This means that the farmer, usually the owner of the land, hires workers to engage in various forms of agricultural labor alongside him (or her) on the farm. (A farmer who does not participate in direct production is exclusively engaged in capitalism.) A portion of the fruits of these wage workers' labor (i.e., the surplus) is appropriated by the farmer *cum* capitalist. The surplus here takes the form of profit.

Capitalist production, whether in agriculture or manufacture, is guided by profit maximization and the competitive dynamic that requires constant expansion and reorganization. Farmers engaged in independent production began to hire wage workers because they responded to market signals and government pressures to expand their holdings of land and machines. As I have indicated, the seasonal nature of agriculture coupled with competitive pressures cause the capitalist/petty producer to incur large debts.[4] This increases the costs of production and thus the risks. Sometimes such a gamble leads to great profits. At other times, when revenues are insufficient to cover costs, the farmer risks losing ownership or access to the land, the *sine qua non* of independent production in agriculture. This is the basis for the conflict between the needs and tendencies of petty production versus capitalism in agriculture. The petty producers' claim on the surplus and their very survival depends on their continued ownership and/or control over the resources of production. But simultaneous participation in capitalism for these producers often necessitates competitive gambles that can jeopardize this condition.

The tension between the process of petty production and the capitalist class process (implied by my conceptual interpretation) supplements the previous discussion of the background of the crisis. Furthermore, it might help clarify observed trends in recent statistics on the agricultural sector as follows.

Agricultural statistics for 1900–1970 show a few clear trends. During that period, the percentage of the labor force in agriculture declined from 41 percent to 3.5 percent (U.S. Department of Commerce 1975, 126–127). The total number of farms decreased, while the average acreage per farm increased. Between 1970 and 1980, these trends intensified, and the tendency toward concentration has become even more apparent. For example, during this period there were enormous increases in the number of farms that had annual gross sales exceeding $40,000, with the largest percentage increase among those with annual gross sales above $500,000; the number of farms with less than $40,000 annual gross sales dropped sharply (Belden 1986, 24–25).

The discussion in the previous section also explained the many pressures existing in the 1970s and early 1980s that encouraged farm owners to expand acreage and attempt to produce and sell more commodities, largely through borrowing. By 1985, agricultural areas where debt levels were highest included huge sections of Iowa, Nebraska, North Dakota, South Dakota, Minnesota, and Wisconsin (Spencer 1986, 442)—much of the grain belt. These were precisely the areas where government and private banks encouraged expansion. Grain accounts for at least 50 percent of all agricultural exports. By expanding, through debt, to grow more grain, these farms increased the possibility that they would be jeopardized.

Finally, even the elusive figures on agricultural labor indicate a trend toward concentration and increased wage-labor usage over the past ten to twenty years. (Statistics on wage labor in agriculture are hard to collect because large numbers of migrant workers are "undocumented.") It is important to note that the states with the largest expenditures on agricultural wage labor are not in the grain belt (where the farm crisis is most severe). This is because of the high degree of mechanization possible in grain cultivation. Over the past fifteen years, the largest expenditures on wage labor have been in California, Florida, Texas (Belden 1986, 48), North Carolina, and Washington (Vogeler 1981, 229). In these states, workers are employed in the more labor-intensive process of fruit, vegetable, tree, and cotton harvesting, as well as tending to animals on dairy, poultry, or egg farms. In fact, the U.S. Agricultural Census shows that those farms that produce grain were the only ones to hire less labor in 1979 than in 1974! Wage labor increased in all other crops discussed (Holland and Carvalho 1988, 18).

A significant percentage of agricultural wage labor (perhaps more than 35 percent) is used by the largest 2 percent of all farms, that is, farms with annual gross sales over $250,000 and in most cases over $500,000 (Belden 1986, 48). These are, for example, the large fruit orchards and vineyards of California, Washington, and Florida. Although, as I have indicated, agriculture is highly concentrated today, many of these large farms (i.e., those with over 1000 acres in cultivation and/or $250,000 in gross sales) are not held by agribusiness processing corporations such as Cargil, Dole, or Ralston Purina. In most instances, these large farms are family corporations that originated as "family farms" in the Midwest or as larger units in the Far West (MacLennen and Walker 1980, 31). These farmers are the temporary victors in the capitalist competitive tournament of the past fifty years. As in most tournaments, everyone cannot be a winner, and last year's winners must meet this year's challengers.

Some Implications of Theory

Competitive pressures in the 1970s and earlier propelled many farmers initially engaged in market-oriented petty production to expand acreage, hire workers, and acquire huge debts—that is, to engage in capitalist production. This group of decisions "set farmers up." The greater their dependence on the market, their crop specialization, their expenditures on costly and harmful pesticides and chemical fertilizers, the more debt incurred and the higher the risk of failure. As the figures indicate, the very process of capitalist competition in agriculture generated its opposite—a high degree of concentration of agricultural holdings. As farmers engaged in petty production *and* capitalism, they attempted to expand their level of market production and thus jeopardized the very basis of their existence.

Perhaps these nascent capitalists should take their cues from the large agribusinesses that echew the risks of farming. That is precisely why agribusinesses contract out.

This analysis suggests that the exclusive dependence on market imperatives by agricultural producers is dangerous. It is dangerous to farmers because it increases their risk of bankruptcy. But it is dangerous to the U.S. population as well. In order to maximize profits, agribusinesses demand that contract farmers resort to harmful practices (e.g., keep chickens under twenty-four hours of light in cramped quarters or use land so intensively that it leads to soil erosion). Even if they are not bound by a contract, farmers who are totally specialized after years of competition often sacrifice healthful growing practices for a guaranteed maximum yield at the right moment.

My analysis suggests that along with market forces, oligopsonistic agribusinesses, federal government policies, and the hazards of nature, the decisions of individual farmers to expand helped create the crisis that is now destroying them. Rural activists who agree with this understanding (and many do) have been developing political campaigns that focus on government agencies at the state and federal levels, and on the values and ideas that guide decision making on individual farms.

Solutions: New Ideas and Political Activism in Farm Country

Rural activists have responded to the farm crisis in a number of ways. On the one hand, a significant amount of energy has been devoted to immediate relief and the prevention of further concentration of farmland. This effort includes demands for a moratorium on foreclosures, an increase in federal assistance to the Farm Credit System, federally mandated and/or voluntary supply management (of agricultural products), as well as counseling and support for families facing the direct results of the crisis—depression, suicide, divorce, and poverty. Many groups on the local, state, and national levels are engaged in such activities.

Simultaneously, other groups are more research oriented, paving the way for the future—developing a blueprint for "sustainable agriculture." By this term they mean the kind of food production that sustains (rather than destroys) the soil, the genetic variety within species, the water supply, and similar environmental factors of food production. Among other things, they are engaged in experiments involving organic farming, the formation of land trusts to preserve farmland,[5] the passage of statewide laws that limit corporate monopolization of farmland, and the development of legal/financial devices that would preserve the family farm. They are shaping a new vision and at the same time actively working to put the foundation pieces of a new agriculture in place.

Federal Farm Policy and Activist Organizations

State and federal governments have been involved in the "farm economy" for a long time. Specific policies aimed at protecting farm prices and limiting production levels came out of the New Deal and the attempt to aid smaller farmers. These policies were drafted in an attempt to guarantee parity between urban and rural products. For example, if the costs of products that rural producers must buy increased by 10 percent, the prices they received for their commodities should have increased by this amount as well. In this way, the standard of living for rural producers could be maintained. Also, at that time, new governmental institutions charged with providing cheap credit, such as the Farmers Home Administration, were created.

In the conservative political climate of the 1950s, the farm programs of the New Deal, especially those concerned with supply management, were attacked as "bolshevik" or "socialist market planning" and were virtually dismantled ("Crisis in Agriculture" 1988, 23). This led to a period in which huge surpluses often pushed commodity prices down significantly. The low commodity prices benefited the agribusiness merchants and processing companies, and were especially profitable for the international grain merchants, who could undercut overseas competitors. But the producers of the commodity, the midwestern grain farmers, suffered from both the unpredictability of the market price and its general decline. In the late 1960s and 1970s the federal government aided farmers by paying them a subsidy, that is, an amount to close the gap between the price floor (or loan rate,[6] the price paid to farmers by agribusiness) and the "target price," calculated to reflect the average cost of producing a particular crop. Thus, federal policy satisfied the needs of the grain merchants and grain producers at the expense of the "taxpayer."

The laws related to agriculture today include supports for family farms as well as outright giveaways to particular commodity producers. They reflect not only the vision of the New Deal era but the strength of various lobbies, such as the American Dairy Association, along with more recently formed rural people's coalitions such as the League of Rural Voters or the National Save the Family Farm Coalition. Thus, after decades of congressional logrolling, lobbying, loud protests, and tractorcades, the resulting legislation is a hodgepodge of contradictory programs. The most recent pressures on Congress and on state legislatures come from these same groups and reflect the many and conflicting needs and interests within agricultural production and processing.

Rural activists have formed many local and statewide organizations in areas where the agricultural crisis is felt most severely. Some, discussed in this paper, have been largely successful in combining the service function with broad political activism. They include the North American Farm Alliance (NAFA) headquartered in Iowa; Groundswell in Minnesota; Women Involved in Farm Economics (WIFE): Prairie Fire/Rural Action in Iowa; the Farm Unity Coalitions of Iowa, Michigan, and Wisconsin; the Farm Alliance of Rural Missouri and Illinois; and the Center for Rural Affairs in Walthill, Nebraska.

The NAFA is a coalition of U.S. and Canadian farm groups that attempts to build bridges with labor unions, peace groups, and other progressive forces. Members explain the farm crisis as one that affects urban consumers as well as farmers. On the local level, they provide a farm crisis hotline and legal referrals, as well as an informational clearinghouse and speakers' bureau. Their national agenda includes a return to parity pricing (through federally sponsored cost-of-production price floors), a serious supply management program, and a program for soil and water conservation. These ideas are widely supported by the groups and coalitions discussed here. They were incorporated into the 1985 Farm Policy Reform bill, which was not enacted. Instead, the Reagan administration passed the so-called Food Security Act of 1985, which, although it included a strong conservation provision, caused significant reductions in price floors and in subsidy payments to medium-sized (family) farms. Many of the provisions of the progressive but unsuccessful 1985 legislation have been incorporated into a Save the Family Farm bill, introduced by Senator Tom Harkin and Representative Richard Gephardt. Portions of this bill were finally passed as part of the omnibus Farm Spending Act (HR 1425) in 1988.

Prairie Fire/Rural Action, based in Iowa, is an interesting and multifaceted group. It is a resource and training center for farm advocates across the nation. In Iowa the group helped to pass a limited farm foreclosure moratorium law in 1985 and to establish the Iowa Farmer–Creditor Mediation Service, along with legislation that requires mediation before foreclosure. The group has organized an active crisis hotline and a series of Farm Unity Survival Committees throughout the state. They have also used their resources to oppose racist and anti-Semitic groups that have attempted to organize distressed farmers based on simplistic explanations of the crisis. Prairie Fire is an active member of the Iowa Farm Unity Coalition, which includes farm groups as well as church groups, and the populist Iowa Citizen Action Network.

The Center for Rural Affairs in Nebraska has developed a unique combination of activism and research. It has organized a successful campaign to limit corporate farming in Nebraska. Through a 1982 law, which required a state constitutional amendment, both corporate landownership and farm operation were limited (Strange 1988b, 5). The center devotes many of its resources to research that deals with environmental conservation, land stewardship, and the technology necessary to sustain small-scale agriculture through the twenty-first century. We look briefly at some of the center's ideas through the work of one of its co-directors, Martin Strange, in the next section.

On the national level, many agricultural coalitions have developed. They include the American Agricultural Movement (this group organized the tractorcades of the 1970s in Washington, D.C.), the Working Group on Farm and Food Policy, the Rural Coalition, the League of Rural Voters, and the National Save the Family Farm Coalition.[7] These groups have coalesced to create a permanent presence in the nation's capital. But these groups are also concerned with various kinds of federal legislation, such as tax policy or trade policy, that could have significant effects on rural life, along with farm policy.

From the perspective of a political or economic conservative, all these proposals simply constitute unwarranted interference in the operation of the market. The conservative argument describes the agricultural crisis as a "shaking out" of farms that made poor business decisions or that lack the capital to use the latest technology.[8] While the above is an abbreviated version of the conservative "small government is good government" argument, it makes the basic points, all of which can be readily refuted.

First, the farms that are in trouble today are not facing foreclosure because they are "inefficient." Research by private economists and the U.S. Department of Agriculture has suggested that smaller farms are no less productive per acre than their larger corporate competition (Kline 1981). They simply lack the market power and the financial and other advantages of larger farms. For example, as former Secretary of Agriculture Robert Bergland pointed out in a much heralded 1978 report, "A Time to Choose," federal policies tend to help larger farms more than small farms. In 1978, 3 percent of all farms received 46 percent of the benefits paid by federal farm programs (Kline 1981). In other words, the more land a farm has, the more it can get paid not to grow a particular crop or the more it can benefit from specific price supports. The subsidies received by larger farms in the recent past have been enormous and have been the subject of much public discussion (Robbins 1987a).

The very agricultural interests that sometimes call for a "free market" approach, such as the American Farm Bureau Federation or international grain merchants, have no philosophical compunction about reaping the benefits that government tax policy bestows in the form of "tax farming"[9] or trade policy.

Future Directions for a New Agriculture

In tandem with efforts to address the immediate problems of foreclosed farm families, diverse groups of rural activists are looking at agriculture for the long run. These agricultural "rebels" are numerous, and their pursuits are crucial. They do not always speak with one voice, although they have certain characteristics in common. All recognize that the rules, values, or rhythms guiding agricultural production and decision making must be other than competitive market requisites. Some emphasize loosely defined laws of nature; others, religious or spiritual assumptions; and still others, decidedly anticapitalist economic values. Obviously, these categories are not mutually exclusive.

Farming methods have received a great deal of attention from research institutes such as the Rodale Center in Maxatwany, Pennsylvania, and the Land Institute in Salinas, Kansas. The Rodale Institute studies current food production throughout the United States as well as various methods of organic or regenerative agriculture. Regenerative farming attempts to renew soil productivity and guard against erosion through such methods as systematic crop rotation, including a nitrogenous legume cycle, and the use of organic (rather than chemical) soil additives. These alternative methods help break the dependence of farms on toxic and expensive supplies and the corporations that produce them. The organic, or regenerative, approach has gained many adherents in the past decade. "In 1986, the U.S. Department of Agriculture estimated that 30,000 of the nation's 22 million farms now use some regenerative techniques" (Schneider, Russell, and Weyrich 1986, 106).

The critique of current agricultural practices lodged by the organic farming movement has further implications. In the United States today, a significant portion of the fruits and vegetables eaten in one place have been grown hundreds, perhaps thousands, of miles away. Transportation costs are high, and nutrient losses are also high during periods of transportation and storage. Thus, many adherents of regenerative agriculture encourage the local production of foodstuffs (see, e.g., Berry 1985–1986; "Everything in Its Place," 1987).

Wes Jackson, a plant geneticist and a founder and co-director of the Land Institute, presents an even more profound critique of current farming practices than the "organic farming movement." He is engaged in research that challenges the most basic assumption of modern agriculture: tillage of the soil. He believes that current techniques of cultivation destroy natural resources and involve unnecessary expenditures of energy. Jackson posits a model of agriculture close to "gathering." "What he's after is a sort of domesticated, super productive wild meadow: a pasture that performs like a wheat field" (MacFadyen 1984, 182). Jackson is therefore engaged in research that might produce herbaceous perennial seed-bearing polyculture. This is a plant that can grow freely without active cultivation and that has the same nutrient characteristics as such staples as wheat, rice, and corn. The discovery of such a seed could have revolutionary implications; it might challenge the need for farming as we now know it.

Advocates of sustainable agriculture recognize the need for state and federal policy intervention to support their efforts. One such researcher–activist is Martin Strange, co-founder and co-director of the Center for Rural Affairs in Nebraska.[10]

To support the development and survival of family farms in the face of market forces that require expansion, Strange suggests a series of policies that would end subsidies to capital, that is, decisions that substitute machines for labor. For example, he opposes all tax policies that support tax-loss farming or that allow "farm corporations to deduct salaries and benefits paid to major stockholders" from taxable income (Strange 1988, 263).

Strange, along with other progressive agricultural organizers, agrees with conservative critics that many of the current price support and commodity programs are wasteful and contradictory. Unlike the conservatives, however, he proposes a supply management program that benefits farmers, not farm acreage, and that rewards farmers for the quality of their farming practice (such as diversification), rather than for the quantity of commodities they produce. For example, he suggests a series of federally sponsored, mandatory, nontransferable production quotas that would be allocated to producers based on need, not on previous yield history.

Strange also recommends state and federal initiatives that would block further concentration of agricultural land in a few hands. For example, he suggests that more states pass laws that restrict corporate farming (as Nebraska and other states have done). Adjustments in state property tax laws toward greater progressivity and federal taxes on inherited wealth in land might also discourage concentration.

Finally, Strange is among those who question the direction of agricultural research, especially in publicly funded institutions. He maintains that much research (often jointly supported by private agencies such as agribusinesses or chemical companies) is done to expand the high-tech, capital-intensive approach to agriculture. This investment of human energy and public funds does little to assist family farms and/or sustainable agriculture. Therefore, he suggests greater public accountability on the part of agricultural universities, as well as the earmarking to the needs of family farms. This issue has received much attention recently.

In 1987 the Center for Low Input Agriculture was established by the U.S. Department of Agriculture with monies from the 1985 farm bill. This center has funded grants in a few regions of the country to explore various sustainable or low-input methods (Forster 1988, 26). Also, in 1988 in California, where large farms predominate, a judge determined that the publicly funded agricultural research and experimental stations did not do enough to support the needs of small farms and thus violated the Hatch Act of 1887 (Levine, 1988, 9). Judge Raymond March ordered the University of California to devise a plan that would meet the needs of the state's smaller farms.

Thus the issue at this stage of the game, for rural activists, is not whether governmental policies are needed, but what governmental policies ought to be demanded. Given the complex nature of the economy and the agricultural system, federal and state governments are the only agencies with the resources and powers necessary to address some of the problems associated with the farm crisis, through tools such as tax policy, credit policy, production control, and soil conservation. The ideas and decisions of individual farmers and farm communities are crucial here as well.

The preservation of the middle-sized (family) farm is of more than sentimental significance. Its survival offers the possibility for developing new, nontoxic, noncorporate/capital intensive methods of producing food—as long as there is sufficient government support so that farmers do not have to respond only to market imperatives. Here, however, the identity of the middle-sized farmer as a "self-made man," an entrepreneur, and an independent comes into conflict with the realities of agricultural production in an advanced capitalist society. The policies needed to change the future of American agriculture (both for the farmer and the consumer) run directly counter to generally accepted principles that are identified with basic American freedoms. The unrestricted freedom to buy and sell land (as a resource of production) based on market price rather than considerations of social utility, the primacy of the market in determining input costs and product prices, and the identification of "efficiency" with the bottom line of the business ledger serve to increase and consolidate the power of the multinational corporations that control so much of contemporary American agriculture.

There are several implications of the foregoing analysis of the farm crisis for rural community organizing. Like the housing crisis, the farm crisis arises, in part, out of the normal functioning of capitalism. Exacerbated at times by international events or federal policies, the crisis experienced at the level of the community—farm foreclosures and dying rural towns—is part of the structure of national, even global, economic trends toward a concentration of capital. Unlike the housing crisis, however, the problems faced by owners of middle-sized farms and their communities are problems of production, not of collective consumption. Although historically the United States has accepted at least some degree of social democratic welfare state policymaking with respect to collective consumption, the production arena is hedged with an ideological minefield. Governmental involvement in agricultural production has been confined to counterbalancing unfavorable market conditions or using agricultural surpluses as part of international trade policy. As pointed out in this essay, even these policies have been considered dangerously "bolshevik" during reactionary times. Thus the task of organizing in rural communities on the basis of agricultural issues involves serious ideological conflicts that cannot be wished away.

On the positive side, the issues confronting rural organizers today are issues that touch everyone; they are no longer purely agricultural issues. The late-nineteenth-century Populists failed to persuade urban workers that the dream of a republic of smallholders offered solutions to the problems of industrial life, but today the problems of agriculture are tied to environmental issues that concern all of us. In this respect, 1988 was an important year: People recognized the environmental destruction created by human misuse of soil, water, and air as the dumping of wastes into the ocean closed many beaches on the Atlantic coast; the ozone layer that protects our planet from excessive exposure to the sun's ultraviolet rays was pierced, scientists believe by certain chemicals and the buildup of carbon dioxide wastes; and much publicity surrounded explanations of the dangers of food "enhancers," such as alar in apples. Large segments of the population, not just the usual environmental organizations, began to experience the effects of technological decisions that did not take the future into account. To the extent that this growing awareness is applied to agricultural production, new links may be forged between the experience of the rural community, the experience of the urban consumer, and the structures that connect their respective grievances.

Notes

1. The sources are many and the number vary. Kline (1981) has suggested that since 1950, an average of 2000 farms have been lost each week. The National Agricultural Statistics Service for 1985 has estimated that approximately 117 farms a day, or 819 a week, have gone under. (The latter figures are taken from Prairiefire's 1987 report.)

2. Market contracts stipulate the type of commodities that must be produced while production contracts indicate conditions which must be met in the process of raising the commodity. For more discussion of contract farming, see Vogeler (1981) and Wilson (1986).

3. I rely here on the class concepts developed by Stephen Resnick and Richard Wolff (1987).

4. The figures on farm debt are astonishing. For example, in February 1986, the *New York Times* reported that the Farmers Home Administration had begun to notify 65,000 farmers that they must restructure or renegotiate their loan payments or face foreclosure. This agency is trying to recover $568 billion in delinquent loans.

5. For further explanation of this legal mechanism, see Gerard and Johnson

(1984, 126–134) and MacFadyen (1984, 122–143). A land trust is a legal mechanism that breaks down landownership rights into parts (i.e., the right to clear the land, the right to build on the land, etc.). A conservation-oriented land trust in effect buys the owners' right of certain types of development, thereby preventing any future owners of the land from exercising this portion of the ownership package. For example, land trusts can be structured so that the land in question is used only for agriculture.

6. The loan rate is the amount of money a farm can receive for a specific commodity that it stores in a government-approved storage facility. At the end of the loan period, the farmer can repay the principal and interest and retrieve the commodity or can give it up in exchange for the loan. The loan rate is set below the market price by the Federal Commodity Credit Corporation.

7. Each of these coalitions includes a broad scope of farm organizations, activist research organizations, denominational and interfaith action committees, civic groups, and individuals. The Working Group on Farm and Food Policy produced a very thoughtful and provocative report called "Beyond Crisis: Farm and Food Policy for Tomorrow."

8. For a clearly presented conservative analysis of the farm crisis, see Worth (1985, 128–132) or, among his other writings, Bovard (1988).

9. For a detailed explanation of this phenomenon, see Vogeler (1981, 147–161). In his words, "Tax loss farming—or how to lose at farming and still make a profit, is one source of federal subsidy to corporations and wealthy urban investors. Rather than work the land a hazardous business in the best of years, they milk the tax laws . . . [the idea is to] lose money in farming and write those paper losses off against real non-farm income."

10. For a more extensive analysis, see Strange (1988a).

References

"Ag Banks Seek a Bailout." 1986. *Dollars and Sense*, January–February.
"Amber Wave of Grain." 1982. *Dollars and Sense*, September.
Belden, Joseph. 1986. *Dirt Rich, Dirt Poor: America's Food and Farm Crisis*. New York: Routledge and Kegan Paul.
Berry, Thomas. 1985–1986. "Wonderworld as Wasteworld: The Earth in Deficit." *Cross Currents*. Winter.
Berry, Wendell. 1983. *The Unsettling of America: Culture and Agriculture*. San Francisco: Sierra Club Books.
"Big Farms to Get Huge U.S. Subsidies." 1986. *New York Times*, July 27.
Breimyer, Harold F. 1982. "Agriculture, Return of the Thirties?" *Challenge*, July–August, 334–340.

Bovard, Joel. 1985. "The Fat of the Land: What Is the Farm Crisis?" *Policy Review*, no. 32 (Spring).

———. 1988. "Buying Off the Farm." *New York Times*, August 14.

Burbach, Roger, and Patricia Flynn. 1980. *Agribusiness in the Americas*. New York: Monthly Review Press.

Comstock, Gary, ed. 1987. *Is There a Moral Obligation to Save the Family Farm?* Ames: Iowa State University Press.

Congressional Quarterly. 1984. *Farm Policy: The Politics of Soil Surpluses and Subsidies*. Washington, D.C.: CQ Press.

"Crisis in Agriculture." 1988. *Multinational Monitor* 10, nos. 7–8 (July–August).

"Debt Crisis in Agriculture: Reagan's Policies Hit Below the Corn Belt." 1985. *Dollars and Sense*, May.

Dennison, Mike. 1985. "The Grain Shippers Role in the Farm Crisis," *In These Times*, March, 20–26.

"Everything in Its Place: The Bioregional Approach to Decision Making." 1987. *New Internationalist*, May.

"Farm Population Lowest Since 1850s." 1988. *New York Times*, July 20.

Forster, Thomas. 1988. "Sustainable Agriculture and Food Production: Finding an Oasis in Time of Drought." *Food Monitor*, nos. 4–5 (Fall): 24–27, 38.

Fox, Michael. 1986. *Agricide: The Hidden Crisis That Affects Us All*. New York: Schocken Books.

Gates, Paul. 1960. *The Farmer's Last Frontier: Agriculture, 1815–1860*. New York: Holt, Rinehart and Winston.

Gerard, Jennie, and Sharon Johnson. 1984. "Sunshine Agriculture and Land Trusts." In *Meeting the Expectations of the Land*, edited by Wes Jackson, Wendell Berry, and Bruce Colman. San Francisco: North Point Press.

Hady, Thomas F. 1987. "Is There a Farm Crisis?" *Journal of Economic Education* 18, no. 4 (Fall): 409–420.

Handlin, Oscar, and Mary Flug Handlin. 1969. *Commonwealth*. Cambridge, Mass.: Belknap Press.

Hicks, J. D. 1961. *The Populist Revolt*. Lincoln: University of Nebraska Press.

Holland, David, and Joe Carvalho. 1985. "The Changing Mode of Production of American Agriculture." *Review of Radical Political Economy* 17, no. 4 (Winter): 1–27.

Hurley, Judith. 1986. "U.S. Farmers and the Third World," *Fellowship* 52, nos. 4–5 (April/May): 18–21.

Jackson, Wes, Wendell Berry, and Bruce Colman. 1984. *Meeting the Expectations of the Land: Essays in Sustainable Agriculture and Stewardship*. San Francisco: North Point Press.

Kline, David. 1981. "The Embattled Independent Farmer." *New York Times Magazine*, November 29.

Lappe, Frances Moore, and Joseph Collins. 1978. *Food First, Beyond the Myth of Scarcity*. New York: Ballantine Books.

————. 1983. "Trading the Future," *Food Monitor*, no. 34. (July/August): 16–20.

Levine, Howard. 1988. "Small Farmers Win One in the Halls of Congress and Win in a California Court." *In These Times*, February 3–9.

Lewontin, R. C., and Jean-Pierre Berlan. 1986. "Technology, Research and the Penetration of Capital: The Case of U.S. Agriculture." *Monthly Review* 38, no. 3 (July–August): 35–47.

MacFadyen, J. Tevere. 1984. *Gaining Ground: The Renewal of America's Small Farms*. New York: Ballantine.

MacLennan, Carol and Richard Walker. 1980. "Crisis in U.S. Agriculture: An Overview," In *Agribusiness in the Americas*, edited by Roger Burbach and Patricia Flynn, 20–40. New York: Monthly Review Press.

Merrill, Richard. 1976. *Radical Agriculture*. New York: Harper Colophon.

Moberg, David. 1986. "The Reagan Administration's Farm Policy Comes a Cropper." *In These Times*, January, 22–28.

————. 1988. "Should We Save the Family Farm?" *Dissent*, Spring, 201–211.

Morgan, Dan. 1980. *Merchants of Grain*. New York: Penguin.

Perelman, Michael. 1977. *Farming for Profit in a Hungry World*. Totowa, N.J.: Aljanheld, Osmun.

Prairiefire. 1987. "The Continuing Crisis in Rural America: Fact vs. Fiction," A Prairiefire research report, May.

Resnick, Stephen, and Richard Wolff. 1987. *Knowledge and Class: A Marxian Critique of Political Economy*. Chicago: University of Chicago Press.

Reynolds, Maura. (1988). "Jewish Groups Examine Farm Crisis," *New York Times*, February 29.

Robbins, William 1985. "Farm Crisis Endangering Rural Towns." *New York Times*, October 14.

————. 1987a. "Limits on Subsidies to Big Farms Go Awry, Sending Costs Climbing." *New York Times*, June 15.

————. 1987. "No End in Sight for Annual Harvest of Debt." *New York Times*, January 4.

————. 1988. "American Farm Crisis: The Weather, Economic and Otherwise, Is Improving." *New York Times*, February 14.

Russonello, John. 1985. "Farm and Food Policy in Congress: An Update." *Minimonitor 2*, no. 3 (Summer).

Schwab, Jim. 1985. "The Shaky Farm Credit System." *Nation* 240, no. 18 (May 11).

Schneider, Keith. 1987. "Economics, Hate and the Farm Crisis." *New York Times*, December 7.

————. 1987. "Farming without Chemicals: Age-Old Technologies Become State of Art." *New York Times*, August 23.

Schneider, Keith, Dick Russell and Noel Weyrich. 1986. "Is Organic Agriculture a Solution to the Farm Crisis?" *Utne Reader*, October/November.

Spencer, Milton. 1986. *Contemporary Economics* New York: Worth.

Strange, Martin (1988a). *Family Farming: A New Economic Vision*. Lincoln: University of Nebraska Press, and San Francisco: Institute for Food and Development Policy.

————. 1988b. "Family Farming: Faded Memory or Future Hope?" Food First Action Alert, San Francisco.

————. 1989. *Family Farming: Conflict and Hope in American Agriculture*. Lincoln: University of Nebraska Press, and San Francisco: Institute for Food and Development Policy.

U.S. Department of Commerce, Bureau of the Census. 1975. *Historical Statistics of the United States: Colonial Times to 1970*. Series D 11–23. Pt. 1. Washington, D.C.: GPO.

"U.S. Farmers in Struggle." 1983. *Food Monitor*, no. 31 (January/February).

Vogeler, Ingolf. 1981. *The Myth of the Family Farm: Agribusiness Dominance of U.S. Agriculture*. Boulder, Colo: Westview.

Wessel, James with Mort Hantman. 1983. *Trading the Future*. San Francisco: Institute for Food and Development Policy.

Wilson, John. 1986. "The Political Economy of Contract Farming," *Review of Radical Political Economy* 18, no. 4 (Winter): 47–70.

Worthy, Ford S. 1985. "Getting Uncle Sam Off the Farm." *Fortune*. March 8.

Young, John A. and Jan M. Newton. 1980. *Capitalism and Human Obsolescence: Corporate Control vs. Individual Survival in Rural America*. Montclair, N.J.: Allanheld and Osmun.

CHAPTER 8

Two Roads Left

Strategies of Resistance to Plant Closings in the Monongahela Valley

**Sidney Plotkin
and William E. Scheuerman**

Capitalism, wrote Joseph Schumpeter, is a "process of creative destruction" (Schumpeter 1947, 81–86). Expanding unevenly and violently, it can hurl once mighty industries and great cities aside as if they were cardboard empires. But for all the disruption it brings in its wake, capitalist development has no rationale for resistance. On the contrary, the market esteems dynamism as progress and its celebrants excoriate those who would stand in the way. In George Gilder's words, people who oppose economic progress are "faithless and shortsighted"; they form "the prime obstacle to the survival of civilization" (Gilder 1981, 279). In one sense, Karl Marx's view was not altogether different from Gilder's. In the *Communist Manifesto* both he and Engels lambasted segments of labor that fought only to protect themselves and their jobs from the inevitable modernization of capital (Marx and Engels 1948). The great socialist challenge was to advance the struggle for a new society, not to waste precious energy struggling to preserve moribund technologies.

This paper examines the efforts of people who refuse to accept the logic of capitalist modernization and the massive social disruptions that accompany rapid economic change. It examines political opposition to the virtual shutdown of the steel industry in the Monongahela Valley of western Pennsylvania in the early 1980s.

Fundamentally, we recognize that the decline of steel in the Mon Valley, as its residents call it, represents one piece of a more general crisis of disaccumulation and restructuring in international capitalism (Scheuerman

1986). Looked at in relation to this global context, the act of opposing plant shutdowns in the Mon Valley, or anywhere else for that matter, holds little promise of success. But we also believe that workers and citizens do not have free choices about the scale and scope of possible political action. They are socially and historically bound to the community and industry in which they must produce to exist. Their fight, if they are to make one, must, at least initially, take place locally against the companies, policies, and executives they know, aided by the unions, community groups, and political resources they have traditionally employed to defend their interests. This essay, then, does not focus on the question of the viability of local resistance as a rational strategy for social change. Instead, it examines the kinds of local actions that actually manifest themselves in the immediate circumstances: the goals and strategies selected; the steps taken, and their effectiveness. [1] In short, this essay examines the dilemmas inherent in any course of action taken by community organizers and organizations. At bottom, we want to explore what possibilities, if any, the chosen strategies open for the achievement of intermediate objectives, objectives whose realization might lay a base for the continuity and expansion of organization and, ultimately, for progress and liberation in the forms of community life.

Activists and workers in the Mon Valley have tried to engage the process of disinvestment, to examine it critically and to call it into question. Some in the valley argue that public pressure should be used to force the major remaining steel company—USX Corporation (formerly U.S. Steel)—to keep its steelmaking operations going. Others believe the corporate decision to abandon basic steel is irreversible; their goal is to create a new, publicly owned industrial base for the region, one built on the shards of the old nineteenth-century plants. Although the strategies and goals of the various opponents of disinvestment clash, they all reject the "natural" workings of the marketplace as the final arbiter of the region's future. Viewing capitalist logic as less than inherently rational, inevitable, or publicly beneficial, opponents of disinvestment believe that effective political action could change basic economic decisions. In examining the politics of resistance, how it came to take the forms that it did, and what it reflects about understandings of change and possibility in contemporary U.S. society, this paper looks at strategies of opposition to plant shutdowns in the Mon Valley, the paths that organizers and workers are attempting to chart in conflict with some of the region's biggest and most influential corporations. We focus on political goals and methods, on ideas of politics and political resistance as they developed in the course of local efforts to do something about vast economic dislocation. In the broadest sense, we wish to learn something about how people begin to change themselves, their values, and their goals as they confront gigantic disruptions in their lives and futures; about how they come to organize themselves to resist; and finally, about the nature of institutional responses to such opposition.

The first section of this essay places our concerns within the context of existing work on urban political movements. We identify and contrast different schools of thought in the literature of urban political sociology and relate these to conflicting estimations of the potential for radical social change. The second part offers a sketch of the decline of the U.S. steel industry and an empirical account of political resistance to plant shut-downs in the Mon Valley from 1983 to 1988. This section identifies two conflicting strategies of resistance—the "agitational" and "institutionalist" approaches—and examines their development and impact in the valley. The paper concludes with a brief reconsideration of the two roads left in relation to the literature on urban social change.

Theories of Resistance

The literature of urban political sociology has become increasingly con-cerned with questions of the organization and direction of radical urban movements. For purposes of this analysis, we identify three characteristic schools of thought that can help clarify the issues and implications of the kind of oppositional politics recently found in the Mon Valley. Each can be associated with a particular viewpoint on the radical potential of urban social change.

Possibility 1: The Inevitability of Defeat

Piven and Cloward's (1977) extended analysis of urban poor people's move-ments in the United States leads to the sorriest conclusions about the chances for urban radicalism. They argue that lower-class groups, led by large-scale militant organizations, have failed to transform society because the bureaucratic organizations formed to carry on the battles tend to obstruct the expansion of issues and conflict. Militant organizations, in their view, inevitably become hierarchical, rigid, and subject to penetration and cooptation by elites. As with Michels (1949), Piven and Cloward insist that radical political organizations tend to mimic the structure and behavior of the conservative organizations they seek to replace. But Piven and Cloward draw their conclusions as much from their working theory of power as from bureaucratic theory and their empirical evidence. For them, social power is an essentially ahistorical phenomenon. That is, they make universal claims about the organization of social power, independent of the particular historical character of the society they want to analyze. In their words, "the roots of power *in any society* . . . tend over time to be drawn together within one ruling class" whose control of the means of production and coercion become virtually insurmountable (Piven and Cloward 1977, 1; italics added). Accordingly, they conclude, the structures, institutions, and norms—in a word, the culture—of established society masks a vast organization of repression against the chances of liberationist change. Although the exploited may periodically rebel, the dominance of existing institutions and forms of life and the confinements of lower-class experience and education all limit any emerging resistance to the achievement, at best, of marginal economic benefits and petty symbols of political status. Indeed, Piven and Cloward see dominant power groups as sufficiently well organized and class conscious to absorb the most passionate dissent from below. By contrast, they see the underclass as politically unsophisticated and lacking the wherewithal to organize itself for sustained resistance. Not surprisingly, Piven and Cloward conclude that short bursts of spontaneous, militant, and passionate agitation offer the best—in fact, probably the only—chance for lower-class people to improve their lives at the margins.[2]

Possibility 2: Radical Enlightenment

A very different possibility is held out by more orthodox class analysis. In this view, localized economic conflicts are seen as structurally inseparable from the basic class relationships and contradictions of the larger social formation (Mingione 1981).[3] The dynamic of these contradictions is transformative: It contains the potential for the transcendence of the existing social order and its replacement by a classless society (Miliband 1977, 17). The prevailing ideology and political forms of a given society mediate and obscure the repressive nature of existing class relationships, as Piven and Cloward insist, often leading the exploited to fight in ways that do not challenge the nature of exploitation itself. But as long as the taproot of the oppressive experience lies in the basic class relations of the society, political resistance to the consequences of oppression can open the way to a more acute experience and understanding of the situation, especially when the experience is subject to a reflection that is urged and guided by theoretically and ideologically sensitive leaders (e.g., community organizers, union leaders, party workers) (Fisher 1984). In this analysis, local situations, however opaque, potentially serve as the basis, through critically informed action, for deeper probes and challenges to the system. Here, radical change of the class structure remains a difficult but winnable project, and there is no theoretical reason why it cannot begin with local action.

Possibility 3: The Urban Movement as a School for Change

Manuel Castells's analysis of urban movements offers a somewhat different, more clouded outlook on urban radicalism than either of the above models (Castells 1984). Unlike political scientists such as Piven and Cloward, Mollenkopf (1983), and Katznelson (1981), all of whom draw their dim conclusions about urban radicalism mainly from studies of 1960s'-brand participatory politics in the United States, Castells introduces a comparative, historical view of urban movements, studying examples in Europe and Latin America as well as the United States. For Castells, urban radicalism is indeed hemmed in by the power of prevailing structures and institutions. But this premise warrants neither the pessimism of Piven and Cloward nor the opposite belief that urban economic conflicts can be transformed into class struggle.

Although, like most Marxist urbanists, Castells sees the emergence of differentiated urban movements forming against the backdrop of global structural changes, he breaks with orthodox class analyses that situate the most important changes in the economy alone. To Castells, innovations in information and communication technology (culture) and state organization (politics) are equally critical to the shaping and dynamics of urban movements.

The variety of structural developments and pressures leads Castells to conclude that urban movements arise in resistance to what he understands as a triptych of major developments: the intensified commodification of cities by global capital; the increasingly obvious hegemony of cultural meaning and social understanding by the international mass media; and the administrative centralization of political power and policy by modern states. Obviously, such developments are hardly independent of one another. But, for Castells, the key point in analyzing urban radicalism is to note how these tendencies are experienced, not so much as a single massive systemic threat from above, but as more or less discrete institutional and cultural challenges to the capacity of urbanites to create meanings of their own out of the welter of urban life. The result, especially in the United States, is that isolated issues tend to be pursued by interest groups at the expense of challenges to the general social structure by broad-based class and community alliances (Castells 1984, 124). Following the lead of Marcuse a generation ago (1964), Castells attributes the containment of contemporary urban radicalism to the "absence of effective channels of social change" in advanced capitalist society, especially radical political parties. Urban radicals—economic, cultural, and political—fight their battles in the names of neighborhood, ethnicity, and community not because their local institutions are especially utopian, but because they lack any significant political vehicle for comprehending and challenging the main compulsions of capitalist, state, and cultural hegemony from above. In short, they lack an alternative mechanism, or *vehicle*, of social *struggle* and transformation. Although the vehicles to globalize and radicalize the issues and discourse of national politics do not now exist, Castells still believes that "urban movements do address the real issues of our time, although neither on the scale nor terms that are adequate to the task" (1984, 331). Refusing to foreclose possibilities, he argues that radical urban movements "are the organizational forms, the live schools, where the new social movements of our emerging society are taking place, growing up, learning to breathe." They are the agents "potentially capable of superseding these contradictions" (1984, 331).

Not surprisingly, perhaps, given his reliance on organic metaphors, Castells does not develop these ideas systematically. But his work is a reminder that urban oppositional politics can be a rich, multidimensional activity, one whose implications for change may hit at a number of sore spots in the structure of domination. Thus cultural and political battles that seem far away from central institutions might well turn out to have unexpectedly subversive implications. In the same vein, local attacks on economic power, which on the surface seem doomed from the start, may in fact contain illuminating lessons about how to mount further challenges to systemic power. Of course, Castells is careful to make no promises. The analysis of urban movements remains indeterminate insofar as it can make no *a priori* statements about the nature of any particular instance apart from an empirical analysis of the case.

With our three broad frameworks as backdrop, the following sections present a picture of the vast and rapid decline of the U.S. steel industry and the opposition it generated in the form of our two strategies of resistance, the agitational and institutionalist models.

The Great Steel Collapse

Stoked by the unceasing requirements of international warfare and aided by government's willingness to offer its helping hand, the U.S. steel industry emerged from World War II as the globe's most powerful producer, accounting for some 61 percent of world steel production (U.S. Congress, Senate Committee on Finance 1967; Scheuerman 1986). Nevertheless, in the late 1950s, when the United States became a net importer of steel, the first symptoms of a deadly sclerosis had appeared. Today the disease has run its course: The U.S. industry is in ruins. Plant closings reduced industry employment from a 1966 peak of nearly 550,000 workers to the current low of 185,000. The mighty U.S. Steel Corporation, once referred to as "the corporation," has become the more generic-sounding USX Corporation, and now threatens to pull out of steel operations all together. The nation's second-largest producer, LTV, the Wheeling-Pittsburgh, number six, have already gone bankrupt. Number three, Bethlehem Steel, and number five, Armco, teeter on the edge of default; and the fourth-biggest producer, Inland Steel, cannot raise its share of the capital to build a much needed cold rolling mill in conjunction with Japan's Nippon Steel.

The underlying causes of domestic steel's collapse represent a textbook case of the negative impact of private oligopoly on public community. Since its emergence as a concentrated industry at the end of the nineteenth century, the handful of large steel companies avoided the specter of overproduction, falling prices, and declining profits by controlling output and regulating prices (Adams 1977; Reich 1984). Private industrywide planning, established in the form of price leadership by U.S. Steel, enabled the steel giants to flourish, particularly in the decade and a half following World War II. During the first nine months of 1957, for example, U.S. Steel earned $18 after taxes on every ton of steel it shipped, almost three times more than it earned in 1941 (U.S. Congress, Office of Technology Assessment, 1980). But despite their high profits, the companies neither paid out handsome dividends to their shareholders nor invested in more modern and efficient plants and equipment. Instead, in anticipation of future steel shortages, domestic producers purchased new raw material holdings and financed a spate of mergers and joint subsidiaries with other steel companies. Indeed, a study by Daniel Fusfeld revealed that as of December 13, 1956, integrated steel firms, in various combinations, controlled fifty-three intra-industry joint-venture subsidiaries, as well as an additional seventeen in other industries (Fusfeld 1958). In short, by the mid 1950s the domestic steel industry was heavily oligopolistic, although the industry would continue to centralize for the next two decades.

The turning point for domestic steel producers came in 1959 when a lengthy (126 days) steel strike forced consumers to buy foreign steel. In 1959 (and ever since) the United States became a net importer of steel. Corporate officials responded to imported steel with allegations of unfair competition, a position initially rejected as a hoax by the United Steel Workers of America (USWA). But as imports consumed increasingly larger shares of the U.S. market, the steelworkers fell into line. By the mid 1960s integrated steel producers and the union had joined forces to become a formidable political force that lobbied Congress to pass import-quota legislation.

The corporate–labor coalition for protectionism failed because large free trade interests believed steel import quotas would trigger a damaging trade war. But the coalition's efforts were not in vain. In 1969 President Johnson cajoled Japanese and European producers to curtail steel shipments to the United States. The Voluntary Restraint Agreement (VRA) of 1969, renewed for an additional three years in 1972, allowed the Japanese and European producers to divide the U.S. market as part of an international steel cartel.

The steelworkers' union's decision to wage a protectionist battle with their corporate overlords had consequences that union leaders did not anticipate. Justified as a necessary respite to allow steel companies to modernize aging facilities, VRAs gave steelmakers the impetus to pull out of the steelmaking business. Immediately following the 1969 agreement, investment declined. Steel increased its diversification efforts, closed plants, and several major producers eventually went into bankruptcy.

From corporate perspectives, such investment decisions were matters of private business policy. They bore no public imprint and there was no case for public accountability. Yet the economic decisions of Big Steel had unmistakable social and political effects, and nowhere more graphically than in the Monongahela Valley of western Pennsylvania. The situation of U.S. Steel symbolizes the valley's plight. U.S. Steel's Duquesne mill, for instance, became the company's first facility to shut down totally, and whereas twenty years ago the corporation employed 50,000 steelworkers in the valley, today fewer than 5000 work for USX. Overall, unemployment in the Mon Valley is officially calculated at 9.5 percent, although a study sponsored by the Pittsburgh Catholic Diocese Task Force on Unemployment suggests that 17 percent of the workforce is jobless. Fully 55 percent of the region's household heads are out of work. Suicide rates are double the national average, while crime rates, divorce, wife and child abuse, and the use of drugs and alcohol all mount (Scheuerman 1986). This is the context for the buildup of resistance to plant shutdowns in the Mon Valley.

Political Response to Economic Crisis

The steel crisis shattered the political base and power of the region's USWA locals and paralyzed the area's local governments by throwing them into an immediate fiscal crisis. More, the decisions upended a whole way of life for thousands of individual steelworkers, their families, and their communities. But with the conservative triumph of President Ronald Reagan in Washington, Mon Valley workers could find little sympathy in the nation's capital.[4] Instead, the major political response to the valley's economic crisis was an infusion of welfare, social security, unemployment, and Trade Readjustment Assistance Act funds designed to keep workers and their families going in the immediate aftermath of the shutdowns.

This income certainly helped economically, though just as surely it contributed to the spread of a broad sense of quietude and acceptance among steelworkers, a passive resignation in the face of what appeared to be an inevitable fate (Buss and Redburn 1983). In mediating the workers' experience of crisis with essential resources, the national welfare state almost certainly limited the feelings of desperation and oppression that Marx saw as necessary ingredients of radical political action. Spontaneous uprisings of workers, such as those of the unemployed committees of the 1930s, were preempted, as were riots and other forms of collective violence (Piven and Cloward 1979), though crimes by and against individuals increased.[5] Instead, the combination of welfare state programs and appeals to market ideology produced what Poulantzas called an "effect of isolation" on workers in the valley, as well as on the valley itself in its relation to the rest of society (Poulantzas 1975). What forms of resistance occurred, then, began as pockets of militancy within a larger framework of class defeat. The organizers' first task and goal was precisely to create where they did not exist the beliefs that job losses were not inevitable, that something could be done to save the valley as a blue-collar industrial center, and that action must be started from below by workers themselves, for the region's official political and economic leadership showed no inclination to change its economic course. The debate centered on the nature of the action to be taken and its goals. Below the surface, however, the issues really hinged on more basic conflicts over the nature of the situation the workers faced.

Responses to these questions took two very different forms. One major approach was "agitational." Influenced heavily by the community organization theory of Saul Alinsky (Alinsky 1947, 1969), agitators saw the plant closings as an act of irresponsible corporate power. They aimed at forcing the leading steel corporations and banks to acknowledge their moral responsibility to the valley by reinvesting in steel. Since steel industry executives would not voluntarily recommit capital, the agitators urged local workers to shame and embarrass top-level officials into reversing their investment plans. In effect, the agitational approach reflects something of Piven and Cloward's belief in the possibilities of heightened militancy as a short-lived but effective means of gaining the recognition of elites. By contrast, the alternative model was essentially "institutionalist" in that it sought not to change the behavior of corporate elites but to introduce a new political–economic organization in the valley to substitute for the corporations. Based on traditional progressive ideas about the gradual development of class consciousness, institutionalists focused on the irrationalities of the private economy itself by initiating moves toward a smaller-scale, regional, publicly owned steel industry. In short, the agitators directed their efforts at "bad" leaders, while the institutionalists focused on creating an alternative to the systemic or structural problems of corporate capitalism, albeit *within* that system.

The Agitators

Initially guided by the tenets of the priestly ministry—the task of bringing peace and comfort to their congregations—the agitational strategy grew out of efforts by Mon Valley clergy to aid steelworkers with traditional sources of priestly aid: spiritual replenishment, emergency food relief, family counseling, and, more generally, the feeling that community institutions shared the workers' pain and were trying to help. At a somewhat more advanced level, some churches began to sponsor job-training services. Soon, however, a number of activist Protestant ministers, mainly Lutherans and Episcopalians, came to believe that treating the symptoms of dislocation was not enough. Beginning in 1980, and with the support of their church leaderships, they met to organize more comprehensive responses. Calling themselves the Pittsburgh Area Mission Strategy (PAMS), the ministers hired a local community organizer who had once worked for the city's Catholic church, Charles Honeywell. An Alinsky disciple, Honeywell infused the young ministers with the lessons of empowerment and direct action he had learned at the Alinsky training ground—the Industrial Areas Foundation in Chicago. But such lessons were introduced only gradually, as PAMS at first continued to supply the priestly services of food, counseling, and education to get the workers back on their feet.

As economic conditions worsened in the valley—the ministers were especially moved by the near bankruptcy of the town of Clairton in 1982— and urged on by Honeywell, PAMS clergy reviewed their strategy. Gradually they came to see the limits of the priestly ministry in coping with what they now identified as something much greater than a series of essentially private misfortunes. Changing their name to the Denominational Ministry Strategy (DMS), they recognized that from a political as well as a moral viewpoint, it was necessary to locate the people responsible for the basic conditions of unemployment and long-term disinvestment that plagued the region. As one of the ministers, the Reverend James Von Dreele, suggested, nothing would change for the workers until their suffering was traced back to the decision makers whose choices had caused the pain.

As a first step, Honeywell and the ministers petitioned Pennsylvania Governor Richard Thornburgh to declare the valley an economic disaster area. When this failed, DMS decided to challenge the centers of private corporate power themselves, namely, the leaderships of U.S. Steel and the other major steel companies, as well as Pittsburgh's Mellon Bank. The clergyman approached nearly fifty industrial and financial chieftains. According to Von Dreele, the group received a standard reply. As executives at Mellon Bank put it, "We're too powerless to do anything. . . . We're only lenders, not investors."

DMS soon recognized that their opponent—the city's corporate elite— was impervious to the soft-spoken appeals of the priestly ministry. As Honeywell explained their new awareness, Scripture teaches that actions to alleviate suffering are not enough. In the presence of evil, the priestly ministry fails. It is akin to "feeding Jews through the fence" of the concentration camp. Moreover, because its passivity strengthens evil, mere priestly action is itself immoral. Rather than "adapt to evil," Honeywell urged the ministers to undertake a much more activist and critical prophetic ministry that accepts the moral responsibility of "agitating the pharisees" and provoking the institutional evildoers into reactionary responses that would make churchgoers aware of their existence. In Von Dreele's words, "To educate the congregation [we] must use tactics that outrage the culture."

The ministers attempted to galvanize their congregations by urging collective economic pressure against Mellon Bank. They directed their anticorporate campaign against Mellon because, in their words, "Mellon Bank, more than any other institution, determines the economic destiny of the greater Pittsburgh area" (1397 Rank and File 1984). Mellon, they argued, had chosen to abandon the Mon Valley by investing in foreign steel companies rather than in the regional steel complex. The agitators substantiated their position by pointing to the millions the bank poured into a number of Japanese companies, including Kawasaki, Kobe Steel, Sumitomo, and Mitsubishi, and simultaneously foreclosed on a $13 million loan to Mesta Machine Company, a Mon Valley producer of steel mill equipment. The Mesta shutdown cost more than a thousand workers their jobs.

Working with a small group of rebel unionists from Local 1397 of the USWA, DMS encouraged unemployed steelworkers and local residents to withdraw their savings from Mellon. Von Dreele estimates that depositors removed about $5 million, although bank officials insist the amount came to no more than $100,000. When this tactic brought no response, DMS turned to harsher actions. As Honeywell saw it, the important thing was to attract attention to the issue, in E. E. Schattschneider's sense, "to expand the scope of conflict" (Schattschneider 1969). It was not even a question of building support; DMS just wanted to focus attention to the issue. As Honeywell explained, "We're not concerned with a good press." To the contrary: "Bad press causes reaction, half against us, half against them." In fact, "you only win with bad press." "It's an image war," added Von Dreele, one in which outrageous images are the political equivalent of rubber bullets.

DMS introduced a kind of guerrilla theater into the politics of industrial decline. They attempted to disrupt business at local Mellon branches by depositing dead fish in safe-deposit boxes. The agitators barged into church services attended by corporate officials, confronted steel executives at their suburban homes, berated church hierarchy at their altars. DMS people even went so far as to toss containers of skunk oil during a children's Christmas pageant at one of the city's most affluent churches. At the same time, the clergy urged their parishioners to lend political and financial support to prophetic ministry. As the campaign intensified and tactics became more extreme, however, resistance grew in some congregations against the ministers rather than the steel companies, especially at Pastor Douglas Roth's Trinity Lutheran Church in Clairton. Angry congregants petitioned Bishop Kenneth May, leader of Mon Valley Lutherans, to investigate Roth's activities. After the minister refused to tone down his rhetoric, the synod's executive board called for his transfer to another parish. Roth declined to step aside. Bishop May regarded his refusal as a direct challenge to his and the synod's authority and ordered Roth to leave the church at once. The minister held his ground and, accompanied by the parish's executive board, locked himself inside the sanctuary. Lawyers for the synod—from the firm of Reed, Shaw, Smith, and McClay, which also represented Mellon Bank and U.S. Steel—obtained an injunction, and on November 13, 1984, the county sheriff removed the minister and jailed him. Refusing to change his ways, Roth spent 112 days in a Pittsburgh cell. Ultimately, he lost control of his church and was defrocked by the Lutheran hierarchy.

With Roth's imprisonment, questions of unemployment, disinvestment, and "corporate evil" became inextricably fused with the issue of the right of DMS to practice the prophetic ministry. The theological struggle over ministerial roles soon overshadowed the economic and social problems that sparked the creation of DMS. The more the established hierarchy rejected prophetic ministry, the more the DMS clergy came to believe that theological attacks marked the beginning of challenges to corporate power. As the Reverend John Groppe, perhaps the most outspoken of the DMS ministers, explained, the "scribes and pharisees [are] standing with Mellon Bank against Roth so that they can continue their evil. . . . Christ never stood on the side of the powers that be and condoned them, but that's exactly where the national church stands." When others on the local political left urged DMS not to allow church politics to prevail over the politics of steel, DMS accused its progressive critics of complicity with the steel corporations. DMS also suggested that some of its leftist critics had communist leanings. By now DMS saw enemies and demons everywhere. The evil forces of corporate capital, the Mafia (Honeywell's special fascination), and the Communist party were joined in a secret cabal against the forces of good. DMS began to look and sound more and more like a cult; its leaders, with limited political experience, were caught up in a passion play of symbols and icons whose meaning took on a demonic life of their own wholly independent of the gritty realities of unemployment and social change.

For all practical purposes, Douglas Roth's imprisonment ended whatever influence DMS had as a rallying point for progressive politics in the Mon Valley, although the organization still exists, and remains defiant. Roth, for example, now conducts religious services at a small pentecostal church across town from his former congregation, still vowing to return to his old Clairton church. "It's just a matter of how much more . . . they want to lose before I win," he says. And mocking U.S. Steel's recent name change, DMS renamed itself DMX. It still makes occasional protests, and the ministers continue to claim influence. "We're upsetting and making all sorts of impact without having to lift a finger," proclaimed one DMX minister at a rally reported by the *New York Times* ("Dismissed and Defrocked . . ." 1988). In fact, DMX has all but faded into the shadows of local radicalism. Lacking labor or church support, and without credibility, DMX no longer has the power to command sustained attention from a symbol-hungry media. Bogged down in the traditional values of Christian morality, DMX could not address the larger structural issues of economic change. This presented the organization with what proved to be a fatal dilemma: The ministers found themselves in the position of promoting agitation without a program. Failure to resolve this contradiction rendered the organization irrelevant to the cause of social change in western Pennsylvania.

The Institutionalists

Institutionalists worked from a very different theory of political change than the prophetic ministers of DMS, although on at least one score the two groups agree: The key to change lies in the political awareness of the valley's workers. Institutionalists seek to change political understandings by enlisting worker support for and participation in new arrangements of policy and power, rather than through dramatic "actions." Institutionalists confront the problem of power and participation. With Tocqueville, they believe that action is possible only when citizens come to experience in direct and intimate ways the exercise of meaningful power. In the institutionalists' view, the theatrics of outrage do not provide the basis for radical change. Instead, community activists must link proposals for change to concrete analyses of the processes that lead to the destruction of communities; they should develop programs that create counterinstitutions of power, institutions capable of giving hopeless people control over the forces that matter in their lives.

Economically, institutionalists tend to agree with the established ortho-doxy that private capital accumulation has run its course in the steel industry and that hand wringing, moral indignation, and public arousal will not reverse this fact. But they sharply disagree with the mainstream economic belief that governmental and corporate efforts to build a service economy in the region will do much to improve the lives of steelworkers and their families. This strategy, it is argued, will produce few payoffs for the working class. Not only are traditional blue-collar workers ill prepared for the new jobs—jobs whose wages promise to be substantially lower than those historically won by the USWA—but, more profoundly, the high-tech ap-proach promises only to recentralize power over industrial and financial choices, leaving the region's workers as dependent on irresponsible deci-sionmakers as in the past (Lynd 1983; Massey 1985). If at least a part of the area's industrial working class is to survive over the next several decades, the valley must retain a part of its traditional manufacturing base. As the core of what he calls a "brownfield strategy," Staughton Lynd, a major institutionalist theorist, urges the establishment of a smaller, publicly owned, regionally scaled steel industry to serve mainly local needs. To achieve this, he calls for the use of existing legal powers, such as eminent domain, as well as federal financing, to underpin a public industrial author-ity—a Steel Valley Authority (SVA)—able to carry on production in the public interest (Lynd 1983; Tri-State Conference on Steel, n.d.).

Although New Deal planning along the lines of the TVA furnishes a historical example for the institutionalists' proposed Steel Valley Authority, the idea of an SVA evolved in direct reaction to massive plant closings in Youngstown, Ohio, the heart of the Mahoning Valley (Lynd 1982). The Mahoning shutdowns, which cost approximately 10,000 jobs in the late 1970s, inspired local residents to form a coalition of unemployed steelwork-ers and local business and church leaders. The coalition sought to reopen plants under community ownership. It raised millions in "Save Our Valley" pledges, and hired consultants to design a rebuilding program that many experts considered feasible. But U.S. Steel's refusal to sell its property, and the Federal government's failure to provide guaranteed loans, proved too much for the community activists. The coalition, now called the Tri-State Conference on Steel, could not save Youngstown. But as the spate of plant closings spread to the Mon Valley, Tri-State took the plan for a Steel Valley Authority eastward into the next battleground of steel closings, the Monongahela Valley of Pennsylvania (Lynd 1983; Marcus 1986).

Building on a base of community organizers, local union officials (the hierarchy of the USWA also came on board), and progressive Catholic clergy, especially Father Garrett Dorsey, Tri-State worked quietly and steadily in the scattered and fragmented little towns of the Mon Valley surrounding Pittsburgh to accumulate support for SVA among workers, local business owners, and politicians. As Dorsey put it, "When the great corporate center of Pittsburgh shrugs its shoulders, when the financial center of Pittsburgh shrugs its shoulders, you need some public intervention to encourage and promote industry and growth for employment and jobs."

Gradually, Tri-State managed to form alliances with local and state officials and even with many small business owners. A major breakthrough came in response to U.S. Steel's plan to close its huge Duquesne facility and raze its highly productive Dorothy Six blast furnace. After U.S. Steel rejected a union plan to avoid the closing, the steelworkers' union, lead by Duquesne Local 1265, joined forces with Tri-State. Now even the international union, which had previously resisted Tri-State's efforts in Youngstown, was working with the community group to save steel jobs in the Mon Valley.

Tri-State raised money from the international union, the city of Pittsburgh, and Allegheny County to conduct a feasibility study of the Duquesne plant. Yet, even though the study confirmed Tri-State's idea that the plant could be turned around, U.S. Steel's chief executive officer, David Roderick, held fast. The company would close the plant and raze the Dorothy Six furnace, thus denying Tri-State the backbone of any modernization plan. A series of legal battles and mass demonstrations followed, but Roderick finally had his way: The wreckers' ball smashed Dorothy Six to bits.

The Dorothy Six razing represented a major defeat for Tri-State. But the group continued to organize and to press its case for a democratic restructuring of steel through the establishment of a Steel Valley Authority. In January 1985 the Pennsylvania legislature responded to Tri-State's call by agreeing to charter a Steel Valley Authority, giving it the power of eminent domain to take over plants by compensating owners. Crucially, though, the state failed to appropriate the funds to pay for takeovers. Clearly, without funding, the SVA added up to little more than a symbolic gesture of state concern for a ravaged region. But in keeping with their gradualist strategy, the institutionalists' had gained an important new foothold for the principle of a community-based industrial authority with the power to interpose a public voice in major private disinvestment decisions. With a mantle of legitimacy, Tri-State could now offer SVA to local politicians and citizens as a working framework for a new industrial order in the region.

Nine municipalities soon joined the SVA, including the city of Pittsburgh, which committed $50,000 in seed money. This was not much in comparison with the probable costs of a plant compensation claim, but it was a start. Not long after, the SVA won an important legal victory. In the battle to prevent the closing of Pittsburgh's WABCO and Union Switch and Signal companies, the Federal District Court of Western Pennsylvania upheld the SVA's right to condemn properties in the public interest. The court refused, however, to prohibit the companies from removing equipment from the plants, since the rule otherwise would require the SVA to demonstrate its capacity to pay compensation for a takeover, a capacity it did not have.

While the SVA unsuccessfully challenged this part of the court's decision, it is now moving to deal with the funding issue head-on. The SVA and Tri-State have urged the state legislature to establish a Pennsylvania Industrial Development Finance Corporation (PIDFC). According to Tri-State, "PIDFC's aim is to pool state and local funds for investment in industrial plants and mines" controlled by local public entities such as the SVA. Under the plan, which follows similar approaches in Michigan and Massachusetts, the state would furnish $10 million in start-up capital to PIDFC. The agency "would then work to attract investments from state public employee pension funds and institutional and individual investors . . . to provide equity financing for industrial projects" (Tri-State 1988a, 7). Early in 1988, the PIDFC bill, with the backing of a number of labor, church, and business groups such as the Pennsylvania Coal Association, passed the legislature's Business and Commerce Committee by a 16–2 vote (Tri-State 1988a, 7).

As its fight for a capital fund goes forward, Tri-State maintains its effort to save individual plants. Early in 1988, for example, a long-awaited regional Metals Retention Study was completed. Pushed by Tri-State after the Dorothy Six disaster and financed by the City of Pittsburgh and Allegheny County, the study concluded that LTV's South Side Electric furnaces could be reclaimed, and with them, 350 new steel jobs. Tri-State, the SVA, the USWA, and a host of other groups are "currently involved in the campaign to restart the electrics using a public-private-worker ownership structure" (Tri-State 1988a, 1).[6]

With its mixed record of success in keeping plants open, and fully aware of the obstacles it faces, the SVA's proponents have no illusions about the ability of their institution to restore steel to its former primacy. Thus, "Tri-State does not say that every manufacturing facility could or should be saved" (Tri-State 1988a, 1). Its leaders admit that, in the words of board member Bob Erikson, "It's not going to put a hundred thousand people back to work." And they know that a significant battle was lost when Dorothy Six was destroyed. But a public steel authority does exist, and it has the legal right "to intervene when good manufacturing facilities are in danger of being abandoned or torn down." More, the SVA joined the kindred groups from other regions of the United States in February 1988 to form a national Federation for Industrial Retention and Renewal. The group will assist specific anti-shutdown efforts in towns and cities across the nation and try to shape a national policy "to challenge de-industrialization" (Tri-State 1988b).

Conclusion

It is clear that, measured against the scale of dislocation brought on by the breakup of the steel industry, neither the agitational nor the institutional models have produced major victories. DMS has all but disappeared as a significant voice in the valley, and the Steel Valley Authority has a long way to go before it turns out a single bar of product. There is no evidence that corporate executives, however pained they might feel personally about the consequences of disinvestment, are prepared to let private feelings dictate corporate policy, while the paucity of resources in the local public sector does little to encourage hopes that public investment can really stem the tide. It would not be unreasonable to conclude that the case for the political, let alone economic, rationality of resistance to plant shutdowns remains to be made. As we have argued elsewhere, it may well be that the only effective power communities and regions have to protect themselves against ruinous change is to demand the legal responsibility of corporations when they set their roots down in an area, not when they are desperate to leave (Plotkin and Scheuerman 1986; Plotkin 1987). But, as noted at the outset, the politics of opposition to economic change needs to be seen not only from the standpoint of policy consequences but also from the perspective of its impact on the political consciousness and organization of those who make such opposition. Indeed, it was in this sense that we introduced our three perspectives on urban radicalism. It is necessary, therefore, to review briefly our account from the viewpoint of what each perspective might suggest about our findings.

Given the fate of DMS and the slow progress of the SVA, the pessimism of Piven and Cloward seems well founded. From their perspective, the militant agitational style of prophetic ministry might well be a reasonable strategy. Taken further, it might have created enough disruption in the valley to compel corporate and government elites to buy social peace by pressing Congress to give increased emergency welfare and unemployment benefits to jobless workers and their families. But instead of urging workers to believe in and fight for their rights to increased benefits—the only victory workers could reasonably have won, for Piven and Cloward—DMS ministers fought to change corporate behavior. Incapable of transcending their religious outlook, DMS was more absorbed with the moral responsibility of elites than it was with politicizing workers and their congregations, which helps explain why the clergy found itself ultimately caught up in intrachurch battles at the expense of larger political and economic issues. By contrast, Piven and Cloward might argue, the Tri-State Conference on Steel made all the predictable mistakes in believing that sustained bureaucratic organization could alter the basic conditions of the poor and unemployed. Thus the Pennsylvania state government did provide for the shell of a public industrial authority—but without supplying the necessary capital to allow the SVA to buy steel plants, the state ensured that workers would inevitably feel let down, without winning anything real. It is possible, of course, that Tri-State will win passage of the PFDIC and gain some seed capital for investment. Without this money, the SVA stands a good chance of fading innocuously into the institutional woodwork of state government.

From a class analysis perspective, DMS might be praised for aiming its wrath at corporate capital, the true holders of power in the valley. But since the wrath was uninformed by a theoretical or historical understanding of the nature of capitalist crisis, the prophetic ministers could be said to have engaged in futile, self-destructive actions that had no impact on the political understanding or class consciousness of workers, except perhaps to reinforce their sense of alienation and helplessness against corporate power.

Tri-State leaders, by contrast, well understood the nature of the capitalist system they were dealing with, but they also made no effort to define the issues in explicitly class terms. They proposed the SVA as a mechanism to save the region's industrial jobs and preserve the valley as a home for its traditional steelworker families. Tri-State's ideology, to the extent that it has one, is essentially a fusion of populist democratic and communitarian themes. It has defined its program not in terms of resistance and struggle *against* the class enemy, but in terms of a great regional coalition *for* the Steel Valley Authority. Indeed, by accepting the logic of the shutdowns as inevitable and focusing their attention on a change in political institutions, they may well have helped to take the corporations off the political hook. For these reasons it is unclear, from a class perspective, what workers themselves might have learned from the battle for the SVA, and what they are learning in the process of its development.[7] Because the stress thus far has been on a positive program of coalition building and legislative politics, the big issue of who runs the national political economy and for what ends remains unspoken. It is, of course, true that the idea of a regional steel authority is a serious alternative to market domination, but the SVA has had much more difficulty gaining support for this notion than for its efforts to save individual plants. Where, then, the class analyst would ask, does the SVA lead: to the rescue of isolated factories or to new principles of democratic socialist planning? And what real role will workers have in the management of whatever plants are saved? Like DMS, after all, the SVA has been an institution controlled and led by organizers, intellectuals, and activists, not by the workers themselves. And finally, is the SVA really designed to bring about social change, or is it, as some Tri-State leaders often suggest, mainly an effort to keep the working-class valley economically alive as Pittsburgh gears up for the new service capitalism? In short, the class implications of the SVA remain hazy at best.

Nothing in the Mon Valley case would appear to undermine Castells's two central observations about American examples of urban opposition: that such instances tend "to happen at the level of immediate experience without relating to the corresponding level of a broader social structure" and to occur in the form of relatively narrow interest-group politics rather than class or even multiethnic movements (Castells 1984, 124). Nonetheless, given Castells's sensitivity to the cultural dimension of urban protest, he might well be impressed by the spirit and zeal of the prophetic ministry, the emotional power of its attack on corporate Pittsburgh, and its dramatic use of evocative religious symbols to arouse moral indignation. But surely he would be no less disappointed at DMS's muting of the "empowerment" theme, typical of Alinsky-style community struggles. Absent the call for community power, it would be hard to see, from Castells's perspective, how the group's efforts at guerrilla theater served the political education of workers and citizens. The SVA, on the other hand, could well represent, for Castells, a more serious example of the fusion of class and territorial interests in a sustained drive for the creation of new urban and regional understandings and institutions. Until now, though, the group has functioned largely as a conventional interest group. More research is surely needed on the extent to which Tri-State has managed to attract support among the various subcommunities and ethnic groups of the area's working class and on the kinds of appeals it has made. It is also necessary to get a better picture of how local and state politicians view Tri-State and the SVA. At the same time, it is still not clear whether Tri-State seeks or will be able to develop a new regional ideology of working-class interests. Nor is it clear what such an ideology might mean for the interests, self-understanding, and political power of small capitalists whose support is essential to any effective regional coalition, not to mention the interests of big capital, labor in other regions, and the outlook of the national state. Castells would likely share the reservations of a class analyst about the contribution of the SVA.

We are compelled to conclude that, ultimately, the opposition to plant closings in the Mon Valley may well amount to little more than a sad political footnote to the decline of the steel industry in America. In that case, it might be fair to call this essay a study in comparative desperation. But the case is also an illustration of the persistent human refusal to lie down before power. At the least, what Marcuse called the spirit of negation set a defiant human face against the seemingly objective tide of the end of steel. And it is by no means clear that the defiance will end in total defeat.

Notes

1. For a critical analysis of localism as a base of radical environmental politics see Plotkin, Chapter 9 in this volume.

2. Writing within a more conventional functional perspective, Apter and Sawa (1984) come to conclusions strikingly similar to those of Piven and Cloward. For them, the emergence of "extra-institutional protest" as a major form of organized political action in liberal democracies is an important development, although it is not likely to change the system in fundamental ways. An analysis of the often violent Narita airport protests in Japan leads these authors to conclude that "extra-institutional protest . . . may well be an important element in the way democracies can listen and hear what they might otherwise ignore" (p. 241). But listening and hearing are not the same as acting, responding and changing. And Apter and Sawa offer no reason to believe that "extra-institutional protest" can force advanced

214Where the Action Is

capitalist states to change their policies, much less their direction, in fundamental ways. Instead, "extra-institutional protest" may well expand and supplement the channels of accountability in liberal capitalist democratic states and thus, in however rocky a fashion, contribute to legitimation. In this sense, Apter and Sawa parallel the Piven–Cloward view that urban protest represents an aggressive but still relatively impotent means of achieving lasting radical change.

3. As Foucault has rightly argued, however, Marxists always hedge their bets on the support of local conflicts: "If one accepts that the form—both general and concrete—of struggle is contradiction, then clearly everything which allows the contradiction to be localized or narrowed down will be seen as a brake or a blockage" on revolutionary action (1980, 143). Local action can be supported within a class perspective only insofar as it is subjectively and objectively connected to systemic consequences. Although this is not the place for a detailed examination of his work, Foucault rejects such notions of localized structural contradiction as well as notions of structural power. For him, just as modern power systems are best seen as highly differentiated and localized networks of control, so "resistances" are inherently specific to localized mechanisms, capillaries and micronetworks of power. Foucault, however, says little or nothing about the concrete historical nature of resistance or where it might lead (Foucault 1980).

4. By contrast, when Democratic politicians in the 1980s wanted to symbolize their concern for downtrodden labor, the unemployed steelworker became an appropriate cliché for political consultants. According to one, Charles Guggenheim, the Democrats' 1984 presidential nominee, Walter Mondale, missed a useful television opportunity when he failed to do a spot with unemployed steelworkers. In Guggenheim's words, a steelworker spot might have produced "a piece of film that's fairly emotional" (Diamond and Bates 1988, 316–317).

5. As Newton (1978) argues, the prominence of interpersonal violence and crime in economically ravaged American cities is closely connected to the absence of urban institutions to articulate grievances in class terms. Or, to use a phrase popularized by Jesse Jackson, in the absence of effective political organization, "economic violence" leads to personal violence.

6. At the same time, however, the Metal Retention Study, performed by Hatch Associates and A. D. Little, also concluded that the reopening of a number of other plants, including USX's Homestead Works, would not be economically rational. In Tri-State's view, this conclusion was seriously distorted by the analysts' assumption that each plant should be reviewed from the standpoint of its profitability as a stand-alone operation. It has been Tri-State's idea from the beginning to insist that the region's steel facilities should be evaluated as a potentially integrated complex serving the region's public needs for steel as well as, perhaps, wider private markets. Indeed, the national steel market has improved somewhat recently. According to one recent report, U.S. mills are "planning to increase their spending for new plant and equipment by 23.3%" in 1988, "on the heels of a 39.2% boost in 1987" (Gleckman 1988). In this context, as well as in terms of the longer-term national

need for reconstruction of the country's battered roads and bridges, "it is essential," says Tri-State, "that the facilities be safely 'moth-balled' until they can be re-opened. Once they are dismantled they can never be brought back" (Tri-State 1988a, 2).

7. Sugestively, the *New York Times* headlined an article on the Mon Valley's posture in the 1988 Pennsylvania presidential primary with these words: "Steel City Tires of Politics and Promises (1988b). The *Times* article noted that local steelworkers "say they no longer expect much from their Government," while "radical solutions have little appeal" either (1988b).

References

Adams, Walter. 1977. "The Steel Industry." In *The Structure of American Industry*, edited by W. Adams. New York: Macmillan.

Alinsky, Saul. 1946. *Reveille for Radicals*. Chicago: University of Chicago Press.
———. 1971. *Rules for Radicals*. New York: Random House.

Apter, David, and Nagayo Sawa. 1984. *Against the State: Politics and Social Protest in Japan*. Cambridge, Mass.: Harvard University Press.

Buss, Terry, and F. Redburn. 1983. *Shutdown at Youngstown*. Albany: State University of New York Press.

Castells, Manuel. 1984. *The City and the Grassroots*. Berkeley: University of California Press.

Diamond, Edwin, and Stephen Bates. 1988. *The Spot, the Rise of Political Advertising on Television*. Rev. ed. Cambridge, Mass.: MIT Press.

"Dismissed and Defrocked, ex-Pastor Still Divides Lutheran Parish." 1988. *New York Times*, April 7, A25.

Dorsey, Reverend Garrett. 1986. Interview with authors, August 5.

Erikson, Robert. 1986. Interview with authors, August 1.

Fisher, Robert. 1984. *Let The People Decide: Neighborhood Organizing in America Boston:* Boston: Twayne.

Foucault, Michael. 1980. *Power/Knowledge: Selected Interviews and Other Writings, 1972–1977*, edited by C. Gordon. New York: Pantheon.

Fusfeld, Daniel R. 1958. "Joint Subsidiaries in the Iron and Steel Industry." *American Economic Review*. May, 578–587.

Gilder, George. 1981. *Wealth and Poverty*. New York: Bantam.

Gleckman, H. 1988. "Commentary: So Yon Thought Tax Reform Would Kill Capital Spending." *Business Week*, June 27, 31.

Gorz, Andre. *Farewell to the Working Class*. Boston: South End Press.

Gropp, Reverend John. 1985. Interview with authors, January 25.

Honeywell, Charles. 1985. Interview with authors, January 24.

Katznelson, Ira. 1981. *City Trenches: Urban Politics and the Patterning of Class in the United States*. Chicago: University of Chicago Press.

Lynd, Staughton. 1982. *The Fight Against the Steel Shutdowns: Youngstown's Steel Mill Closings*. San Pedro, Calif.: Singlejack Books.

———. 1983. "Reindustrialization from Below." *Democracy* 3, no. 3 (Summer): 21–33.

Marcus, Irwin M. 1986. "The Tri-State Conference on Steel and the Creation of the Steel Valley Authority." Manuscript.

Marcuse, Herbert. 1964. *One-Dimensional Man: Studies in the Ideology of Advanced Industrial Society*. Boston: Beacon Press.

Marx, Karl, and Frederick Engels. 1948. *The Communist Manifesto*. New York: International Publishers.

Massey, Doreen. 1985. "Which New Technology?" In *High Technology, Space and Society*, edited by M. Castells, 302–316. Urban Affairs Annual Review, vol. 28. Beverly Hills: Sage.

Michels, Robert. 1949. *Political Parties*. Glencoe, Ill.: Free Press.

Milliband, Ralph. 1977. *Marxism and Politics*. New York: Oxford University Press.

Mingione, Enzo. 1981. *Social Conflict and the City*. New York: St. Martin's Press.

Mollenkopf, John. 1983. *The Contested City*. Princeton: Princeton University Press.

Piven, Frances Fox, and Richard Cloward. 1979. *Poor People's Movements*. New York: Random House.

Plotkin, Sidney. 1987. *Keep Out: The Struggle for Land Use Control*. Berkeley: University of California Press.

Plotkin, Sidney, and William E. Scheuerman. 1986. "The Lesson of Mon Valley: Get Them Before They Get You." *Nation*, October 4, 309–311.

Poulantzas, Nicos. 1975. *Political Power and Social Classes*. Translated by T. O'Hagen. London: Sheed and Ward.

Reich, Robert. 1983. *The Next American Frontier*. New York: Times Books.

Schattschneider, E. E. 1960. *The Semi-Sovereign People: A Realist's View of Democracy in America*. New York: Holt, Rinehart and Winston.

Scheuerman, William E. 1986. *The Steel Crisis: The Economics and Politics of a Declining Industry*. New York: Praeger.

Schumpeter, Joseph. 1947. *Capitalism, Socialism and Democracy*. 3rd ed. New York: Harper & Row.

Sinclair, Upton. 1984. *The Flivver King*. Chicago: Kerr.

"Steel City Tires of Politics and Promises." 1988. *New York Times*, April 26, A1.

Tri-State Conference on Steel (Pittsburgh). n.d. "Steel Valley Authority: A Community Plan to Save Pittsburgh's Steel Industry." Manuscript.

———. 1988a. Newsletter. February.

———. 1988b. Newsletter. April.

U.S. Congress, Senate Committee on Finance. 1967. *Steel Imports, Staff Study*. Washington, D.C.: GPO.

U.S. Congress. Office of Technological Assessment. 1980. *Technology and Steel Industry Competitiveness*. Washington, D.C.: GPO.

Von Dreele, Reverend James. 1985. Interview with authors, January 24.

Weinberg, Jay. 1985. Interview with authors, August 1.

1397 Rank and File (Pittsburgh). 1984. "Why Is Local 1397 Fighting Mellon?" Newsletter, USWA, Local 1397.

CHAPTER 9

Enclave Consciousness and Neighborhood Activism

Sidney Plotkin

In the small world of the neighborhood, a sure bet to ignite protest is an outside proposal to change the community, particularly when the plan threatens some permanent shift in the use of land and buildings. Since corporations and government regularly try to rearrange urban land uses as a means of increasing their profits and power, opportunities for urban protest abound (Logan and Molotch 1987; Elkin 1987). Given the structures and pressures of the capitalist city, it is reasonable to conclude that such protest expresses deep-seated tensions between the defenders of neighborhood use values and the exchange value and power interests of public and private development elites (Logan and Molotch 1987, Chap. 4).

If the distinction between exchange and use-value interests were always applied in the streets, community organizers might well be advised to promote urban land-use protest as part of a radical practice. But should community environmental protest be understood solely as a struggle between the defenders of use values and the promoters of exchange values? Probably not, for many neighborhood land protests are animated by the exchange value (or "property value") interests of local homeowners. And tragically, the land-value concerns of homeowners are all too often inextricably mixed up with motives of race and class prejudice, as in the recent conflagration over construction of low-income housing units in Yonkers, New York.

In fact, if we look candidly at the kinds of things rejected by community activism, it is easy to conclude that they do not fall into neat socioeconomic categories. Community activists rarely make political or moral distinctions

A slightly different version of this paper appears in *Comparative Urban and Community Research* 3 (1990).

between the projects they find offensive. As often as not, neighborhood activists are as quick to reject projects aimed at fulfilling social needs—that is, the use-value needs of nonresidents, especially the poor and the sick—as they are profit-oriented projects of corporate elites (Saunders 1981).

Suggestively, Samuel Bowles and Herbert Gintis, two of the more prominent theorists of urban populism, praise community movements precisely because they "deny the separability of [their] economic, moral, and cultural concerns" (1986, 10). For them, community politics is, and should be, practiced as a kind of holistic defense of the neighborhood good. Bowles and Gintis make a strong case; but they also avoid the implications of community activism for neighborhood conceptions of the outside world and wider social needs. This is an important omission because the inseparability of community concerns is often tied to a vision of the outside as an undifferentiated source of antineighborhood dangers and threats, a view that can easily identify all change with destruction. Such outlooks lead many urban protestors to make sharp distinctions between insiders and outsiders, rather than between the various sources or beneficiaries of change. They also encourage protestors to make the category of the unwanted cover a multitude of sinners, including more than a few who have not sinned, such as the homeless, children with AIDS, battered women, or people of color.

From this perspective, one of the most poignant dilemmas of community activism is that the communal language protesters use to make their fights does not favor the crafting of socially enlightened distinctions between social, technical, and political–economic dangers. Threats to health, safety, physical environment, property values, or racial prestige are routinely seen as simply different facets of generalized vulnerability to change. As the popular category for identifying the basis of resistance in local land-use fights, the term *community* papers over such distinctions. Community, after all, is anything but a pejorative term. Its warm and toasty imagery of "we-ness" invites support and sympathy, especially among progressives. But if we take seriously the question asked by Posner in her Introduction to this book—"What does 'community' actually mean in relation to the issues that are the basis of community/neighborhood organization?"—we are forced to come to terms with the restrictiveness of much neighborhood activism. In the arena of community land use, especially, it is necessary to see one meaning of community as defensiveness and exclusion, as a sense of beleaguered membership in an endangered enclave.

This enclave consciousness, I want to argue, is a very large part of the American idea of community. It does not exhaust the idea of community; it does not mean that neighborly good feelings and warm associations do not exist; it does not mean that the idea of community is a sham. The idea of an enclave consciousness means that community is a notion and a practice that should be approached critically and carefully. As an enduring inner theme or dimension of community, the enclave consciousness has tremendous political importance because it urges protesters to frame the varied questions of urban change within separatist or exclusionary perspectives.

The point of this chapter is to explore some of the sources and content of enclave consciousness in the American tradition, and to consider its contribution and limits as an ideology of political opposition. I begin with some general comments about the relation between structure and conflict, using these as a springboard for discussion of what I see as some main sources of the enclave consciousness in the American political tradition. Then I turn to the content, limits, and possibilities of enclave consciousness itself.

Institutions and Conflict

> Neighborhood activism emanates from the structure of social relations in society as a whole, and not merely from forces unique to the living place. (Cox and McCarthy 1982, 214)

The above observation is central to an understanding of the limits of enclave consciousness as a shaper of political action. As Fisher and Kling argue in Chapter 5 of this volume, one of the main dilemmas of activism in America hinges on the difference between the systemic class origins of the problems working people face in their neighborhoods and the tendency of neighborhood activists to identify solutions with local political strategies.[1]

This mismatch of source and agency is no accident. Political conflicts not only happen in specific local contexts but political systems give rise to specific types of motivation, understanding, organization, and action. These elements combine in complex ways to structure the form and range of social grievances. Political systems and cultures vary in the way they give emphasis to the sources of power, agency, and exploitation, including the factor of class. In other words, different political institutions and ideologies "make available, visible, and interpretable socially constructed images of social processes and related interest perceptions," and they also tend to block alternative images and perceptions of interest (Dunleavy 1979, 422; Bachrach and Baratz 1970; Newton, 1978). In some societies, Britain and

France for instance, strong central states long ago turned their municipal governments into administrative subunits of the central power. In these places, where citizens tend not to view their local governments as independent units of government, important political issues come almost naturally to be identified with wider, centralized networks of power, including class power. In the United States, by contrast, with the exception of county governments, local governments have never been seen by the citizenry as merely administrative instruments of high-level authority. In the American political tradition people think of their local governments as institutions of direct democracy in their own right. Americans learn that their local governments are meaningful tools of local popular will. Such traditions help, however subtly, to give essentially local meaning to many key issues.

By creating, fostering, and limiting the powers of local jurisdictions, central states influence the makeup of working-class political consciousness and identity. Central states can thus lay a basis for labor's solidification into more or less stable territorial groupings that focus the struggles of ordinary people on their local political milieux. Depending on the degree of autonomy of the local units in different nation-states, local political organizations may become more or less predominant as sources of political identity and power (Katznelson 1981). Indeed, it is reasonable to suppose that there may be a relationship between the relative political strength of local governments and tendencies for labor to articulate its interests in local terms. As the United States has one of the least centralized political systems among capitalist states, it is useful to begin an analysis of enclave consciousness with a look at the entrenched legal localism of the American tradition.

Legal Localism

Local governments have played an unusually important role in the U.S. political tradition since its beginnings. The creation of American political institutions was strongly influenced by the fact that the first colonists imported from England localist political traditions that reflected that country's feudal past. England, after all, was governed into the late sixteenth and early seventeenth centuries by a "Tudor polity" that strongly favored representation of the local landed aristocracy (Huntington 1968). Although England gradually abandoned the localist representative tradition after its civil war, in the United States there was no need to do so. Here, merchant towns were already equipped with legal power to administer their affairs along capitalist lines; the local bourgeoisie had no feudal aristocracy with whom to settle accounts. Thus, as Gerald Frug notes, American colonial towns were in many ways akin to medieval enclaves, inasmuch as "they were established by people who broke away from existing social restraints and who formed relatively closed societies with new social structures" (Frug 1980, 1097).

At the same time, property-based differences, fueled by varying social and religious traditions and already strong regionalist sympathies, encouraged great distrust of centralized political power. After the American Revolution, when it came time to organize the new national government, the leading interests settled on a compromise that allowed the scattered ruling elites to dominate their local and state bailiwicks pretty much on their own terms (Dahl 1961). Meanwhile, the key national institutions of Congress and the presidency were left to express loose pluralistic coalitions of local powers. As James Madison reminded those who feared an overly strong national government, there was little in the proposed political system to modify the tendency for politicians "to sacrifice the comprehensive and permanent interests of the State [much less the national government] to the particular and separate views of the counties or districts in which they reside" (*Federalist Papers* 1961, 296). From the beginning in the United States political localism was invested with considerable elite as well as popular support.

Ideological Localism

If the legal frame encouraged localism, so did the populist tone of the nation's democratic ideals. There are firm roots for ideological localism in the agrarian protests of the early American farmers, the political philosophy of Thomas Jefferson and Thomas Paine, and not least in the spiritual rebelliousness of the American Protestant tradition. Americans have long believed that society should foster grass-roots political action as the natural field of egalitarian democracy (Seidelman and Harpham 1985, 6; Tocqueville 1945). This tradition, which inspired Saul Alinsky and much of the contemporary populist left, celebrates local association and direct forms of political action as the most appropriate and representative vehicles of democracy. Alinsky may well have stated the key principle of ideological localism when he insisted that "if the people have the power . . . in the long-run they will, most of the time, reach the right decisions" (Alinsky 1946, xiv).

Essential to the populist celebration of direct action is a related set of beliefs holding that "small units of social and political organization" are "the citadels of all the values associated with democracy" (McConnell 1966, 91). Small-scale democracy enjoys this virtue because the majority it seeks to embrace is more homogeneous than the mixed and conflicting populations of larger units. Small jurisdictions are more likely to encompass neighborhood people who think, feel, live, and own more or less alike. Thus small communities tend to an outlook—an enclave consciousness—that sees its primary political conflicts with the outside society, not within. In fact, as critics of small jurisdictions have noted, this way of thinking can end up justifying the repression of minorities as well as majorities while supporting the social power of leading economic interests (*Federalist Papers* 1961, 81; McConnell 1966). As far as the ideology of small-scale populist democracy is concerned, however, such criticisms are beside the point. For the populist democrat, the important thing about grass-roots democracy is that it projects the voice of seemingly united and organic communities against an alien and demanding outside world.

The homogeneity of small grass-roots constituencies has other important political consequences for the content of the political demands made by populist enclaves. Because people who identify with little constituencies regard the interests and values of their neighbors as essentially like their own, members of the enclave are unlikely to generate, on their own, ideological discussions that reexamine or challenge dominant values and interests. Taken as given expressions of homogeneous community preferences, the enclave will seek to transmit its "common" interest outward in very concrete ways. These will typically take the form of demands for specific economic benefits, or for privileged exclusions from the larger society—the typical work of American congressional politics—or, as is typical of urban land-use fights, the exclusion of unwanted industrial or social projects. In other words, small constituencies are even more likely than large ones to reject appeals designed to build linkages and coalitions between different segments of the society, or designed to identify linkages of need and interest between the enclave and the wider society, for such ideas are "less recognizably in the interest of [the] readily definable groups." (McConnell 1966, 115). The populist pragmatism of small constituencies, with its roots in the legal localism of American politics, is thus unlikely to represent serious ideological threats to the established order. In sum, for all the enthusiasm and seeming radicalism of direct-action politics, the political implications of ideological localism tend to be conservative (McConnell 1966, 115; Lowi 1971, Chap. 3).

Economic Localism

Legal and ideological localism favor a diffusion or scattering of ethnic, racial, or political identities. But there is an economic root to American localism too.

The idea of economic localism may seem odd at first, especially in a U.S. context, which has always celebrated the virtues of unified national and even international markets. But it is not hard to understand the logic of economic localism if we remember the dynamism of cities.

Urbanites have a tough time maintaining a given quality of life. The dynamics of economic and social change are extremely powerful, and they regularly threaten household and neighborhood stability. "Each neighborhood experiences constant inflows and outflows of residents, materials and money," and there is not much that individual neighborhoods can do to control such changes (Downs 1981, 1; Harvey 1973; Logan and Molotch 1987). This dynamism is strongly emphasized by the boosters of local growth politics, who regularly strive to open the city to ever greater flows of external investment and change (Peterson 1981; Feagin 1988).

Naturally, local residents struggle against expansion and change. No one wants to see his or her life disrupted (Elkin 1987, 43). But land-use struggles usually end up as efforts to confine the neighborhood to existing members by curbing competition for whatever locational advantages the residents may possess. As Weber argues, when groups try to close their socioeconomic relations in this way they usually take "some externally identifiable characteristic of another group (actual or potential) competitors—race, language, religion, local or social origin, descent, residence, etc.—as a pretext for attempting their exclusion." For this reason, among others, Weber sees neighborhood as "an unsentimental economic brotherhood" for whom socioeconomic separatism is anything but an alien policy (Weber 1978, 1:342, 360f).

This economic tendency toward exclusion is encouraged in modern capitalist cities. In capitalist urban settings the exclusionary rights of private property not only determine the social and spatial organization of the city but form the first legal defense against environmental change (Plotkin 1987). One expression of this economic exclusionism is the Neighborhood Improvement Association tradition of community organizing, which developed primarily "to protect property values and community homogeneity," usually by "excluding members of lower classes and racial minorities" (Fisher 1984, 73).

Economic localism reflects a proprietary aspect of communalism, a kind of possessive communalism. Very much part of the enclave consciousness, possessive communalism suggests a belief that private interests are best nurtured and guarded by their setting in a socially restrictive enclave of kindred properties. The enclave—"our neighborhood"—thus comes to be seen not so much as a warm affective "community" as a collective property for the safekeeping of private possessions. Possessive communalism, in this sense, comes not from organic traditions but from the private, individual motivations of property, what MacPherson (1962) called the liberal ethos of "possessive individualism." Possessive communalism reflects an understanding that the private economic and social interests of neighborhood members are joined inextricably together by the residents' common occupation of an area. These interests, the residents believe, can best be protected if they act as if their locale was a kind of communal private property in need of joint regulation (Nelson 1980). Justifying the militant antibusing efforts of one working-class Brooklyn neighborhood, a local activist invoked this idea of possessive communalism with a suggestion that his community was a private membership club. "You have to do it to keep out the undesirables," he explained. "It's a cooperative effort of neighbors. They have the right to pick their neighbors" (Rieder 1985, 82).[2]

Legal, ideological, and economic localism strengthen and shape the "strong forces working toward cultural heterogeneity and territorial differentiation in the urban system" (Harvey 1973, 84). They help to explain a political context that gives rise to parochial rather than class activism, to closed rather than open social relationships (Weber 1978, 1:43–46). To look at the situation in such terms is necessary for understanding how urban social conflicts are culturally structured (Smith 1988). But these ideas do not get us close enough to the content of enclave consciousness itself. For this, we need to move from frame to substance.

The Enclave Consciousness

In the enclave consciousness, people see their neighborhood as home territory, a familiar environment of people, buildings, and space, surrounded by alien threats. The enclave consciousness is first of all a political orientation to the defense of such a place (Cox and McCarthy 1982, 196). As opposed to a politics of ideological commitment, the enclave consciousness reflects the desire "to give politics first a location rather than simply an abstract structure" (Morris and Hess 1975, 9). Based on a sensibility of firm interconnection between social relations and the urban built environment of houses, sidewalks, yards, stores, churches, parks, lots, and streets, the enclave consciousness has much to do with the spirit, custom, and collective self-understanding of a more or less well-defined neighborhood. The result is "a tenacity of neighborhood sentiment" (Logan and Molotch 1987, 101).

The place-bound confines of neighborhood constitute the relevant "environment" of community land-use protest. Although much of the environmental literature has tended to elide the point, the social historian Samuel P. Hays has seen these local sensibilities and grass-roots feelings as singularly important thrusts behind recent environmental protest. "In its initiative and its direction," writes Hays, "the environmental impulse in America after World War Two came from the grass roots." More, "the emotion, the drive, the persistence of what is often called environmental activism stems from the meaning of environmental values at this primary group context of life" (Hays 1982, 721). Other studies of local no-growth movements have come to similar conclusions (Popper 1981; Nelson 1980).

We should be careful, however, not to exaggerate communal feeling and territorial identity as elements of the enclave consciousness. Especially in the privately oriented culture of the United States, sentiments of possessive communalism are bound to be linked closely to feelings of possessive individualism. We need not wholly reject the idea of community to see that it can serve as a political mask for what are felt to be primarily individual, family, or household interests (Frieden 1979). Indeed, what lends the enclave consciousness its peculiar social character is the way in which possessive individualistic elements are combined and blended in the American context with social and economic ties to neighborhood and place.

Tocqueville caught one aspect of this fusing of private and social identities when he noticed that in America democratic individualism rarely meant isolation from others. Individualism, he argued, did draw people away from society at large, but it also attracted them to smaller social circles, inclining them toward family and friends, not atomism and blind self-seeking (Tocqueville 1945, 21:104). Thus "many values of popular individualism are really familistic with control, security, comfort and convenience being sought for the family." (Gans 1988, 3). The private household, in this sense, is the magnetic center of community.

The neighborhood can lend valuable support to the varieties of family and household in modern American life, of course (Logan and Molotch 1987, 103–110), but for the enclave consciousness, these are primarily gifts to the safekeeping of household interests. Thus, while celebrating

community, neighborhood households that embody the enclave consciousness also regularly strive to preserve privacy and social distance between
themselves in order to retain their individual, apolitical character. This
instrumental connection between household and neighborhood is an important factor behind the strongly protective or defensive cast of much community activism. It helps explain why effective political and social action is
likely to require the presence of an immediate common threat (Weber
1978, 1:361). As one protestor explained, the possibilities of community
organization around more abstract ideals are remote. Attacks on children
and property form the most reliable reasons for activism. "There's only one
kind of activism you can have in Canarsie: you can organize [people] around
protecting their bucks or their kids" (Rieder 1985, 173).

As an ingredient of the enclave consciousness, the importance of threat
cannot be overemphasized. With instability and change as normal features of
urban capitalist life, households and communities are genuinely "vulnerable
places" (Rieder 1985, Chap. 3). Residents feel they must remain alert to
external dangers emanating from the wider society and market. Control,
security, and minimization of risk are constant preoccupations of the enclave
consciousness. As Gans writes, "the goal of popular individualism is hardly
separation from other people," especially inasmuch as others are needed to
watch out for and fight against unwanted changes in the environment (Gans
1988, 3–4). Like the plebs of Machiavelli's Florence, today's urban protest-
or's use collective action not so much to gain power for themselves as a
group but to be left alone in their neighborhoods and to avoid domination
by the powerful (Machiavelli 1970, 116).

Neighborhood independence is a central theme of the enclave consciousness. Like the private household, the neighborhood should be able to stand
on its own two feet. Buttressed by beliefs in its hard-earned independence,
members of the enclave feel they owe little to the larger society. Except,
perhaps, for religious commitments to a wider church community, or the
call of an emergency and therefore temporary coalition, the enclave consciousness rejects ties to other neighborhoods, much less to wider units of
political association such as mass movements, trade unions, or political
parties.[3] Some writers argue, in effect, that the enclave consciousness
predominates in America today, as "the concept of national community,
while of vital significance in wartime, has failed to gain popular acceptance"
(Savas 1987, 304; Gans 1988, 114).

In place of "national community," the enclave consciousness offers
the distinctively autarkic ideal of communal independence, leading many

urbanites to believe they have "a right to avoid entanglement in the affairs of the larger society" (Rieder 1985, 95). A New Jersey protester, for example, animated by state efforts to move AIDS patients into a nearby nursing home, said as much when he declared. "These AIDS people come from a decadent society. . . . I'm talking about sex and degenerates passing drug needles in Newark . . . NIMBY! [not in my backyard] You said it, NIMBY! That's what we believe" (quoted in *New York Times*, April 3, 1988). But even when the enclave consciousness takes more humane forms, as illustrated by one recent study of community activism in Paris, it seems devoutly to crave communal separateness. When student architects working with the neighborhood sought to give graphic representation to the residents' urban longings, their vision was of "an island of communal life, with gardens and patios surrounded by medium-rise housing" (Body-Gendrot 1987, 135).

Like the Paris protesters, the anti-AIDS activist in New Jersey apparently believes that his own neighborhood is an "island," that it has the potential to be a stable, internally coherent, and decent place, a setting capable of regulating its own, quite healthy affairs. Neighborhood, for the enclave consciousness, thus becomes something close to a complete expression of essential relationships, one with a happy integrity of its own that is distinct from metropolitan or national systems. In other words, the modern enclave consciousness has much in common with the world view of preindustrial country–town life, which Robert Weibe so well captured with his phrase "the island community." Like their rural forbearers, members of today's urban enclaves still manage "to retain the sense of living largely to themselves" (Weibe 1967, 2).

The enclave's yearning for independence is laden with anxiety. Feelings of neighborhood marginalization and exploitation can run rampant when centralized institutions make surprise announcements of new development projects or suddenly warn of long-simmering environmental threats (Apter and Sawa 1984, 235). Nor is the prime lower-class threat—urban crime— just the statistical hyperbole of conservative politicians. Working- and middle-class urbanites understandably feel that their enclaves are squeezed between the economic depredations of the corporate and political elite and the random street attacks of drug users. For the enclave consciousness, the city is manipulated by greedy forces from above and beset by uncontrollable violence from below. It is an external arena of predatory interests, a conflict-ridden system aimed at controlling, exploiting, and destroying the enclave.

Enclave struggles become a matter of "them" against "us." The enclave consciousness reflects a "subordinate value system" that neither fully supports nor radically rejects the dominant value structure (Parkin 1971, 88). This subordinate outlook adapts to the outside social structure by maintaining a posture of tense skepticism with respect to external authority and militant rejectionism when it comes to the lower classes. Nor does such contempt work only in one direction. The enclave consciousness leaves plenty of room for black as well as white racism, as well as color-blind class prejudice. In this context, all externally induced changes become suspect, and the wider society is seen to have no justifiable reason for ever altering the neighborhood. As one progressive city planner explained after meeting with a group of neighborhood opponents of a new industrial park, the protestors seemed to believe that "there are never circumstances that justify forcing some residents to move," even to make way for a project beneficial to workers in the city as a whole (Clavel 1986, 102). Clearly, the end result of the enclave consciousness is a policy of "beggar thy neighbor" as community groups regularly seek to export or exclude the perceived "bads" of urban life while fencing in the goods (Harvey 1973; Stone 1987, 9).

Such tendencies, rife in Alinsky's influential theory of community organization, are a commonplace of neighborhood self-defense fights (Alinsky 1946; Fisher 1984; Castells 1983, 60–65). At its core, Alinsky's approach can be read as a systematic effort to awaken the enclave consciousness, although rarely to inform it with an explanation of the forces that make the larger social system tick. Cleveland's recent experiment with urban populism—in the form of the Kucinich administration's effort to take on the city's banks and utilities—is a case in point. There was nothing in the Alinsky theory of activism to prevent Kucinich from moving toward racist appeals when his political future was in peril (Swanstrom 1985). And as Feagin suggests for the case of Houston, working-class racism is so endemic to that city's political culture that a class-oriented community politics has been virtually stymied (Feagin 1988).[4]

Inspired and energized by moral outrage against elite manipulation and lower-class depredation, the enclave consciousness channels political activism and resistance mainly into demands to "leave us alone." With its characteristically defensive, exclusionary, and reactive character, the resulting politics is a "geopolitics of local community," in which "deterrence, counterforce, holding ground, securing borders, flanking maneuvers, and standing fast" are "central organizing concepts" (Rieder 1985, 234). Each enclave becomes a mini-Pentagon, always prepared for the next big fight, though without the requisite store of strategic weapons. As the siege mentality prevails, all efforts are concentrated on restricting the power of elites or the underclass to penetrate the community. As Harry Boyte notes, much community organizing in the 1970s reflected a "marked localism, or tendency to concentrate on those problems closest to home and to be suspicious and skeptical about involvement in any broader or larger organizational forms and coalitions addressing 'bigger issues' " (Boyte 1980, 191).

In sum, the enclave consciousness tends toward a rigid and undifferentiated exclusionism. It is a consciousness reluctant to make social or moral distinctions between environmental dangers arising from the physical and technical processes of urbanization and extreme fears of strangers. But even where the focus of community action is not racial exclusion or opposition to a proposed land-use change but a suddenly discovered, internal environmental threat, the typical enclave demands center on corrective action by external institutions or a buyout of the affected homes, not basic changes in patterns of social – economic planning, decision, and investment (Freudenberg 1984).

Not surprisingly, then, a good deal of the inspiration and focus of urban environmentalism is distinctively reactionary, a response to decisions, policies, and activities conducted by corporate- and state-sector managers that are seen to threaten the neighborhood health. Thus Freudenberg's study of 110 community organizations revealed that the most common problems cited by community activists were "toxic dumps, pesticide or herbicide spraying, and air pollution" (Freudenberg 1984, 445). It is certainly true that many of the groups concerned themselves with nonhealth issues as well—taxes, utility rates, and housing, for instance. But the study found that nearly half were originally organized to confront an imminent health threat. Health-based environmentalism is an important element of contemporary enclave politics.

Such reports complement Hays's argument that a crucial "personal and grass-roots tendency in environmental affairs stress[es] self-reliance in matters of health protection," a motive that closely "dovetails with the protection of place" (Hays 1981, 723). Such findings also conform with abundant poll data revealing an apparently well-established belief in advanced industrial societies that safety from the harms of pollution is a virtual "entitlement" of the welfare state. There is now felt to be a community right to a safe environment, a right that is to be statutorily guaranteed by the central authority of the welfare state, but is factually to be defended by the neighbors (Mitchell 1984, 58; Nelson 1977).

In defense of such rights, the enclave consciousness supports much more than ritualistic participation in electoral or interest-group politics. Indeed, given the dissipation of local party structures and the wiring of a mass electorate into the modern system of telepolitics, militant forms of direct action have emerged as prime strategy for the enclave consciousness. The siege mentality, coupled with a penchant for exciting urban dramas to attract the camera, encourages activists to shout No! to power. Protest meetings, angry denunciations of city and corporate leaders, referendum and petition campaigns, marches to and around the centers of urban power, rent strikes, sit-ins, lie-ins, and assorted other forms of bureaucratic sabotage are now familiar features of "street-fighting pluralism" (Yates 1977). Expanding the intensity, if not always the scope, of conflict has become the name of the game in the geopolitics of enclave defense. Nevertheless, it is worth noting that much of the noise of street demonstrations can be a "facade that is more imposing than the substance behind it" (Henig 1986, 225), for community activist groups are themselves often divided by social and political conflicts and only weakly representative of community sentiment (Rieder 1985).

Functional Unruliness: A Diminutive Refusal

Enclave consciousness is a historical product of diverse cultural traditions and deep-seated political–economic patterns that have profoundly shaped the experience of labor in America. It is one reason the "many signs of ferment and social conflict in American cities remained largely within segments of the working class" (Smith 1988, 79). And it may well be that radicalism in America meets its limit at the enclave. The enclave consciousness is a weak link in the chain of labor history, but for all that, it is still important as a defense against the totalization of power by modern capitalist society (Habermas 1973). Perhaps it would be worthwhile, then, to count some of the blessings of the enclave consciousness as a precursor to comments about possible connections to an urban class consciousness.

First, at a time when "we are witnessing a shrinking of the realm of the possible and a shrinking of the realm of the public" (Henig 1986, 243), the enclave consciousness is one force that actually keeps open the public space of dissent and oppositionism in American culture. For all its limitations, the enclave consciousness inspires a kind of functional unruliness in urban politics, functional, that is, to the continuation of politics and the making of popular demands in an increasingly apolitical and privatized society. This consciousness contains more than a little of what Veblen once described for the English case as a stubborn "spirit of insubordination" (Veblen 1954, 102). As a legacy of old-fashioned democratic belief, the enclave consciousness supports the making of what amount to irrationally rational demands to be let alone by, rather than to participate within, institutions of domination. That is why the so-called politics of NIMBY—Not In My Backyard—poses uniquely puzzling dilemmas for centralized state and corporate power. The exclusionary demands of NIMBY are simply not as subject to cooptation as were the participatory demands of the 1960s (Katznelson 1981; Plotkin 1987). Today, central and urban governments can continue to "engage in regressive social engineering," but now they must expect street fights before they get their way (Mollenkopf 1983, 294; Huntington 1984).

More, for all its restrictiveness and negative-mindedness, the enclave consciousness does offer a powerful rationale of empowerment. Community resistance is evidence against the dour image of politics taught by sociologists of "the mass society" (Mills 1956). Citizens who fight to secure their homes and communities from intervention by high-level controllers manifest alienation, but not apathy. They show a will and a capacity to question authority. Their actions belie what Marcuse, following Mills, saw as the repressive quiescence of a "one-dimensional" citizenry, whose powers of reasoned criticism have been wholly incorporated by the centralized media empires, including the national state (Marcuse 1964). Political consciousness in the lower ranks of society, even in its unreconstructed enclave form, is a little less flat and quiescent than critical theory has suggested.

Clearly, community opposition to environmental dangers does not exemplify what Marcuse called "The Great Refusal." But, as a more diminutive refusal, enclave politics is not without consequence for crucial human interests—the preservation of community and nature, the protection of life and health, the reduction of socially unnecessary human misery, and ecological waste. These are not secondary values. The unruliness of the enclave consciousness is functional to their preservation, too, at least in the short run.

Finally, if the enclave consciousness helps to spawn a politics of exclusion, exclusion can sometimes give way to more socially responsible perspectives. Under certain conditions, urban enclaves have forged alliances with other groups and pursued more universalistic goals. To take one example that I have discussed elsewhere: Mexican Americans from the poor west side of San Antonio, Texas, who used Alinsky-type organizing strategies to defend *barrio* interests, did not let the enclave perspective prevent them from joining cause with white middle-class environmentalists to fight a regional shopping mall that threatened the city's sole source of water (Plotkin 1987). And what is doubly important about this illustration is the way Mexican American organizers developed a practical understanding of the connections between environmental issues and issues of corporate-led urban development. The defenders of the *barrio* joined the mall fight not only to protect the city's pure water but as a means of regulating capital flight from downtown to the suburbs; they saw the mall issue as one way to raise larger questions about the social as well as spatial planning of their city.

Similarly, in the very different context of Laurinberg, North Carolina, poor blacks, whites, and Native Americans joined forces to fight location of a treatment plant for hazardous wastes. According to the town's white mayor, it was not only environmental fears that brought the town together but a sense of exploitation by arrogant outside elites. The treatment plant people came here "because they thought we were ignorant," said the mayor, "they thought we would roll over and die a long time ago." Instead, according to a *New York Times* report of April 1, 1986, the town's battle expanded the conception of the enclave; it "produced a growing sense of unity and strength among blacks, whites and Indians in an area where racial divisions had been the norm." And in a number of American cities, neighborhood organizations have taken on economic issues with much broader than merely enclave significance, such as tenants' rights and rent controls, redlining by banks and insurance companies, ownership of municipal facilities, and corporate disinvestment (Clavel 1986; Swanstrom 1985; Plotkin and Scheuerman, see Chapter 8 in this volume). Can we identify conditions that make such alliances more likely?

Building on Clavel's work on recent urban progressive movements, it is possible to identify three key conditions for movements of political expansion beyond the enclave (Clavel 1986, 16–18). First, there needs to be a widespread economic or environmental rationale for an alliance of enclaves. Urbanites are most likely to see beyond the enclave only when they experience issues that directly touch the economic and environmental security of many neighborhoods at once. Issues such as the regional mall or waste plant threaten the plausibility of everyday assumptions about the independence of enclaves. Such issues offer openings for discussion and education about the relation between enclave needs and public needs. By their very nature, such "trans-enclave" issues demand alliance as the condition of victory, and once alliances are formed, there is always the possibility, however slim, for movement on to other citywide, system-related issues.

Second, alliances of enclaves are more probable if they aim at getting control of politicians and local governments. Obviously, there is tremendous potential for quick burnout here and for cooptation. But the logic of functional unruliness may create a more independent momentum for urban residents. In some cases it can lead them to build organizations that are better prepared for sustained surveillance of city government and that see the need for a more liberal, not to mention radical, national politics, even in the inevitable days when the pace of action slows and political interest wanes.

Finally, for Clavel, urban progressivism is most likely to develop with the help of a local planning community that is able to frame issues in trans-enclave, redistributive terms, both within and outside local government. I would go beyond a narrow definition of professional planners here and stress the importance of political organizers and activists in general. In the first analysis, organizing in American communities means organizing the enclave. The cultural, economic, and political biases make this all but inevitable. Activism, organization, and planning, therefore, have to be seen by progressives as ideological and pedagogical activities, not only as practical matters. A disruptive experience may move people to do things in politics they would otherwise not ever think of doing, such as going to public meetings and demonstrations. But experience, of itself, does not broaden political vocabulary or confer new categories of analysis. That is where the role of the organizer comes in and where political education will always count for the most in shifting perspectives beyond the enclave.

Final Thoughts

There is no question that in America's cities, new populism is more in tune with what many people want to hear than is the traditional radical call for class struggle. But in making demands on the political system, new populists tend to forget the demands that people, including activists, need to make on one another to think clearly about the causes of their ills. There is more to the question of democracy than "empowerment" and "participation." The radical tradition has always understood, particularly in its European variants, the cognitive dimension of democracy and freedom (Neumann 1957). In other words, to fight for their rights effectively, people need to know something about the social system in which they are struggling. They need to have ideas about what established power is for and against, how organized power is related to their needs, and how those needs are related to the needs of others in a similar class situation. "To understand the changes of many personal milieux," said Mills, "we are required to look beyond them" (Mills 1959). This need to look beyond the milieus of the enclave implies that radical politics must have an ideology that is also a pedagogy.

A key political function of the concept of class for such a pedagogy is that it offers a way of making social, and even moral, distinctions about the nature of urban environmental threats, distinctions that are not possible within the enclave consciousness. Radical concepts of class, after all, not only identify capital as the predominant factor behind most urban ills but also establish a rational basis for understanding the community of weakness and insecurity experienced by the urban majority as whole, whatever their particular residential enclave. By offering unifying explanations of how urban majorities really share their community of vulnerability, the concept of class becomes a way of making distinctions between the heightened skepticism with which the majority should greet the plans of the local business leadership and the social responsibility that members of the endangered majority owe to one another. Class, in other words, affords a way of articulating differences between projects expressly designed to serve the profit and power interests of the dominant class, those intended to patch the environment, and those whose purpose is to shelter the weak. From a class perspective, organizers can work confidently with community organizations to resist the profit/power projects, demanding in exchange for their acceptance, perhaps, some real measure of private repatriation of profits to the urban public sector. Environmental installations—the notorious waste facilities and incinerators, for example—can become powerful lessons in the need for a "Not in Anybody's Backyard" strategy that aims at alternative patterns of energy supply, investment, and use. Finally, and this is certainly the hardest but in some ways the most important case, there are the social facilities designed to serve the weakest elements of the working class—low-income housing, drug and AIDS shelters. For these instances, the notion of class as community of vulnerability offers at least the glimmer of a possibility for asserting the common weakness of all members of the urban majority and thus the need for a sense of social responsibility among the better-off workers for the weakest of the weak.

Notes

1. As Raymond Williams has observed, "All significant social movements of the last thirty years have started outside the organized class interests and institutions. . . . But there is not one of these issues [ecology movement, campaigns against poverty and homelessness, etc.] which, followed through, fails to lead us into central systems of the industrial-capitalist mode of production and among others into its system of classes" (1983, 172–173)

2. The existence of possessive communalism does not mean that we are entitled to reduce neighborhood action to economic action. The health and safety concerns of working-class neighborhoods are real enough, as are the social affections and animosities that are everywhere mixed up in the complex motivations of urban separatism (Weber 1978, 1:43–46). But we cannot avoid the fact that private property economic structures are nearly everywhere connected with the social forces favoring closed relationships. Even in poor neighborhoods, where the activists are tenants rather than owners, the impulses of exclusionary property are felt quite powerfully, as the neighbors come to see their interests in the restrictive terms of the segmented city. After all, where the city itself is little more than an organization of property interests, the exclusionary consciousness of property stamps the outlook of all classes (Plotkin 1987).

3. Logan and Molotch (1987) correctly point out that such tendencies were much less true for black protest in the 1960s; then, "the activist thrust was against the larger system" (p. 138). However, even the systemic radicalism of black protest was not immune to territorial forms of cooptation (Katznelson 1981).

4. The tragic findings of such case studies are backed up by broader national samplings of opinion. A National Opinion Research Center study found that for most white ethnics group in the United States, 43% or more of those questioned believed that "white people have a right to keep blacks out of their neighborhoods if they want to"; for Eastern European Catholics, the percentage agreeing was 58% (Harrigan, 1985, 79). No surprise, then, that Jimmy Carter could run for the presidency in 1976 by declaring his commitment to protect the "ethnic purity" of American neighborhoods, or that, twelve years later, George Bush would make a black rapist the unifying symbol of political fear in white working-class communities.

References

Alinsky, Saul. 1946. *Reveille for Radicals*. Chicago: University of Chicago Press.
Apter, David E., and Nagayo Sawa. 1984. *Against the State: Politics and Social Protest in Japan*. Cambridge, Mass.: Harvard University Press.
Bachrach, Peter, and Morton Baratz. 1970. *Power and Poverty: Theory and Practice*. New York: Oxford University Press.

Body-Gendrot, S. N. 1987. "Grass-roots Mobilization in the Thirteenth Arrondisse-ment of Paris: A Cross-National View." In *The Politics of Urban Development*, edited by C. N. Stone and H. T. Sanders, 125–143. Lawrence: University of Kansas Press.

Bowles, Samuel, and Herbert Gintis. 1986. *Democracy and Capitalism: Property, Community and the Contradictions of Modern Social Thought*. New York: Basic Books.

Boyte, Harry. 1980. *The Backyard Revolution*. Philadelphia: Temple University Press.

Castells, Maxwell. 1984. *The City and the Grassroots*. Berkeley: University of California Press.

Clavel, Pierre. 1986. *The Progressive City: Planning and Participation, 1969–1984*. New Brunswick, N.J.: Rutgers University Press.

Cox, K. R., and J. J. McCarthy. 1982. "Neighborhood Activism as a Politics of Turf: A Critical Analysis." In *Conflict, Politics and the Urban Scene*, edited by K. R. Cox and R. T. Johnston, 196–219. New York: St. Martin's Press.

Dahl, Robert. 1961. *Who Governs?* New Haven: Yale University Press.

Downs, Anthony. 1981. *Neighborhoods and Urban Development*. Washington, D.C.: Brookings Institution.

Dunleavy, P. 1979. "The Urban Basis for Political Alignment: Social Class, Domes-tic Property Ownership, and State Intervention in Consumption Processes." *British Journal of Political Science* 9: 409–443.

Elkin, Stanley L. 1987. *City and Regime in the American Republic*. Chicago: University of Chicago Press.

Feagin, Joe. 1988. *Free Enterprise City: Houston in Political and Economic Perspec-tive*. New Brunswick, N.J.: Rutgers University Press.

The Federalist Papers. Edited by Clinton Rossiter. 1961. New York: Mentor. Pp. 77–84, 294–300.

Fisher, Robert. 1984. *Let the People Decide: Neighborhood Organizing in America*. Boston: Hall, Twayne.

Freudenberg, Nicholas. 1984. "Citizen Action for Community Health: Report on a Survey of Community Organizations." *American Journal of Public Health* 74: 444–448.

Frieden, B. J. 1979. *The Environmental Protection Hustle*. Cambridge, Mass.: MIT Press.

Frug, G. 1980. "The City as a Legal Concept." *Harvard Law Review* 93: 1053–1154.

Gans, Herbert J. 1988. *Middle American Individualism: The Future of Liberal Democracy*. New York: Free Press.

Habermas, Jurgen. 1973. *Legitimation Crisis*. Boston: Beacon Press.

Harrigan, J. J. 1985. *Political Change in the Metropolis*, 3rd ed. Boston: Little, Brown.

Harvey, David. 1973. *Social Justice and the City*. Baltimore: Johns Hopkins University Press.

———. 1982. *The Limits to Capital*. Chicago: University of Chicago Press.

Hays, S. P. 1981. "The Structure of Environmental Politics Since World War II." *Journal of Social History* 14: 719–738.

Henig, J. R. 1986. "Collective Responses to the Urban Crisis: Ideology and Mobilization." In *Cities in Stress*, edited by M. Gottdiener, 221–246. Beverly Hills, Calif.: Russell Sage.

Huntington, Samuel P. 1968. *Political Order in Changing Societies*. New Haven: Yale University Press.

———. 1984. *American Politics: The Promise of Disharmony*. Cambridge, Mass.: Harvard University Press.

Katznelson, Ira. 1981. *City Trenches: Urban Politics and the Patterning of Class in the United States*. Chicago: University of Chicago Press.

Logan, John R., and Harvey L. Molotch. 1987. *Urban Fortunes: The Political Economy of Place*. Berkeley: University of California Press.

Lowi, Theodore J. 1979. *The End of Liberalism*. 2nd ed. New York: Norton.

McConnell, Grant. 1966. *Private Power and American Democracy*. New York: Random House.

Machiavelli, Niccolo. 1970. *The Discourses*. Edited by Bernard Crick. Baltimore: Penguin.

MacPherson, C. B. 1962. *The Political Theory of Possessive Individualism*. New York: Oxford University Press.

Marcuse, Herbert. 1964. *One-dimensional Man*. Boston: Beacon Press.

Marx, Karl, and Friedrich Engels. 1948. *The Communist Manifesto*. New York: International Publishers.

Mills. C. Wright. 1956. *The Power Elite*. New York: Oxford University Press.

———. 1959. *The Sociological Imagination*. New York: Grove Press.

Mitchell, R. C. 1984. "Public Opinion and Environmental Politics in the 1970s and 1980s." In *Environmental Policy in the 1980s: Reagan's New Agenda*, edited by N. J. Vig and R. Kraft. Washington, D.C.: CQ Press.

Mollenkopf, J. H. 1983. *The Contested City*. Princeton: Princeton University Press.

Morris, D., and K. Hess. 1975. *Neighborhood Power*. Boston: Beacon Press.

Nelson, R. H. 1980. *Zoning and Private Property Rights: An Analysis of the American System of Land-use Regulation*. Cambridge, Mass.: MIT Press.

Neumann, Franz. 1957. "The Concept of Political Freedom." In *The Democratic and the Authoritarian State*, edited by Herbert Marcuse, 160–200. New York: Free Press.

Newton, K. 1978. "Conflict Avoidance and Conflict Suppression." In *Urbanization and Conflict in Market Societies*, edited by K. R. Cox, 76–93. Chicago: Maaroufa Press.

Parkin, Frank. 1971. *Class Inequality and Political Order*. New York: Praeger.

Peterson, Paul. 1980. *City Limits*. Chicago: University of Chicago Press.

Piven, Frances Fox, and Richard Cloward. 1979. *Poor People's Movements: Why They Succeed, How They Fail*. New York: Random House.

Plotkin, Sidney. 1987. *Keep Out: The Struggle for Land-use Control*. Berkeley: University of California Press.

Popper, F. J. 1981. *The Politics of Land-use Reform*. Madison: University of Wisconsin Press.

Poulantzas, Nicos. 1975. *Political Power and Social Classes*. Translated by T. O'Hagen. London: Verso/New Left Books.

Rieder, J. 1985. *Canarsie: The Jews and Italians of Brooklyn Against Liberalism*. Cambridge, Mass.: Harvard University Press.

Saunders, P. 1981. *Social Theory and the Urban Question*. New York: Holmes and Meier.

Savas, E. S. 1987. *Privatization: The Key to Better Government*. Chatham, N.J.: Chatham House.

Schattschneider, E. E. 1960. *The Semi-sovereign People*. New York: Dryden Press.

Schwartz, N. L. 1988. *The Blue Guitar: Political Representation and Community*. Chicago: University of Chicago Press.

Seidelman, R., and E. J. Harpham. 1985. *Disenchanted Realists: Political Science and the American Crisis, 1884–1984*. Albany: State University of New York Press.

Smith, M. P. 1988. *City, State and Market: The Political Economy of Urban Society*. New York: Blackwell.

Stone, C. N. 1987. "The Study of the Politics of Urban Development." In *The Politics of Urban Development*, edited by C. N. Stone and H. T. Sanders. Lawrence: University of Kansas Press.

Swanstrom, Todd. 1985. *The Crisis of Growth Politics: Cleveland, Kucinich and the Challenge of Urban Populism*. Philadelphia: Temple University Press.

Tocqueville, Alexis de. 1945. *Democracy in America*. Vol. 2. Edited by P. Bradley. New York: Random House.

Veblen, Thorstein. 1915. *Imperial Germany and the Industrial Revolution*. New York: Viking Press.

Weber, Max. 1978. *Economy and Society*, 2 vols, edited by Guenther Roth and Claus Wittich. Berkeley: University of California Press.

Weibe, R. H. 1967. *The Search for Order*. New York: Hill and Wang.

Williams, Raymond. 1983. *The Year 2000*. New York: Pantheon.

Yates, D. 1977. *The Ungovernable City*. Cambridge, Mass.: MIT Press.

C H A P T E R 10

The Agony and the Equity
Strategies for Building Low-Income Housing

Tony Schuman

Criticism of self-help is heretical in Western moral and social thought. It flies in the face of biblical injunction, the Puritan work ethic, and the pioneer spirit. Indeed, who can offer anything but encouragement to those who, unable to compete for housing in the private market and neglected by inadequate public programs, provide shelter for themselves and their families through the sweat of their brows? But a problem arises when this individual solution to the housing question is elevated to programmatic dimensions suggesting wide

This short essay has a long history. It was solicited in 1980 as a critique of a self-help rehabilitation project in Harlem sponsored by the Urban Homesteading Assistance Board (UHAB), which remains a primary source of technical assistance to New York City's neighborhood housing and development organizations. It was published as "Commentary on UHAB/Self-Help" in *The Scope of Social Architecture*, ed. C. Richard Hatch (Van Nostrand Reinhold, 1984), a book that encouraged a socially motivated professional practice by documenting a wide range of interventions by architects. Five years later, the essay was revised for inclusion in *Critical Perspectives on Housing*, ed. Rachel Bratt, Chester Hartman, and Ann Meyerson (1986), a compendium of analytical and programmatic writings by progressive "housers." Because the article sought to link design and construction at the building scale to broader issues of housing policy and social theory, the central argument remains unchanged. Discussion of the community organizing effort of ACORN (Association of Community Organizations for Reform Now) in the East New York section of Brooklyn is included in this revision as an example of the possibilities and problems of a self-help approach to housing.

The article's ten-year history covers a shift among low-income housing advocates from an initial enthusiasm for a "pure" self-help model largely independent of government intervention to an increasing dependency on public subsidies and contracted labor. In the process, the central issue shifts from the inherent values of self-help to the relationship between local initiative and broader strategies for empowerment. These issues are exemplified in the community organizing of ACORN. The tension between a local focus and a broader concern with structural change sits at the heart of the dilemmas of activism. There is probably no area where these dilemmas are more intertwined than self-help housing.

applicability and success on a mass scale. And although the optimism that attended early self-help housing experiments has abated somewhat in the face of time and financial pressures, the allure of small-scale, grass-roots direct action remains powerful. This essay attempts to suggest directions that might strengthen self-help housing and lead to a more generalizable response to the housing question in the United States.

The Growth of Self-Help

The cooperative, self-help tradition in the United States may be traced to barn raising and the quilting bee in the years of westward expansion, but its application to multifamily urban housing is recent (Kolodny 1986). Several factors explain this upsurge. The cycle of disinvestment (leading to housing abandonment) and reinvestment (by a new urban "gentry") has resulted in the displacement of hundreds of thousands of households.[1] At the same time, the rapid increase in tax foreclosures has put many buildings in city hands, potentially available to tenants at low cost.[2] This combination of pressure and opportunity has promoted self-help as a means of preserving both the housing stock and the community profile of low-income neighborhoods.

The scope of resident-initiated housing activity is broad, ranging from rent strikes and tenant management to development and sponsorship of rehabilitation and new construction. Self-help housing, more particularly, involves two programmatic ideas: the desire to reduce construction and operating costs by investing "free" labor, and cooperative ownership of buildings to guarantee security of tenure. These ideas are clearly combined in the sweat-equity approach pioneered by the Urban Homesteading Assistance Board (UHAB) in New York City, now codified in New York's municipal homesteading program.[3] Since this approach serves as a model for similar efforts in other cities, it is of more than local interest to examine the pitfalls and shortfalls of sweat equity.

Benefits of Self-Help

Four potential benefits are claimed for self-help housing:

1. Reduced construction and operating costs. Savings result from the donated labor of the participants in construction (and eventual maintenance) and the use of public subsidies to produce below-market mortgage interest rates.

2. Employment and skills training. Residents working under the supervision of experienced builders learn skills useful in building construction, management, and maintenance, and are prepared for employment in the construction industry and related fields.

3. Control of urban land. With the housing shortage forcing rents upward and making working-class neighborhoods ripe for redevelopment, cooperative ownership offers the hope of retaining a part of the housing stock for low- and moderate-income families.

4. Strengthening of community and individual identity. The effort required to carry out a rehabilitation project in the face of adverse economic conditions, bureaucratic red tape, and inevitable construction snags is a powerful molder of collective consciousness and self-esteem. The process serves to decommodify both labor power and housing (assuming nonspeculative resale restrictions), providing an opportunity for dignified work whose product is appropriated directly by the workers. Self-help housing also offers design flexibility capable of meeting the needs of nontraditional user groups ill served by conventional housing programs.[4]

Pitfalls

All the potential benefits have been realized to some extent in every self-help project, and this is the great merit of the approach. At the same time, each has also revealed serious problems, suggesting that self-help housing will need greatly increased assistance to become a viable option and that much more radical programs must be developed if we are ever to realize the promise of a decent home for every American. The problematic aspects can be explored by reference to the benefits described above.

1. Reduced costs. Recent trends indicate that the gap between housing costs and income continues to grow. According to the *New York Times* of April 20, 1982, during the 1970s median rents rose 125 percent nationally, while median incomes went up only 98 percent. More recent figures for New York City indicate that housing costs continue to rise faster than inflation and that although rent–income ratios have remained constant over the past three years (at 29 percent) this statistic understates the dramatic loss of low-rent units.[5] Despite a net gain of 50,000 jobs in the city in 1988, nearly one-quarter (23.2 percent) had incomes below the poverty level set by the federal government ($11,611 for a family of four). Samuel M. Ehrenhalt, regional commissioner of Labor Statistics, observed in the *New York Times* on February 28, 1989, "I think this kind of challenges some cherished notions of the past that economic growth would be adequate to pull people out of poverty." The net result is that those who need it most are increasingly unable to afford even self-help housing, despite the reduction in initial costs and the economies involved in cooperative management and maintenance.

There is no reason to believe that the gap between income and housing costs will narrow. On the contrary, the historical inability to correlate costs and incomes indicates that the discrepancy is a structural aspect of capitalism, viewed as a long-term secular trend (Stone 1986). Because housing costs are affected much more by mortgage rates than construction costs, sweat labor itself is unable to solve the dilemma posed by the rent–income gap. As a result, self-help housing is increasingly dependent on government subsidies. New York City's Homesteading program has been obliged to increase their subsidy from $6000 per unit in 1982 to up to $45,000 in grants and loans on current projects. Neither the economic nor the political climate suggests that these subsidies will soon be available in sufficient quantity.[6]

2. Employment. The potential benefits here are restricted at the outset to the younger and more energetic of the poor. Excluded are the elderly, the disabled, women with child-care responsibilities, and employed people who could not support themselves and their families on the modest stipends that were initially available to self-help labor through vehicles like the defunct Comprehensive Employment Training Act (CETA) program. For participants in self-help, training in the building trades offers little beyond its eventual application in building maintenance. As the minority groups most active in self-help housing have historically been excluded from the construction trade unions, there is little likelihood that self-help training will lead to permanent employment. The result is that in employment terms, the experience is perhaps more valuable in terms of basic job skills than in construction work directly. Several homesteaders have found jobs with public and community agencies concerned with housing and related programs.

It has been argued that there are more than enough potential construction jobs available in rehabilitating the housing stock of our beleaguered cities to employ the self-helpers and ease the unemployment problem generally. The idea is appealing for both economic and social reasons. Nevertheless, there are substantial obstacles to realizing such a program on more than a token scale. First, there would be competition from the construction unions wanting a piece of the action. Second, with the virtual elimination by the Reagan administration of direct federal housing subsidies, housing rehabilitation is largely restricted to gentrifying areas attractive to private capital. If the rehabilitated housing were to meet the social goal of sheltering low- and moderate-income households, it would require not only construction subsidies but also deep operating subsidies and a commitment to the right of people to remain in their communities regardless of their status in the economy.[7] This last concern goes right to the heart of the question of control of urban land.

3. Control of urban land. Despite the efforts of New York City's innovative Alternative Management Programs, several of which aim at the disposition of city-owned housing to tenant cooperatives or not-for profit community organizations (Kolodny 1986), the amount of housing thus retained for low- and moderate-income households is negligible compared with the wave of coop conversions and gentrified brownstones that is transforming the class and racial character of New York's older neighborhoods.[8] In more remote and derelict communities, such as the South Bronx and central Brooklyn, where gentry fear to tread, a policy of "planned shrinkage" has been proposed to spur the out-migration of poor residents.[9] From an accounting standpoint, this would rid the city of dependent, service-consuming tenants and open up vast tracts of land for redevelopment. In these outlying areas, the absence of private-market interest in the land has facilitated their availability for community-based affordable housing initiatives, although the absence of a neighborhood retail and service infrastructure remains a problem. Conversely, in neighborhoods like Clinton and Valley on Manhattan's West Side, both under intense development pressure, the clustering of buildings in the city's Alternative Management Programs helps the neighborhoods hold the line against complete gentrification.

What is at issue here is the very definition of a city. While community residents see the city as a place to live and work, raise children, and pursue their educational, cultural, and recreational needs, the private real estate sector sees the city as an opportunity for investment, a locus for the accumulation of capital. Commenting on proposals to rehabilitate low-rent housing in the West Side Urban Renewal Area in New York, the *New York Times* editorialized on December 1, 1979, that it would be irresponsible to permit continued low-yield use of the land when private investors stood ready to renovate the area for high-income families: "The city's obligation is to demolish the obsolete buildings and sell the land for as much as possible."[10]

Municipal policy in older industrial cities, such as New York and Newark, New Jersey, is to recapture the housing stock as a tax-paying resource, even if this objective puts housing beyond the reach of low-income families. As these cities reorganize their economies in the face of massive industrial flight, the captive pool of unskilled labor is seen as a liability rather than a resource. Put crudely, unskilled workers are superfluous to an increasingly service-sector economy, and so is their housing. In this context, the ability of the urban poor to remain in the city at all depends on their willingness to subsidize their own existence. But self-help housing cannot compete with private interest. A few buildings may be salvaged, but urban land is controlled by capital.

4. Community and individual identity. Self-help housing is an intense, energizing, and creative undertaking. In the absence of public or private support, community residents have taken a stand in defense of their communities. People have been "reborn" in a socially conscious and collective manner.[11] Newly rehabilitated buildings stand as rays of hope amid piles of rubble.

The impact of the self-help experience on its participants is difficult to measure and varies widely from group to group. The most passionate advocate of self-help is the English architect John F. C. Turner, whose book *Freedom to Build* has been a Bible for the movement. His view stresses the values of self-sufficiency, autonomy, and decentralization, and suggests that self-help housing is an expression of individual liberty. Adherents of this viewpoint present optimistic assessments of the process, and support the concept with a fervor approaching "sweat ecstasy." There is an implicit assumption that small communities can be sustained internally and independent of larger economic and political forces. The model calls for an expanding number of local efforts, leading to the eventual incorporation of like communities in a new, self-governing network—society is transformed from the bottom up.

This view reflects both a populist orientation, distrustful of a government controlled by a giant corporations, and a conservative anarchist perspective, wary of centralizing tendencies in large-scale organizations. But to the extent that self-help is seen as a starting point for transforming society, there are several instances in which it works at cross-purposes to this goal.

There is an inherent tendency in self-help to reduce the value of labor power, to have a depressant effect on wages, despite a general agreement that the maldistribution of income is a primary source of our housing problems to begin with. The willingness of self-help workers to labor for low wages, or even without compensation, competes with the demand for an adequate living wage.

By assuming the burden of providing shelter for themselves, self-help groups reduce pressure on government to maintain its legitimacy by alleviating the failures of the private market with social programs.[12] This implicit willingness to manage the contradictions of the capitalist housing market is sometimes acknowledged explicitly by the participants.[13]

The absorption of discontent through self-help housing activity also has a dampening effect on accumulated grievances, which might erupt into social conflict with broader implications. Major efforts at reform in the United States have generally followed open social strife, from the Draft Riots of the Civil War to the Great Society programs that followed the urban rebellions in the late 1960s. The point is not lost on advocates of the status quo.

The precarious financial picture of self-help housing has led community groups to entertain a variety of agreements with private investors to preserve and expand the stock of low- and moderate-rent housing. Until the Tax Reform Act of 1986 removed the depreciation allowance as a tax shelter for outside income, a number of not-for-profit community groups entered joint-venture limited-partnership agreements with private investors through the sale of equity shares.[14] Since the tax reform, attention has shifted to various developer give-back schemes (internal cross-subsidies or contributions for off-site affordable housing) which trade zoning concessions and tax credits for housing assistance. These approaches, while outside the pure sweat model, demonstrate the pressures to conform to the private market for housing. Although no neighborhood group can be faulted for seeking critical financial assistance, there is at least an element of irony in the attempt to solve housing problems by reinforcing the tax code and zoning incentives that maintain a housing system based on profit rather than need.

Because the same economic forces that threaten the viability of self-help housing on a project basis prevent its applicability on a large scale, the question of consciousness is a critical one. The natural desire for control over one's housing does not alter the fact that self-help groups do not command sufficient economic resources to make it work. Likewise, recognition of the indifference and inefficiency of the central government does not alter the fact that the government alone has the political power and economic resources to provide housing for those unable to compete in the private market. If the pitfalls of self-help housing are predominantly economic in nature, the shortfalls stem from its failure to challenge the structure of the economy. The root of the dilemma is the privatization of the housing question, the attempt to solve a collective social problem—

the provision of decent, affordable housing—at the level of an individual building.

Shortfalls

Because the housing question arises from the disparity between housing costs and income, there are three logical means of addressing the problem: raise wages, lower costs, or subsidize the difference.[15] As self-help groups complete the construction phase and take on the management and mainte-nance of their housing, the underlying economic problems come to the fore. It is especially instructive, therefore, to see how the groups approach the question of financial solvency.

As self-help groups tend to view the housing problem as outside the labor market, issues of wage levels and income distribution are generally not addressed. Instead, a number of proposals have been put forth aimed at further lowering production costs. There have been a few attempts to lower the cost of materials through cooperative purchasing or the creation of small shops to fabricate items such as kitchen cabinets. Most efforts focus on easing the size and terms of the mortgage itself. While production subsidies ease the debt burden, they do not address the issue of long-term maintenance and operating (m&o) expenses. In the case of public housing, for example, where capital costs are financed through bond issues repaid through general tax revenues, tenant incomes are not sufficient to cover m&o costs, even exclusive of any debt burden. The general manager of the New York City Housing Authority estimates that rental income, where rents are limited to a maximum of 30 percent of gross household income, covers only two-thirds of the operating budget, the balance coming from additional federal subsidies under the Brooke amendments (Shuldiner 1989).

In this light, the most encouraging development in self-help housing circles is the call for permanent operating subsidies. While not actually closing the cost–income gap, this demand at least acknowledges its exis-tence. It marries a practical response to the problem with a historical and theoretical understanding of our capitalist housing system. The underlying premise is that rents should be based on income—an obvious point of unity with all low- and moderate-income tenants. The idea itself is hardly radical. Both public housing and the recently curtailed Section 8 subsidy program are based on the principle that tenants should not have to pay more than 25 to 30 percent of their income in rent.[16]

The demand for permanent operating subsidies is attractive for several reasons. First, it is national in scope and addresses the housing problems of millions of needy families in addition to the relatively small number engaged in self-help. Further, the subsidy issue raises three questions that go to the heart of our socioeconomic structure: the nature of present housing subsidies, the ideology of homeownership, and the financing sources for additional operating subsidies.

The prevalent notion is that existing housing subsidies are for the poor. This is not so. The present beneficiaries of federal housing subsidies are overwhelmingly middle- to upper-income investors, landlords, and home-owners rather than low-income housing consumers. The principal vehicle for subsidy is the Internal Revenue System, which offers highly regressive deductions to homeowners for property taxes and mortgage-interest payments and gives housing investors generous deductions for depreciation (Dolbeare 1986).

Just as important as the issue of unequal benefits through tax policy is the way in which these subsidies have reinforced the idea of homeownership as symbolizing the success of the free-market system in housing. In the words of Herbert Hoover, an enthusiastic booster of the "own your home" campaigns in the 1920s, "To own one's own home is a physical expression of individualism, of enterprise, of independence, and of freedom of spirit."[17]

In this regard, it is not surprising that self-help housers are so taken with the idea of ownership. They are hostile not only to private for-profit ownership of housing but also to public ownership. The obvious alternative to indifferent public agencies or rapacious private landlords, however—control through cooperative nonprofit housing—turns out to be an illusion when residents cannot meet carrying costs. And while New York City has been generous in its tax abatements for builders of luxury housing, there has been little public discussion of tax relief for low-income housing cooperatives. Ownership may in fact mean control when we are talking about giant corporations that command enormous capital resources and government attention, but it does not mean control for the disenfranchised poor.

The recognition of the need for permanent operating subsidies can shift attention from the ideological issue of ownership to the practical question of control in terms of security of tenure. To provide this security, new public financing mechanisms will be necessary to provide the requisite level of ongoing subsidy. The National Low Income Housing Coalition proposed replacing the present tax-*deduction* mechanism with a tax *credit*, which would have provided more equitable assistance to moderate-income home-owners and would have increased federal tax revenues by an estimate $3.5 billion in 1982 (Dolbeare 1981).

Organizing for Self-Help Housing Programs: ACORN in New York

The dilemmas that pull organizers back and forth between class and commu-nity, received and derived ideology, and voluntarism and reliance on state action are clearly limned in the recent homesteading program launched in New York by ACORN (Association of Community Organizations for Reform Now). As a brash newcomer to local housing issues, the group's successful squatting action in the East New York section of Brooklyn led to important innovations in housing delivery systems, and raised equally important ques-tions about organizing strategies.

Beginnings

From its modest beginnings in 1970 as an organization of welfare mothers in Little Rock, Arkansas, ACORN has expanded in the past two decades to become a national, multi-issue organization with over 75,000 members in twenty-seven states. The group's strategy is to build a "mass community organization" that must be permanent, membership based, employing direct action tactics to achieve the overriding social goal of empowerment (Delgado 1986, 63). Despite the tight organization and multi-issue focus, it was not until 1985 that ACORN launched a major organizing drive in New York City. It did so, however, in a big way.

The first ACORN organizing team arrived in New York in 1982 and set up shop in the poor neighborhoods of central Brooklyn. Focusing quickly on the housing problem, ACORN sought for three years to convince the city's Housing Preservation and Development (HPD) agency to convey to them title to vacant abandoned buildings for a homesteading program. In August 1985, impatient with the lack of progress and drawing on tactics that had been successful in Philadelphia and other cities (Borgos 1986), ACORN organized a squatting action in twenty-five vacant city-owned buildings. In the context of a desperate housing shortage and in the midst of an election-year primary battle between Mayor Edward Koch and City Council President Carol Bellamy, ACORN orchestrated a brilliant media campaign. Drawing clergy and elected state and local officials to the site, several of whom were arrested along with squatters, ACORN's pressure brought a response from the borough president's office to help negotiate a solution that saved both face and houses. The deal was simple: The city would stop trying to evict the squatters and would work with them on a homesteading program if they, in turn, would disavow squatting as a tactic. As Felice Michetti, then first deputy commissioner at HPD, was quoted in the *New York Times* of October 12, 1987, "Once ACORN was willing to recognize that squatting is illegal and not an answer, it paved the way for a mutual sharing of ideas and financing by the city."

While ACORN had considerable expertise in community organizing, they had little experience in housing development. In this regard, the involvement of the Pratt Institute Center for Community and Environmental Development was critical. Pratt Director Ron Shiffman, based on his long experience with New York City government and a more recent involvement with ACORN, brokered the no squatting/no evictions agreement. More important, Pratt's sophisticated grasp of housing and development economics led to the proposal for a mutual housing association (MHA) as the vehicle for carrying out both the transfer of title and the renovation of the buildings.

Mutual Housing Association

In essence, an MHA is a private, not-for-profit corporation chartered by the state for the purpose of providing new or rehabilitated housing at below-market rates through various forms of public assistance and membership contributions. While MHAs have been in widespread use in Western Europe since the turn of the century, ACORN's establishment of the Mutual Housing Association of New York (MHANY) represents the first municipally sponsored effort in New York City to move beyond the proposal stage.[18] Membership is open to any household whose family income does not exceed 80 percent of the New York metropolitan area median. As of January 1989 there were 60–70 families occupying thirty-eight predominantly two- and three-family buildings as homesteaders; an additional 150–160 families are on a waiting list. Three- quarters of these households earn less than $15,000 per year, and their median income in $9600 (Wood 1989). Member households are required to make an annual contribution of $32 and to designate at least one household member to perform fifty hours of voluntary "sweat" labor. There is a one-time cost of $250 to purchase the dwelling unit (the buildings are sold to MHANY by the City of New York for $1 a building). In addition to the buildings currently occupied, the city has committed to transfer title to 20 more buildings, for a total of 180 units.

In order to preserve the affordable character of the housing for future residents, MHANY retains ownership of the land and places restrictions on the deed to the house that limit the resale price to the initial $250 investment plus receipted expenses for approved improvements to the dwelling. If the homesteading family wishes to move, they are obliged to offer the unit to MHANY for repurchase so that MHANY can transfer the occupancy to another member household. Viewed from the perspective of housing affordability, this limited-equity arrangement is the most significant part of the program. It decommodifies housing while retaining the security of tenure associated with homeownership. As Shiffman noted in the *New York Times*, October 12, 1987, mutual housing represents "a new form of social contract between the city and its poorer residents, who get buildings at a nominal fee while giving up their right to speculate and maximize profit. The transfer of property in return for the promise of housing for low-income residents in perpetuity is a good one." MHANY thus accomplishes two goals at the same time: The MHA institutionalizes ACORN's presence in the neighborhood (through their ownership of the land), and the resale restrictions institutionalize the nonspeculative character of the renovated housing.

Even if speculative profit taking on resale is eliminated, however, long-term affordability depends on monthly operating and maintenance costs as they correlate to homeowner income. ACORN's MHANY project has benefited from an unusual level of public subsidy, reflecting both the successful organizing campaign and the skilled resources of the Pratt Center and the Consumer-Farmer Foundation, which provides financial administration services to MHANY. The benefit package includes below-market and forgivable loans (under an income-based formula), construction grants for MHAs and rehabilitation grants from city, state, and federal sources.[19] The combined impact of this assistance is a projected monthly operating cost of under $100 per unit, with a maximum of $130 a unit. This includes taxes, insurance, a reserve fund, and a $10 monthly administrative fee to MHANY (which increases to $30 after granting of the Certificate of Occupancy). By agreement with the city, the tax burden will remain at current (prerenovation) assessment levels for a period of ten years. This figure does not reflect debt service or building maintenance.

Although several of the first homesteading families invested considerable sweat labor in renovating their homes, the present model is for the "sweat" component to be limited to trash removal during demolition and finish work after occupancy, with the balance of the work contracted out. This shift away from a pure sweat model is congruent with the experience of other homesteading programs in New York and reflects the inherent financial and physical problems of the process: It often takes four years or longer to rehabilitate a building using nonskilled, part-time labor; low-income families are limited in their ability to purchase materials directly or to get credit from lending institutions; the pace of construction is restricted by the number and physical capacity of the household members. In the MHANY program, the sweat component is limited typically to less than 10 percent of the construction cost.

Ideology

The great merit of the MHANY project is the immediate benefit to the homesteading families and the safeguarding of benefits for future families. Since MHANY requires resale to the association itself, the transaction is controlled directly. The response of the homesteaders and the contribution to citywide housing organizing represented by ACORN remain to be seen. Early indications are that the homesteaders are primarily (and understandably) interested in decent, affordable housing with security of tenure. In newspaper interviews, they speak not of global issues of economic and social justice but of individual hard work, pride, and sacrifice. "I've tried to train my sons to be serious, to do serious work and take care of their families," observed one homesteader in the *New York Times* of October 12, 1987. Another explained, "Little by little, I've put a lot of money into this house, and I didn't want to lose it."

The translation of this intensely personal experience into a broader level of community action will depend ultimately on the consciousness of the homesteaders. As the process moves more toward outside contracting and tackles multiple dwellings where households will be cooperators rather than homeowners, this consciousness will be even more difficult to induce and maintain.

A Strategic Role

Despite its shortcomings, self-help is a currently necessary activity and a useful training ground for local activists. Participants are brought into direct confrontation with market forces and financing schemes. In this sense, it is precisely because self-help does not "work" as a solution that it has potential. The self-respect and fighting spirit of the self-help housers, coupled with their manifest commitment to preserving their neighborhoods, inevitably leads them to defend their physical and emotional investment. As they come to grips with the high cost of housing operation, they are obliged to consider various cost-reducing strategies, including mortgage and tax default. They are also pushed to act in coalition with other self-help groups and to reach out to other low- and moderate-income tenants.

A demand for permanent operating subsidies anticipates the pressures to default and can help the self-helpers concentrate on issues that are, in fact, within their control—the day-to-day decisions regarding the management of their housing, from tenant selection and eviction policy to maintenance and repair priorities.

This demand socializes the housing question. It insists on housing as a matter of need and of right, on housing as a necessity and not a luxury, on housing that must, therefore, be treated as a public good and not as a commodity (Achtenberg and Marcuse 1986). By themselves, of course, subsidies cannot solve the housing question. The social context for housing includes issues of employment, education, health services, and discrimination by race and gender. But the demand is a practical one that can be implemented incrementally and that can provide an ongoing experiment in public responsibility with local control.

Self-help groups, for example, are in an excellent position to demand targeting of existing housing subsidies for buildings in not-for-profit cooperative, community, or public ownership. The groups will also be in the forefront of the demand for greatly increased housing subsidies, having demonstrated that hard work cannot surmount the failure of the private market.

It has been argued by some that advocacy of self-help is a dangerous diversion, shunting attention from the structural aspects of the housing program into a bottomless pit of small-scale self-exploitation. To the extent that self-help is seen as a solution to the housing question, these fears are well grounded. But the key, as always, is to bring the conflicting foci of the dilemmas of activism to as common a point as possible. In the absence of a national mass movement for decent housing as a public responsibility, therefore, self-help programs, coupled with some understanding of the structural nature of the housing problem, constitute an important aspect of the struggle for social and economic justice.

Notes

1. A 1982 study of displacement, defined as "people losing their homes against their will," estimated that 2.5 million Americans are affected each year and that, beyond this total, "some 500,000 lower-rent units are lost each year, through conversion, abandonment, inflation, arson, and demolition" (Hartman, Keating, and LeGates 1982, 3).

2. The foreclosure process has produced its most dramatic results in New York City, where nearly 8000 buildings were under municipal ownership as of January 1989. Of this total 4358 buildings were occupied, making the city the unhappy landlord for almost 50,000 occupied units (48,821) housing over 150,000 people (Kiefer 1989).

3. The Urban Homesteading Assistance Board (UHAB) is a nonprofit housing service establishment in 1973 to advocate and provide technical assistance for self-help housing groups. The initial UHAB approach was to use voluntary "sweat" labor to perform most of the construction work, under the supervision of paid, skilled (and licensed) professionals. UHAB helped the groups secure legal and architectural assistance and negotiated grants and low-interest loans for seed money and construction costs. For an account of UHAB's history, and a case study in self-help housing rehabilitation, see Laven (1984). With UHAB's assistance, New York City's Department of Housing Preservation and Development (HPD) launched an Urban Homesteading Program in 1981, with the city performing work requiring professionals and the homesteaders doing demolition, roofing, carpentry, and interior work.

4. This design flexibility could be in the form of unit size and mix or in the provision of special facilities such as day care, workrooms, greenhouses, or even a mosque (see Laven 1984).

5. According to the most recent triennial Housing Vacancy Survey, median gross rent in New York City rose 21.5% from 1984 to 1987, compared to an 11.6% rise in the Consumer Price Index (Stegman 1987). While the overall net loss of

renter units during the three-year period was relatively modest at 8000, the loss of low-rent units was considerably more dramatic: 67,000 units were removed from rent-controlled status (the category of city housing with the most stringent rent increase provisions), and although most of these were moved into rent-stabilized status (with modest rent increases negotiated annually for one- and two-year leases), there was a net loss of 8000 stabilized units. On the other hand, more than 54,000 unregulated rental units were created (through new construction and vacancy decontrol of existing units). The percentage of units renting for less than $300 a month dropped from more than 32% in 1984 to 17% in 1987; those renting for $500 a month or more jumped correspondingly from 17% of the stock in 1984 to 30% in 1987 (Weitzman 1988). As George Sternlieb, former director of the Center for Urban Policy Research at Rutgers University, observed in the *New York Times* on June 6, 1981, "We lose housing from the bottom and replace it at the top." The rise in homeless individuals and families is only the most visible and appalling consequence of this transformation in the local housing market (although homelessness stems from a number of factors exogenous to housing issues per se).

The general picture for New York tenants is even more precarious for tenants in city-owned housing. According to Stegman (1987), nearly 40% of these tenants pay over 35% of their income for rent (as against official federal policy, which sets 30% of income as a maximum reasonable percentage for rent). Median income for these tenants is $7848 versus $16,000 for all renters, so the rent as percentage of income ratio has even greater impact on household standard of living.

6. The rehabilitation budget includes $15,000 per unit in the form of a 30-year loan at 1% interest from the city (to allow the groups more control over contracted work than under grant financing and to make them eligible for tax-abatement programs) plus $20,000 to $30,000 in loans from the New York State Housing Trust Fund which are forgivable if the household meets applicable income-eligibility requirements. Since its inception in 1981 and through 1988, the Urban Homesteading program has processed a total of 49 buildings containing 396 units (Kiefer 1989). The city's current 10-year plan projects an additional of only 370 units through this program over the next decade ("Ten-Year Housing Plan" 1989, 7).

7. Housing abandonment and neighborhood decay are, of course, by-products of fluctuations in the free-market economy produced by the mobility of capital. The social impact of plant closings, capital flight, and other encumbrances of a capitalist economy are highlighted in Bluestone and Harrison (1982). A study by Homefront (1977) underlines the relationship between abandonment and shifts in the local labor market in terms of availability of mortgage financing and the profitability of rental housing in New York.

8. While the Division of Alternative Management (DAMP) at HPD may be justly proud of the 15,420 units in 669 buildings at present headed for continued low-income occupancy under private, not-for-profit, or cooperative ownership, this is still a drop in the bucket compared with the 7975 buildings in the city-owned inventory, most of which are headed for demolition. The city took title to 4773

occupied multiple-dwelling buildings in the six years from 1983 to 1988 (Heitler 1989). DAMP's ten-year total sales of 628 buildings with 16,280 units represents only a small percentage of the total city-owned inventory. Over the same period, 93,850 units were removed from the rental housing stock through conversion to condominium or cooperative ownership (Stegman 1988).

9. According to the *New York Times* of February 3, 1976, the phrase "planned shrinkage" was coined by then New York City Housing Administrator Roger Starr in proposing a triage approach to urban redevelopment. Although the notion was roundly criticized by community advocates and never became official city policy, it has become a de facto reality due to abandonment, arson, and service cutbacks. The result is acres of land in areas like the South Bronx and East New York, which stand ready for redevelopment through mechanisms such as enterprise zones.

10. The controversy over the West Side Urban Renewal Area continues. The debate over the last available building site focuses on alternative strategies to generate private-sector subsidies for low- and moderate-income housing. Both involve the granting of higher than as-of-right densities in exchange for developer contributions. According to the *New York Times* of February 1, 1989, the logic, says Abraham Biderman, commissioner of Housing Preservation and Development, is that "in gentrifying neighborhoods, you take revenues from the sale of land and reinvest those revenues." The local Community Planning Board approves of the strategy but rejects the density as an excessive burden on the neighborhood.

11. For an upbeat account of the impact of collective housing action on a group of Lower East Side tenants, see *The Heart of Loisaida* (1979), a half-hour film by Marci Reaven and Beni Matias. *Squatters: The Other Philadelphia Story* (1984), by Charles Koppelman, recounts a successful organizing campaign led by ACORN (Association of Community Organizations for Reform Now). Both films are available from Cinema Guild, 1697 Broadway, New York, NY 10019.

12. The argument follows James O'Connor: "The capitalistic state must try to fulfill two basic and often mutually contradictory functions—*accumulation* and *legitimization*. This means that the state must try to maintain or create the conditions in which profitable capital accumulation is possible. However, the state also must try to maintain or create the conditions for social harmony" (O'Connor 1973, 6). The point here is that self-help housers, in some measure, absolve the state of its responsibility to maintain its legitimacy through social expenditures for housing.

13. See, for example, architect Rod Hackney's account of a neighborhood-based redevelopment project in Macclesfield, England (Hackney 1984). Significantly, Hackney is past president of the Royal Institute of British Architects (RIBA) and mentor to Prince Charles in his much-publicized defense of "community architecture."

14. Early efforts using this mechanism are Inquilinos Boricuas en Accion (IBA) in Boston's South End, and Los Sures in Brooklyn's Williamsburg neighborhood.

15. These options were identified over a hundred years ago by Frederick Engels. "Capital does not *want* to abolish the housing shortage," Engels wrote, "even if it

could; this has now been finally established. There remain, therefore, only two other expedients: self-help on the part of the workers, and state assistance" (Engels 1872, 57; italics in original).

16. The rent–income ratio of 25% was not scientifically derived but emerged as a "reasonable" cap until President Reagan upped the ante to 30% in 1982 (Hartman 1986, 368). An alternative method of calculating income available for housing, by first subtracting all nonshelter necessities from household income, shows that for millions of families, even 25% of income for housing is far too high (Stone 1986, 46).

17. Quoted in "Signs of Life: Symbols in the American City," published in conjunction with an exhibition organized and designed by Venturi and Rauch, Architects and Planners, for the Smithsonian Institution, 1976. See also Wright (1981).

18. An Artists Mutual Housing Association was incorporated in 1985 but was unable to secure title to city-owned buildings and has yet to become fully operational. An important precursor to the MHAs was New York's trade union–sponsored limited-equity cooperative housing movement.

19. MHANY has secured over $4 million in grants and loans for the rehabilitation work in addition to a technical services contract to cover architectural and construction supervision work by the Pratt Institute Center and *pro bono* legal services. The bulk of the funding is $2.7 million in below-market and forgivable loans from HPD through the New York State Housing Trust Fund. Additional funding came from Rental Rehabilitation grants through the Department of Housing and Urban Development, the New York State Affordable Housing Corporation, and the New York Landmarks Conservancy. The breadth and level of funding demonstrates the ingenuity of MHANY and their advisers as well as the level of public subsidy required to make "self-help" work.

References

Achtenberg, Emily Paradise, and Peter Marcuse. 1986. "The Causes of the Housing Problem." In *Critical Perspectives on Housing*, edited by Rachel Bratt, Chester Hartman, and Ann Meyerson, 4–12. Philadelphia: Temple University Press.

Bluestone, Barry, and Bennett Harrison. 1982. *The Deindustrialization of America*. New York: Basic Books.

Borgos, Seth. 1986. "Low-Income Homeownership and the ACORN Squatters Campaign." In *Critical Perspectives on Housing*, edited by Rachel Bratt, Chester Hartman, and Ann Meyerson, 428–447. Philadelphia: Temple University Press.

Bratt, Rachel, Chester Hartman, and Ann Meyerson, eds. 1986. *Critical Perspectives on Housing*. Philadelphia: Temple University Press.

Delgado, Gary. 1986. *Organizing the Movement: The Roots and Growth of ACORN*. Philadelphia: Temple University Press.

Dolbeare, Cushing. 1981. Statement Before the Committee on Ways and Means, U.S. Congress, March 31.

————. 1986. "How the Income Tax Subsidizes Housing for the Affluent." In *Critical Perspectives on Housing*, edited by Rachel Bratt, Chester Hartman, and Ann Meyerson, 264–272. Philadelphia: Temple University Press.

Engels, Frederick. 1872. *The Housing Question*. 1970 ed. Moscow: Progress Publishers.

Hackney, Rod. 1984. "Community Architecture and Self-Help." In *The Scope of Social Architecture*, edited by C. Richard Hatch, 94–103. New York, Van Nostrand Reinhold.

Hartman, Chester. 1986. "Housing Policies under the Reagan Administration." In *Critical Perspectives on Housing*, edited by Rachel Bratt, Chester Hartman, and Ann Meyerson, 362–378. Philadelphia: Temple University Press.

Hartman, Chester, Dennis Keating, and Richard LeGates. 1982. *Displacement: How to Fight It*. Berkeley, Calif.: National Housing Law Project.

Hatch, C. Richard, ed. 1984. *The Scope of Social Architecture*. New York: Van Nostrand Reinhold.

Homefront. 1977. *Housing Abandonment in New York*. New York: Homefront.

Kiefer, Simon. 1989. Interview with the author, January 13. Kiefer is director of intergovernmental relations, Division of Alternative Management Programs (DAMP), Department of Housing Preservation and Development (HPD).

Kolodny, Robert. 1986. "The Emergence of Self-Help as a Housing Strategy for the Urban Poor." In *Critical Perspectives on Housing*, edited by Rachel Bratt, Chester Hartman, and Ann Meyerson, 447–463. Philadelphia: Temple University Press.

Laven, Charles. 1984. "Self-Help in Neighborhood Development." In *The Scope of Social Housing*, edited by C. Richard Hatch, 104–117. New York: Van Nostrand Reinhold.

O'Connor, James. 1973. *The Fiscal Crisis of the State*. New York: St. Martin's Press.

Reynolds, Sue. 1989. Interview with the author, January 10. Reynolds was a planner at the Pratt Institute Center for Community and Economic Development.

Shuldiner, Joseph. 1989. Remarks at the "Robert Moses' New York" Conference, Columbia University, February 13. Schuldiner is general manager of the New York City Housing Authority (NYCHA).

Stegman, Michael A. 1988. *Housing and Vacancy Report*. New York: Department of Housing Preservation and Development (HPD).

Stone, Michael. 1986. "Housing and the Dynamics of U.S. Capitalism." In *Critical Perspectives on Housing*, edited by Rachel Bratt, Chester Hartman, and Ann Meyerson, 41–68. Philadelphia: Temple University Press.

"Ten-Year Housing Plan: The City's Numbers." 1989. *City Limits* 14, No. 1 (January).

Turner, John F. C., and Robert Fichter, eds. 1972. *Freedom to Build*. New York: Macmillan.

Weitzman, Philip. 1988. "State of the Stock." *City Limits* 13, no. 7 (October): 12–15.

Wood, Peter. 1989. Interview with the author, January 10. Wood is executive director, Mutual Housing Association of New York (MHANY).

Wright, Gwendolyn. 1981. *Building the Dream: A Social History of Housing in America*. New York: Pantheon.

C H A P T E R 11

Changing the Conversation
Reconstructing Public Discourse about Education

Svi Shapiro

New Directions for the Sociology of Education: Toward a Politics of Educational Change

It is time for an important shift in the focus of critical educational studies and the sociology of education. While there can be no denying the spectacular advances that have been made in the last decade and a half in a whole variety of areas impinging on, and constituting the field of, education, we are still far from knowing how we might convert our insights into a genuine politics of educational change. We do not know, and until now have little explored, how public imagery and discourse about education is constructed, and how we might intervene to change them. Put more directly, we have not begun to theorize the process through which a (progressive) agenda for educational change might be employed—one that has the capacity to capture the ideological and linguistic high ground from the dominance of the political right. Despite our critical understanding of pedagogy, curriculum, and knowledge, of the hidden curriculum, of the production of texts, of the structure of class, race, and gender divisions, and of the role of the state, we have little focused, at a popular level, on how educational issues are so defined, how a public language about what schools should or should not do comes to hold sway, or how a politics that effectively articulates educational concerns develops.

Drawing on my own empirical studies as well as the work of people like Geoff Whitty, who have similarly surveyed the effects of radical sociology of education in Great Britain (Whitty 1985, Shapiro 1987), I have concluded that despite the immense theoretical production of recent years, the impact on public discourse has been sparse. Obviously, many factors limit interventions of a radical or critical left character; nonetheless, this should not excuse the existence of important lacunae in the work of critical educational theorists. Our failure must be compared, on the one hand, to the relative openings that have been created in public discourse around left issues— for example, those concerning the environment, feminism, sexuality, anti-imperialist struggles, peace and global justice, homelessness, poverty, and medicine. And, on the other hand, the extraordinary success of the right in constructing popularly resonant discourses about education that appeal to powerful impulses in American life—choice, freedom, accountability, opportunity, moral standards, hard work, and rigor. Put more bluntly, what is the use of our exquisitely elaborated emancipatory pedagogues if we lack the capability to mobilize significant public support for and affirmation of them? We still have fully to confront the fundamental question of how we are to constitute an alternative (or counterhegemonic) vision of education. I am concerned with a discourse that might effectively mediate our radical hopes in the form of an agenda capable of winning the allegiance of working- and middle-class parents and other citizens in the society—if not all of them, at least significant elements among them. What educational images, ideas, philosophies, and policies can together harness the needs and inter-ests of these constituencies so that, in Gramsci's terms, a "popular bloc" might be politically constituted, one concerned with a democratic and emancipatory reorientation in the purpose and nature of schools in the United States. There has yet to be formulated a critical *politics* of education conceived in these terms.

Such a politics must start from a recognition that within critical social, moral, cultural, and economic situations, there is a continuing ideological contest over how situations are to be defined and understood, and through what discursive logic they are to be placed and made sense of. Politics, in our society, notes Stuart Hall, is either conducted ideologically or not at all. The power of the right's political project is that it has been willing and able to make thematic a whole range of crises in ideological terms that support its own economic, political, cultural, and sexual logics. It has been able to harness the real problems, concerns, and needs facing the majority of the people, and ideologically to construct them in terms of a conservative philosophy. Hall, for example, describes how the National Health Service crisis in Britain is constituted as about the "politics of choice" (note the similar process at work around the issue of tuition tax credits for private schooling in the United States), and links the popular desire for choice to the mechanism of the "free market." Of course, there is nothing natural or automatic about this connection. Hall notes that it is possible to reconstruct the idea of choice in relation to such different themes as the growing diversity of society, the widening of access, or the empowerment of ordinary people (Hall 1988, 35). It reflects the relative weakness of the left that such discursive alternatives are almost invisible. In similar ways, in an "over-bureaucratized, over-managed, under resourced society" (Hall 1988, 33), notions of "privatization" and "deregulation" represent potent ideological responses—ways of defining and explaining oppression as well as appearing to deal with it. In all of this we are drawn back to the powerfully interpretive dimension of politics. The struggle over how we should "name" the crisis we are facing is central to the process of political contestation. Since the political character of people's ideas cannot be guaranteed by our class positions or by any set of social relations, it is perfectly possible for the right to construct a politics that speaks to people's experience, that resonates with some of their everyday aspirations. Such politics, of course, ultimately "hegemonizes" their interests—that is, it reincorporates subjects into their subordinate social relations. But we need to recognize that in no sense do social interests give rise to a particular kind of politics; interests are never *given*, they have to be politically and ideologically *constructed*.

The power of the hegemonic ideology is precisely that within it can be inscribed a vast range of different social positions and interests; it seems to represent a little bit of everybody (Hall 1987?, 19). It is the illusion of the intellectual, says Hall, to believe that ideology must be coherent, each part of it fitting together neatly when in fact the whole purpose of what Gramsci called an organic ideology (one that is historically effective) is that it articulates into a configuration, different subjects, different identities, different projects, different aspirations. It does not reflect a unity, it constructs a "unity" out of difference. This is what we see in the politics of a Reagan or a Thatcher: the capacity to stitch together into an apparently unified discourse a series of different voices and identities—that of the freewheeling entrepreneur, managers of corporate capital, the respectable patriarchal male, the aggressive patriot, responsible wives and mothers, hard-pressed parents, moral zealots of the evangelical right, the independent farmer, and the blue-collar populist, among others. All of them are constructed as a unity—a collective political subject unified around a discourse that appears and feels as if it addresses *their* distinct fears, anxieties, and concerns. The success of a hegemonic political project is precisely that it offers a political agenda that seems to express a multitude of needs and contains them within social images that capture their interests in vivid and resonant language.

Public Language and Popular Mobilization: Constituting an Effective Educational Discourse

It seems to me that Hall's analysis and frame of understanding alerts us to the crucial ingredients of a politically effective discourse on education. It enables us to identify the principles that structure an educational language that mobilizes wide and popular support—a language that provides ideas, images, meanings, and a conceptual and practical logic that captures the imagination of the public around matters of schooling and education. In the first place, this analysis compels us to recognize the way in which a politically effective discourse on education must mediate larger, widely felt concerns that arise in the society and the culture. It must, in other words, address (or appear to address) popularly experienced problems, anxieties, conflicts, needs, and so forth. Education must respond (or appear to respond) to the contradictions of our social lives and ideologies; it must offer some redress to the crises that have emerged out of the circumstances of our economic, moral, cultural, communal, familial, and spiritual existence. Of course, the proposed educational ideas and practices do not usually directly deal with, or address, these crises. The circumstances that give rise to them must be interpreted or defined, and the crises explained in particular ways and remedies proposed. Education, in this context, can be, and frequently is, a crucial aspect of the process of ideological definition. Education itself can help define what the problem or crisis is about, and how it has come to exist in the forms that it does.

One example of this is the way in which the economic and communal decay of inner-city life in the major urban centers of the United States is explained in terms of the deterioration of urban education. The ineffectiveness of schools comes both to define the larger social problem and to offer a potential resolution to it. With this example in mind, and following Hall, it is certainly possible for education to play a role in redefining a critical situation so that people are allied with the power bloc or, alternatively, are in radical opposition to it. The declaration of an "educational emergency" in our cities leaves open the possibility that the crisis stems from a community culture grown pathological from overdependence on welfare institutions or, alternatively, from the effects of capital flight and corporate irresponsibility and callousness. The former explanation contributes to a "populist unity" that might favor a conservative retrenchment of the welfare state and cuts in social spending.

In all of this it is clear that contests over the discourse concerning education are ideological. They provide a theme that covers a whole range of crises, but in terms that are supportive of a larger political project. When successful, educational discourse is able to harness the real problems, concerns, and needs facing people and ideologically to construct them in terms of this political project. Of course, where this political project is conservative, needs and concerns have been incorporated in such a way that subjects are maintained in subordinate roles and social relations.

But in order to be politically effective, educational discourse must do more than mediate popular concerns. It must also constitute a collective political subject. It must create, or contribute to the creation of, a social bloc in which diverse groups somehow come to see themselves as confronted by similar problems and in need of a common educational agenda. As we have seen, this social bloc is not homogeneous; these groups are different in terms of their interests, needs, and social positions. It requires a discourse within which this diversity can be inscribed—one that "seems to represent a little bit of everybody" (Hall 1987, 19). It must provide a language that is sufficiently elastic or fluid that it can construct a unity out of difference. Its philosophical, ethical, cultural, or other message must be capable of sounding finite and clear and at the same time of speaking to a diverse range of people. Far from finding strength in cohesion and consistency, its discursive power lies in the capacity to be, if not all things to all people, then at least to have a liability of meaning that allows it to speak in and to a multiplicity of voices while maintaining an apparent unity of meaning.

How, concretely, can this be done? In what follows I have sought to illustrate the process by looking more closely at one area of the currently dominant educational discourse, that which speaks to questions of "excellence" and "standards" in schools. By looking at this area, I believe it is possible to show how political effectiveness can be achieved through precisely the means described above. By now there can be few who are not aware of the way in which the language of "excellence" has invaded public discussion of education to the point where it has seriously undercut and displaced other historically significant language (e.g., that of democracy or equity). At every level, from national reports to state plans, from national

political campaigns to school board elections, this language has hegemon-
ized the educational debate. It has done so, I believe, precisely through its
ability to speak not just to educational concerns but to wider, popularly
resonant aspirations and issues. And to the way in which it has been possible
to crystallize out of this diversity an apparently unified discursive moment
around which a powerful, political–ideological will could be constructed
and focused.

The Clamour for Excellence: The Educational Politics of Economic Decline

With the 1983 publication of the "nation at risk" report, the discourse of
excellence reached its most publicly acknowledged position. Not since the
late 1950s had the kind of language associated with this discourse achieved
such prominence. A decade or more of reaction against the humanistic and
equity-oriented discourses of the 1960s and 1970s was finally exploded in
this media-trumpeted report. Issues of falling educational standards and
mediocre schools were given a spectacular platform, and a full-scale ideological event was constructed by opinion makers in the media and by politicians
and their intellectual henchmen. It needs no genius to recognize the principal ideological underpinnings of this report (as well as related reports
working within discourses of a similar nature). Questions of declining standards and achievement are of concern because of their impact on the eroding
position of the U.S. economy vis-à-vis other capitalist economies:

> Knowledge, learning, information and skilled intelligence are the new raw
> materials of international commerce and are today spreading throughout the
> world as vigorously as miracle drugs, synthetic fertilizer, and bluejeans did
> earlier. If only to keep and improve on the slim competitive edge we will
> retain in world markets, we must rededicate ourselves to the reform of our
> educational system. (National Commission on Excellence in Education 1983)

Whatever the hand wringing over declining civic awareness, artistic or
literary accomplishments, cultural understanding and sensitivity, the real
cause for alarm lay in the way that education was failing to prepare a
workforce suitably equipped with the skills and knowledge to ensure continued U.S. hegemony in the world market. Excellence in this context became

equivalent to the schools' ability to supply corporations with higher levels of human capital; the ability to prepare and train workers needed by advanced technological sectors of American business. Without a rigorous and demanding type of schooling, this report and others like it claimed, the nation would be unable to recover from its declining industrial competitiveness. Higher productivity in the workplace, it was argued, depended on educational reforms that ensured the highest standards of academic performance. Notwithstanding the fact that this "crisis" is discursively composed as "national," it is actually a sectoral one. The discourse of excellence serves very specific class interests—particular segments of capital. Although the "what's good for GM is good for America" ideology runs deep, we must be careful that the specific national interests that are really at risk are delineated. There may well be a crisis of schooling, but it has, in this context, been shaped politically and ideologically to give a national–popular character to what, in effect, are the needs and concerns of an unrepresentative, though powerful, section of the society. As a result, public education is expected to conform ever more assiduously to the ideological and material logic that such needs and concerns dictate.

Also, within the context of economic crisis, there can be little doubt that the notion of excellence has special appeal to working-class and intermediary groups that face what Robert Kuttner has described as the "declining middle" (Kuttner 1983, 60–72)—the shrinking prospects for middle-class incomes and jobs. The restructuring of American labor identified by Kuttner, Lester Thurow, and others has provided the critical economic context that has made this kind of educational discourse especially appealing.

Facing a sharp contraction in the prospects for upward mobility, educational practices that seem to embody greater selectivity are easily connected to the anxieties and resentment of the "respectable" white working class. Excellence becomes the coded ideological promise of policies that will impose greater restrictions on entry into upper-level programs and tracks by those who appear to have benefited disproportionately from the egalitarian educational interventions of the past two decades. In this context, excellence, and the call for raised standards, represents a discursive and practical weapon through which the clamour of minorities, immigrants, and other groups in the American underclass might be stifled. It is a focal point for educational reforms that erect a dramatically expanded infrastructure of testing and evaluation, that legitimize the designation and funding of special elite public schools as well as programs for so-called gifted students, and that demands new graduation requirements that pile on extra courses and time. In all these ways, the economic crisis is addressed—but through a recipe that displaces the origins of the crisis from the investment priorities of big business and the state, and the widespread de-skilling of labor, to what is argued as declining standards in the classroom. Such a displacement carries with it racist, sexist, and nativist undertones, as well as shifting the blame from those who occupy the "commanding heights" of the economy to the inadequacies of teachers and students. Through a series of subtle but powerful ideological displacements, the very real crisis is converted into a crisis of teaching, and of cultural laxity that too readily rewards and indulges those who are really not deserving of achievement. The crisis is defined in terms of schools that have become too easy or indulgent, rather than of a society that is unable to provide an adequate supply of decently paid, secure, and satisfying jobs. There is no doubting the appeal of such arguments to a working and middle class concerned about future prospects for their children, but prone to a politics of class and racial divisiveness as the means of struggling to maintain their well-being and security.

Educating for excellence in the context of contemporary working-class and middle-class struggles is thus the coded signification for a conservative politics of education—one that holds out a solution of sorts to the precarious and eroding possibilities for intergenerational social mobility through the effects of an intensified regime of educational selection. This regime promises a more emphatic stratification and a more rigid hierarchy of opportunities and achievements within and between working-class and middle-class groups. Such a politics of education is an extension of the social struggle being waged between subordinate and intermediary groups in the United States that has focused on the welfare state. Here, as in education, middle-class and white working-class groups have perceived that social policies and legislative actions have supported those further down in the social structure at their expense. There is certainly evidence that supports this perception (Cloward and Piven 1982; Edsall 1984). After all, the American welfare state, alone among Western industrial states, does not provide universal social benefits such as national health care or child allowances. Regressive tax policies and inflation have seemed to make the middle class carry the lion's share of taxes. White working-class and middle-class resentment is the inevitable consequence of a welfare state that in its means-tested parsimony appears to, and frequently does, provide its heavily taxed working and middle classes with meager benefits. Far from augmenting, through a "social wage," the sense of labor solidarity, the welfare state can spawn a politics of racial and intraclass rage. No matter how minimal the

AFDC payments, how limited the effects of affirmative action, how scarce the affordable day care, a politics of reaction is produced in which racial minorities, the poor, women, and children are victimized. A combination of the divisive ideological effects of the welfare state and the crisis of middle-income jobs and incomes has made a discourse of excellence in schools especially relevant. It effectively harnesses the sense of middle-class social injustice and apprehension at the "downward equalization" of intermediary groups with those traditionally below them. It is certainly those feelings that, as Thomas Edsall points out, have been reflected in the political realignment that has been under way in the United States since the late 1960s (Edsall 1984).

Authoritarian Populism: Combating the Erosion of Social Authority

The tendency among progressive educators and critics to dismiss conservative attacks on the educational reforms of the 1960s as nothing more than mystification or ideological distortion misses the very real consequences for schools. Notwithstanding the hysterical overreaction of such critics as Alan Bloom, who have inferred that a radical transformation (and debacle) of the system took place during this time, real changes in education (conjoined with changes in the economy and in social relations) certainly did have an impact on working- and middle-class life. Curriculum changes, challenges to testing, opportunities for wider access by excluded and marginal groups, and so on, indeed changed some of the ideological and institutional conditions that structured class, race, and gender relations in America. The intense democratic and egalitarian pressures unleashed throughout the society threatened, even undermined, some of the relatively privileged aspects of middle-class life and the position of some members of the working class. In this sense, a call for excellence and higher standards is a coded reference to the demand that schools reassume their role of providing and legitimating a particular social hierarchy.

Of course, in this sense, the focusing of larger social and economic conflicts on issues of education is deeply rooted in American political life. "Culture wars" have historically represented the displacement into the school arena of intense social struggles. Against a wider diffusion of cultural capital achieved through the struggles of the excluded and the marginal (women, blacks, immigrants, the handicapped, and other minorities), conservative demands that schools once more ensure proper respect for the traditional academic curriculum and high educational standards find a political resonance among those made insecure by the erosion of the curricular–cultural underpinnings of the social order. Made uneasy by the clamour for rights, opportunities, and justice, groups struggle to hold the line against encroachments on their economic advantages. They provide a popular base of support for a cultural politics that decries the erosion of traditional standards and academic excellence. The social struggle is displaced into insurgencies against social promotion, mainstreaming, bicultural and bilingual education, and declining test scores. Ready support is given to policies that promise to produce and enforce stratification within and between schools through the intense use of tests and curricula that emphasize achievement and competency. "Standards," "excellence," "rigor," and "basics" are rallying cries for working- and middle-class Americans, embattled on the economic front and alarmed by a shutting down of prospects of upward mobility for their children, who choose a strategy that would increase the differentiating and hierarchical effects of schooling (instead of a struggle against corporate investment priorities and for increased economic justice). The strategy gives support to pedagogies, forms of evaluation, and curricula that intensify the competitive aspects of education and that reassert the culturally advantaged position of children from the middle class and their peers from white and native working-class backgrounds. Among these groups, excellence becomes an extension of a competitive and individualistic discourse of survival in the context of a de-industrializing and de-skilled economy.

The discourse of raised standards and excellence has come to express not only the struggle for economic survival but also a cultural resentment. Raised standards and excellence have become attached to the agenda of a populist conservatism that identifies them as weapons with which to fight the moral and cultural disintegration that has undercut the structures of social authority in America. Symptoms of this disintegration are not hard to find. Upheavals in social relations prompted by civil rights struggles, the women's movement, youth unrest, and so on, have unsettled traditional hierarchical relations involving blacks and whites, men and women, young and old. Successive government scandals from Watergate to Iran-Contra have repeatedly called into question the legitimacy of political authority and the ethical character of national leadership.[1] Notions of appropriate and correct sexual and marital behavior have become separated from ideas of unequivocally fixed propriety. Drugs and alcohol reach into all social strata, corroding the image of bourgeois respectability. The ethic of consumption— hedonism, immediate gratification, novelty, ostentatious display, and restless anxiety—contradicts the message of traditional Protestantism with its emphasis on duty, persistence, sobriety, modesty, and hard work. The cultural crisis to which the discourse of standards provides some response must not be underestimated. Its most visible protagonists might be the dispossessed southern and rural working class with their evangelical zeal, but its effects reach deeply into middle-class life. *Habits of the Heart* showed us the decimation of the language of commitment among this latter group, throwing a powerful light on the pervasively anomic underbelly of American culture (Bellah et al. 1985). The contemporary landscape of adolescent existence with its epidemic of teen suicides and childbearing attest (in obviously different ways) to the widespread forms of alienation among the young.

Quite clearly, the right has effectively articulated this moral crisis. Notwithstanding the widespread criminal culpability of members of the Reagan administration, or the sexual scandals of the religious right (or, of course, the larger responsibilities in regard to the expansion of poverty at home or renewed militarism abroad), it has succeeded in "explaining" the crisis and offering legislative directions that purport to resolve it. Not surprisingly, explanations and solutions are presented in terms of "returning" to prior high standards—of imposing discipline and renewing demands on young people. While the crisis is recognized as a broad social one, it is described as a personal one—of lax individual behavior and permissive family and school values. In all of this the culpability of the school is central. In the 1960s and 1970s the moral terrain was captured, so the argument goes, by the liberals and humanists who fomented the culture of "anything goes." Today an authoritarian populism seeks, through the schools, to reinstate a moral order without the ambiguities, uncertainties, and contingencies that apparently accompanied the culture of liberalism. As a footnote, it must be said that despite eight years of Reaganism, the authoritarian populist agenda has floundered badly. Although there has been an increase in the censorship of books, greater restrictions on the public school's press freedoms and student rights, no transformation has occurred. No new religious or moral agenda has been introduced into the schools. The struggle for a minute of prayer in public schools and the battle over "creationism"[2] signaled the way in which the very real cultural struggles of subordinate groups were siphoned off into a trivializing and marginal discourse.

The Urban Crisis: Conservative Pedagogy for Liberation?

An important variation of the discourse of excellence, one that is related to but distinct from what we have analyzed, is the crisis of urban schooling. From this "otherworld" of American education, with its shocking statistics of dropout rates, violence, absenteeism, classroom disruptions, and illiteracy, comes a particular version of the discourse structured by this specific ideological and material context. In important ways, it certainly resembles familiar conservative pedagogy. Its most grotesque embodiment is Joe Clark, the high school principal who patrolled the school halls, bat in hand, and was ready, in order to preserve an ordered learning environment, to expel any and all "hooligans" or drug pushers found in his school. Clark received firm support from within the black community and, not surprisingly, from the Reagan administration. The discourse of urban school authoritarianism also takes as its theme the degeneration of social life in the nation's inner cities, considering it a matter of personal immorality and degeneration of character. It articulates the will to improve oneself, in spite of the decrepit conditions of contemporary urban life, through individual resolve and commitment to rigorous and demanding standards. It is the puritanical component of the Jesse Jackson campaign that decries in the harshest language the use of drugs and teenage promiscuity. It echoes black critics like Louis Farrakhan, who acknowledge the debilitating moral and cultural consequences of ghetto life. Against idleness, passivity, dependence, and psychological debility, it insists on a radical personal transformation in which the exercise of discipline, responsibility, and commitment is central.[3] Ideologically inscribed in the pronouncement that "I am somebody" is the assertion of the possibilities for a better life for those able to discipline themselves (sexually, intellectually, etc.) and dedicate themselves to hard work and the highest standards of achievement. It prescribes an agenda of conservative schooling for radical ends: doing one's homework, working for the highest grades, behaving in class. In my home city of Greensboro, North Carolina, it is poignant testimony to the resonance of this discourse that the school system's optional "traditional" middle school—a school instituted as

a result of parents' criticism of the too-liberal ethos of the city's schools—
is now predominantly black. Yet the struggle for better education among
urban minorities can never be completely divorced from the pursuit of a
different agenda, one that distinguishes it from what, until now, has been
seen as a very conservative set of demands. Alongside the language of
discipline and standards is the demand for social justice. Alongside Jesse
Jackson's conservative recipe for school effectiveness and success is a more
radical call for political and economic empowerment: "Three million high
school seniors will graduate this May and June. You should come across
that stage with a diploma in one hand symbolizing knowledge and wisdom,
and a voter card in the other hand symbolizing power and responsibility"
(Jackson 1984).

For dwellers of the inner city, the crisis in schooling (or anything else)
cannot be put only in individual terms. The effects of economic decline,
corporate rapaciousness, inequalities in race and class and ethnicity, government indifference to poverty, collectively experienced homelessness,
poor medical care, inadequate nutrition, and the rest produce a recognition
of the inseparability of a discourse of excellence from that of the need for
greater social justice. In this sense, of course, the excellence movement in
urban schools can never be fully absorbed into a right-wing agenda. Equity
and excellence, as the Carnegie Foundation (1988) report on urban education noted, cannot be separated.

Contradictions of Reform: Excellence and the Professional Bureaucracy

Even a concern with issues of equity and justice does not guarantee a
progressive educational agenda. Recent conflict in the Philadelphia school
district makes this clear. Concern over inequities and low standards in that
city led district officials to develop a K–12 standardized curriculum with an
extraordinary degree of hierarchy and control over the work of teachers. The
curriculum outlines a scope and sequence for instruction in each subject,
and a "packing schedule" that suggests how much time teachers should
spend on each topic. In addition to this is a series of standardized tests
developed to monitor instruction. The majority of the school district's teachers oppose the new curriculum because of its hyperrational pedagogic
framework, authoritarian approach to teachers, and de-skilling and de-

intellectualizing of teacher's work, but the curriculum's supporters, who include not only school officials but members of the Parents Union, see it as strongly connected to concerns about equity. Its ostensible aim is to ensure that all students who graduate from the city's schools have a mastery of "essential skills and knowledge." The new policy's architect, Rita C. Altman, associate superintendent for curriculum, was quoted in *Education Week* of March 23, 1988, as saying that the curriculum "addresses the issue of equity." It "provides that which is due every child in the school district, regardless of where the child attends schools, or what his or her socioeconomic background is."

In Philadelphia, paradoxically, the quest for greater equality gives legitimacy to a rigid, standardized, positivistically oriented curriculum. There can, perhaps, be no more powerful example of the way in which hegemony is not so much imposed as superimposed on the real concerns and struggles of subordinate groups in the national culture. Social justice becomes the driving force for educational practices that are ever more authoritarian and dehumanizing.

One consequence, evident in the Philadelphia case, is that the movement for higher standards leads to an increase in power for the professional educational bureaucracy. This constituency certainly can be viewed as one that has an intense stake in how high standards and excellence are to be defined and given practical shape. The professional educational bureaucracy, too, contests the discursive and material form of educational reform. It struggles to articulate its interests in the educational crisis. Linda McNeil demonstrates this process clearly in her study of the "Contradictions of Reform" (McNeil 1988, 478–485). In an attempt by both the state and the school district to respond to concerns over factors such as the uneven quality of education, grade inflation in weak schools, and variations in teacher competence, policy changes resulted that moved the locus of knowledge and control ever further away from teachers and placed it in the hands of the administration. The changes emphasized a great subordination of the curriculum to measurability and standardization. McNeil's description of the process is worth quoting:

> The curriculum components were taken apart, sequenced, numbered, and sub-numbered in a manner reminiscent of the transformation of factories by "efficiency experts" early in the century. For each semester's work, a private testing firm designed tests of student outcomes that were multiple-choice and computer-gradeable. A teacher who followed the prescribed curriculum in

sequence, keeping pace with the district guide, would "cover" the material in time for the test. All lesson plans were to be numbered to match appropriate proficiencies, and some principals required that the day's proficiencies be posted for students to see. Teacher merit pay, building principals' bonuses, and newspaper comparisons of school scores were all linked to student performance on the proficiencies. (McNeil 1988, 483)

We must understand this process as more than irrational or mindless behavior. Bureaucracy, we know well, develops its distinct set of interests, acting in ways that are relatively autonomous from other power structures in society. It is no accident that the nettle of reform thrust on it is grasped, but it is then transformed into a set of strategies and intentions whose effect is to augment the power and authority of the bureaucracy. Whatever else comes to pass as a result of the movement for higher standards and excellence, the professional bureaucracy aims not to be a loser in the process.

The struggle against these tendencies can and must be fought at the community level. Local groups and individuals must support teachers (like those in Milwaukee and St. Louis associated with the Democratic Schools Collaborative) who insist that we are engaged in a process that is not enhancing but downgrading teaching. The constant de-skilling and de-intellectualizing of teaching in places such as Philadelphia do nothing to reverse the pervasive apathy and alienation of students in city schools. Parents can and do respond to the idea that the "dumbing-down" of teachers' work in no way adds to the vitality or interest of the students' experience. Good teaching requires, not mindless technicians, but people encouraged to act as thoughtful, responsible, and creative workers. We also have to insist that test-driven, quantifiable, and fragmented curricula do nothing to overcome the widespread boredom or hostility found among students. These changes are making things worse in the classroom, not better. They are producing, not excellence, but disinterest and failure. In particular, the point must be made that whenever schooling becomes more test oriented, it produces more losers among poor and minority students. Finally, in contesting the engineered, bureaucratic equalitarianism found in Philadelphia and elsewhere, we must insist that the real value of social justice is that it promotes democracy. The purpose of equity in our schools is that it enhances conditions under which all students become developed, critically intelligent, and responsible human beings. The kind of standardized "banking" education espoused by the bureaucracy betrays the black tradition of empowering education. It violates the liberating promise of education in a democracy. Our criteria for a quality education become, then, radically different from those offered by the bureaucracy. Our concern is ensuring that young people have "voices" with which to participate actively and assertively in determining the direction of their lives. We measure skills, knowledge, and intelligence by the extent to which they empower the young to challenge and reconstruct their decaying communities. Community groups must denounce the idea that education is, or can be, a neutral, objective, or impartial process. Education is always a political process. What remains to be determined is whose ends it will serve—the interests of the community or the corporate interest in a pool of workers accommodated to the proliferation of low-paying, dead-end jobs.

Cultural Conservatism: The Restoration of a "Regime of Truth"

For one last group we should consider, a group we might call "cultural conservatives," the discourse of excellence and higher standards promotes a "return" to an age of settled commitments, an established and certain moral order, and a culturally unified and organic community. For this group, curricular changes in schools can play a crucial role in transmitting "true, tried, and tested" meanings, knowledge, and values that can help reestablish the firm foundations of the moral and cultural order. In place of the uncertainty and relativism that plagues the postmodern world view, cultural conservatives propose an education dedicated to absolute values and an indisputable hierarchy of worthwhile knowledge. The purpose of curricular change is to reestablish the authority of what Foucault calls a "regime of truth," to replace the cacophony of voices that challenge and fragment the formerly unified and settled grammar of American life. Our present chaotic and unruly condition is viewed as primarily the result of the 1960s with its insurgencies against established values, social relations, and cultural conventions. It is the disintegrative symptoms that cultural conservatives seek to address, not the contradictory structures of our economic and political life that lie behind them.

No more disturbing example of conservative rage, an analysis that attends mainly to symptoms, and prescriptions that evoke the return to some golden age of academic excellence is to be found than Alan Bloom's (1987) enormously successful book, *The Closing of the American Mind*. In Bloom's

furious attack on liberal values he castigates all those things that the right
has associated with moral decline in America: affirmative action, equal
opportunity, rock music, the 1960s, the young, and permissive sex. Most of
all, he assaults the deleterious influence of democratic values on education.
Indeed, as William Barber (1987) argued in a review of the book, *The
Closing of the American Mind* seems to qualify as one of the most profoundly
antidemocratic books ever written for a popular audience. American society
needs protection from "openness," which produces relativism and nihilism.
American education needs protection from democratic intrusions, affirmative action, and progressive curricular reform, which undermine the authority of those who constitute that special community of the intellectual elite—
"the community of those who seek the truth, of the potential knowers."
(Bloom, cited in Barber 1987, 64).

In a different tone, E. D. Hirsch's (1987) best-seller, *Cultural Literacy*,
builds its educational prescriptions on philosophical and social foundations
that mirror those of Bloom. There is something of enormous consequence
missing in our national life, something that reflects the failure of our schools.
Young Americans are coming of age without the requisite body of shared
information needed to maintain the cultural viability of the national community (Hirsch 1987, 18). Schools are failing their fundamental acculturative
responsibility to ensure the conditions for the preservation of our communal
life. Our shared language, beliefs, and understandings have been put at
risk by the educational policies promulgated during the 1960s. Essential
ingredients for a "common basis for communication" have fallen into disre-
pair. The *fundamental* social problem is the absence of an effective language. The root cause of our political, economic, and social difficulties is
to be found in the failure of schools to provide a common discourse. The
real threat to the nation comes from the fragmentation of our communal life,
which is a consequence of the present lack of widely shared meanings,
ideas, and facts. A wider exposure to these things (not political struggle or
ethical vision) is the *sine qua non* for reconstructing a viable communal life.

Not surprisingly, Hirsch dismisses the notion that the particular discourse
he has in mind represents the cultural capital of a privileged class or section
of the population. The discourse he speaks of, he assures us, belongs to no
one specific group more than any other. "Each group," he says, "participates
and contributes as much as any other" (Hirsch 1987, 11). The fantastic
nature of this claim will be left to sociologists of culture and language to
answer. His functionalist explanation of the spread of national systems of
education and language conjures up misleading images of cultural transfor-

mations that have spread their advantages in a beneficent and fair manner to all parts of the nation.

Hirsch's vision is shared by former Secretary of Education William Bennett (1988), who proposed a core curriculum that stresses the acquisition of language skills and a "shared body of knowledge." Bennett argues that "there remains a common ground that virtually all our schools can reach and inhabit . . . and most Americans agree about what that common ground is."

Like that of Hirsch, Bennett's report reflects a certainty of what properly constitutes the character of the public language and culture—an authoritative assertion of the nature and character of valuable and worthwhile knowledge. It is, for example, clear what constitutes the "recognized masterworks of Western literature" (Bennett, cited in *Education Week*, January 13, 1988); the relative importance of mathematics and music, art, and physics; and the amount of time that should be allocated to any particular area of study. For Bennett and his ideological allies, it is time to end the equivocation and uncertainty about what must be taught, what is important, what is to be viewed as significant or great. We know exactly where we must go, and Bennett has provided the definitive map.

Not surprisingly, Bennett's cultural and epistemological certainty about what constitutes the canon of great or classic work has resulted in his castigation of scholars who question the scope or legitimacy of the existing curricular canon. Such questioning represents what he calls a "curriculum debasement" (Bennett, quoted in the February 17, 1988, *Chronicle*). The attempt in literature to include the voices of women or blacks, for example, or to dispute the clear demarcation of what can be considered high or low culture, must be regarded as academic irresponsibility and leads to the "irreparable damage" of higher education and the sullying of intellectual standards (Bennett, quoted in the February 17, 1988, *Chronicle*).

A well-publicized study by Diane Ravitch and Chester E. Finn, Jr., *What Do Our 17-Year-Olds Know?* offers the same series of explanations and perceptions found among other conservative cultural critics of education. There is dismay at the decline of an established curricular canon and the inference that schools and society have lost their hitherto sound moral and cultural moorings as a result. Of course, the now pervasive moral, cultural, and social uncertainty is the result of antiauthority insurgencies during the 1960s. Such insurgencies were driven by hedonistic and permissive impulses that contested all forms of discipline, including those demanded in the academic life. A demand for the restoration of an authoritative curriculum is thus also a demand for the restoration of a disciplined way of life. And there is the belief in a golden age that preceded the turbulent 1960s—a time when education provided the firm foundation for what is truly excellent in our tradition. The result of these changes is the decline of commitment, of ethical conviction, and of trust in established authority—effects that constitute, for cultural conservatives, the social crisis of our time.

Conclusions: Toward an Alternative Educational Discourse

What conclusions or lessons can be drawn about the possibilities of constructing a viable left educational agenda? In the first place, it is clear that at least part of what is compelling about an educational discourse is its capacity to address widely perceived problems in our social, economic, political and moral life. In this sense, there are no right-wing issues, only right-wing discourses. That is, it does no good discounting what are held to be the major issues or concerns in our lives as merely "false consciousness." Drugs, the disintegration of authority, declining literacy, the need for religious practices in schools, concerns about basics, and so on, are real problems in the eyes of many parents. If we wish to affirm Gramsci's insight that ordinary people know something about their world and their lives, then we must be ready to see the validity of specific concerns. A left agenda that wishes to be taken seriously must acknowledge and reflect these real-life concerns. What is at question, however, is the need to recompose the discourse in which these issues have been situated. We must both affirm the reality of the concerns and attempt to reconceptualize them so that their genesis and potential resolution can be understood in new and different ways. A vivid and at least partially successful example of this tactic can be seen in Jesse Jackson's embrace of the drug problem. Embarrassing to some on the left because he is taking up what is, typically, a right issue, Jackson has affirmed the reality of the problem. Yet he has also, insistently, attempted to recompose the discourse in which the drug issue usually finds itself. He wants the drug issue to be seen as the direct consequence of urban neglect, corporate irresponsibility, and the alienation and despair that results when populations are thrown on the economic and social slag heap. Thus the problem is real, but the explanations and meanings attached to it point to a politics of economic justice and social concern, not moralistic excoriation or simplistic individual solutions ("Just say no"). Redefining an issue is, of course, possible across a wide range of issues. In an outstanding new book, David Purpel (1988) argues that one does not have to belong to the religious right to believe that there is indeed a moral and spiritual crisis in American education. The tragedy is not that this group has foisted a mystifying ideology on the society but that the issue of a very real spiritual or religious crisis in our schools has been monopolized by the right. We can affirm that there is a crisis while struggling to construct it in other ways. We need, Purpel argues, a religious commitment in our schools (not to be confused with a denominational one)—not the kind that mandates a minute of prayer or some other trivializing response, but one that insists on an education that teaches, in the spirit of liberation theology, the values of community, compassion, social justice, and peace.

Our analysis of the discourse of excellence also illustrates how a collective agency for educational change is politically and ideologically constructed. The discourse represents no automatic or necessary expression of some preexisting material interest or social class. On the contrary, the collective agency was born of a complex melding of diverse, even contradictory, social groups. Each of them was able to find in the language something they could identify with, something that seemed to speak to their particular needs and circumstances. To speak of a "popular bloc" in these circumstances is to recognize that a political unity has been, at least temporarily, created out of a range of groups very different in terms of their material interests and social positions. To recognize this is to realize the necessity for a language that offers a focal point for a shared ideological campaign sufficiently broad and fluid so that it lends itself to a flexible discourse that can speak to, and for, a variety of voices. This lability of meaning provides the possibility of aggregating diverse groups into a collective will. No words or ideas will have this effect. We must know something about the issues that confront people, and about the deeply rooted and evocative traditions in the national popular culture. We have seen some of these themes developed in the language of excellence.

There is a dialectic in all of this between an issue-specific, programmatic kind of educational language and a discourse that connects directly to a larger social vision. In this sense, the left has much to learn from the right. A politically effective discourse requires the enunciation of a moral vision that speaks unabashedly in a language of hope and possibility, in utopian images of what could and ought to be. It is not enough critically to analyze and uncover what oppresses, dehumanizes, and produces suffering. There must also be an affirmation of the purpose of human existence and of how we ought relate to one another. In seeking to mobilize support for educational change, a radical agenda must place this moral vision at the center of any political discourse. This is what it means to call into question the purpose of education, what is important to know or understand. These are fundamental moral–political questions that mark the difference between a technical discourse about education and a discourse that raises essential human and social concerns. Through our insistent emphasis on these questions, we can make clear the social philosophy that distinguishes *our* educational concerns and aims from those of others. Despite the all-too-evident hypocrisy and the abuse of moralism, we must recognize the critical necessity of a clearly enunciated ethical vision to an effective politics of educational change.

Notwithstanding the importance of ethical ideals and a moral vision, what ultimately matters is the actual nature of educational practice. The litmus test of change is the pedagogical experience itself. It is clear that broad moral commitments, no matter how important they are for mobilizing political support, in no way generate specific forms of practice. In our inquiry into the discourse of excellence, we saw how wide a range of practices might be included under the rubric of a single discursive frame. It is true, too, when one looks at other powerful discourses, say, "accountability," where it is possible to find stipulated serious forms of parental and community involvement in schooling as well as (more commonly) highly bureaucratic forms of professional control. Similarly, the language of "individualization" spawns genuinely emancipatory forms of pedagogy as well as (more commonly) the reductionist and behaviorist curricular forms associated most often with what special educators call the Individualized Education Plan. We have also seen the possibilities and ambiguities associated with the recently popular notion of "empowerment," a term that is at the same time structurally or institutionally vague and yet evokes powerful imagery concerning a militant assertion of democratic rights. Although in many contexts advocates of empowerment mean something very much less than a fundamental and democratic transformation of the existing pedagogic and organizational relations, empowerment can provide teachers with ideas and language that contradict the taken-for-granted authoritarianism of schools. Within the curriculum, the notion of education for "citizenship" certainly has a history associated with the collective effacement of minority and immigrant cultures. Yet it can also serve as a springboard for demands to link the classroom to a critical interrogation of mass mediated culture.

While we reemphasize the importance to a strategy for educational change of addressing, through education, popular social, economic, political, and moral issues and concerns, and of connecting these to a broad set of moral commitments and a future vision, there is no substitute for a programmatic agenda that supports specific forms of pedagogic and curricular practice. In this sense, recent developments in the critical pedagogy of literacy and in social studies make enormous contributions to our agenda. To these we must add educational practices that can address other broadly felt concerns. For example, we cannot dismiss the concern to link education to work as merely the unfortunate consequence of the dominant pragmatic and utilitarian outlook. In the present economic climate, being skilled, even if it is only for doing dead-end, low-skilled labor, is better than being on the dole. In such a situation, parents have to take this side of education seriously. Progressive and socialist educational traditions do take this relationship seriously, and speak in relevant and significant terms to the issue of work (Castles and Wustenberg 1979, Jones 1983). Naturally, the goal here is a kind of knowledge and understanding different from the typical vocational or technical training with its narrow, de-intellectualized focus. Interestingly, as a number of commentators have noted, the current movement to restructure labor in the American economy has created some openings in the direction of a radical reconceptualization of what it means to be educated for the workplace (Carnoy and Levin 1985). Elsewhere, the crisis in media exploitation of our children and youth has created openings to a pedagogy concerned with the critical exploration of popular culture and the mass media. The precipitous decline in voting among the eligible electorate offers possibilities for a civic education that aims to teach active democratic participation in, and responsibility for, governance of the community. The threat of nuclear war has already opened the doors of many schools to parent-supported peace and global education projects. The erosion and fragmentation of communal life, along with the increasing perception of new social and racial divisions, are encouraging experiments in community service and community education. And the crises in moral and sexual life have opened a broad arena for educational interventions that, so far, have been monopolized by the right.

We have run through a series of issues, but we do not mean to produce a shopping list of proposed curricular changes. The notion of an educational agenda suggests something that is both specific in its program and broad in its image, immediate in its orientation and visionary in its concerns. It seeks, most of all, to link education to the pressing social, economic,

Where the Action Is

political, and moral concerns of our lives while grounding the resolution of these concerns in a moral vision and the future image of a world made better by virtue of being more just, more compassionate, more democratic, and more free. The danger is that our agenda might get out of balance. We might become bogged down in producing a new curriculum for every crisis and problem; or the brilliance of our vision might overawe the day-to-day work of professional educators. Of course, there is a much greater danger—that critical educational scholars might fail to become public intellectuals at all, willing and able to translate their insights into a language of popular hopes and aspirations and a strategy for effecting change.

Notes

1. For an excellent discussion of the relationship between a right-wing populist politics and the cultural disintegration of the 1960s and 1970s, see Phillips (1982) and Bell (1976).

2. For a brilliant analysis of the way "creationist" ideology has expressed the resentment and bitterness of southern working-class groups toward the "new capitalism" of the South, see Peller (1987).

3. In this context, as well as in Third World situations, there is often the widest gulf between middle-class radical morality with its libertarian spirit and that adopted as part of the revolutionary ideology of the lumpen class. The latter invariably emphasizes the need for a severe, puritanical, and disciplined moral regime as part of the struggle against the debilitating emotional and spiritual effects of colonial domination.

References

Ayers, W. 1987. What Do Our Seventeen-Year-Olds Know: A Critique. *Education Week* 7, no. 12: 18, 24.

Barber, Beryanin. 1988. The Philosopher Despot. *Criticism* 29, no. 1: 61–65.

Bell, Daniel. 1976. *The Cultural Contradictions of Capitalism*. New York: Basic Books.

Bellah, Robert N., et al. 1985. *Habits of the Heart*. New York: Harper & Row.

Bennett, William J. 1988a. *James Madison High School: A Curriculum for American Students*. Washington, D.C.: U.S. Department of Education.

————. (1988b). "James Madison High School." *Education Week* 7, nos. 15–16:27–30.

Bloom, Alan. 1987. *The Closing of the American Mind*. New York: Simon and Schuster.

Canoy, Martin, and H. M. Levin. 1985. *Schooling and Work in the Democratic State*. Stanford: Stanford University Press.

Carnegie Foundation for the Advancement of Teaching. 1988. "An Imperiled Generation." In *The Report of the Trustees of the Carnegie Foundation for the Advancement of Teaching*. New York: The Foundation.

Castles, S., and W. Wustenberg. 1979. *The Education of the Future*. London: Pluto Press.

Cloward, Richard, and Frances Fox Piven. 1982. *The New Class War*. New York: Pantheon.

Edsall, T. 1984. *The New Politics of Inequality*. New York: Norton.

Hall, S. 1987a. "Blue Elections, Election Blues." *Marxism Today*, July, 30–35.

————. 1987b. "Gramsci and Us." *Marxism Today*, June, 16–21.

————. 1988. "Thatcher's Lesson." *Marxism Today*, March, 20–27.

Hall, S., and M. Jacques. 1983. The Politics of Thatcherism. London: Lawrence and Wishart.

Hirsch, E. D., Jr. 1987. *Cultural Literacy*. Boston: Houghton Mifflin.

Jackson, J. 1984. *New York Times*, February, 27, A18.

Jones, K. 1983. *Beyond Progressive Education*. London: Macmillan.

Kuttner, B. 1983. "The Declining Middle." *Atlantic Monthly* 252, no. 1: 60–72.

McNeil, L. M. 1988. "Contradictions of Reform." *Kappan* 69, no. 7: 478–485.

National Commission on Excellence in Education. 1983. *A Nation at Risk*. Washington, D.C.: The Commission.

Peller, G. 1987. "Creation, Evolution, and the New South." *Tikkum* 2, no. 5: 72–76.

Phillips, K. 1982. *Post Conservative America*. New York: Vintage.

Purpel, D. E. 1988. *The Moral and Spiritual Crisis in Education*. South Hadley, Mass.: Bergin and Garvey.

Ravitch, Diane, and Chester E. Finn. 1987. *What Do Our Seventeen-Year-Olds Know?* New York: Harper & Row.

Shapiro, H. S. 1983. "Class, Ideology and the Basic Skills Movement: A Study in the Sociology of Educational Reform." *Interchange* 14, no. 2: 14–24.

————. 1987. "Educational Theory and Recent Political Discourse: A New Agenda for the Left." *Teachers College Record* 89, no. 2: 171–200.

————. 1988. "Beyond the Sociology of Education: Culture, Politics and the Promise of Educational Change." *Educational Theory* 38: 415–430.

Shor, Ira. 1986. *Culture Wars*. Boston: Routledge and Kegan Paul.

"Teachers vs. Curriculum in Philadelphia." 1988. *Education Week* 7, no. 26: 1.

Whitty, Geoff. 1985. *Sociology and School Knowledge*. London: Methuen.

Working-Class Women, Social Protest, and Changing Ideologies

Ida Susser

This article focuses on community activities in which women were involved in the Greenpoint–Williamsburg section of Brooklyn, New York, between 1975 and 1978. The instability of employment opportunities for both men and women and the increasing role of the state in providing life-supporting services for the poor have stimulated a new challenge, a new adversary, and a new set of activities and responsibilities for working-class women. In what follows I first review some of the literature on U.S. working-class women with respect to this kind of grass-roots activity. I then trace the community activities of poor women in one locality, linking the growing instability of the household economy to the development of particular forms of neighborhood organization.

Since the early nineteenth century, working-class women have played a significant role in the labor force and have been involved in community organizations and protest movements (see e.g., Cantor and Laurie 1980; Kessler-Harris 1982; Eisenstein 1983; Socks and Remy 1984). Despite women's long involvement in labor and community action, sociological research concerned with "blue-collar" women and "workingmen's wives" (from the 1950s through the 1970s) presents a different picture (e.g., Komarovsky 1964; Rainwater et al. 1959). It almost entirely fails to note these women's direct relationship to the "neighborhood" or "community" and their clear presence in the public sphere. Thus, although recent works on and biographies of working women document their involvement in neigh-

Reprinted from *Women and the Politics of Empowerment*, ed. Ann Bookman and Sandra Morgen (Philadelphia: Temple University Press, 1988), 257–271. Portions of this paper appeared in an earlier version in the *American Ethnologist* 13, no. 1 (1986), under the title "Political Activity among Working Class Women in a U.S. City."

borhood organizations and protest (Ackelsberg 1984; McCourt 1977; Serfer 1976; Kaplan 1982; Castells 1984; Joseph 1983; Morgen 1984; Piven 1984; Wolf 1984; Gilkes 1980; Nelson 1974), most earlier research contains little hint of such a dimension to their activities.

There are at least two explanations for these omissions. First, the problem may be *methodological*. Studies relying on structured interviews rather than participant observation will not yield data concerning women's involvement in community activities unless the relevant questions are asked and their import is recognized by the informant. Such studies certainly catch little of the texture of the community life. Second, the research may represent accurate historical descriptions of women's behavior and ideas under different *phases* of a changing national economy.

In many of the earlier studies (e.g., Ruben 1976; Komarovsky 1964; Rainwater et al. 1959), working-class women are portrayed as miserable, isolated, and passively accepting of their husbands' decisions. They survive just over the borders of poverty. They cook and clean for their husbands and take care of the children. In these descriptions, working-class women daily fight a desperate battle against loneliness and frustration. They live in fear of the awful descent into poverty should their husbands become ill, lose their jobs, or leave. Working women are seldom described in such research. When they do appear, they seem to be regarded as somewhat "deviant" cases. Epidemiological studies of women tend to reinforce this impression. One class study finds that women who live in damp, rundown housing and who have many financial problems exhibit a greater tendency toward depression than women who have more money and live in better housing (Brown and Harris 1978). Major factors in the depression of working-class women were low income and three or more children under fourteen years old at home. Once again, however, the positive impact of community involvement is not considered, and the psychological resilience of working-class women under changing conditions may be underestimated. Thus it is possible that because of the limitations of interview techniques, we have been presented with a "partial reading" of the actual experiences of working-class women.

Obviously, it is not often that working-class women (or women of any class) rise to high office in business, government, or even academia (Githens and Prestage 1977). The dearth of women in the higher echelons of political parties or union bureaucracies, or other positions of power, has been well documented (Center for the American Women and Politics 1980; Stacey and Price 1981). Under certain conditions, however, women have been involved in leadership roles in informal neighborhood organizations the constituencies of which seldom reach beyond the local or city level and rarely "make news" (Gutman 1976; Seifer 1976; Castells 1984). It remains unclear whether these activities were present in the communities described in the studies discussed above and failed to be documented simply for methodological reasons. It is likely, however, that particular historical periods generate different levels and kinds of community organization, and this is the point that is developed here.

Women, Work, and the State

It has often been noted that in industrial societies working-class women have historically served as a low-paid labor force and have also provided unpaid domestic labor (Gordon 1972; Quick 1977; McIntosh 1978; Beechey 1978). These activities are seen as integrated and facilitated by the shared household of husband, wife, and children (see, e.g., Secombe 1974; Oppenheimer 1970; Barrett 1980; Brenner and Ramos 1984). The husband supposedly has a higher-paying job and a better chance to find employment than his wife. The wife, tied down by domestic responsibilities and discriminated against in the job market, has fewer alternatives and earns lower wages, being pulled into the work world in periods of high employment or to fill particular niches.

Certainly, involvement in low-paid labor and unpaid domestic work are salient characteristics of women's work in Greenpoint–Williamsburg. But differential employment opportunities between men and women are not so clear-cut. Male unemployment is high, and unionized manufacturing jobs are disappearing (Sternlieb and Hughes 1977, 145–165). Under these conditions, household structures are more flexible than suggested in the above model, and single-parent, sibling, and multigenerational households are common. A more central and related problem is evident in the above model of gender relations in the economy. Such an analysis neglects the pertinence of remittances that people (and more specifically at this time in the United States, women) obtain from the state. It is here that women's collective action in demanding resources from the state—their direct political action—becomes particularly relevant. The political activities carried out by women to secure resources from the state are far more significant than might be predicted from an analysis that sees women only in terms of labor-force participation or domestic responsibilities.

Shifts in the structure of the American economy have created a new situation: a subpopulation made up predominantly of women and children who depend on state financing in some form. This population may see its political interests in terms of affecting state policies, and not only in terms of employer–employee relationships or male–female domestic–economic relations.[1]

In documenting women's involvement in community organizing, I draw on my fieldwork in Greenpoint–Williamsburg from 1975 to 1978.[2] In order to conduct the research, I lived in this neighborhood from September 1975 until September 1976, and in the following two years I continued to visit people informally, conduct interviews, and participate in neighborhood events. In the course of this research I spent time with many families and accompanied people in search of work, housing, public assistance, and other services, and I traced the development of a variety of community organizations. I also observed in detail such political events as the election campaign of candidates for the local school board and the protest over the closing of a firehouse (briefly outlined below). Racial and ethnic differences are reflected in significant social and geographic divisions in the area. I attempted to work with people from a variety of backgrounds and to trace divisive and cooperative processes among groups in the community.

Greenpoint–Williamsburg is an old industrial working-class neighborhood that is a casualty of the departure of manufacturing industries from New York City and of shifts in the world economy (Tabb and Sawers 1978; Alcaly and Mermelstein 1977). It is currently characterized by a diversity of ethnic and racial groups, high unemployment, and low-paying service jobs. Women and men find themselves in unstable jobs, in and out of work, and on and off public assistance. For this reason, it is imperative to view those who are at any one time dependent on public assistance as part of the working class, rather than to see them as a separate category such as "underclass" or "lower class."

Many of the women with whom I worked in Brooklyn had extensive financial and personal problems. Whether or not they lived with their husbands, they never had enough money for essentials. They were pursued by bills, electricity turn-offs, and evictions notices. They had to face days without food for themselves or their children, lack of money for health care, and major problems among themselves and their children. They had to cope with unemployment, alcoholism and drug addiction, wife beating, and child abuse—a full assortment of personal and social ills.

These problems cannot be ignored, and I would not underestimate their impact. Nevertheless, in spite of—or even because of—them, the lives of women I studied were characterized by much more than passive suffering. Above and beyond the difficulties of their daily lives, the people in Greenpoint–Williamsburg were political actors.

In order to demonstrate the importance of historical changes in the economy and state regulations and the way these can interact with a woman's life cycle to influence her involvement in political activities, I outline the careers of two women from the neighborhood. One was a black woman in her mid-fifties and the other a white woman in her early forties. Each was a leader in her own area of activity.

The first woman I will call Jackie Williams. Born in 1926, she worked in the cotton fields as a child and came to New York City with two young children in 1955. She left her husband after a series of damaging conflicts. In the South she had worked as a milliner; in the North she worked in a laundry at very low pay. Neighbors cared for her children while she was at work. After many years, she was offered a job in a local voluntary agency. From there she moved to a variety of jobs funded by the Office of Economic Opportunity (OEO) and then to a Comprehensive Employment Training Act (CETA) job. With the CETA cutbacks, she became unemployed.

From 1965 on, when her children were in their teens, Jackie Williams became an articulate and extremely active community spokeswoman. She supervised and cooked practically all the free senior citizen lunches provided daily by her agency, organized a protest against rent raises, and attended numerous meetings protesting budget cutbacks. She was not afraid to speak out in public and rallied supporters who covered the full racial and ethnic spectrum of Greenpoint–Williamsburg.

I will call the second woman Mary Sanchez. Born in Brooklyn in 1938, she married a man from Puerto Rico in 1954, and they had four children. In 1959, her husband left her and the children. After that, she would leave her children with her sister while she went out to work in a dyeing factory. When the factory moved from New York City in 1970, she stopped working and applied for Aid to Families with Dependent Children (AFDC), a federal public assistance program. Mary Sanchez received AFDC assistance until 1977, when she again returned to work—this time cleaning in factories after hours. From 1975 to 1978, she, her children, and her grandchildren were the main force behind the organization and distribution of summer lunches on Norman Street in Brooklyn. As I point out, this was an act with greater political implications than is immediately apparent.

Neither of these women lived with men while they were politically active, and in both cases their children were over ten years old at the time. Both were dependent in some form or other on state funding while they were involved in collective action. Though these characteristics are in no way universal among the politically active women I studied, they are significant in that they led to varying degrees of political involvement. Among women with younger children, day care and the particular form it took became an overriding factor in their political participation. Similarly, among married women, the husband's employment or lack of it was a significant determinant of the wife's involvement. Women whose husbands were unemployed or employed in low-paying, insecure service jobs appeared to be more active in neighborhood organizations than those who were living with apparently stable, well-paid, unionized workingmen. This may explain the variations in working-class women's activism found in the literature. As we enter a new phase of experience in the American economy, in which many of the former stable working class are insecure, women have become more politically active.

A second point that emerges from the careers of Jackie Williams and Mary Sanchez is that both women were politically active in the late 1960s and through the 1970s, the period when extra funding was available from the OEO. Their public careers must be understood, then, in relation to their own stage in the life cycle and to their employment experiences and forms of financial support, each of which was shaped by the historical period in which they were active.

Women's Groups: Resources for Political Action

Most families on Norman Street in Greenpoint–Williamsburg during the period of my research were living on low incomes. Social contacts tended to be restricted to the street and a few surrounding blocks, but these were not the only important connections. People had numerous "institutional contacts" (welfare, the penal system, city services, the military). Even distant relatives played a role in local functions. Nevertheless, the street was the local meeting place, and it was by spending many hours on the block that I became familiar with the lives and problems of the families there.

In three years of interaction with the residents of Greenpoint–Williamsburg, I assembled a mass of data testifying to the frequent involvement in collective action of working-class women in this urban community. Women participated in block associations and tenants' associations. They mobilized to demand health care, day care, and adequate schools, and to prevent the demolition of local housing. Collective-action strategies ranged from demands for the provision of community service to outright confrontation. Whatever the nature of the community's action, each action required that people evaluate needs in the community, identify gaps in government services, and work collectively to overcome them. Thus, even the least confrontational community activities led people to perceive problems as issues to be approached collectively rather than individually.

Such cooperative efforts, as we see in the case of the lunch program described below, generated their own ideology or cultural interpretations that did not correspond with the "victim blaming" or individual-centered explanations underlying many service-providing institutions. In addition, the participation of poor women in local associations and activities developed and strengthened links between families, friends, and neighbors that were often the basis for future, more obviously political mobilization (as we see in the case of the firehouse, outlined below). From this perspective, community activities such as participation in block associations and tenants' associations or running a play street or lunch program can be seen as political. In many instances, these activities may reflect community resistance to hegemonic values and the redefinition of local problems in collective terms. Such actions seldom proved successful, and successes proved limited and rarely long lasting. They usually did not "make news." Nevertheless, persistent efforts to control the environment, with whatever small success, were a significant feature of life.

The basis for women's collective action on the block was to be found in the daily round of domestic responsibilities. Child care, for example, constituted an important way by which women developed social groups that later proved effective in local organizing. In these small groups, patterns of cooperation, communication, and analysis were established, and the value of collective effort was opposed to individual competitiveness was experienced. These values were expressed in concern for "the block" or "the neighborhood" and in reminiscences about growing up in the same area. An emphasis on one's responsibilities to kin was extended to responsibilities for the community.

The need for assistance with young children was widespread and crucial to the women of Norman Street. For working women, child care was essential, but there were times when it was important for a mother to have additional help with her children. If a woman appeared overwrought and likely to abuse her children, her sister, mother, or a neighboring relative would offer to take the children. Wives, sisters, and mothers, as well as brothers and uncles, all aided the working mother on Norman Street, although brothers and uncles watched children more rarely than sisters or aunts or grandmothers. Women took these responsibilities as a matter of course. The existence of a support group, based largely on neighbors and kin on the mother's side of the family, in which each individual provided small amounts of assistance, was combined with a high degree of flexibility in household structure. Assistance might be limited and the household fraught with conflict, but there was, nevertheless, a firm base of kindred to provide for members in need. Those same kindred, as we later see, were mobilized for more direct political action. As Rapp has noted, "kinship networks are part of 'community control' for women" (Rapp 1982).

Neighborhood women watching children spent many hours together. They also kept "an eye out" for every child in the vicinity. The constant hours spent together formed the basis for strong friendships among the women on Norman Street. This was the meeting ground through which other levels of cooperation and reciprocal aid formed and were reinforced in daily interaction.

As they sat on the block, women traded information about money problems, compared bills, and discussed eligibility for, and the methods they used to obtain, Medicaid benefits. They discussed what they were going to cook for supper and the problems they had in managing to feed their husbands and children. They calculated whether they might have enough money to go to Bingo, where they might possibly win the "windfall profits" they could find nowhere else and keep alive the vain hope that they might escape from it all. They also kept a general watch on everything that people on the block were doing. And it was here that small but essential loans might be negotiated.

Young mothers on the block received advice from experienced mothers—and were constantly teased about their pregnancies and their (mostly nonexistent) affairs. Men, in contrast, did not spend time on the street. They visited local bars or sat in front of television sets with their beers. Social groups for them were not centered in the neighborhood—except as they involved their wives or kindred. Young, unemployed men did congregate on street corners and were often in trouble with the law. But though they were reprimanded and criticized by the women on the street, they were seldom enlisted in the women's collective activities. I would suggest that it was, in part, the absence of clearly defined responsibilities (other than employment for money, which was not easy to come by) that led to this adversarial but not clearly directed behavior on the part of the young men.

Long before their involvement informal neighborhood politics, the women of the neighborhood exercised "local control." For example, they had known the local street gang members from infancy and did not hesitate to confront them. Several times during my stay, they intervened in dangerous fights between groups of young men and boys. They kept these conflicts from escalating into neighborhoodwide brawls.

The Summer Lunch Program

The organization of a program to distribute bag lunches to children during summer vacation demonstrates the resistance to media and government perceptions of a problem and the emergence of cultural reinterpretations generated by the collective efforts of poor people to improve conditions in their community. It indicates the way in which the provision of community services by local women was itself political and took place within a highly politicized context.

In 1973, New York City established a summer program to provide lunches for children in the neighborhoods of New York. In 1976, Mary Sanchez and six other women, who formed a friendship group, requested the summer lunches for their block and supervised their distribution. They made numerous independent but collective policy decisions that reflected the needs of the community, but not the legal priorities of the state. There were needy persons in the neighborhood who were not children. The program provided them with free lunches too. The elderly and disabled, in particular, were a target group for the women. Lunches were distributed to children but were eaten by household members and kin. Women would collect the lunches and store them for their evening meal. For some, the summer lunch program provided the major part of the household's nutrition.

Throughout New York City, the lunch program became the target of defamatory news reports accusing the poor of scattering food in the streets. The lunch program was vilified daily on local television. Contrary to the image portrayed by the media, the lunch program was valued by the people who received food, and its importance was reflected in the energy they expended in maintaining it. Street cooperation reached a high level in administering the lunch program—and the priorities were established by the women who administered the program.

These women on the block, building on their kin and neighborhood groups, exhibited strong collective control of the program in the face of a variety of threats to report illegal behavior to the city administration and in spite of the many bureaucratic inefficiencies on the part of the agencies hired by the state to deliver the food. The women allocated resources according to their own values and their own evaluation of community needs, in direct contradiction to priorities established by state legislation. In other words, they created their own cultural and political context for the identification of community needs and distributed resources according to collectively negotiated priorities. In so doing, poor women reinforced views of their problems as rooted in social rather than individual shortcomings and constructed local ties based on such common interpretations. The development of such cultural reinterpretation and community links in a wide variety of activities provided the basis for more demanding, long-term, and out-of-the-ordinary events, such as the mobilization around the threatened loss of fire protection described below.

The Firehouse

A more dramatic, and grueling, activity, which also depended in part on preexisting links between women, was the takeover of the firehouse. In 1975 the city, as part of fiscal cutbacks, announced plans to remove the neighborhood's fire engine. This was a period of an extremely high incidence of arson, and the removal of the truck was a genuinely life-threatening matter.

The response from the neighborhood was rapid. A siren was sounded from the firehouse, and concerned residents, recognizing the signal, telephoned their friends and neighbors to call them to action. Before the fire engine could be removed, a large crowd of neighborhood residents had gathered in front of the firehouse to prevent the truck from driving out. A man of Polish immigrant parentage who had just suffered an injury at work and was unable to return to his job took leadership at this point. He, his wife, and their four children moved into the firehouse, where they stayed, with widespread community support and numerous other visitors, for more than a year. This man's mother also moved in and brought in her wake many of the elderly people who supported the takeover to spend time and play chess in the firehouse. Neighboring women assisted with cooking, laundry, collecting children from school, and generally helping the family in the firehouse to continue under particularly harrowing conditions. Ultimately, the community mobilization proved successful; the firehouse was reopened.

An earlier experience of women involved in defending the firehouse was an important factor in the success of this mobilization. In 1972, when the S&S Corrugated Paper Machinery Company planned to expand, it was given permission by the New York City administration to pull down nineteen houses in Williamsburg, the homes for ninety-four families, to make room for plant buildings. Residents of Williamsburg (specifically residents of the "North Side," where the firehouse was also located) organized to try to prevent the destruction of their homes. In the face of highly visible protests and demonstrations, the company proceeded with the demolition. Angry and despairing residents sat in the streets in front of the bulldozers in a final attempt to prevent the destruction of their homes. Finally, S&S was forced to build fourteen new three-story houses that were designed as "moderate-income cooperatives" and could be bought by the displaced residents. In spite of the loss of the nineteen houses, this outcome was viewed as a major success in the neighborhood. The strength of community links forged in this previous struggle, the political experience (in public speaking and political negotiation), and the common culture generated in antipathy to the decisions of the New York City administration, combined with the overall sense of the possibility of success, provided important groundwork for the later firehouse demonstrations.

A second significant factor in the case of the firehouse was that the household around which the demonstration was organized was partially supported by state funds. The husband received disability benefits, while his wife was employed as a meat packer. In this case, although it was the man, rather than the woman, who was receiving state funds, once again dependence on the state helped shape the nature and target of political activism. A third factor was that the wife's women friends and neighbors continued their support and increased their aid in maintaining the household in the firehouse. The patterns of cooperation and the links the women had utilized in their daily lives were activated in the firehouse takeover.

The firehouse demonstration was, however, different in significant ways from the smaller events described earlier. It was orchestrated and perpetuated partly with the help of male community organizers and community spokespeople. This was a stronger and more effective movement than any of the other demonstrations, for several reasons. First, the coalition was built between community residents and the firefighter's union, and this link broadened and deepened the constituency of the action. Another factor contributing to the success of this activity was the pressure brought to bear on local politicians to support the neighborhood's demands. This pressure was applied at a pivotal time, just before elections. Thus it could be more effective, especially as voting participation in the areas around the firehouse and in Greenpoint was higher than in even poorer areas of Williamsburg.[3] In this instance, both men and women residents were active in picketing and demonstrating, in blocking the Brooklyn-Queens Expressway (a major intercity artery), and in other protest activities.

It seems likely that it was the *coalition* of work and community interests combined with the relationships forged with city and state Democratic politicians that gave the firehouse demonstration its uniqueness and its strength. It has been suggested that divisions between men and women in U.S. society are reflected in divisions between work and community (Acklesberg 1984). In this instance, the women of Greenpoint–Williamsburg did not take a separatist or particularly feminist approach. Nevertheless, the collective experiences and values among women in the community, combined with the differing experiences of men, specifically with unions in the workplace, made effective resistance possible.

Discussion

On the basis of this research, let us now reexamine the issues raised in the introduction to this article. I would suggest that the difference between the descriptions of working-class women in the 1950s and 1960s and those presented here can in part be understood in terms of phases of historical development in neighborhood action in relation to the changing experiences of America's working class. This experience is conditioned by the disappearance of stable, male-oriented jobs and a concomitant, growing dependence of families on the state. The working-class political movements of the 1970s and 1980s frequently became bitterly adversarial in relation to the state (as in the case of the movement around the firehouse) with the worsening of conditions and the deepening severity of the "crisis" faced by the national and world economy.

Neighborhood movements in recent decades have incorporated direct action and collective protest into their strategic vocabulary. Such movements show some similarities to the "bread and meat" riots of the early twentieth century (Gutman 1976). Like civil protests early in the century, they involve direct action and, frequently, open conflict. But the movements of the 1970s and 1980s differed from these and earlier voluntary associations in that they presupposed the *welfare state* and the historical changes wrought by the Roosevelt and Johnson eras.

During the presidency of Franklin Delano Roosevelt, a variety of measures were introduced to combat mass economic misery and in response to the development of militant unions and populist movements. These included the Social Security Act of 1935, which created retirement pensions and unemployment insurance, income maintenance for specific groups, aid for dependent children and aid to the blind, as well as funds for maternal and child health services. Although aspects of the welfare state (such as workers' compensation) already existed, the 1930s represents a watershed in the provision of social services and the legitimation and expectation of government assistance.

A second major shift occurred during the presidency of Lyndon B. Johnson with the War on Poverty. The reforms of the 1960s can be seen partly as a response to the burgeoning civil rights movement and the ghetto riots, but they also represent changes that had been taking place since World War II in every advanced industrialized nation. In 1965 the Social Security Act was amended to include Medicare and Medicaid funding. Similarly, the Older Americans Act (Public Law 89–73), also in 1965, established nutrition programs and senior citizen centers for the elderly. All these programs provided assistance for the care of household members that had previously been regarded as the responsibility of women household members. These acts also established the right to health care, nutrition, and caretaking in old age for all members of American society. Whether or not such care is currently provided, the legislation enacted in the past fifty years has created a fundamental legitimacy for demands that the government provide caretaking services for the needy.

Now, rather than focus on the distribution of resources or the ownership of production, people demand that the *state* take action to ameliorate bad conditions. Women have begun to mobilize communities to demand action and funding from state agencies. They have been demanding that a broad range of services be funded by the state *as a right*.[4]

In Greenpoint–Williamsburg, women were involved in the formulation and organizing of political demands. They took leadership roles. They became presidents of local block associations; they made speeches, coordinated demonstrations, organized food distribution, and dealt with politicians—both local and national.

These women seldom expressed a coherent political ideology. They certainly regarded it as their duty to cook for their families, do the shopping, and take primary responsibility for the children whether or not they were also employed outside the home. The expectations and ideology surrounding women's domestic work have not changed dramatically as more women have been going to work (Hunt 1980). Studies from all over the world show that when women work, they take on paid employment as an extra job.

Nevertheless, neighborhood organizations and the demand that the state finance caretaking activities represent in themselves a rejection of the full range of duties assigned to women in this society. The fact that women are central in the organizing of these movements reflects both their concern with their "traditional" duties and the changing nature of their experiences. Although the movements focus on what are now regarded as women's "traditional concerns"—the care of the young and the disabled, for example— they demonstrate women's ability to build on their collective experience for organizing purposes and to demand collective goods and services from the state. Women are demanding that the state take over caretaking activities that are commonly thought to be women's responsibility.

Conclusion

Historians have analyzed the changes in the form of political expression corresponding to the emergence of industrial society (see, e.g., Thompson 1966; Brody 1960; Scott 1974). Such studies, however, have been largely concerned with men and their political activities. In a sense they may have contributed to the idea that women did not participate in industrialization and that their traditional role has always been that of homemaker. Recent feminist scholars have begun to redress this imbalance (see Eisenstein 1983; Sacks and Remy 1984; Tax 1983; Kessler-Harris 1982).

Women's participation in community organizations has seldom been subjected to historical analysis.[5] Clearly, women's work and unemployment experiences have been very different from men's, and it was to be expected that women's collective action would have emerged at different times and in different ways. If one is to understand the ways in which women's protest has differed from men's, however, one must understand these differences in terms of a changing relationship among corporate power, working-class people, and the state. Within this context, one must be sensitive to the consequences of the changing nature of and demand for labor as well as the changes in the demand for reproduction of the labor force.

In this context, I have shown that neighborhood and community organizations have their own history and have evolved their own forms, parallel to, but in no way subsumed by, collective action at the workplace. Here, too, women have developed methods for extracting more goods and services from the state and sometimes even from corporations (e.g., the S&S Corrugated Paper Machinery Company) in their efforts to raise the value of wages by supplementing them with public financing of the collective needs of the community.

Working-class women have acted on the basis of their common experiences and assigned child-care roles in society to develop effective collective action and to both demand increased financing from the state and protest reductions in the maintenance of community services. Whether or not they have become leaders on a national level, such women are still significant for their reinforcement of collective values, their exercise of local control, their actions in redistributive activities, and their persistent demand for public services. In their participation in conflict within neighborhoods, they contribute to changing definitions of the responsibilities of the state to the growing sector of nonworking or low-paid workers in our economy. In neighborhoods where services are deteriorating and people are suffering a loss of political influence because they have lost their employment, the ability to influence events through recognized channels is also declining.

With the decrease in employment opportunities, the major route by which working-class people were able to maintain some control over the conditions of their lives is lost; union membership and support are also disappearing. In this context, we see women's collective organization becoming more focused and the resort to direct action more frequent as women fight to maintain the few remaining services allocated to the working poor. The local protest movements of the past two decades are the result of women's fighting to make up for the departure of industry and the loss of stable, well-paying jobs.

The firehouse movement in Greenpoint–Williamsburg is particularly significant in that it demonstrated the effectiveness of coalitions built between the residents of a working-class community (both men and women) and workers concerned for their continued employment. The important theoretical issues raised by current changes in the U.S. economy (marked by increasing unemployment and declining industrial work) concern the ways in which the growing unemployed, nonworking, or low-paid and state-supplemented sectors of the population mobilize to extract resources from the state and negotiate a redefinition of government priorities. I would suggest that the collective activities of working-class women and their changing experiences and expectations are central to this endeavor.

Notes

1. It is not entirely correct to see this population that is reliant on state funding as new. It is more accurate to view it as greatly expanded and more visible. Black women have been in this situation for a much longer period, and the impact of this on community mobilization can also be traced. See also Stack (1974) and Valentine (1978).

2. For a more complete account of working-class life in Greenpoint–Williamsburg, see Susser (1982).

3. This issue is discussed in more detail, including its implications for minority representation and access to political power, in Susser (1982).

4. Piven makes this point and sees it as the explanation for the much-discussed "gender gap" in the voting patterns of men and women of the 1980s, as well as a basis for a mass movement of women.

5. However, see Kaplan (1982) for one such analysis.

References

Ackelsberg, M. 1984. "Women's Collaborative Activities and City Life: Politics and Policy." In *Political Women: Current Roles in State and Local Government*, edited by J. Flammang. Beverly Hills, Calif.: Sage.

Alcaly, R., and D. Mermelstein, eds. 1977. *The Fiscal Crisis of American Cities: Essays on the Political Economy of Urban America with Special Reference to New York*. New York: Random House.

Barrett, M. 1980. *Women's Oppression Today*. London: Verso Books.

Beechey, V. 1978. "Women and Production: A Critical Analysis of Some Sociological Theories of Women's Work." In *Feminism and Materialism*, edited by A. Kuhn and A. Wolpe. Boston: Routledge and Kegan Paul.

Brenner, J., and M. Ramos. "Rethinking Women's Oppression." *New Left Review* 144 (March–April): 33–72.

Brody, D. 1960. *Steel Workers in America: The Non-Union Era*. Cambridge, Mass.: Harvard University Press.

Brown, G., and T. Harris. 1978. *Social Origins of Depression*. New York: Free Press.

Cantor, Milton, and Bruce Laurie, eds. 1980. *Class, Sex, and the Woman Worker*. Westport, Conn.: Greenwood.

Castells, Manuel. 1984. *The City and the Grassroots*. Berkeley: University of California Press.

Center for the American Woman and Politics. 1980. "Women in Elective Office, 1975–1979." Fact sheet issued by the National Information Bank on Women in Politics, Eagleton Institute of Politics, Rutgers University.

Eisenstein, S. 1983. *Give Us Bread but Give Us Roses*. Boston: Routledge and Kegan Paul.

Gilkes, C. 1980. "Successfully Rebellious Professionals: The Black Woman's Professional Identity and Community Commitment." *Psychology of Women Quarterly* 6.

Githens, M., and J. Prestage, eds. 1977. *A Portrait of Marginality*. New York: McKay.

Gordon, D. 1972. *Theories of Poverty and Unemployment*. Lexington, Mass.: Lexington Books.

Gutman, Herbert. 1976. *Work, Culture and Society in Industrial America*. New York: Vintage.

Hobsbawm, E. 1955. *Primitive Rebels*. New York: Norton.

Hunt, P. 1980. *Gender and Class Consciousness*. New York: Holmes and Meier.

Joseph, S. 1983. "Working-Class Women's Networks in a Sectarian State: A Political Paradox." *American Ethnologist* 10, no. 1.

Kaplan, T. 1982. "Female Consciousness and Collective Action: The Case of Barcelona, 1910–1918." *Signs* 7.

Kessler-Harris, A. 1982. *Out to Work*. New York: Oxford University Press.

Komarovsky, Mirra. 1964. *Blue-Collar Marriage*. New York: Random House.

McCourt, K. 1977. *Working Class Women and Grass Roots Politics*. Bloomington: Indiana University Press.

McIntosh, M. 1978. "The State and the Oppression of Women." In *Feminism and Materialism*, edited by A. Kuhn and A. Wolpe. Boston: Routledge and Kegan Paul.

Milkman, R., ed. 1985. *Women, Work and Protest: A Century of U.S. Women's Labor History*. Boston: Routledge and Kegan Paul.

Morgen, S. 1984. "Women and Community Organizing: The Intersection of Gender and Class in a Grassroots Health Action Coalition." Paper presented at "U.S. Women and Resistance in the Community and the Workplace," symposium, American Anthropological Association, Denver.

Nelson, C. 1974. "Public and Private Politics: Women in the Middle Eastern World." *American Ethnologist* 1 (August): 551–565.

Oppenheimer, V. 1970. *The Female Labor Force in the United States*. Berkeley: University of California Press.

Piven, Frances Fox. 1984. "Women and the State: Ideology, Power and the Welfare State." *Socialist Review* 74 (March–April): 13–23.

Rainwater, L., R. Coleman, and G. Handel. 1959. *Workingman's Wife*. New York: Oceana.

Rapp, Rayna. 1982. "Family and Class in Contemporary America." In *Rethinking the Family*, edited by B. Thorne. London: Longman.

Rubin, Lillian. 1976. *Worlds of Pain*. New York: Basic Books.

Sacks, K., and D. Remy. 1984. *My Troubles Are Going to Have Trouble with Me*. New Brunswick, N.J.: Rutgers University Press.

Scott, J. 1974. *Glassworkers of Carmaux*. Cambridge, Mass.: Harvard University Press.

Secombe, Wally. 1974. "The Housewife and Her Labor under Capitalism." *New Left Review* 83: 3–24.

Seifer, Nancy. 1976. *Nobody Speaks for Me*. New York: Simon and Schuster.

Stacey, M., and M. Price. 1981. *Women, Power and Politics*. London: Tavistock.

Stack, Carol. 1974. *All Our Kin*. New York: Harper & Row.

Sternlieb, G., and J. Hughes. 1977. "Metropolitan Decline and Interregional Job Shifts." In *The Fiscal Crisis of Cities*, edited by R. Alcaly and D. Mermelstein, 145–165. New York: Random House.

Susser, Ida. 1982. *Norman Street: Poverty and Politics in an Urban Neighborhood*. New York: Oxford University Press.

Tabb, W. 1978. "The New York City Fiscal Crisis." In *Marxism and the Metropolis*, edited by W. Tabb and L. Sawers. New York: Oxford University Press.

Tax, M. 1983. *The Rising of the Women*. New York: Monthly Review Press.

Thompson, E. P. 1966. *The Making of the English Working Class*. New York: Vintage.

Valentine, B. 1978. *Hustling and Other Hard Work*. New York: Free Press.

Wolf, J. 1984. "A Rising Vote of Thanks: Afro-American Women, Club Activities and Social Welfare in the 1920s." Manuscript.

CHAPTER 13

Transformative Populism
and the Development of a Community of Color

Marie Kennedy and Chris Tilly
with Mauricio Gaston

The neighborhood of Roxbury is Boston's ghetto. Roxbury is the center of Boston's black community, and of a growing Latino community. Roxbury is also the economically poorest neighborhood in Boston, with a per capita income only two-thirds of the Boston average in 1980.[1] Over the past ten years, there has been a tug-of-war between two insurgent strategies for community development in Boston's poor and working-class communities in general and in Roxbury in particular. Both strategies are left populist, but there the similarity ends. One approach is a narrow version of populism that we call redistributive populism, which suppresses nonclass differences such as that of race, seeks to unite "the people" around a least-common-denominator program based on traditional ideology, and holds out redistribution of resources as the central goal. The second approach, transformative populism, differs markedly: It emphasizes and even celebrates diversity as well as unity, explicitly introduces derived ideology in a process of mutual education of coalition members, and targets as its central goal the transformation of consciousness through empowerment.

We use a case study of community development in Roxbury to weigh the

Mauricio Gaston passed away in 1986. He was not directly involved in the analysis of populism presented in this paper. However, the main source of data for the paper is a detailed case study of the Roxbury community that Gaston conducted with Kennedy over a period of years. We dedicate the paper to his memory and his vision. We would like to thank Jim Green, Gus Newport, Charlotte Ryan, Bob Terrell, Chuck Turner, and especially Mel King for numerous discussions (including comments on earlier drafts from Green, King, and Ryan) that influenced our thinking as reflected in this paper. The opinions expressed are our own, however, and do not necessarily reflect those of any of these people.

merits of the two populist approaches. We argue that transformative populism is a superior strategy for achieving progressive goals related to community development, including the goal of redistribution. This superiority is especially evident in communities of color, as the case of Roxbury illustrates. We offer a limited comparison between the two strategies, but our main emphasis is on the innovative contributions of transformative populism as they have emerged in Roxbury's community struggles over the past several years. The task of comparison is complicated by the fact that a redistributive populist leader, Raymond Flynn, was elected mayor of Boston in 1983 and again in 1987. Thus, redistributive populism has held a piece of state power (in this case, on the municipal level) in recent years, while transformative populism has remained a movement in opposition.[2]

We present the case in five steps. First, we summarize the history of Boston and Roxbury that has created the context for current community development struggles. Second, we sketch the two populist strategies as they have developed in Boston. Both strategies, we argue, are responses to the class–community dilemma—the problem that important aspects of class oppression are experienced by people as members of multiclass communities. Third, we contrast the ways in which the two populisms have dealt with the relationship between traditional ideology—the "common sense" that people bring to daily life—and derived ideology—conscious left ideology. Fourth, we describe how Boston's redistributive and transformative populist movements have approached the state, in particular the local state, which has been the arena for important conflicts over community development. Finally, we offer brief conclusions.

Boston and Roxbury: From Disinvestment to Displacement

The need for community development in Roxbury follows from a thirty-year history of disinvestment. Roxbury has experienced tremendous losses of housing and industry at the hands of the market, and added assaults at the hands of the state, through urban renewal and highway clearance. In one area of the neighborhood, known locally as the "Bermuda triangle," 70 percent of the housing stock was lost to abandonment and arson in two decades. All the signs of intense poverty are evident in Roxbury: high unemployment, low participation in the labor force, low educational levels, a high crime rate, flourishing drug traffic, a high dropout rate from school, and a high rate of teenage pregnancy. Some of Roxbury's census tracts are among the poorest in the country, on a par with the poorest counties in Mississippi and with Indian reservations in the western United States.

To a large extent, the devastation of Roxbury was a by-product of the revitalization of Boston. Forty years ago, Boston was one of the most economically depressed cities of the Frostbelt. In the intervening decades, Boston has been transformed into a regional and even national center of services and finance. This economic transformation was facilitated by major highway construction and one of the most vigorous urban renewal programs in the country, orchestrated by the Boston Redevelopment Authority (BRA).

But Boston's economic renaissance entailed a three-pronged attack on Roxbury's well-being. First, downtown investment came at the expense of investment in poor communities and particularly communities of color. Neighborhoods like Roxbury were "redlined" by the banks. Roxbury properties were overassessed for tax purposes (until tax laws changed in 1982) and denied services in a deliberate policy of neighborhood "triage," whereas downtown developers were given tax breaks and city services were concentrated on developing downtown areas. Second, the booming service industries created a much more polarized labor market than the manufacturing and transport industries they replaced. People of color were, and are, largely confined to very-low-wage jobs in the hotels, hospitals, restaurants, and stores that constituted much of "New Boston's" economy. Third, Boston's programs of highway construction and urban renewal physically destroyed much of Roxbury. For example, highway planners working on a new Southwest Expressway (I–95) and Inner Belt circumferential road managed to cut a broad swath through industrial, commercial, and residential buildings in Lower Roxbury and along Columbus Avenue, a major Roxbury artery, before a popular movement stopped construction. Major urban renewal projects in Madison Park and Washington Park resulted in massive demolition of housing and displacement, despite the construction and renovation of subsidized housing.

Today, investment in downtown Boston has almost reached its physical limits. But pressure for investment continues, posing a new threat of displacement for outlying neighborhoods such as Roxbury. The pressure for investment is due both to the demands of capital and to the fiscal crisis of the local state, exacerbated by a statewide tax-cutting referendum passed in 1979. Roxbury's large amounts of publicly held land, its location only minutes from downtown, and its transportation connections to downtown make it an ideal new turf for capital. And indeed, since 1985, BRA has been nursing a number of development plans for Roxbury, including the $750 million Dudley Square Plan, bringing together twenty-one developers to redevelop the commercial and cultural center of Roxbury. Although the development plans are posed in terms of the "revitalization" of Roxbury, they are likely to lead to a massive displacement of current residents (Gaston and Kennedy 1987). Even the simple announcement of the plans has caused the displacement of current residents by speculators engaging in blockbusting, speculative purchases, and even arson.

Roxbury's cycle from disinvestment to impending displacement represents, in a particularly extreme form, the problems faced by all of Boston's low-income neighborhoods. To some extent, all these neighborhoods have suffered from neglect, and to some extent all of them are now at risk from the overflow of downtown development. In fact, this cycle typifies low-income urban neighborhoods across the country, although other neighborhoods occupy different points in the cycle. Thus the challenge facing Roxbury activists is a universal one: how to develop the community in a way that serves the people that make up the community, instead of displacing them.

Class, Race, and Community: Two Populist Responses

Community development in low-income communities requires directing and harnessing private and public investment. It pits poor and working people against capital in a class conflict. But this class conflict is played out and experienced at the level of the community. Community members perceive a variety of forces, both impersonal (e.g., bank redlining) and personal (e.g., slumlords) that threaten their community. The embattled community includes landlords and business owners as well as unemployed people, welfare recipients, and people living from hustles, not just "pure" proletarians. Organizers must find ways to develop and link community-based identities and struggles in a fashion that challenges capital. This is the class–community dilemma, as defined by Posner in the Introduction to this volume.

But, as Jennings points out in Chapter 5, there is another dimension to the dilemma: race. Race adds complexity to the situation on two levels. For one thing, racial distinctions color the relationship of capital to a given community. Capital as employer seeks to maintain communities as stable sites for the reproduction of the labor force, but seeks to limit community stability and cohesion to the extent that this cohesion serves as a basis for mobilization. Capital as user of physical space balances preserving communities within given neighborhoods as sources of income flows (rent, interest, profits) against displacing communities in order to convert the space to more profitable uses. In communities of color, both balances are tipped further toward instability. Much of the black and Latino labor force falls into a secondary labor market where flexibility, rather than stability, is at a premium, or even into the labor reserve. And because communities of color tend to be poor, current income flows to capital from these communities are small, making alternative land uses more attractive.

At a second level, race affects the possibilities for political mobilization. Where neighborhoods are relatively segregated, as in Boston, racial identities can foster unity within communities, but division among them. Where neighborhoods are mixed, racial splits can fracture coalitions within a community. Given these effects of racial divisions, and given the concentration of people of color in the inner cities of the United States, the class–community dilemma often becomes a class–race–community dilemma.

In Boston, community activists have responded to this dilemma with two divergent strategies. Both strategies are left populist; they seek to unite "the common people" to do battle with the forces of corporate greed, real estate speculation, and government indifference or corruption. In both cases, the class content of the strategy is implicit, not explicit. But the two populisms are quite distinct, particularly regarding the racial dimension of the dilemma.

The first strategy is what we call *redistributive populism*. Redistributive populism builds unity by emphasizing what people have in common, and downplaying or even overlooking differences such as race. Redistributive populists take an integrationist or assimilationist view of race, arguing that racial divisions will fade into insignificance as poor and working people pursue common goals. The strategy also assumes that people will only change their views incrementally, through participation in struggles in which they have already taken sides. Redistributive populists avoid raising issues that pose broad challenges to their constituency's world views, or proposing struggles that their constituents are not already committed to. Such populists value community organization as a means to the end of redistribution of resources and economic justice. In general, redistributive populists also hold the goal of transforming people's world views and relationships to one another, but they see this as a long-term goal to be achieved as a by-product of the accumulation of short-term redistributive struggles.

Although redistributive populism as we have described it is an ideal type, we believe that most of the new populism, as defined by Evans and Boyte (1986) and others, can be classified within this approach. In Boston, the redistributive populist coalition ranges from the Fair Share grouping of progressive community organizations to a variety of elected and appointed officials who see themselves in the tradition of Boston's populist James Michael Curley, who was repeatedly elected mayor earlier in this century. White Irish populist politician Ray Flynn, along with his campaign organization before the 1983 mayoral election, and his staff once he became mayor— including many Fair Share activists—has led redistributive populism to electoral victory in Boston.

The second strategy is *transformative populism*. Transformative populism emphasizes diversity as well as unity. Transformative populists seek to unite people based on their common oppression, but also seek to use the resulting coalition to battle each group's distinct oppression. In this strategy, people must learn not only from their own struggles but from the struggles of others—and therefore organizers confront coalition members with issues designed to stretch the members' world views. Instead of expecting and working for the disappearance of distinctions such as race, transformative populists project a "salad bowl" model of the good community in which differences are preserved and valued. Transformative populism views community organization—and the resulting transformation of people's consciousness—as an end in itself as well as a means toward redistribution. Even in the short term, the goal is liberation, not simply economic justice.

Transformative populism has a strong base in Boston, particularly in Roxbury. The black populist Mel King and his supporters, who formed the Boston Rainbow Coalition after King lost the 1983 mayoral election, make up the electoral arm of transformative populism in Boston. A variety of community organizations, many of them grouped in Boston's Community Control Coalition, also espouse some form of transformative populism.

The difference between the two populisms was thrown into sharp relief during the 1983 mayoral race, when Flynn and King ran against each other.[3] The difference between the political histories of the two candidates speaks volumes. Both were Boston natives of working-class parents. But their routes to the mayoral candidacy were utterly different. Flynn became a state representative from white, largely Irish South Boston by combining an appeal to the economic underdog, which has mobilized Boston's Irish since the days of Mayor James Michael Curley, with extreme social conservatism. Flynn sponsored antiabortion legislation and helped lead the movement against court-ordered school desegregation. Flynn went on to join the Boston City Council, and garnered the top vote totals in the 1981 council election by broadening his economic appeal—stressing affordable housing and cultivating his ties to organized labor—without moderating his positions on social issues.

King, in contrast, rose to prominence as a community activist and then state representative from the integrated, largely black South End. Although he initially focused on neighborhood issues such as street gangs, school desegregation, employment discrimination, and affordable housing, King soon became a leading advocate on a wide range of issues including women's liberation, gay liberation, peace, and opposition to U.S. intervention abroad. King's legislative initiatives ranged from the construction of a community development finance apparatus to the divestment of Massachusetts pension funds from companies doing business with South Africa.

To the surprise of virtually all political observers, these two candidates became front-runners and then finalists in the 1983 mayoral race. Two populist groupings coalesced around the candidates. Flynn sharpened his image as a populist, proclaiming that the issue of the election was the struggle between the neighborhoods and a greedy "downtown." He shifted his stands on social issues somewhat—for example, avowing support for the Equal Rights Amendment—while avoiding any shifts that might alienate his base in South Boston and other socially conservative white neighborhoods. The progressives who joined Flynn's campaign believed that it was essential to build a coalition that brought in the white working-class communities that make up the majority of Boston's population, even if this meant setting aside a whole range of "noneconomic" issues. This coalition was almost entirely white, although there were some exceptions—for example, a Fair Share chapter from the black neighborhood of Mattapan signed on.

King also staked out a populist campaign, using such slogans as "We may have come here on different ships, but we're all in the same boat now." He made a particular effort to reach out to white working-class neighborhoods on issues of housing, jobs, and development. But, he continued to stress noneconomic issues, from racism to gay rights. As a result, he attracted active supporters from a wide range of communities and movements: blacks, Latinos, Asians, gays and lesbians, feminists, peace activists, and housing activists, among others. The result was the Rainbow Coalition, a term coined by King a year before Jesse Jackson adopted it. On the left, King attracted those who embraced what we call transformative populism—those who saw addressing noneconomic issues as the key to an effective populist coalition.

The most striking difference between the two campaigns was on the issue of race. Boston has long been a racially polarized city, and that polarization has been especially public and violent since the 1974 court-ordered school desegregation. But Flynn asserted in a television debate that "the real problem is economic discrimination," adding that "there are poor whites and blacks who do not have access to the political structure in this city." He insisted that the problems of white South Boston and black and Latino Roxbury were identical. King, in contrast, targeted racism as a serious problem in its own right and challenged whites and blacks to confront the problem.

Flynn won the election. Although King won 95 percent of the black vote, 67 percent of the Latino vote, and 20 percent of the white vote, this amounted to only one-third of Boston's mainly white electorate. Redistributive populism defeated transformative populism at the polls. But in the years since the election, black, Latino, Asian, and white activists have continued to nurture transformative populism. And in the recent struggles over community development in Roxbury, the contributions of transformative populism have become increasingly clear.

Of the dozens of groups working on community development in Roxbury, a half dozen—with overlapping personnel—work within a transformative populist framework. Because of the imminent threat of displacement, the transformative populists have focused on organizing for community control over the planning process and specifically over land use. But the groups have undertaken this organizing at many different levels. Certain groups, such as the Dudley Street Neighborhood Initiative and the Washington Street Corridor Coalition, target community control over development in areas that cross conventional neighborhood boundaries. The Greater Roxbury Neighborhood Authority (GRNA) is attempting to establish democratic community control over development in all of Roxbury (Gaston and Kennedy 1987). A variety of groups, including the Greater Roxbury Incorporation Project (GRIP) and Project FATE (Focusing Attitudes Toward Empowerment) have campaigned for referenda proposing that Roxbury incorporate as the separate city of Mandela, independent of Boston (Kennedy and Tilly 1987). The Center for Community Action trains organizers of color and sponsors community forums. Most of these groups are connected to citywide coalitions: the electoral Rainbow Coalition, and the Coalition for Community Control of Development, initiated by the GRNA and now including groups from all but two of Boston's major neighborhoods. The struggles led by these groups have highlighted two areas of difference between the two populist strategies: ideology and the role of the state.

The Dilemma of Ideology

In addition to the class–community dilemma, Posner in her introduction to this volume identifies the dilemma of the tension between traditional ideology and derived ideology—between common sense and critical analysis. As noted in the previous section, the two populisms approach this tension in different ways.

Redistributive populism calls for uniting people around traditional ideology. In practice, this leads to an ideological dichotomy. The organizers of redistributive populist movements are generally leftists, motivated by derived ideology.[4] But they mobilize their constituency using much more limited discourses that reflect "where people are at." Once more, the example of racism provides an apt illustration.

Charlotte Ryan, a community organizer in the racially mixed Boston neighborhood of Dorchester, was interviewed by Green (1984). She commented (in Green's paraphrase): "While many individual organizers in Fair Share were personally concerned with fighting racism, they did so in a private way. . . . By taking a strictly economic approach to problems that would yield 'quick victories,' 'they ignored and sometimes denied the racial component of issues' " (p. 26). This dichotomy between privately held and publicly expressed views implies a certain elitism on the part of the organizers.

Mel King pointed out the problem in addressing a white Dorchester community meeting during the mayoral campaign: "Look, the other candidates won't come here and talk to you about the problem of race. And that's because they don't respect you enough to think you can deal with the issue" (Green 1984, 30).

By pulling people together using traditional ideology, redistributive populists build a broader coalition than might otherwise be possible in the short run. But the coalition is riven by hidden conflicts. To hold the coalition together, redistributive populist leaders—even those who hold radical, transformative views—constantly defer transformative goals. The pressure to maintain and broaden the coalition leads inexorably to politics founded on the least common denominator.

Transformative populists, in contrast, explicitly attempt to bridge the gap between traditional and derived ideology. But how? The recent organizing in Roxbury provides some answers.

It is important to note that even redistributive populist organizing in black and Latino Roxbury could not take the same form as organizing in white areas of Dorchester. Whereas ignoring race may be expedient in parts of Dorchester, it is impossible in Roxbury. Thus the functional equivalent of an "economic fair share" approach in Roxbury would be a "racial fair share" approach: an assimilationist strategy aimed at obtaining more resources for blacks and Latinos.

But some transformative populist Roxbury activists have moved beyond this redistributive approach in several ways. First, they have linked Roxbury residents' immediate experiences as members of a subordinate racial group to broader concepts and struggles: international issues, class analysis, and the importance of self-determination.

The main international connection drawn by Roxbury organizers is between the situation of blacks and Latinos in Roxbury and that of blacks in South Africa. Boston's Black United Front (BUF, an organization that no longer exists) set a precedent for solidarity in 1968. After riots in the wake of Martin Luther King's assassination, the liberal Polaroid Corporation announced its intention to present BUF with a check to assist in rebuilding Roxbury. But Polaroid had been targeted by black activists for selling South Africa photographic equipment used to produce the hated "passes" designed to control the movements of black South Africans. BUF held an all-night drop-in meeting to decide how to respond to Polaroid's gift. The next day, as television cameras rolled, Chuck Turner (now director of the Center for Community Action) accepted the check on behalf of the Black United Front, and immediately signed the check over to the African National Congress.

Activists have continued to voice the connection with South Africa and other anticolonial struggles. At the GRNA's first mass meeting to develop strategies for effective opposition to the Boston Redevelopment Authority's Dudley Square Plan, black public housing activist Regina Placid and black School Committee member Jean McGuire compared Boston's treatment of

Roxbury with South Africa's bantustan policy. The Center for Community Action's organizer training curriculum routinely includes material on South Africa.

The need for class analysis is posed by class divisions within Boston's black community. One example arose with BRA's opening salvo in the current development plans for Roxbury, on a piece of land known as Parcel 18. BRA, under the leadership of a Flynn-appointed director, Stephen Coyle, proposed high-rise office towers for the site, a plan that seems certain to lead to displacement in neighboring areas. In the face of community opposition, a Flynn-initiated "redistributive" solution gave a 30 percent share of the project, as well as the downtown development to which this parcel is linked, to a coalition of black, Latino, and Asian developers headed by a black-owned company. Flynn, in chorus with the local media, stressed the fact that this was the first time in Boston that minority developers would share in Boston's downtown development boom. Is this community control over development? No, answered GRNA and other groups. Commented GRNA's Bob Terrell, "It's nice that [black] individuals have mobility from Boston's investment boom, but the masses of black folks don't. . . . To move everybody forward, we need community control" (Kennedy and Tilly 1987, 17).

Roxbury's transformative populists project an agenda based on self-determination, not assimilation (see Chapter 5 for further discussion of the importance of this distinction). The most striking instance of this stand arose with the debate over the 1986 "Mandela" ballot proposal to incorporate Roxbury as an independent city. From the standpoint of the redistributive populists in the Flynn administration and the black leaders they mobilized against incorporation, this proposal was not only racially divisive but insane. Roxbury residents would be staking claim to the most disinvested, economically barren parts of Boston. But transformative populists, including GRIP, GRNA, Mel King, and others, saw the matter differently. They recognized that Roxbury was ripe for reinvestment and that community wealth—the transformative potential of a community of people—was largely untapped. Transformative populists concluded that incorporation would provide a lever for community control over the potential flood of new investment, as well as more effective utilization of existing resources, both human and material. Liberal critics charged that the Mandela advocates' slogan of "Yes we stay; no we go" was deceptive, given that a yes vote favored the separation of Roxbury from Boston. But, in fact, the slogan served to popularize the idea that self-determination was the only alternative to displacement—

and helped to win over the one-quarter of Roxbury voters who eventually supported the referendum (Kennedy and Tilly 1987).

A second element of the transformative populist Roxbury organizers' approach to the dilemma of ideology is the recognition that the relationship between derived and traditional ideology runs in both directions. Activists armed with a left ideology have something to teach their constituents, but they also have something to learn from them.

Recent Roxbury community development struggles yield examples of both aspects. On the one hand, GRNA activists seized on the theory of uneven development and of cycles of disinvestment and reinvestment (as described earlier in this paper), and translated it into the popular notion that "Roxbury already paid for the downtown boom; now we're owed." This insight—far from obvious to the residents of an impoverished neighbor-hood—has become commonplace for those involved in Roxbury's community development movement.

On the other hand, a group of mainly white left housing experts (including author Kennedy), who had historically opposed homeownership because it atomizes communities and promotes a petty bourgeois "investor" mentality, were forced to reevaluate their position by the insistent support of Roxbury residents for homeownership. The result of discussions among intellectuals and activists was a program for nonspeculative homeownership, which maintains security of tenure and the right to alter one's living space physically but places controls on resale. In turn, Roxbury groups have begun to implement parts of the program as they develop housing (Stone 1986).

This two-way ideological street begins to break down the elitism implicit in the redistributive populist approach. Respecting ordinary people enough to believe that they can change their world view when exposed to new ideas means respecting them enough to believe that they see important parts of reality that the left does not.

A final contribution of Roxbury's organizers to solving the dilemma of ideology is their adoption of a broad concept of empowerment, emphasizing process as well as product. For redistributive populists, the criterion for success in the foreseeable future is in fact redistribution: How effective are community groups at redirecting resources toward their communities? In order to maintain momentum and keep people involved, these populists pursue what organizer Ryan calls "quick victories," believing that education will spontaneously occur as a by-product. Their long-term vision rests on the belief that enough redistributive victories will lead to a transformation of consciousness. Roxbury's transformative populist organizers instead define empowerment in terms of a change in mass consciousness—"making a break from a dependency model to work on what would ultimately be an interdependency model," as Mel King has put it. Thus these organizers seek to cultivate a patient, long-term view of struggle. In this view, building a unit of low-income housing or improving trash pickup are victories, but adding new groups to a coalition or popularizing a radical analysis of development may be even more important victories. This difference in view spills over to conflicting populist views of the role of the state, and it is to this that we turn next.

The Role of the State

The disjuncture between community-based mobilization and societywide transformation arises most sharply when we consider the role of the national state, as Posner points out in her introduction to this volume. But a smaller version of this dilemma is played out at the local level. Community development struggles in Roxbury have most directly involved Boston's municipal government.

It would be overstating the case to claim that redistributive populists hold local power in Boston. The power of the mayor is hemmed in by that of other elected officials, such as members of the City Council and The School Committee; appointed officials such as BRA's board of directors; and a vast bureaucracy, largely staffed by holdovers from former mayor Kevin White's liberal but hardly populist regime. Even so, the mayor occupies an extremely powerful position in Boston. Furthermore, Mayor Flynn has appointed avowed populists—in many cases, former organizers from Fair Share or other organizations—to key leadership positions in the bureaucracy. And substantial minorities in both the City Council and the School Committee are populists of various stripes.

Thus, when we contrast the redistributive and transformative populist approaches to the local government, we are making an asymmetrical comparison between redistributive populists largely within and working through the local government and transformative populists chiefly located outside the local government. Within the limits of this comparison, recent struggles over the role of local government in Roxbury have reproduced the split between redistribution and transformation that has come up repeatedly in this paper.

The contrast is sharp. Flynn's redistributive populists are sincerely committed to redistributing wealth. But they balk at redistributing power— the power to plan and to control land use. They seek to use the power of government to provide a set of material benefits—chiefly housing and jobs— for low-income people, but not to change the power relations between the government and low-income people. Redistributive populists have proven unwilling to encourage a movement that challenges the local government as well as supports its progressive initiatives. Their vision of community development is a narrowly economic one, measuring development by the number of housing units, jobs, or dollars. In short, the redistributive populists in power emphasize representation, not participation. There are two reasons for this emphasis. First, it appears to be the most "efficient" way to achieve redistributive goals. Thus, Flynn administration officials argue that militant movements making broad demands jeopardize the limited redistributive compromises that are possible. These officials espouse the "politics of the possible." Second, minimizing mobilization and participation lessens the risk that more conservative elements of the populist coalition will actively oppose progressive initiatives. When city officials plan reforms that go beyond the basis of the coalition—a recent example is integrating public housing in predominantly white areas of Boston—it is easier to carry them out from above than to lead an ideological struggle that may split the coalition.

In contrast, Roxbury's transformative populists hold that redistribution of power is essential. Activists have identified the politics of the possible as a trap. Organizer Chuck Turner recently commented, "We have to look at how we define material reality." He noted that the mainstream view of Boston's economic reality is founded on a scarcity of resources, but that if Roxbury's residents accept this view and simply fight for their share of these scarce resources, they have already lost half the battle.

Transformative populists work with a broad definition of community development, akin to their broad definition of empowerment. They emphasize that community development consists not simply of developing the neighborhood where people live but, first and foremost, of developing the people who make up a community. In the words of Tanzania's Julius Nyerere,

A country, or a village, or a community cannot be developed. It can only develop itself. For real development means the development, the growth, of people. Roads, buildings, the increases of crop output, and other things of this nature, are not development; they are only tools of development. . . . A man is developing himself when he grows, or earns, enough to provide decent conditions for himself and his family; he is not being developed if somebody gives him these things. A man is developing himself when he improves his education—whatever he learns about; he is not being developed if he simply carries out orders from someone better educated than himself without understanding why those orders have been given. A man develops himself by joining in free discussion of a new venture, and participating in the subsequent discussion; he is not being developed if he is herded like an animal into the new venture. (Nyerere 1974)

Three examples demonstrate how these two views of the relation between state and movement have clashed. First, consider the struggle over federally subsidized housing. In 1985, a large amount of housing subsidized by the U.S. Department of Housing and Urban Development (HUD) in Boston, most of it located in Roxbury and other black areas, was foreclosed. In the disposition of this housing, both the tenants and Mayor Flynn's staff were concerned that the housing be repaired and remain subsidized. HUD's representatives at the federal level seemed intent on selling off the housing to interests that would thwart these goals. Tenants in a number of these developments started a massive organizing drive; the mayor's office began secret negotiations with HUD. Flynn's populists-in-office reacted with dismay to the organizing. In fact, at one point a city official, a former tenant activist himself, essentially asked author Kennedy and her colleague Muricio Gaston to convince the tenants to stop organizing and making noise because it was threatening the negotiations. The tenant organizing continued, and eventually a deal was struck between the city and the federal government, but not without considerable ill feeling between community activists and city officials.

A second conflict is over the scope of community participation in development planning. Compare the Flynn administration's implementation of a "community participation" process in the Parcel 18 development project with GRNA's demands for community participation. Parcel 18 is the largest development parcel in the Southwest Corridor, the land cleared for the never-built Southwest Expressway. The parcel enjoys a strategic location, adjacent to a new subway station on a recently relocated line, and near Dudley Square. Over a ten-year period, the Parcel 18 Task Force, a coalition of tenants, community development corporations, black developers, agencies, and abutting institutions, researched, planned, and explored development alternatives for the site. After studying the various proposals for development articulated by the Task Force, BRA representatives literally said, "Thank you for your input," and proceeded to unveil a fully developed plan centered on two thirty-story office towers—a plan radically different from anything the task force had in mind. A black populist associated with the BRA explained the BRA's position: The "process" is irrelevant as long as the "development content" benefits the community (Gaston and Kennedy 1987).

GRNA made it clear that this sort of participation was not satisfactory. At a point when the city government sensed the level of popular support harnessed by GRNA, the BRA floated a proposal to create a Project Advisory Committee (PAC) for the Dudley area, with members appointed by the mayor and with only advisory power over development. GRNA countered by organizing constituency caucuses of small merchants, clergy, tenants, neighborhood associations, community development corporations, and other groups, identifying representatives from each sector, and presenting them for ratification at a Roxbury "town meeting" of more than five hundred people, as a popularly elected "interim PAC" that would serve until broader elections could be held.

City officials were forced to deal with the interim PAC. Negotiations between the interim PAC and the mayor's office resulted in a twelve-point agreement that included an expanded interim PAC (including eight mayoral appointees in addition to the thirteen community-elected representatives), community elections for a PAC within a year, and substantial review and veto powers for the PAC. Mayor Flynn, put on the spot in front of another community meeting of five hundred people, was forced to endorse the agreement, but the BRA's board of directors (holdovers from the former mayor's administration) refused to accept the PAC's expanded powers. The matter remains unresolved, but interestingly, a number of the mayor's appointees to the PAC have joined a GRNA lawsuit to compel the BRA to meet the agreement.

A third point: Roxbury activists have stated that sometimes the best development plan is no plan at all—or at least no specific, immediate product. At a 1986 Boston housing conference bringing together progressive housing professionals from City Hall, the universities, and community agencies, a top BRA official formulated what amounted to a "trickle down" approach to housing. He argued that since Boston has a severe housing crisis and the federal government is providing no funds to build affordable housing, the city government's goal should be simply to build whatever housing it was possible to finance on city-owned vacant land in Roxbury. If only high-priced housing could be built, he reasoned, at least it would increase the supply of housing and bring down the price. Ken Wade, a GRNA leader, responded, "No way! We should build nothing at all on that land until we can build what the community needs. We should just put all that land in a community land trust, and when we can build affordable housing, that's when we'll do it." This development strategy directly challenges the product-oriented "politics of the possible."

Redistributive populist attempts to redistribute resources without changing who has control over the resources are likely to backfire. In the case of the HUD-owned housing, it seems likely that in the absence of tenant mobilization, the city would have been less able to negotiate a favorable deal.[5] As for the development of Roxbury, the Flynn administration's haste to funnel development funds into the neighborhood has already led to displacement as land values around Dudley Square and the Southwest Corridor rise. Further development along the same lines will create new housing and jobs in the neighborhood of Roxbury, but a large part of the community of people currently living in Roxbury will be displaced and therefore will not share in these resources.

Conclusion

This case study contrasts redistributive populism to transformative populism in the arena of community development in a community of color. In our view, transformative populism has proven superior to redistributive populism as an approach to community development in this setting, and this superiority is likely to extend more broadly to other arenas of social change.

This judgment depends on one's view of community development. Certainly if one defines community development primarily in terms of the development of people, the transformative approach is more appropriate. But we would argue that even redistributive populism's own stated goals—building a community-based movement for social change that can effectively carry out redistribution of resources—are better met by a transformative strategy. The evidence for this claim comes from the two strategies' different approaches to the dilemma of ideology and to the role of the state.

Redistributive populism is in some sense an "easier" strategy than transformative populism. Demands framed solely in terms of redistribution of resources are easier to formulate; broad support for such demands is easier to amass; "quick victories" are temptingly easier to claim.[6] In addition, the entire approach can be more easily meshed with the timetable of electoral or legislative strategies. Indeed, left community organizers tend to fall back reflexively on the redistributive strategy because it is the path of least resistance—despite their long-term transformative goals.

But the ease of pursuing redistributive populism comes at a cost. Support for a narrowly redistributive movement may be broad, but it is shallow. Redistributive populism's commitment to the use of least-common-denominator traditional ideology leaves populist movements disarmed before the very real divisions of race, class, gender, and so on. Transformative populism's insistence on understanding and valuing diversity, and on dealing with all kinds of inequality and injustice, not just the one type that affects the largest number of people in a community, may drive some potential supporters away, but it builds a popular consciousness that makes it more difficult to shatter or coopt a coalition. This is important even when organizing at the level of a single community—particularly a community of color, where the reality of racial divisions is unavoidable. The emphasis on dealing with diversity becomes even more crucial when building multicommunity coalitions that are diverse along racial and other lines. At a time when in the United States as a whole white poverty rates are declining but black and Latino poverty rates are increasing (Center for Budget and Policy Priorities 1988), calling for "the greatest good for the greatest number" simply is not sufficient.

The transformative strategy requires placing one's trust in the common people to wrestle with difficult issues and come to positions that may be at odds with their traditional world views. This trust also implies a willingness of organizers and intellectuals to learn from the people being organized, leading to creative solutions to seemingly intractable problems, and alternatives to apparently unavoidable tradeoffs. In a situation where immediate material victories are severely constrained by economic and political forces, transformative populism's emphasis on nurturing a long-term view and measuring success by movement building and consciousness raising can enable a community to sustain ambitious goals.

Transformative populists see the main progressive role of the state as empowering and building people's movements, not simply presiding over a fair redistribution of scarce resources. We do not claim that it is inevitable that redistributive populists in office will seek to suppress popular mobilizations, sacrifice long-run possibilities to achieve short-term material results, and avoid effective community participation—as redistributive populists in Boston's Flynn administration have done. Nevertheless, the redistributive populist emphasis on product over process—redistribution rather than transformation—makes them likely to fall into these patterns.

In general, without a movement toward community empowerment, a reform government lacks the popular mobilization necessary to carry out substantial, lasting redistribution. The government remains hemmed in by "not enough money," unable to make more aggressive demands on capital or to stimulate self-help initiatives. The "gifts" from the city government to disadvantaged communities turn out to be small, poorly planned and delivered, and most likely temporary. In some cases, "redistributive" assistance from a progressive-minded government can be downright destructive—as the development assistance directed toward Roxbury by the Flynn administration has been.

Finally, a transformative populist approach is better equipped to confront the deep questions of structural change that successful social movements must sooner or later answer. We believe that in order to achieve lasting change, a movement for the development of poor communities must question not only existing strategies for economic growth but the value of growth as currently defined. It must challenge not only the policies of current governments but the entire political system that rests on massive nonparticipation and an extremely restricted set of electoral choices. In doing so, it must link up with other movements concerned with these issues. While Roxbury's transformative populists have only begun to scratch the surface of these problems, they and others like them seem more likely to come up with solutions than is a redistributive populist movement.

We have coined the terms "transformative" and "redistributive" for this paper. Without using these names, most Boston activists sense the importance of the differences in approach we have outlined. Regardless of what terms are used, we believe it is important for activists in Boston and elsewhere to become conscious of the distinction and to explicitly develop what we have called transformative populism. It is easy to fall into redistributive populism, and the clear understanding necessary to avoid this goes well beyond what this paper has to offer. The continued efforts of activists and intellectuals working together can make this understanding possible.

Notes

1. The boundaries of Roxbury are variously defined from one governmental agency to another and by different community organizations. We are generally referring to the 1980 Boston Neighborhood Statistical Areas 9 (North Dorchester/ Dudley), 30 (Franklin Field), 38 (Egleston Square), 52 (Highland Park), 53 (Lower Roxbury), 54 (Sav-Mor), and 55 (Washington Park). Per capita income in Roxbury in 1979 varied from a low in Lower Roxbury of 52% of the citywide per capita income to a high of 73% in Sav-Mor.

2. Several readers of earlier drafts of this paper argued that we are "too easy on the Flynn administration." We would like to emphasize that this paper in no way constitutes an evaluation of the accomplishments (or lack thereof) of the Flynn administration or of opposition groups. In order to pose the contradictions in the case most clearly we have assumed a best-case scenario for the Flynn administration and the broader movement it represents. The primary question posed is this: If what we are terming redistributive populists acted in good faith on the stated intentions of their most progressive spokespeople, how would their strategy compare with the alternative transformative populist strategy?

3. Much of this discussion draws on Green (1984).

4. According to a Flynn staffer, even Ray Flynn has confidentially identified himself as a socialist.

5. In a related example outside Roxbury, Flynn government officials proposed development of housing on vacant city-owned land in the South End. The city officials initially stipulated that only 35% of the housing be developed for low- and moderate-income residents, fearing that proposing a higher level of affordability would arouse political opposition from middle-class South End residents and developers. Community activists responded by forming the Ad Hoc Housing Committee. Over opposition by city officials, they won a more participatory process. In the course of this process, the Ad Hoc Housing Committee built majority support— including most of the representations of the South End's middle class—for a formula of one-third low-income, one-third moderate income, and one-third market rate. The city belatedly endorsed the formula. Without the mobilization from below, city officials never would have gone beyond the original 35% target, despite their avowed support for affordable housing.

6. Of course, dogmatic left sloganeering is also easy; transformative populism must avoid this trap as well.

References

Boyte, Harry, and Sara Evans. 1986. *Free Spaces: The Sources of Democratic Change in America*. New York: Harper & Row.

Center for Budget and Policy Priorities. 1988. *Still Far from the Dream: Recent Developments in Black Income, Employment and Poverty*. Washington, D.C.: The Center.

Gaston, Mauricio, and Marie Kennedy. 1987. "Capital Investment or Community Development? The Struggle for Land Control by Boston's Black and Latino Community." *Antipode* 19, no. 2 (September): 178–209.

Green, James. 1984. "The Making of Mel King's Rainbow Coalition: Political Changes in Boston, 1963–1983." *Radical America* 17 and 18.

Kennedy, Marie, and Chris Tilly. 1987. "A City Called Mandela: Secession and the Struggle for Community Control in Boston." *North Star*, no. 5: 12–18.

Nyerere, Julius. 1974. *Man and Development*. New York: Oxford University Press.

Stone, Michael. 1986. "Nonspeculative Homeownership." Roxbury Technical Assistance Project, Working Paper, Center for Community Planning, University of Massachusetts at Boston.

For Further Reading

Following are publications we found helpful in analyzing community development struggles in Boston's Roxbury. This list is in no way exhaustive, as we did not do a literature search in the usual sense.

Any analysis of the effectiveness of community development strategies needs to be framed in the context of postindustrial restructuring of urban environments and the labor force in the United States and, to some extent, internationally. Books we recommend on this topic follow.

Fainstein, Susan S., Norman I. Fainstein, Richard C. Hill, Dennis Judd, and Michael P. Smith, eds. 1986. *Restructuring the City*. Rev. ed. New York: Longman.

Hartman, Chester. 1984. *The Transformation of San Francisco*. Totowa, N.J.: Rowman and Allanheld.

Mollenkopf, John. 1983. *The Contested City*. Princeton: Princeton University Press.

Palen, John, and Bruce London, eds. 1984. *Gentrification, Displacement and Neighborhood Revitalization*. Albany: State University of New York Press.

Smith, Michael P., ed. 1984. *Cities in Transformation: Class, Capital and the State*. Urban Affairs Annual Reviews No. 26. Beverly Hills, Calif.: Sage.

Smith, Neil. 1984. *Uneven Development*. Oxford: Basil Blackwell.

Smith, Neil, and Peter Williams, eds. 1986. *Gentrification of the City*. Boston: Allen and Unwin.
Tabb, William, and Larry Sawers, eds. 1978, 1984. *Marxism and the Metropolis*. 1st and 2nd ed. New York, Oxford University Press. The two editions have a number of different selections, and both editions are interesting.

Works helpful in elaborating the race–class component of community development struggles include the following:

Boston, Thomas D. 1988. *Race, Class and Conservatism*. Boston: Unwin Hyman.
Harrison, Bennett. 1974. "Ghetto Economic Development: A Survey." *Journal of Economic Literature*. March.
Goldsmith, William. 1974. "The Ghetto as a Resource for Black America." *Journal of the American Institute of Planners*. January.
Jennings, James, and Mel King, eds. 1986. *From Access to Power*. Cambridge, Mass.: Schenkman.
King, Mel. 1981. *Chain of Change: Struggles for Black Community Development*. Boston: South End Press.
Marable, Manning. 1983. *How Capitalism Underdeveloped Black America*. Boston: South End Press.
Radical America. 1987. Special Issue on "Race and Community Control, Media, Politics." Vol. 20, no. 5.
Tabb, William. 1970. *The Political Economy of the Black Ghetto*. New York: Norton.

Sources useful in thinking about organizing and about progressive municipal policy include the following:

Castells, Manuel. 1983. *The City and the Grassroots*. Berkeley: University of California Press.
Clavel, Pierre. 1986. *The Progressive City: Planning and Participation, 1969–1984*. New Brunswick, N.J.: Rutgers University Press.
Cowley, John, Adah Kaye, Marjorie Mayo, and Mike Thompson, eds. 1977. *Community or Class Struggle?* London: Stage One.
Radical America. 1983–1984. Special Issue on "The Mel King Campaign and Coalition Politics in the Eighties." Vols. 17 and 18, nos. 6 and 1.

The following bibliography may be useful on the general subject of community development:

Tilly, Chris, with Yohel Camayd-Freixas, P. Clay, Bellen Daniels, and Frank Jones. 1985. *Fifteen Years of Community Development: An Annotated Bibliography, 1968–1983*. Bibliography No. 156. Chicago: Council of Planning Librarians.

On the case study of community development in Roxbury, we have also written the following:

————. 1987. "Blueprint for Tomorrow: The Fight for Community Control in Black and Latino Boston." *Radical America* 20, no. 5.

————. 1987. "Capital Investment or Community Development?" *Antipode* 19, no. 2 (September).

Gaston, Mauricio, and Marie Kennedy. 1985. "Dudley in 2001: After the El . . . Center for Whom?" Community Service Program, College of Public and Community Service, University of Massachusetts at Boston. January.

————. 1985. "From Disinvestment to Displacement." Roxbury Technical Assistance Program, College of Public and Community Service, University of Massachusetts at Boston. August.

Kennedy, Marie, and Chris Tilly. 1987. "A City Called Mandela." *North Star*, no. 5 (Spring).

————. 1987. "The Mandela Campaign: An Overview." *Radical America* 20, no. 5.

About the Authors

Robert Fisher is associate professor of history at the University of Houston–Downtown. Since his days as an undergraduate, he has been active in the peace monement and community organizing efforts.

James Jennings is associate professor of political science and senior fellow of the William Monroe Trotter Institute at the University of Massachusetts, Boston. Jennings is a long-time activist with grass-roots organizations in the Boston area, including the 1979 and 1983 Mel King mayoral campaigns and the 1984 and 1988 presidential campaigns of Jesse Jackson.

Ira Katznelson is dean of the graduate faculty and Henry and Louise Loeb Professor of Political Science at the New School for Social Research.

Marie Kennedy is an associate professor in the Center for Community Planning, College of Public and Community Service, University of Massachusetts at Boston. For over twenty years, Kennedy has been a community activist in the Boston area, combining activism and research in her work with the late Mauricio Gaston, with Chris Tilly and with Mel King on community development.

Joseph M. Kling teaches in the Government Department at St. Lawrence University in Canton, New York. For many years, Kling worked in Brooklyn, New York, as a youth worker and community organizer.

Bruce Palmer is associate professor of history at the University of Houston, Clearlake. Palmer worked as an organizer in Rochester, New

York, and served as a member of the research and education staff to the Student Nonviolent Coordinating Committee (SNCC) in Atlanta, Georgia, and Jackson, Mississippi. Palmer was co-organizer and treasurer of the University of Houston/Clear Lake American Federation of Teachers Local 4033.

Sidney Plotkin is associate professor of political science at Vassar College. While teaching at the University of Texas at San Antonio, Plotkin was active in environmental and civil rights issues.

Prudence Posner is director of the Liberty Partnership Program of Associated Colleges in Canton, New York. She has taught high school in Brooklyn and worked at the United Community Centers in Brooklyn as a community organizer, youth worker, and director of research and education.

Rayna Rapp is chairperson of the graduate department of anthropology at the New School for Social Research and has long been active in the women's movement.

William E. Scheuerman is professor of political science at the State University of New York at Oswego and is currently serving as vice-president for academics of the United University Professions, the nation's largest higher education union.

Tony Schuman is a registered architect and associate professor of architecture at New Jersey Institute of Technology. Schuman has been a founding member of numerous professional, advocacy, and activist organizations offering technical assistance, research, analysis, and program and policy recommendations on housing and community development issues. He is currently chairperson of the New York chapter of Architects/Designers/Planners for Social Responsibility.

Svi Shapiro is a faculty member at the Greensboro School of Education of the University of North Carolina. Shapiro worked as an educator for the Inner London Education Authority, taught junior high school in Philadelphia, and served as regional coordinator on a special project for the Massachusetts Department of Education, Division of Special Education.

Ida Susser is associate professor at the School of Health Sciences at

Hunter College and is currently working on a book about the emergence of the environmental movement in Puerto Rico.

Chris Tilly is assistant professor of economics at the University of Lowell in Massachusetts. Tilly has been active in student, community, and labor organizing in Boston and San Francisco and serves as a member of the editorial collective of *Dollars and Sense* magazine.

Rona Weiss is associate professor of economics at Iona College in New Rochelle, New York. Weiss has been active in the antiwar movement, the struggle for public funding for higher education in New York and Massachusetts, as well as initiating peace and justice activities at Iona College.

DILEMMAS
OF ACTIVISM

Class, Community,
and the Politics
of Local Mobilization

Edited by
Joseph M. Kling
and Prudence S. Posner

Through the 1980s, collective resistance to
conditions of economic deprivation, social
insecurity, and political control have become
more parochial, fragmented, and reactive,
rather than transformational. In order to
challenge these trends activists need to sort
through the understanding and practice they
bring to their work in communities and
organizations. The essays in *Dilemmas of
Activism* contribute to that reexamination.

The collection looks at the ways in which
both class and community create frameworks
for activism at the local level. The editors
select three dilemmas that, they argue,
inherently shape the issues and strategies
around which people mobilize. These include
the opposing pulls between class and
community, derived and inherent ideology,
and state action and local control.

The editors use the concept of "dilemmas" in
order to emphasize the way in which
competing social-change theories, identified
respectively as new populism and Marxism,
are in fact complementary ways of
understanding the same set of processes.
They are inseparable and equally necessary,
both for the activist who wishes to move
beyond organizing for traffic lights at busy
corners where schoolchildren cross, and for
the theorist who wishes to explore the
practical implications of ideas about
community change.

Part I is theoretical and includes essays that
set out the concepts necessary to a general
understanding of social action, such as